Action-Based Book Features

QR Codes

Use your mobile phone to take a picture and go to the webpage and videos for each chapter. Internet access is required. Roaming charges may apply: check your mobile phone service contract or mobile network conditions.

 SHARE IT

Hashtags and tags for various networks are included in this book to facilitate conversation.

Stories and Case Studies

The beginning and end of each chapter include stories and case studies. In some examples a précis of the story or case study has been provided with indication that the full artifact is available online.

Social Networks

Learning networks for you to join.

 ADD FRIEND

Easily add the educators, administrators, and leaders in this book to your Twitter or your RSS reader. The first time a person is mentioned, we share their friend information. *(This is not to ask you to find people on Facebook you don't know.)* See the index for those mentioned twice.

Flat Classroom™ Framework

The framework given in this book is used to help you determine which projects are best for you.

 WEBSITES

Key web addresses.

 tweetable

The Flat Classroom Fifteen **15**

Fifteen actions (and a few bonuses) to turn this book into a live learning experience connecting you to other learners.

Definitions

 New terms are defined the first place they appear and are also in the glossary at the back of the book and online. Look these words up and use them with others in conversation to cement your learning.

Flat Classroom Diaries

Diary Entry Stories from the authors, teachers, and students involved in Flat Classroom projects. In some examples a précis of the diary entry has been provided with indication that the full artifact is available online.

Digital Citizenship Area of Understanding

These icons highlight the four rays of understanding as shared in the digital citizenship model in Chapter 5 of this book.

ISTE STANDARDS

ISTE NETS standard alignments for students and teachers are noted throughout the chapters.

21st CENTURY SKILLS

C21 Skill alignments are noted throughout the chapters with their standard numbers.

 **PDToolkit**

PDToolkit for Flattening Classrooms, Engaging Minds

Website with media tools that provide the tools (together with this text) to prepare for global collaboration.

WHAT REVIEWERS ARE SAYING ABOUT THIS BOOK

"Insightful, innovative, and practical, this book is a must read for any educator interested in preparing competent global citizens."

—YONG ZHAO, Ph. D, Presidential Chair and Associate Dean, College of Education, University of Oregon

"Open the door and find a new world! In this significant contribution to global education, Julie and Vicki have produced a resource for teachers that contains much needed information, challenges education thinking, and provides resources on each and every page. This is a book a teacher can read and immediately open a global door for their students. For me, it is so exciting (and a relief!) to see that the voice of change in education thinking is the voice of our students."

—TONY BRANDENBURG, Fellow, Australian Council for Computers in Education

"In a hyperconnected world, it's imperative that students gain deep, rich understandings of other peoples and places. This book demonstrates in concrete detail how every classroom can be a global classroom."

—DR. SCOTT McLEOD, University of Kentucky, Founding Director of the UCEA
Center for the Advanced Study of Technology Leadership in Education (CASTLE)

"Thomas Friedman described a new way of looking at our world through the lens of globalization. Lindsay and Davis have mapped out a new geography for schooling, one that ignores borders and boundaries, and empowers learning through access to global communities, tools to enhance and extend that access, and reasons to care about it."

—DAVID WARLICK, The Landmark Project

"This book has everything you need to start collaborative projects in your classroom. From educators to follow to ongoing projects you can join today, Julie and Vicki do a great job of walking you through how to get started with collaborative projects in your own classroom. With links, ideas, and steps to keep both you and the learning focused. This book has enough people, links, and resources to keep you clicking for days."

—JEFF UTECHT, Apple Distinguished Educator, Google Apps for Education Certified Trainer, Consultant, Author

"A 'book without boundaries' that allows the reader to engage beyond the covers of the book, much like the global classroom project."

—JAMIE LANIER, Instructional Technology, Secondary Schools, Johnston County Schools, Smithfield, NC

"This book provides the impetus and support to begin a new journey in global collaboration. You feel the authors will be by your side aiding the teacher with practical help."

—BENJAMIN J. FOSTER, Director of Instructional Technology, Russellville School District, Russellville, AR

Flattening Classrooms, Engaging Minds

MOVE TO GLOBAL COLLABORATION ONE STEP AT A TIME

Julie Lindsay

Vicki A. Davis

Boston • Columbus • Indianapolis • New York • San Francisco • Upper Saddle River
Amsterdam • Cape Town • Dubai • London • Madrid • Milan • Munich • Paris • Montreal • Toronto
Delhi • Mexico City • São Paulo • Sydney • Hong Kong • Seoul • Singapore • Taipei • Tokyo

Editorial Director: Jeffrey Johnston
Vice President, Editor in Chief: Aurora Martínez Ramos
Senior Acquisitions Editor: Kelly Villella Canton
Editorial Assistant: Annalea Manalili
Executive Marketing Manager: Krista Clark
Project Manager: Karen Mason
Manufacturing Buyer: Megan Cochran
Text Designer: Electronic Publishing Services Inc.
Manager, Rights and Permissions: Tim Nicholls
Image Permission Coordinator: Annie Pickert

Manager, Cover Visual Research & Permissions: Diane Lorenzo
Cover Designer: Jenny Hart
Cover Art: Photo by: Erika Bautista. Pictured: Ali (Qatar), Erika (Mexico), Katie (USA), Saud (Qatar), and Sonwabile (Ethiopia)
Media Director: Sacha Laustsen
Full-Service Project Management: Electronic Publishing Services Inc.
Composition: Jouve
Printer/Binder: Edwards Brothers

Credits and acknowledgments borrowed from other sources and reproduced, with permission, in this textbook appear on appropriate page within text.

Photo credits: p. 1, Michael D. Brown/Shutterstock.com; pp. 7, 80, 113, 127, 134, 169, 170, 171, 172, 199, 226, 240, 271, Julie Lindsay and Vicki A. Davis; p. 18, Cybrain/Shutterstock.com; p. 21, V. S. Anandhakrishna/Shutterstock.com; p. 31, Marinini/Shutterstock.com; pp. 52, 285, ZouZou/Shutterstock.com; p. 62, Cifotart/Shutterstock.com; p. 97, Lightspring/Shutterstock.com; p. 109, Naluwan/Shutterstock.com; pp. 126, 259, Shutterstock.com; pp. 145, 215, 244, Zurijeta/Shutterstock.com; p. 158, Stoonn/Shutterstock.com; p. 165, Amahuron/Shutterstock.com; p. 197, Africa Studio/Shutterstock.com; p. 210, Distinctive Images/Shutterstock.com; p. 222, Blend Images/Shutterstock.com; pp. 228, 298, Jaimaa/Shutterstock.com; p. 235, Alex Mit/Shutterstock.com; p. 249, Franck Boston/Shutterstock.com; p. 268, Ancroft/Shutterstock.com; p. 272, Hung Chung Chih/Shutterstock.com; p. 293, Orla/Shutterstock.com

Note: In order to use the QR Code feature, Internet access is required. Roaming and/or data charges may apply: check your mobile phone service contract.

Library of Congress Cataloging-in-Publication Data

Lindsay, Julie.
   Flattening classrooms, engaging minds: move to global collaboration one step at a time / Julie Lindsay, Vicki A. Davis.
      p. cm.
   Includes bibliographical references and index.
   ISBN-13: 978-0-13-261035-3 (pbk.)
   ISBN-10: 0-13-261035-3 (pbk.)
  1. Internet in education.   2. Education and globalization.   3. Students—Social networks.   4. Motivation in education.   I. Davis, Vicki A.   II. Title.
   LB1044.87.D385 2013
   371.33'44678—dc23

2011036986

10 9 8 7 6 5 4 3 2 1

ISBN 10: 0-13-261035-3
ISBN 13: 978-0-13-261035-3

FROM BOTH OF US

To all of the students, teachers, parents, and educators around the world who understand the importance of connecting in positive ways so we can build a brighter future.

FROM JULIE LINDSAY

I dedicate this book to my family for their patience when I am always "at the computer": John, who has always believed in me and supported every new idea, and Violet Rose, who has grown up as a third-culture kid literally living the flat classroom in and out of class. This book is also dedicated to my extended family back in Australia, who is always there for me even if we are miles apart. I give a special dedication to my friend Vicki for having the same energy level as me and the same desire to change the world, one classroom at a time.

FROM VICKI DAVIS

To my husband, Kip, who believes I can reach the sky,
And my three incredible children, who give me the reason to try,
To my Mom and Dad who gave me the wings to fly,
And The Teacher who gives me a plan from on High.
To you I dedicate this book.
To my friend Julie, through the miles, the smiles, the tears, and the cheers,
we have grown stronger, closer, and done things classroom teachers aren't
supposed to be able to do. Here's to you.

JULIE LINDSAY
@julielindsay
http://learningconfluence.com

JULIE LINDSAY

Julie's achievements include: MA Music (La Trobe University in Melbourne), MA Educational Technology Leadership (George Washington University in Washington, DC), ADE (Apple Distinguished Educator), ISTE Ambassador and International Representative on the Board of Directors, Member of Horizon Report Board of Advisers 2008–2011, co-founder of Flat Classroom™ Projects LLC and Flat Classroom™ Conference and Live Events Inc., Chair of the Educator Advisory Board for the Global Education Conference 2010.

Julie is an enthusiastic, global-minded education leader and innovator. Originally from Melbourne, Australia, where she gained recognition as a music educator, over the past 14 years she has been teaching and leading the use of technology in schools in Zambia, Kuwait, Bangladesh, and Qatar, and is currently E-Learning Coordinator and MYP Coordinator at Beijing BISS International School, China.

Julie is recognized worldwide for her innovative programs using a wide array of Web 2.0 tools to transform learning for the emerging digital, "world-is-flat" educational landscape. From ubiquitous mobile technology programs to the Flat Classroom project, Julie leads the way in connecting communities and brings front-line experiences to share with teachers, school leaders, and policy makers alike.

Learn more about Julie from her website, portfolio, and blog at http://learningconfluence.com.

VICKI DAVIS
@coolcatteacher
http://coolcatteacher.blogspot.com

VICKI ADAMS DAVIS

Vicki Davis is a full-time teacher and IT Administrator at Westwood Schools in Camilla, Georgia, where she has taught for 10 years. Wikis, blogs, virtual worlds, videography—if there is a technology tool, it is likely that she has used it in her internationally recognized classroom. Her work has been profiled by Edutopia, Pearson Education, and Laureate, and her Cool Cat Teacher blog (http://coolcatteacher.blogspot.com) is consistently ranked among the top educational blogs in the world, winning the Edublog award for best teacher blog in 2008. She is also co-winner with Julie Lindsay of ISTE's SIGTEL's Online Learning Award 2007 and Taking IT Global Best Online Learning Project 2007 for the Flat Classroom project.

Vicki's passion is to encourage classroom teachers to improve their teaching even in tough times with limited resources, and she believes in the importance of connecting every classroom on a global basis. She also takes time to speak, travel, and work with educators around the world.

Although Vicki has been in the classroom for over 10 years, she did not get there through the traditional route, receiving her degree in Management from the Georgia Institute of Technology where she graduated first in her class and was named Outstanding Management Major. She was a businesswoman and a general manager in the cellular telephone business in the 1990s and a web design entrepreneur. Vicki was a member of Leadership Georgia Class of 2001, past president of the Camilla Chamber of Commerce, and recipient of the Rotary District 6900 Governor's Award of Excellence.

She is a Google Certified Teacher, a Discovery STAR Educator, and an Adobe Education Leader and has served as a judge in Microsoft's Innovative Educators Program. Vicki lives in Camilla, Georgia, with her husband, Kip, and three children.

Her full biography and efolio are available at http://www.coolcatteacher.com.

CONTENTS

PART 2: SEVEN STEPS TO FLATTEN YOUR CLASSROOM

CHAPTER 3
Step 1: Connection   31

CHAPTER 4
Step 2: Communication   62

CHAPTER 5
Step 3: Citizenship   97

CHAPTER 9
Step 7: Celebration 215

PART 3: PROJECT DEVELOPMENT

CHAPTER 10
Designing and Managing a Global Collaborative Project 235

CHAPTER 11
Challenge-Based Professional Development 268

CHAPTER 12
Rock the World 293

WELCOME TO THE WORLD OF GLOBAL COLLABORATION!

High-speed Internet, social media, and mobile devices have opened up a remarkable world of connection and collaboration. Global economies are now increasingly intertwined. Multinational teams are becoming the norm in the workplace. Yet most schools are unchanged.

As schools struggle to engage students with learning and disengage them from their cell phones and social networks, there are some schools leveraging technology and social media to launch learning forward. By implementing global collaborative practices, we are building the bridges today that the society of tomorrow will walk across. We can change society for the better from the bottom up, while improving education and student engagement.

We want students and educators to be able to connect and get along with other people globally without losing their own identity and sense of belonging to a country or culture. We are forging new pedagogies. We question current education systems that place value on content above process. We believe that collaboration and community learning increases understanding as a valuable part of what classrooms are already doing. Global collaboration is not a choice between current pedagogies *or* global collaboration. Rather, it is an "*and*" proposition. We should use current teaching pedagogies *and* effective global collaboration pedagogies as part of the complete, healthy classroom ecosystem. You can get your classrooms and schools there one step at a time. This book will teach you how.

WHAT THIS BOOK IS ABOUT

This book is *not* just about technology, it is about the learning as well as the cultural and academic advantages of embedding global collaboration into the classroom. Learn to redefine education to be holistic, cross-cultural, and technology-rich in order to scaffold new learning paradigms for enhanced engagement and real-world problem solving.

Since that day in November when we connected our classrooms—Julie's in Dhaka, Bangladesh, and Vicki's in Camilla, Georgia, USA—our global projects and project-based conferences have connected thousands of students. We believe in creating rich learning experiences that harness the power of social media and spring from the emerging grassroots connections of educators around the world.

ISTE STANDARDS

NETS.T 1.D
Facilitate and Inspire Student
Learning and Creativity

Although global connections have existed since the modem gained wide use in the 1980s, student content co-creation across the globe is the new frontier of education in an increasingly collaborative world. In many respects, writing and releasing this book is long overdue; however, it has taken time, development, and replication to provide a working model that we've proven can be implemented at all levels of education.

The content in *Flattening Classrooms, Engaging Minds* shares more than just our projects—it also shares experiences from the many other educators, researchers, and administrators who have achieved excellence in this field. We share pedagogy and design principles, but this book, when used correctly, is an experience. It is a journey of discovery that will ultimately

tweetable

By implementing global collaborative practices we are building the bridges today that the society of tomorrow will walk across. #flatclass

change what you do and how you do it in the classroom. It is an experiential "mashup" designed to provoke conversations and actions.

With this book, you can build bridges from your students to the world. You can also build bridges to your core and interdisciplinary content while instilling the vital competencies that will define the successful 21st century learner.

Readers can study this book in sequential order, or go directly to a "phase" of flattening your classroom as needed. In addition, online places where we collaborate and communicate about all topics provide an organic home for further sharing and networking.

Book Organization with Flat Classroom™ 15 Challenges

Part 1: Meet the Flat Classroom™

CHAPTER 1
Flattening Classrooms through Global Collaboration

CHAPTER 2
Impact on Learning: Research in the Global Collaborative Classroom

Part 2: Seven Steps to Flatten Your Classroom

CHAPTER 3
STEP 1: Connection
#1: Set Up Your RSS Reader
#2: Set Up Your Blog
#3: Connect and Reflect

CHAPTER 4
STEP 2: Communication
#4: Communicate with New Tools
#5: Go Mobile!

CHAPTER 5
STEP 3: Citizenship
#6: Create a Classroom Monitoring Portal
#7: Empower Digital Citizenship Action

CHAPTER 6
Step 4: Contribution and Collaboration
#8: Collaborate and Communicate
#9: Assess

CHAPTER 7
Step 5: Choice
#10: Give Students a Choice

CHAPTER 8
Step 6: Creation
#11: Align Your Projects to Standards

CHAPTER 9
Step 7: Celebration
#12: Celebration and Summation

Part 3: Project Development

CHAPTER 10
Designing and Managing a Global Collaborative Project
#13: Global Project Design

CHAPTER 11
Challenge-Based Professional Development
#14: Challenge-Based Professional Development

CHAPTER 12
Rock the World
#15: Tell Your Story

(See full-size version on inside front cover.)

HOW THIS BOOK IS ORGANIZED

VOICE

While we are two authors, we have written this book in first person. For clarity in our examples, you'll see us say "in Julie's classroom" or "Vicki says."

PARTS OF THIS BOOK

This book is separated into three main parts. In Part 1 you will hear stories of collaboration, learn about the authors and the projects, and read about current research into the benefits of effective global collaboration in the classroom.

Part 2 takes you through the seven steps to bring a classroom or school into effective global collaborative practice. As shown in Seven Steps to Flatten Your Classroom, each step is broken into three parts to move you from personal learning (Self), into implementation (School), and into your classroom (Students).

In Part 3 we discuss the framework for planning global collaborative projects and project-based professional development experiences. We end by inspiring you to move forward!

Seven Steps to Flatten Your Classroom

The chapters comprising 7 Steps to Flatten Your Classroom (as shown in Part 2 of this book) are each broken down into three parts: SELF, SCHOOL, and STUDENTS and include the content as shown.

SELF	SCHOOL	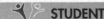 STUDENT
• Definitions, research, background on the chapter's topic • Relate the topic to what you are doing now • Self-assessment survey to help you create a personal plan	• Relate the step to your school and district • Learn how to build relationships with other schools and within yours	• Apply chapter concepts to the classroom and collaborative projects • Understand practical classroom and project examples relating to this topic

Appendix A describes rubrics for project assessment. Appendix B is a short guide to collaboration and the International Baccalaureate. We share the two most prominent technology standards in use on an international scale in Appendix C (ISTE NETS.S and NETS.T) and Appendix D (C21 Standards.)

FEATURES OF THIS BOOK

Alignment with Important Standards. To help educators align the book's principles with standards, we have noted alignments with the ISTE NETS for Teachers and Students and the 21st Century Learning Standards (C21) from the Partnership for 21st Century Skills in the margins.

THE FLAT C

The Flat Cla
and explore
Friedman's b
project design

There ar
video. Group
laboratively
on the projec
Educators, bu

The pers
tive. Using or
Mind,[24] a stu

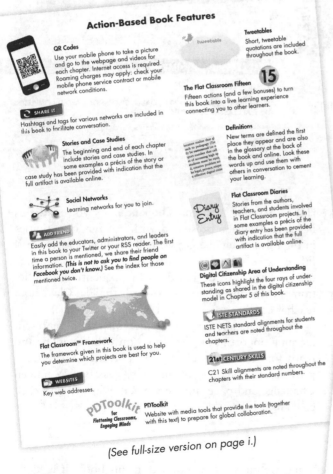

Action-Based Book Features

QR Codes
Use your mobile phone to take a picture and go to the webpage and videos for each chapter. Internet access is required. Roaming charges may apply: check your mobile phone service contract or mobile network conditions.

SHARE IT
Hashtags and tags for various networks are included in this book to facilitate conversation.

Stories and Case Studies
The beginning and end of each chapter include stories and case studies. In some examples a précis of the story or case study has been provided with indication that the full artifact is available online.

Social Networks
Learning networks for you to join.

ADD FRIEND
Easily add the educators, administrators, and leaders in this book to your Twitter or your RSS reader. The first time a person is mentioned, we share their friend information. *(This is not to ask you to find people on Facebook you don't know.)* See the index for those mentioned twice.

Flat Classroom™ Framework
The framework given in this book is used to help you determine which projects are best for you.

WEBSITES
Key web addresses.

PDToolkit for *Flattening Classrooms, Engaging Minds*
PDToolkit
Website with media tools that provide the tools (together with this text) to prepare for global collaboration.

Tweetables
Short, tweetable quotations are included throughout the book.

15

The Flat Classroom Fifteen
Fifteen actions (and a few bonuses) to turn this book into a live learning experience connecting you to other learners.

Definitions
New terms are defined the first place they appear and are also in the glossary at the back of the book and online. Look these words up and use them with others in conversation to cement your learning.

Flat Classroom Diaries
Diary Entry
Stories from the authors, teachers, and students involved in Flat Classroom projects. In some examples a précis of the diary entry has been provided with indication that the full artifact is available online.

Digital Citizenship Area of Understanding
These icons highlight the four rays of understanding as shared in the digital citizenship model in Chapter 5 of this book.

ISTE STANDARDS
ISTE NETS standard alignments for students and teachers are noted throughout the chapters.

21st CENTURY SKILLS
C21 Skill alignments are noted throughout the chapters with their standard numbers.

(See full-size version on page i.)

Action-Based Features. Designed like a social media website, we point out the social networks, friends, hyperlinks, and hashtags and provide QR codes that will let you easily bring content into your online learning network. The chart at left elaborates on all our action-based features and their accompanying icons (see full-page version on page i).

ISTE STANDARDS
If implemented as designed, this project meets all ISTE NET.S standards.

21st CENTURY SKILLS
If implemented as designed, this project meets all C21 standards with various students having different aspects of the interdisciplinary themes based on their research topics.

Chapter Opening Features. Each chapter opens with URL and QR code to our website, a Share It feature with the Twitter hashtag for the chapter, a quotation and a story to set the theme and frame the discussion topics, along with an "Add Friend" icon and information on how to follow the person in the story online.

xv

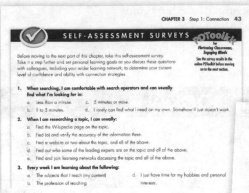

Self-Assessment Surveys. Within Part 2 chapters we have placed self-assessment surveys to help you map your own preparedness to take the steps in that chapter and create a personal action plan. You may find results of these surveys by completing them on the PDToolkit site.

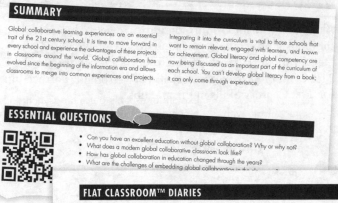

Chapter Ending Features. Chapters end with a Summary, Essential Questions (with QR code and URL) to be discussed in our online communities, specific challenges (with QR code and URL) from the Flat Classroom™ Fifteen (see below), the Flat Classroom™ Diaries (with QR codes and URLs to access the full entries online), and Case Examples of Global Collaboration Projects in Action that round out each chapter to demonstrate how the chapter's principles look in the real world.

Flat Classroom™ Fifteen Challenge. As you read this book you will be presented with a series of activities in the form of challenges we call the Flat Classroom™ Fifteen (see the Flat Classroom™ Fifteen Challenge table). These are designed to be sequential; completion of the entire 15 counts towards the Flat Classroom teacher certification program (a separate course).[1]

Beginners should not feel nervous; these represent learning opportunities for you. You will be taught and ready for each challenge when it is presented. This table provides an overview of the Flat Classroom™ Fifteen Challenge and page numbers where you will find each challenge.

A Note on Tools. Many tools and websites are mentioned in this book. It is likely that as this goes to print that some tools will be renamed, bought out, or just out of business! We've included the websites we mention, their function, and the URL on our book website: http://www.flatclassroombook.com. For simplicity, in this book we will focus on function and may mention the tools but often not the specific website address.

Flat Classroom™ Fifteen Challenges			
Flat Classroom Fifteen Challenge	Summary	When to Complete	Page
1 Set Up Your RSS Reader	Set up RSS and develop your PLN	Step 1: Connection	57
2 Set Up Your Blog	Explore blogging and start your own blog and join the Flat Classrooms educational network (http://flatclassrooms.ning.com)	Step 1: Connection	57
3 Connect and Reflect	Research one or two of the connecting organizations mentioned in this section.	Step 1: Connection	58
4 Communicate with New Tools	Explore and put into use an asynchronous tool and a synchronous tool (preferably with a partner.)	Step 2: Communication	93
5 Go Mobile!	Use your own mobile device in an educational way.	Step 2: Communication	93
6 Create a Classroom Monitoring Portal	Use an RSS reader to create a CMP (classroom monitoring portal) for your classroom	Step 3: Citizenship	121
7 Empower Digital Citizenship Action	Discuss student-empowered digital citizenship with your school colleagues, including "reverse mentoring." *For those not in a school.* Explore social media and student use.	Step 3: Citizenship	121
8 Collaborate and Communicate	Participate in a collaborative wiki project with your class or an online community.	Step 4: Contribution & Collaboration	153
9 Assess	Use available Wiki Rubrics to assess three people from another group in the wiki project you completed in challenge 8.	Step 4: Contribution & Collaboration	153
10 Give Students a Choice	Write a project plan where students are given a choice in their outcome and topic.	Step 5: Choice	194
11 Align Your Projects to Standards	Revise #10 project plan based upon what you have learned and to align with your course or another set of standards such as the ISTE NETS standards or the 21st Century Learning Literacies.	Step 6: Creation	211
12 Celebration and Summation	Participate in a summit and create a graphic to present in the online classroom as you reflect upon what you've learned.	Step 7: Celebration	230
13 Global Project Design	Use your PLN to suggest or join a group of people to pursue a plan for a Flat Classroom–style project. Using the strategies learned in this book and the material from the chapter, design your project.	Designing and Managing a Global Collaborative Project	263
14 Challenge-Based Professional Development	Consider how project-based professional development with educators and students can be used to teach both with mutually beneficial outcomes. Draw up a one-day schedule for your school or a conference.	Challenge-Based Professional Development	287
15 Tell Your Story	You've done it!! Now, it is your job to mentor others and plan projects. Please share with others and us and participate with us at http://flatclassrooms.ning.com!	Rock the World	301

MESSAGE TO OUR READERS

You can do it! It is exciting to embark on a journey. Whether you are experiencing the butterflies of excitement or the fear of the unknown, use your good judgment and the concepts here to safely navigate the waters of global collaboration.

Share the experience of reading and learning from this book across your school, networks, and learning communities. Reach out and join our places and spaces. Contact us and join our projects. Better still, develop the confidence to create your own exciting and rich global learning experiences for you and your students. Then you will be part of the magic we are spreading.

My learning pathway is an ongoing journey that I travel alone as I am the one guiding the direction and yet often others join me, such as this course, and we walk together for a time learning sharing and observing. Eventually, I part ways with my companions but am left far richer by their presence than I was before and often my own journey heads in a new direction.[2]

HEATHER DAVIS,

Flat Classroom Certified Teacher, "A Week in the Life . . ." Elementary Pilot Project Teacher, Beijing China, 2011

PDToolkit FOR *FLATTENING CLASSROOMS, ENGAGING MINDS*

Accompanying this book, there is a website with media tools that, together with the text, provide you the tools you need to prepare for global collaboration that will motivate and engage your students and help them succeed in literacy learning. The PDToolkit for *Flattening Classrooms, Engaging Minds* is available free for six months after you use the password that comes with this book. After that, it is available by subscription for a yearly fee. Be sure to explore and download the resources available at the website. Currently, the following resources are available:

- **Case studies**   Case studies will be posted in their entirety in the PDToolkit.

- **Flat Classroom™ Framework**   We have a sample Flat Classroom Framework that has been completed for you and a blank framework for you to download and use as you plan your projects or map out the pedagogies in existing global projects.

- **Interactive surveys that you complete and see summary of results**   The surveys in the chapters are available in the PDToolkit in an interactive form. Take the survey and have your answers ready for you immediately. Answers are also available online if you use the book to take the surveys.

- **Online glossary**   See the definitions and terms in an easy to search format.

- **Sample student assignments**   View sample assignments online as you prepare your classroom.

- **Downloadable rubrics**   Wiki and digital storytelling rubrics developed in the Flat Classroom projects are available for download and use in your classroom and projects.

- **Enlightened Digital Citizenship**   Download the model for digital citizenship shared in this book.

- **Learning Design Pie Planning Tool**   As you plan projects and examine technology tools, use this tool that will help you reach all learning modalities.

- **Connection Planning Tool**   Download and use this tool for mapping out the global and local connections that will occur in your classroom during each school year to provide balance to your students.

ACKNOWLEDGMENTS

FROM BOTH OF US

http://www.flatclassroombook
.com/acknowledgements.html

We acknowledge that we are the beneficiaries and participants in an enormous global network of teachers who are connecting and learning in powerful ways through the Web. Thank you to all of you who have contributed to our work; this is your book too. Thank you to our manuscript reviewers: Amy H. Blanton, Rutherford County Board of Education; Lawrence H. Fallon, Arlington Public Schools; Joanne Finnegan, Chittenden East Supervisory Union; Jackie Ford, New Albany Schools; Benjamin J. Foster, Russellville School District; Patricia Jackson, Dougherty County School System; Jamie Lanier, Johnston County Schools; Melody Melin, Kasson-Mantorville Schools; and Lisa Suhr, Prairie Hills USD 113; and Flat Classroom certified teachers: your review of this book was invaluable.

A special thank you to Thomas Friedman, Don Tapscott, Dr. Curtis Bonk, Suzie Boss, and Jane Krauss for writing about our work and understanding its importance. Yes Tom, it *is* happening and we *are* doing it, thank you!

Please note a special thank you to Gary Dietz and Rajeev Aurora at Blackboard Collaborate (formerly Elluminate), and Adam Frey at Wikispaces for their continued support of our work and helping these projects to grow.

To Kelly Villella-Canton and all the professionals at Pearson Education and Electronic Publishing Services Inc./Jouve, we extend our gratitude for your advice and work on this book and for believing in the vision that we have to make this book more than just paper but an experience.

To our initial advisors—Terry Freedman, Darren Kuropatwa, Jo McLeay, and Jeff Utecht—thank you for the strong footing and wise advice. To Dr. John Sperandio, CEO at International School Dhaka, thank you for encouragement when Flat Classroom was born. To David Warlick, we express our gratitude for being a continual inspiration and advisor behind the scenes. To Will Richardson, Wes Fryer, Dean Shareski, and also the many K12 Online Conference coordinators, thank you for helping spread the word about these projects. To Lisa Durff, your constant contribution, support, and encouragement is greatly appreciated. To Anne Mirtschin, Steve Madsen, Dr. John Turner, Barbara Stefanics, and Salim al Busaidi, you have been there since almost the very beginning and made these projects better as we pushed ahead. Thank you also to former IB colleagues Paul Fairbrother and Lee Davis for also being there for us. Thank you to Steve Hargadon for your long-standing support, and to Lucy Gray for global collaborative inspiration. To Dr. Ghada at ictQatar, Michael Furdyk and Katherine Walraven from Taking IT Global, and colleagues at Think Global School, we are so very grateful for your support.

To George Haines, Frank Guttler, Andrew Churches, Dr. Leigh Zeitz, Kathy Zeitz, Paul McMahon, Ann Baird, Joan Huntley, Soniiya Jahangir, Chris Chater, Estie Cuellar, Suzie Nestico, Sara Patterson, David Truss, and Craig Union—thank you for supporting us in person as well as virtually! To Mark van't Hooft, Dr. Eric Brunsell, Marcia Alessi, Brian Mannix, Theresa Allen, Eva Brown, Wendy Melnick, Honor Moorman, Fred Haas, Chrissy Hellyer, Nancy von Wahlde, Tina Schmidt, Phil Macoun, Pat D'Arcy, Kevin Crouch, Erica Barclay, Aaron Maurer, Susie Throop, Kim Clayton, Torsten Otto, Lisa Parisi, Cathy Wolinsky, Peggy Sheehy, and David Deeds—thank you for joining in and working so hard for students of all ages.

Thank you to Don Knezek, Lynn Nolan, Anita McAnear, and many others from the International Society for Technology in Education for supporting us through leadership at the inaugural conference and promotion at ISTE events. To Greta Madgwick from HSBC Bank, thank you for sponsoring the first Flat Classroom conference in Qatar. This truly took us to the next level. Thanks to Dr. Greg Hedger, Dr. Ettie Zilber, and Dr. Shabbi Luthra for having the vision to bring Flat Classroom events to your schools (Qatar Academy, Beijing BISS International School, and American School Bombay).

And to all our Flat Classroom teachers who "get it" and will continue to proliferate best practice collaborative pedagogy in learning, we thank you.

FROM JULIE LINDSAY

I have been supported and influenced by so many wonderful people, and I especially want to mention my friends and colleagues at the three International Baccalaureate schools I worked at (International School Dhaka, Qatar Academy, and Beijing BISS IS); I have learned so much from you all. To my Beijing buddies Madeleine Brookes and Heather Davis and, from beyond China, Bernajean Porter and Kim Cofino, thank you for being eternally wise and inspiring. Thanks to all past and present Flat Classroom students, especially the class of 2006. Thank you to the extended Flat Classroom community; teachers, leaders, and workshop and conference participants, it is because of you that I keep going. This book has been an emotional as well as educational journey made possible by your continued participation and support. Thank you.

FROM VICKI DAVIS

To the readers, commenters, and followers of the Cool Cat Teacher blog. No publishing company discovered me: *You did*. I'm forever grateful for your support and confidence and will do my best to encourage you as long as I possibly can.

There are so many people to thank, but I must mention Betty Shiver, curriculum director at Westwood Schools; Ross Worsham, my headmaster; and Dr. Mary Friend Shephard from Walden University. Thank you, students, faculty, parents, and friends at Westwood Schools, the greatest school on the planet (IMHO). I also want to say thank you to Cheryl Oakes, Stephen Downes, Steve Dembo, Alfred Thompson, and Angela Maiers for your influence in my life. To my family (Mom, Dad, Susan, and Sarah; my three wonderful children; and all my nieces and nephews), and especially Kip, without your support this book wouldn't be. I love you.

Flattening Classrooms through Global Collaboration

"We need to educate the 'net generation' differently not so much because 'they' are different, but because the world is different."

DR. ERIC BRUNSELL, College of Education and Human Services, University of Wisconsin, Oshkosh, May 3, 2009, in an email to the NetGenEd™ project

ERIC BRUNSELL
@Brunsell
http://www.teachingscience20.com

CHAPTER 1 WEB RESOURCES
http://www.flatclassroombook.com/introduction.html

SHARE IT

Twitter hashtag for this book:
#flatclass

In the words of Edgar, an Ethiopian student who came to the inaugural Flat Classroom™ Conference in Qatar, 2009:

> What the Flat Classroom is really about . . . [is] connecting and bridging different people and different communities. . . . Learning is not necessarily about learning one plus one, it is about different cultures and learning about the world as a whole. I think it's really important and it helps to make the world more of a global village.[1]

Students also want to make their decisions about one another based on experience rather than media observations. Steve Ramos, from Houston, Texas (another student at the first conference in Qatar), says:

> One thing that really annoys me is when people would react hysterically when I told them I was going to Qatar.

They would say ignorant things like "Ooh, you better take a gun" or "Ooh, hopefully you don't get bombed." And that completely made me mad. I just hate the fact that people are completely blinded by the media and in some ways it sickens me.[2]

When Edgar and Steve met face-to-face, their world views changed. They are not unique. Many of us are finding that students become more open-minded about people from other countries and cultures by simply meeting online. It is not necessary to get on a plane and go to physical places when they can meet on the level plane of online social media spaces. In the words of Miller, a U.S. student in the 2009 Flat Classroom Project (FCP),

I hope to obtain a great knowledge about the flattening of the world through the Flat Classroom Project. I would like to learn what it takes to flatten the world, and the tools that I need to help flatten it. I am excited about getting to make videos about the topics that are contributing factors in the flattening of the world today. I am also eager to meet new people from different countries and get their views on the world and how it is becoming more technologically advanced. I am very excited about the Flat Classroom Project. I am excited to start making a difference.[3]

As evidenced in Miller's words, students feel that they are "meeting" each other when they network in educational spaces. These meetings can be transformative. Students also want to make a difference. These are two of the cornerstones behind the necessity for global collaboration in education.

A GREAT EDUCATION INCLUDES GLOBAL COLLABORATION

tweetable

21st-century skills harness not only the power of technology but the power of people. #flatclass

We believe effective use of technology can build bridges between classrooms, nations, and humankind, and that 21st century skills harness not only the power of technology but the power of people. We need this connection for the future of our planet. It is no longer an option. Students are the greatest textbook ever written for one another and will be travelers on this bridge.

 The Flat Classroom Project is not merely a curricular add-on opportunity for my students. It is an outright necessity in embracing the changes occurring in our world today and as teachers, we are tasked with the challenge of preparing our students for jobs that do not yet exist. The students we teach are the visionaries that will lead my own child someday. Through FCP, my students are not simply learning about cultural diversity, they are living it and doing it. I have witnessed, firsthand, cultural barriers broken and stereotypes disproved through the life-changing Flat Classroom Conference. Unique in its own right, the FCP not only provides a constructivist, collaborative and authentic learning environment, it also provides multiple venues for the celebration of student learning, which is a key element many other projects fail to actualize. I participate repeatedly in this project because of the profound impact it has on many of my students' futures.

SUZIE NESTICO
@nestico
http://coalcrackerclassroom
.wordpress.com

SUZIE NESTICO,
Teacher, Mt. Carmel Area School District,
Pennsylvania, Pennsylvania, Keystone Technology Integrator 2009, personal email

CURRENT HIGH SCHOOL GRADUATES ARE UNDERPREPARED TO COLLABORATE

 I scribbled down four words in my notebook: "The world is flat." As soon as I wrote them, I realized that this was the underlying message of everything that I had seen and heard in Bangalore in two weeks of filming. The global competitive playing field was being leveled. The world was being flattened.[4]

THOMAS FRIEDMAN,
The World Is Flat

Many educators mistakenly view **global collaboration** as an "extra." But visionary educators realize that global collaboration is *not* a curriculum topic but an approach to pedagogy.[5] Using technology, jobs in one country can now easily be **outsourced** (or **offshore outsourced**) to another. When one calls a customer support number, that call can be routed anywhere. The only requirement is that the location have access to high-speed Internet. Global competition for jobs means that today's students must not only be well-educated, creative problem solvers but they must also be equipped to collaborate globally.

Those who wish to be successful must also understand the laws, privacy, etiquette, literacies, and habits of learning that go along with being an effective **digital citizen** of the information era. Research shows that technology plays a key role in succeeding in business, with the ability to connect, network, and collaborate being essential skills.[6] Some people believe that these students who have technological ability at their fingertips just have a natural affinity to "get technology." This simply is not so.

As demonstrated in our digital citizenship model in Chapter 5, technology access and awareness are advantageous starting points. However, being fluent in collaborative people skills online and offline is needed as well. For example, most students in the United States, according to research, are underprepared to work in collaborative teams when they finish high school.[7] The world needs people who can collaborate and collaboration should start as part of the school curriculum beginning in the early years.

LEARNING IS SOCIAL

Learning is a social experience that can be enhanced with **social networking** tools and Web 2.0 technologies. Findings from the *Digital Youth Project: Living and Learning with New Media* tell us that youth currently engage in peer-based, self-directed learning online.[8]

Although adults can be influential in setting learning goals and in functioning as role models, the use of **new media** by youth allows them to learn from their peers. Recent research by the Cisco Learning Network also supports the power of **peer-to-peer learning**. Cisco found that in the case of IT professionals, peer-to-peer learning is necessary and just as important as knowledge coming from the instructor.[9]

According to Steve Hargadon, an expert in social media in education and the founder of *Classroom 2.0* (an **educational network** of over 50,000 educators), the impact of Web 2.0 has changed people's relationships to information and extended personal learning opportunities.[10] Educational networking can minimize isolation in learning and create powerful learning conduits between students.

tweetable

Peer-to-peer learning is necessary and just as important as knowledge coming from the instructor. #flatclass http://tinyurl.com/ciscoresearch

In the Flat Classroom Projects which typically studies technology topics, we see forum posts on topics about novels, history, and other subjects considered to be "core" and not traditionally considered targets for technology integration. Students want to learn from their peers and make learning social! This inclination toward social learning occurs any time we connect students for academic purposes.

The traditional classroom that exists as a distinct entity with one teacher and a group of students can no longer close the door on the world. In fact, a new learning landscape has evolved where responsibility for curriculum, content, and learning is equally shared among all learners (teachers and students).

SHARING UNLOCKS UNLIMITED POTENTIAL

More than enhancing learning, sharing provides great benefits for those who know how to do it properly. Findings by a Metiri Classroom Collaboration study tell us that engagement, pro-school attitudes, and increased achievement are some of the benefits of students working together.[11]

The school where one of the authors (Vicki Davis) teaches received several grants because the teachers have shared what they are doing on their YouTube channel and through Facebook. In fact, this book is a product of the fact that we authors have shared freely much of what we have done via our blogs in a way that has attracted the interest of our publisher, Pearson Education.

ENHANCING EDUCATION WITH CLASSROOM COLLABORATION

Collaboration is working together with one or more others. In a global sense, boundaries are abstract,[12] and more so now that instant publication via wiki, blog, or Facebook is bringing people together from geographically dispersed areas onto common websites.

The aim of global collaboration in education is to improve learning, break down classroom walls, and develop authentic audiences.[13] A global collaborative classroom is able to connect, collaborate, and create products or artifacts with other classrooms anywhere in the world. Furthermore, the use of Web 2.0 has given us a whole new focus and meaning for *global collaboration* by providing collaborative tools that connect and support asynchronous and synchronous work.

DEFINING THE GLOBAL COLLABORATIVE CLASSROOM

A classroom following Flat Classroom project concepts is a classroom that connects and engages with multiple audiences, resources, and tools to create authentic, collaborative learning outcomes. Project outcomes in a variety of media—such as videos, slide shows, presentations, and wikis—add to learning and become part of the **personal learning network (PLN)** of a variety of audiences. These projects and their outcomes also leave a legacy for those who participate. The best projects continually improve by using community input to allow best practices and best learning resources to emerge.

Students can now have a partner in the desk next to them, in India, in China, or elsewhere. Unfortunately, those students who have not collaborated with students in other parts of the world are not going to experience a level playing field after school. Instead, they risk being unable to "speak the language" of communication and collaboration on an international scale, especially if they do not have access to technology tools at home.

The Partnership for 21st Century Skills cites "Collaboration Skills" as an essential skill for students.[14] The International Society for Technology in Education (ISTE)[15] also includes collaboration as an essential standard for students and teachers.

The standards are there. It is time to stop the debate. The walls of the classroom must come down. Well-educated students will immerse in collaborative learning experiences with their peers across the globe.

Knowing how to connect and communicate using "flattened" nonhierarchical methods enabled by the Internet is an essential skill for the 21st century professional and student. This is how the Flat Classroom project started. Without any "official" organizing body behind it, the comment from author Julie Lindsay in Figure 1.1 on Vicki Davis's blog was enough of a spark to ignite the flame of their first collaboration.[16] As a "flat" author, Thomas Friedman, author of *The World Is Flat*, emailed Julie, (Figure 1.2) after finding out about the first Flat Classroom project via her blog.

Flattening means more than just connecting students. It advocates connecting authors, experts, and people throughout the world with common interests. Students who miss out on global collaboration opportunities may just be missing out on their future.

C21 LEARNING AND INNOVATION SKILLS: Communication and Collaboration

NETS.T 3 Model Digital-Age Work and Learning

NETS.S 2 Communication and Collaboration

FIGURE 1.1 Comment from Julie Lindsay to Vicki's Blog on Friedman's *The World Is Flat*

```
JULIE LINDSAY
 ☒ inbox   ▌reply   ▌spam   ▌delete                        10/13/2006

Vicki,
I am also discussing The World Is Flat with my senior IT class. I have some resources
on our wiki page at http://itgs.wikispaces.com/The+World+Is+Flat
This is part of our globalization and cultural diversity topic. The streamed video
from MIT is useful as Friedman gives a good overview of his position.
It would be great if we could interact with your students! Would you be willing/have
the time to participate in an online debate or discussion? my students are Bangladeshi
and Indian nationals and have a perspective from the "other side of the flat world"  ;-)
Have a look at our class blog as well at http://itgsforum.blogspot.com for recent
activity etc. and an overview of the online debate from last year with a school in
Melbourne, Australia.
```

FIGURE 1.2 Email to Julie from Thomas Friedman

```
TOM FRIEDMAN
 ☒ inbox   ▌reply   ▌spam   ▌delete                        11/27/2006

Dear Julie,
I read your blog about the flat world classroom. I was delighted to see it! Tell me
how it goes. Yes, this is really Tom Friedman. Allbest, Tom
```

THE GLOBAL COLLABORATIVE MINDSET

ED GRAGERT, iEARN USA
@iearnusa
http://www.iearn.org

Too often, schools treat connections with the outside world as a nice bonus or filler activity, rather than part of the core mission of a school in the 21st century. Executive Director of iEARN-USA Ed Gragert, who has worked for years to link U.S. classrooms with international partners, says that school cultures must change so that international interaction and collaboration are valued.[17]

In 1976, Edward T. Hall compared culture to an iceberg, having internal and external parts. We have to dig deeper than the picture in a textbook or a video to fully understand our global neighbors because "the only way to learn the internal culture of others is by actively participating in their culture."[18]

TERRY FREEDMAN
@terryfreedman
http://www.ictineducation.org

"The enrichment comes from working with other people who have a completely different culture from one's own. A casual remark or gesture in one country may be deeply offensive, or at least questionable, in another. It is good that young people have the opportunity to make mistakes before doing so in a situation that could have grave and lasting consequences!" says Terry Freedman, ICT leader in the United Kingdom and Flat Classroom advisor since the first project. (For a full case study from Terry, see the end of this chapter.)

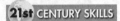

C21 INTERDISCIPLINARY THEME:
Global Awareness

NETS.S 2.c
Communication and
Collaboration

Implementing well-constructed and supported global projects can promote **global awareness** and deeper knowledge of culture than provided in a textbook. Global collaboration should be integrated at every level and in every course to engage students in the benefits of community learning and to instill a globally aware mindset while supporting **global competency** objectives.

WHAT DOES A GLOBAL COLLABORATIVE CLASSROOM LOOK LIKE?

In January 2007, one of my students talked about my global project and said, "I really liked the use of blogs and forums for this project. It really keeps everyone connected even outside of school." This, to me, is an essential component of what makes a classroom great!

Learning used to be confined to the walls around a classroom. Except for the occasional field trip, guest speaker, or video, teaching and learning was defined by the limitations of the classroom space.

Now, the world is our classroom! Our teachers are teachers, students, authors, experts, and parents with whom we have the potential to work when we tear down the walls and open our classrooms to a flat world—where learning has no limits other than the ones we impose ourselves.

Do not go quietly into your classroom. Engage. Be brave![19]

DAVID TRUSS
@datruss
http://pairadimes.davidtruss.com

DAVID TRUSS,
Principal, Dalian Maple Leaf Foreign Nationals School

Students in this environment are taught to be effective digital citizens. Culturally aware, technology-savvy students can contribute and collaborate in meaningful ways as they interact with many different audiences. Given choices of technological tools, they can communicate using audio, video, still photos, or text.

In the modern collaborative classroom project, classes typically "fan out" to cover a subject. With each student having a slightly different research focus, the "jigsaw" of a larger topic comes together as students share learning with each other. The goal is often the creation of rich multimedia and collaborative artifacts that promote higher-order thinking skills and problem solving.

Learning experiences are celebrated as students present and share in online spaces what they have learned. At times, students may be **reverse mentors**[20] for the adults who participate. True global collaboration improves students' understanding and acceptance of one another and produces students who can think and process the overwhelming amount of information in their rapidly changing world.

WHAT IS AN EFFECTIVE GLOBAL COLLABORATIVE PROJECT?

Friedman talks about "**glocalization**" as a "think global, act local" skill that will improve economic advantage.[21] However, in true educational global collaboration, "glocalization" is maintaining local identity in culture and lifestyle while learning about other lifestyles and cultures. An effective global collaborative project is an educational project that flattens or joins classrooms and people from geographically dispersed places within a technology infrastructure built for a common curricular purpose. Interactions foster cultural understanding and global awareness in the process of learning. Local identity is maintained and celebrated.

THE EVOLUTION OF GLOBAL COLLABORATION IN EDUCATION

But aren't we already collaborating globally in the classroom? The concept and practice of global collaboration in the classroom has changed since the development of the Internet. Because of the evolution of tools and Internet speed, we can build a taxonomy that shows an evolution of global collaboration in the classroom (see Table 1.1).

Global Collaboration 1.0. When the possibilities of the Internet emerged in the mid-1990s, astute educators started to reach out and explore collaboration possibilities

TABLE 1.1 Evolution of Global Collaboration

Stage	Connection Speed	Connection Frequency	Type of Connection	Content
Global Collaboration 1.0	Slow	Intermittent	Classroom to classroom	Information exchange
Global Collaboration 2.0	Faster	Intermittent or ongoing	Classroom to classroom; Some student to student through low-bandwidth means	Information and artifact exchange
Global Collaboration 3.0	Faster	Ongoing	Classroom to classroom and student to student	Information exchange and artifact co-creation

around the world. The term *telecommunications* became common and "tele-awards" were issued by companies such as AT&T and the Global SchoolNet.[22] Global collaboration 1.0 generally takes the form of:

- Individual classroom work with some commonalities with partner(s)
- Some sharing via an online website or email
- Coordination by a central body (e.g., Global SchoolNet or ePals)
- Some minimal interaction between participants
- Low-level use of technology and online tools for interaction, but often an opportunity for students to develop web authoring or multimedia skills
- Teacher-directed learning

Global Collaboration 2.0. With expanded Internet speeds and improved technology tools, educators realize the usefulness of online collaborative work by using technology as a scaffold. This stage sees:

- Classrooms getting to know other classes
- Connections and interactions (synchronous and/or asynchronous) that are more common and planned
- Working toward a shared goal (e.g., iEARN Learning Circles)
- Some possible experimentation with Web 2.0 tools
- Teacher-directed learning, with some student independence and connections

Global Collaboration 3.0. At this level, there are high expectations for connectivity and communication. Teachers and students are on the same level and with the focus on student-centered learning. This includes:

- More emphasis on products that are "co-created" and multimedia rich; actions taken by students to make a difference in their immediate or extended community
- Fully engaged teachers who communicate and collaborate online with all participants
- Use of social media tools for communication and interaction
- Classrooms merged into one to study a theme/project, to share research, and to pursue common learning objectives
- High expectations for student and teacher engagement with collaborative expectations (It is not enough to email once a week!)
- Extended community partners (other educators, experts, peers)
- Individual or class/school-based output or products with increasing interdependence on students in other classrooms (outsourcing) for final outcomes
- Teacher- and/or student-initiated collaborations, student-centered learning

The newer forms of global collaboration are about the development of educational networks, finding like-minded people, sharing ideas, and receiving cooperation from different parts of the world. Students work as a team and classrooms work as a single classroom, sharing a pedagogical approach. Friendships and trust relationships emerge with others via online communication rather than face to face.

Room for All Types of Collaboration. Although today's high-speed Internet makes global collaboration 3.0 possible, all levels of collaboration exist in today's schools and have their uses. It should be the goal that before a student goes to college, he or she should participate in projects with 3.0 characteristics. There are, however, uses for all types of global collaboration, and all forms can be transformational. Simple classroom-to-classroom sharing is powerful, but due to time constraints and connectivity requirements, 3.0 may not be possible for all schools.

THE CHALLENGES OF EMBEDDING GLOBAL COLLABORATION

GOING BEYOND THE "WOW!"

Although the so-called hook for many classrooms is the "Wow" of meeting and learning with others who are not face-to-face in the same room, the aim is to make this mode of working common so that "unflat" classrooms become extinct.

There are obstacles to the global collaborative classroom, however. It can be work for teachers to integrate new projects into the curriculum, and it can also be intimidating for students. It can also be an uncomfortable new way for students to learn, especially if a student thrives in the test-based environment.

Despite obstacles, global collaboration in the classroom is a win-win situation. When students are provided choices for learning, we can reach more of them. Students also win when they have interactions that are meaningful and that support authentic problem solving. Teachers know students will be ready to collaborate again after the students learn how the first time. They will have developed lifetime skills. Teachers can also lead the way through modeling good collaboration.

tweetable

Go beyond the "Wow." Embed global collaboration practice into everyday learning so that "unflat" classrooms become extinct. #flatclass

 **ISTE STANDARDS**

NETS.T 1.d
Facilitate and Inspire Student Learning and Creativity

ENGAGING LEARNERS AND LEADERS

In order for students to be fully engaged, teachers must also be engaged. In Julie's experience with her class in Bangladesh, the first students to complete both Flat Classroom and Horizon projects struggled with communication issues, collaboration difficulties, and cultural differences.[23] This new global collaboration enthralled them but, at the same time, the students expressed concerns, wondering if the extra effort was "worth it." This is typical. Many teachers express similar concerns, and have to balance the time needed for enhanced engagement with existing demands on their classroom.

SHIFTING TRADITIONAL PEDAGOGIES

The walls break down when students are part of an inclusive global classroom where expert advisors and peer-group review become a common occurrence, and where the ability to reach out and create friendships with those they *want* to learn with is a reality. Learning globally includes making a difference to the world.

 tweetable

Learning globally includes making a difference to the world. #flatclass

Instead of "lesson plans," many who are collaborating globally create **project plans**. These plans include two things: common deliverables for all students and flexibility for individual teachers to customize other parts of the project to suit the particular needs of their classroom. Some authentic research projects are followed up with action projects, in which students take action based on their learning. The use of social media allows students to have an impact on global issues with creativity and hard work. Student voices can be heard.

HAVING REALISTIC EXPECTATIONS

Learning is not one-size-fits-all, nor does it happen in isolation. Does everyone like geography? Does everyone like mathematics? No! The same can be said for local versus global collaboration (or, for that matter, group work as opposed to working alone). Not everybody likes the same thing. No one method will ever suit all learning styles, so diversity of delivery and audience will help us engage more learners with content.

A LOOK AT THE PROJECTS

The principles in this book may be applied to any age and any subject, including postsecondary education and professional development learning opportunities. Throughout this book we will mention various projects created by the authors and many others.

To give you an overview of the projects in this book we have outlined the Flat Classroom projects. These projects are not meant to be prescriptive, because global collaboration will evolve tremendously in the years to come; however, these descriptions will give you context for where we are now.

THE FLAT CLASSROOM PROJECT

ISTE STANDARDS

If implemented as designed, this project meets all ISTE NET.S standards.

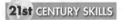

21st CENTURY SKILLS

If implemented as designed, this project meets all C21 standards with various students having different aspects of the interdisciplinary themes based on their research topics.

The Flat Classroom project allows upper middle and high school levels to study and explore emerging trends and "flatteners" in our world as discussed in Thomas Friedman's book *The World Is Flat*. Students learn about technology trends in a project designed to let them experience those same trends firsthand.

There are two main components: a collaborative group **wiki** and a personal video. Grouped in cross-school teams, students conduct **authentic research** and collaboratively edit a wiki on their topic. They can more closely connect with partners on the project's social network through forums, blogs, a live chat, and message walls. Educators, business leaders, or preservice teachers serve as expert advisors on the wikis.

The personal video is a response to the research from a specific creative perspective. Using one of the **six senses of the conceptual age** from Dan Pink's *A Whole New Mind*,[24] a student may tell her or his story using the first-person voice, or another one of the six "senses." Students outsource a section of their video to another student in another classroom. This makes them not just participants studying the forces that make the world flat, but rather those who have lived it. Educators serve as judges to determine the top videos in an awards program at the end of the project. At the

FLAT CLASSROOM™ FRAMEWORK

NAME OF PROJECT: Flat Classroom Project

WEBSITE URL: http://www.flatclassroomproject.net

TWITTER NAME: @flatclassroom

LOCATION: The World

COMMUNICATION: Technopersonal; asynchronous and synchronous

GENERATION: Contemporaries; interactions with older and younger generation

INFORMATION: Students construct personal learning networks (PLNs) to encompass all areas of the learning pathway

LEARNING LEGACY: Public wiki, blogs, and videos; recorded student summits posted online

DIGITAL CITIZENSHIP AREA OF UNDERSTANDING

Safety, Privacy, Copyright, and Legal
Etiquette and Respect
Habits of Learning
Literacy and Fluency

conclusion of the project, students report their reflections on postproject blog posts and student summits in the online presentation room.

We break down this project further in Chapter 10 as we dissect the anatomy of global collaborative project design.

But in the end the dominant focus was not the technologies, or the educational standards; it was the power of the Flat Classroom projects to foster student-centered, student-empowered, student-connected, student-responsible, authentic learning. Student-centered in that students were allowed to be the managers of their own learning. Student-empowered where students forged new relationships. Student-connected in that they worked with people they had not physically met. Student-responsible, it was always apparent who was contributing (and who was not). And authentic in that materials such as the Horizon Report and *The World Is Flat* spoke directly to the students and the world they faced.

JOHN TURNER,
Flat Classroom project teacher, Head of Educational Technology, Canadian International School, Hong Kong
(See a full case study from John at the end of this chapter.)

THE DIGITEEN PROJECT

The Digiteen™ project is a global hands-on project for middle and early high school students. The purpose of the project is to teach and promote effective digital citizenship and responsible online choices. This project studies digital citizenship with students researching current digital citizenship topics and writing a collaborative report on a wiki using the citizenship model shared in Chapter 5 of this book. Using a live social network experience to underpin their research, students experience the technologies they are studying.

After the research, students create action-based educational projects to promote effective digital citizenship, typically at their local schools. This makes the project a representation of Friedman's concept of "glocalization" in that issues that affect digital life and learning are explored and discussed globally, with students taking

JOHN TURNER
@jturner56
http://jturner56.wikispaces.com

ISTE STANDARDS
The research phase of the project meets ISTE NET.S 2, 3, 4, 5, 6. If the teacher allows students to create their own action project instead of creating an assignment for them, it also meets NETS.S 1.

21st CENTURY SKILLS
All C21 student standards except creativity. If the teacher allows the students to design their own action project, creativity is also met.

FLAT CLASSROOM™ FRAMEWORK

NAME OF PROJECT: Digiteen Project

WEBSITE URL: http://www.digiteen.org

TWITTER NAME: @digiteen

LOCATION: The World and Inner Circle (depending on the action project)

COMMUNICATION: Technopersonal; asynchronous, synchronous

GENERATION: Contemporaries; typically action projects include presentations to the younger generation

INFORMATION: Students construct PLNs to encompass all areas of the learning pathway

LEARNING LEGACY: public wiki documenting research and action projects

leadership back in their local community to implement an action. Service learning, "combining classroom instruction with community service to address community needs,"[25] is powerful learning.

THE NETGENED™ (NET GENERATION EDUCATION) PROJECT

This project has been created by the Flat Classroom project team and highly regarded author Don Tapscott. The first NetGenEd project was announced at Flat Classroom Conference 2009 when Tapscott was brought in via Skype to talk to the educator and student participants. In this project, students study the results of the annual Horizon Report[26] (written collaboratively by the New Media Consortium[27] and Educause[28]) and relate them to the characteristics of their generation (called NetGen) from Tapscott's book *Grown Up Digital: How the Net Generation Is Changing Your World.*

Like the Flat Classroom project, students create a collaborative research report via wiki and a personal video. However, in this project, some students assume roles

FLAT CLASSROOM™ FRAMEWORK

NAME OF PROJECT: NetGenEd Project

WEBSITE URL: http://www.netgened.org

TWITTER NAME: @netgened

LOCATION: The World

COMMUNICATION: Technopersonal; asynchronous and synchronous

GENERATION: Contemporaries; interactions with older generation

INFORMATION: Students construct PLNs to encompass all areas of the learning pathway, including the social network and wiki

LEARNING LEGACY: Public wiki, blogs, videos; recorded student summits posted online.

such as **project manager** (PM), assistant project manager (APM), and editors of the various wikis, and therefore student-manage this project. PMs and APMs report weekly to teachers via a survey form to keep everyone apprised of any issues that teachers need to address (such as noncontribution).

After compiling their wiki reports based on current research and encouraged by "expert advisors" (subject matter experts in the industry, as well as other educators), students then create a personal video or multimedia artifact. Similar to the Flat Classroom project, international teams of educators judge the final videos and present awards during an online ceremony.

THE ERACISM PROJECT™

The Eracism Project was the winning project concept by a student team from the inaugural 2009 Flat Classroom Conference held in Doha, Qatar.[29] The project was designed to open possibilities for understanding and realizing solutions to the world's problems through debate. Postconference, we joined with a team of educators, including debate expert Bernajean Porter, to create the project as a global debate using asynchronous tools.

Using Voicethread, schools competed in a double-elimination debate on the topic "Differences Make Us Stronger." The final debate was held online in a virtual world (ReactionGrid using Open Sim) with audience members voting on the winners.

"A WEEK IN THE LIFE . . .": ELEMENTARY FLAT CLASSROOM PROJECT

In this elementary school project, classrooms join globally to explore what life is like in each country and their respective schools through online discussion and real-time linkups where possible. In a short period of time all classrooms collect multimedia, as agreed in their teams, and share this with a view to co-creating artifacts using the collective material. Students build an online learning community as they collaborate

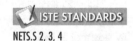

FLAT CLASSROOM™ FRAMEWORK

NAME OF PROJECT: The Eracism Project

WEBSITE URL: http://www.eracismproject.org

TWITTER NAME: @eracismproject

LOCATION: Four schools, none of which is yours; potential for worldwide

COMMUNICATION: Asynchronous debates until the finals

GENERATION: Debate with contemporaries; feedback from older generation

INFORMATION: Teachers as coaches, research is independent by classroom; no common social network or wiki except for debate resources

LEARNING LEGACY: Debates recorded to share with others on Voicethread

21st CENTURY SKILLS

C21 INTERDISCIPLINARY THEMES:
Global Awareness

C21 LEARNING AND INNOVATION SKILLS:
Creativity and Innovation

C21 LEARNING AND INNOVATION SKILLS:
Critical Thinking and Problem Solving

C21 LEARNING AND INNOVATION SKILLS:
Communication and Collaboration

C21 INFORMATION, MEDIA AND TECHNOLOGY SKILLS:
Media Literacy

 **WEBSITES**

Edmodo
http://www.edmodo.com

FLAT CLASSROOM™ FRAMEWORK

NAME OF PROJECT: "A Week in the Life . . ."

WEBSITE URL: http://www.aweekinthelife.org

LOCATION: Worldwide

COMMUNICATION: Technopersonal and interpersonal; asynchronous and synchronous

GENERATION: Contemporaries

INFORMATION: Other learners; teachers as coaches; local classroom resources

LEARNING LEGACY: Private access to Edmodo group through the classroom

on a common set of guiding questions. The project also teaches digital citizenship and introduces students to the concept of a digital footprint.

This project currently uses Edmodo for communication, group creation, and file uploading. The project wiki provides collaborative sharing as well as a learning platform. Many subjects are integrated, such as geography, math, science, technology, social studies, and writing as the students study school time, languages, clothing, housing and transportation, leisure time, food and celebrations, and the environment.

SUMMARY

Global collaborative learning experiences are an essential trait of the 21st century school. It is time to move forward in every school and experience the advantages of these projects in classrooms around the world. Global collaboration has evolved since the beginning of the information era and allows classrooms to merge into common experiences and projects.

Integrating it into the curriculum is vital to those schools that want to remain relevant, engaged with learners, and known for achievement. Global literacy and global competency are now being discussed as an important part of the curriculum of each school. You can't develop global literacy from a book; it can only come through experience.

ESSENTIAL QUESTIONS

- Can you have an excellent education without global collaboration? Why or why not?
- What does a modern global collaborative classroom look like?
- How has global collaboration in education changed through the years?
- What are the challenges of embedding global collaboration in the classroom?

◀ Join in the discussion about these topics @ http://tinyurl.com/flatclass-ch1

THE FLAT CLASSROOM™ DIARIES

Diary Entry 1

DREAMS WHEN WE'RE AWAKE

By VICKI DAVIS
January 2009, Flying home from the first Flat Classroom Conference **Doha, Qatar**

I am nestled amidst the sluggish heaps of jetlagged tourists, entrepreneurs, families, and a mom with one colicky golden haired baby while contentedly listening to Van Morrison about 20,000 feet above the border between Iran and Iraq pondering the meaning of life.

The lady two seats up is watching *Eagle Eye* (a movie) with Arabic subtitles. The man beside me left his seat a while back to remove his Arabic garb and put on a pair of comfortable black flannel sleeping pants. Katie, my exhausted student from south Georgia USA snuggles against a window that, if open, would show her Eastern Europe approaching at a pace of 500 miles an hour.

And that is really how I feel at this moment, with the rush of oncoming air; a vision is coming upon me for what this flat world truly means.

In my whole life, I have never seen what I saw this weekend. I daresay any peacekeeper on earth would sob at the sight of students from the U.S., Qatar, Syria, Ethiopia, Pakistan, Oman, Iraq, India, Australia, and so many other places laughing contentedly together in the midst of Qatar's famous market, the Souk . . . .

Read the rest of this Flat Classroom Diary online.
http://tinyurl.com/flatdreams

Diary Entry 2

AN INTERNATIONAL JOURNEY, A LETTER FROM JULIE LINDSAY

Written in Beijing, China, June 2011

"Come and teach in the real Africa," was the advertisement that inspired my husband and me to apply for and finally accept our first international teaching positions in Zambia, January 1998. Our daughter, Violet, was three. We sold most of our worldly possessions in our hometown of Melbourne, Australia, and left for Africa on our new adventure. We are still out there, over fourteen years and five countries later (Zambia, Kuwait, Bangladesh, Qatar, and now China), experiencing in addition to Australian, also British and International Baccalaureate curriculum while exploring and embracing diverse cultural differences.

My life changed again when Vicki Davis and I started the Flat Classroom Project. I was in Bangladesh in a 1:1 school with wireless Internet access and with students who were studying the impact of technology on society.[30] In addition Web 2.0 was emerging as a platform for communication and collaboration. The time was ripe to embark on something new that could be scaffolded by the new online technologies and could join students across the globe in meaningful learning experiences.

Being an international educator, and having a daughter as a "third-culture kid" (with educator parents[31]), I selfishly want others around the world to experience what we are privileged to live. I want them to be confronted with different religious and cultural beliefs and be immersed in an environment where English (or their own language) is not spoken and where simple communication can often result in highly creative sign language. I want them to

Read the rest of this Flat Classroom Diary online.
http://tinyurl.com/flatjourney

acknowledge and respect differences and learn how to use their personal strengths to create a bond of understanding with new friends. I want them to question, doubt, be amazed, experience alternative lifestyles, treasure similarities, and learn how to get on with other people globally. I want them to be able to do this without losing their own identity and sense of belonging to a country or to a culture, and without feeling superior or inferior to any other person.

Through Flat Classroom we are building bridges, forging new pedagogies, and questioning current education systems that place value on content above process and individual output and gain rather than on collaboration and community learning for understanding. This book is a part of the bridge and we encourage you to learn from the stories and apply it in your own learning situation. I encourage you to embrace your own global journey.

CASE EXAMPLES OF GLOBAL COLLABORATION

Case Study 1

From the Leaders: TERRY FREEDMAN,
ICT consultant and original Flat Classroom Project judge in 2006[32]

PDToolkit
for
*Flattening Classrooms,
Engaging Minds*
Read full Case Studies
in PDToolkit online.

I think this project has gone far beyond its original remit, which, in essence, was to explore Friedman's concept of the "flat world" in ways that exemplified living and working in a flat world. Thus, students and teachers from different parts of the world have collaborated on research and presentation (in the form of a video). This has been both enriching and challenging.

The enrichment comes from working with other people who have a completely different culture from one's own. A casual remark or gesture in one country may be deeply offensive, or at least questionable, in another. It is good that young people have the opportunity to make mistakes before doing so in a situation that could have grave and lasting consequences!

But it has also been challenging, especially for teachers. On a practical level, how do you coordinate the curricula of schools from across the world? How can teachers ensure that the time devoted to such a large project pays dividends in terms of meeting their own nation's targets? What constitutes collaboration, how can it be encouraged, how can it be measured, and how can an absence of (real) collaboration be addressed? And going beyond collaboration, how do we judge if genuine and important learning has taken place? And if it has, will the student remember the lessons learned in a year's time, or in three year's time? The various interactions of the Flat Classroom project have given educators access, in effect, to a vast testing ground in which such issues can be examined.

Case Study 2

Promoting Change in an International Environment[33]
From the Leaders: DR. JOHN TURNER,
Head of Educational Technology, Canadian International School,
Hong Kong

PDToolkit
for
*Flattening Classrooms,
Engaging Minds*
Read full Case Studies
in PDToolkit online.

When the opportunity presented in the early 2000s to be part of the early Flat Classroom projects it was the right opportunity at the right time. With Web 2 taking the classroom even further beyond its four walled limitations here was an authentic educational project of value for students and teachers alike.

Web 2 technologies such as Ning, Elluminate, and particularly Wikispaces have become staple educational tools for many. At the time, though, they were new and challenging.

What they provided in global connections for teachers and students as co-learners was immediate and helped foster even more learning through their array of tools.

The Flat Classroom projects allowed for teachers to connect within the school and around the world as co-learners and educators. At-hand support and communications were vital for problem solving and keeping up-to-date (even if 5:00 am and 11:00 pm meetings to fit in with different time zones are probably not what most teachers see as a professional likelihood).

The opportunity for students to join together generated incredible cultural interchanges and understanding. Be it American, European, Middle Eastern, or Asian students, all could see firsthand that they all shared similar dreams, aspirations, and concerns. Truly a global experience. This carried over into the first Flat Classroom Conference in Doha, which I was part of. Here students saw their online friends up close and stronger connections were made all around.

In conclusion, when I look back, I see the opportunities provided and the strong learning base for taking on change in an ever-changing digital world. For my learning, my students' learning, and for many other teachers and students around this increasingly connected world, the Flat Classroom has been and continues to be a significant contributor.

CHAPTER 2

Impact on Learning: Research in the Global Collaborative Classroom

For the first time in history, our job as educators is to prepare our students for a future that we cannot clearly describe.[1]

DAVID WARLICK

 ADD FRIEND

DAVID WARLICK
@dwarlick
http://davidwarlick.com/2cents

Brian Mannix,[2] seventh-grade social studies teacher at Great Neck South Middle School, USA, says to Julie via email:

> The Digiteen project was challenging for both the students and me, but as you promised we were able to work through the fear and the great challenges faced before us and come out on top. My students have truly risen to the occasion. They are in the process of filming five separate Digital Citizenship videos, collecting money for the creation of an anti-bullying app and have developed an anti-bullying game that will be one piece of that creation.
>
> The students are on track to raise $1,125 to be put toward this Digital Citizenship app that will be created by breaking down and flattening the classroom walls and hiring

an individual overseas to work on the IPhone App creation. In addition to this, students have recorded an anti-bullying song and are in the midst of recording a video for the App.

Finally, students have designed a T-shirt that says "Think B4 U TYPE." We are going to sell that and then put the money toward an "Unplugged Activity" where we promote the dangers of Internet addiction. All of these have been student run and student directed.

Thank you so much for allowing me to enter the Flat Classroom™ world. It has opened my eyes to the tremendous opportunities that lie in front of us as educators and has allowed me to see just how much my students can accomplish in this environment. Thank you for helping to break down the walls.

Brian went on to be named a Tech & Learning leader of the year in the United States for 2010.[3] Already a great teacher, he unleashed the creativity and innovation of his students with the principles advocated in this book. You can do it, too!

BRIAN MANNIX
@mannixlab
https://sites.google.com/a
/greatneck.k12.ny.us/mannixlab

THE VOICES OF CHANGE

What kind of impact do global collaboration and emerging technologies have on the classroom? Let's take a moment to savor the possibilities. While some are dreaming of what education could be, many of us are living the dream. Students around the world are engaging, learning, sharing, collaborating, using higher-order thinking, and employing the skills that business says education is not teaching. It is happening, but just not enough. Some are waiting for more research, which also needs to happen.

The voice of change is heard and shared throughout this book as we explore this impact on teaching and learning. Consider some of the stories we share in this book:

- A young boy with a debilitating speech impediment and autism was unleashed as teachers saw the disability vanish when he filmed himself at home and presented online. He now uses video to communicate flawlessly. (See Chapter 5.)
- Teenagers embarked on a quest to investigate the **virtual worlds** used by their younger brothers and sisters and uncovered findings that had Internet safety experts talking. (See Chapters 1, 6, 7.)
- A boy in the desert of Oman sat under a tamarind tree with a laptop and cellular modem and filmed a movie about the impact of wireless connectivity on a Bedouin tribe as goats, camels, and stick huts scattered the landscape behind him.
- Students were set free to learn and connect as their teachers used **research-based best practices,** technology, and global connections to make their content compelling and relevant to a generation not being reached by antiquated pedagogies.
- Two teachers from separate places in the world linked their small classes of students and now find themselves writing this book and directing international collaborative projects ("in their spare time") for thousands of students every year. This led to the establishment of a nonprofit organization that brings students and educators together for a challenge-based conference that is face-to-face learning the way it should be—less lecture and more hands-on.

"Wireless Connectivity and Bedouin Life" by AhmedM
http://tinyurl.com/fcpbedouin

WHAT STUDENTS SAY

"I [have] decided to form my opinions based on personal experience only, rather than generic typecasts. The common fascination we all share with each other is something valuable and very attainable with an open mind," says Casey Cox, a student who took part in Flat Classroom Project 2006. (See the full case study at the end of this chapter.)

Casey's partner in the project, Cannelle Cuvelier (see case study), says, "Perhaps what struck me most about the project and what surely I will remember most, was the easiness with which my partner and I communicated, in spite of the miles that separated us, the time difference, and the technical difficulties that we encountered. . . . [T]his was how this project changed my view about the use of technology. School work and communication with friends and family using technology wasn't new, but using technology with another student across the world . . . that surely was."

WHAT EDUCATORS SAY

We need more relationships like that between Casey and Canelle. Yes, technology is part of the equation but it is just an operator. The most important variable in the global collaboration equation is *people*. Technology itself is neutral and can be used for good or bad. However, connect one person at a time, build trust, and move forward, and you will see that connecting people in a positive way equals change.

Mrs. Theresa M. Allen, a teacher and the technology coordinator for Cathedral of St. Raymond School in Joliet, Illinois, points out that global collaboration is particularly opportune for children of a certain age: "For students ages 7 to 13, global education satisfies a hunger that grows knowing that there are other students who want to learn just as much as they want to learn about what is beyond their classroom walls. They want to interact, find similarities, common knowledge, and work toward the same goal—together."

Brian Mannix was a participant in Digiteen™ 2010, a Flat Classroom™ project. He writes of the project, "The Flat Classroom experience has led me and my students to scream from the rooftops, 'Mr. Principal. Tear down these walls.' For too long students have been boxed into their own experience with their peers in the classroom and the text on a page. With the filter pulled back in the Flat Classroom, students are able to work together, building upon their skills in order to scaffold for success. It is essential for the future of education for our students in this locally global world."

Eva Brown, a former teacher at River East Collegiate School in Winnipeg, Manitoba, Canada, and a Flat Classroom certified teacher, stresses the absolute necessity of global education today, saying, "Global collaboration is a requirement for digital natives to be competitive in the global economy. It is a literacy that must be in every curriculum."

If we are to solve the pressing global issues, we are going to have to link up people where they are. "Meetings of the minds" are increasingly online. So, we help students as individuals explore the lives, feelings, and motivations of others through online interaction, and respond by sharing our own stories. This has an impact that will change perceptions and practices for the better.

MEASURING THE IMPACT

ANECDOTAL EVIDENCE: DIALOG AND STORIES

Most research begins as a story. Anecdotal observations by teachers or researchers may be made while visiting the classroom but often happen as family or friends have casual conversations. Today's casual conversations happen less over the supper table and more through Facebook, Twitter, blogs, and various other social media. Many of the best researchers are connected through these media sources and are able to overhear the stories and contribute to the dialog around such topics.

The storytellers have now become opinion leaders through social media. Even before any research can be done, there is no doubt that the telling of the stories from the classroom has an impact on classroom practice. Does the telling of the story influence the results? Does the teacher's belief in and enthusiasm for the blogger influence the classroom more than the practices professed in the blog? Does the dialog itself influence classroom practice faster than research can keep up? These are all questions that affect classroom research, particularly on technology and global collaboration, begging for at least a review of the impact of social media on research.

We have many doctoral candidates who contact us about the stories we and our students tell through social media, wanting to look more deeply into the stories we tell. We realize that research must evolve and that research teams may have need for "connected" *and* "disconnected" researchers. (Could the "rock star" status of a particular storyteller bias a connected researcher's findings? Perhaps!) We ask these questions because if we care about doing what is right for education, we must all be willing to open up our practice and admit the imperfections and the need for study of how to improve those imperfections. More research and data are needed, and good online projects will welcome the involvement of researchers.

CORRELATION VERSUS CAUSATION

The Hawthorne studies (from which we get the term *Hawthorne effect*) demonstrated that the very act of conducting a study could cause improvements. Additionally, when someone studies global collaboration, at the heart is typically a highly engaged, well-connected teacher. You could argue that such a teacher is going to improve learning no matter the tools used. We know that one of the greatest influences on learning in the classroom is the teacher.

Additionally, as one looks at global collaboration, one cannot ignore the technology underlying the collaboration. So, as you look at a classroom that is moving rapidly into global collaboration, you will also find a classroom that is rapidly integrating technology in potentially novel ways to the students. Does the impact of learning something new improve learning of the content?

HOW GLOBAL COLLABORATION AND SOCIAL MEDIA ARE TRANSFORMING RESEARCH

RESEARCHERS IN THE ONLINE CLASSROOM

As we look at the stories of change, we must begin to grapple with the evolution of educational research itself. Global collaboration is flattening the classroom for researchers as well. A researcher sitting in the back of the room can have a profound effect on the nature of the classroom, but a researcher observing a blog or wiki may be much less likely to affect what is happening. No one may even know the researcher is there. Thus, with global collaborative learning, researchers have the opportunity to be in classrooms on a daily basis observing the learning in-situ as well as measuring the outcomes. This also provides teachers with the opportunity to reflect and share best-practice leadership.

ACCELERATED RESEARCH THROUGH COLLABORATION

As Macarthur Foundation researcher James Gee acknowledges in his paper, *New Digital Media and Learning as an Emerging Area and "Worked Examples" as One Way Forward,* "I did not get the authors [of the articles he cites] to comment on how they viewed the other pieces of work . . . in fact there really are no mechanisms for this type of cross disciplinary dialog. Journals and other scholarly practices mostly ensure that no such dialog happens and that we respond, at best to people who share our discipline."[4]

It is time for such cross-disciplinary collaboration and dialog among researchers to happen! The human genome was mapped two years ahead of schedule largely because of the collaborative nature of the process. We hope researchers will apply what we've shared in this book about global collaboration to their own research practices. If you are a researcher reading this book, we invite you to contact us. Take stories or questions and turn them into research. The good researcher and good educator both have a strong desire to do what is right to help supercharge 21st century learning.

CITIZEN SCIENTISTS

Forest ecologist Jess Parker of the Smithsonian Environmental Research Center made headlines when he discovered that forests near Washington, D.C., were growing faster than expected. The Smithsonian then partnered with Microsoft and TakingITGlobal to develop Shout to have students band and measure trees around the world. Using statistical analysis, they are able to filter out "noise" from inaccurate readings.[5]

Such analyses are also used in Journey North's Monarch Butterfly Migration Tracking Project. NASA asks for citizen scientists to help improve maps on Mars and says, "**Citizen scientists** have helped to answer serious scientific questions."[6] Other websites, such as Science for Citizens, help researchers and citizen scientists link projects and observations.

Could you imagine classrooms where students are citizen scientists? Where they can report lessons and activities that they like? Where their reviews can be correlated

ISTE STANDARDS

NETS.T 5
Engage in Professional Growth and Leadership

WEBSITES

Shout Citizen Science Tree Banding Project
http://shoutlearning.org /treebanding.html

Monarch Butterfly Project
http://www.learner.org/jnorth /monarch

NASA Citizen Scientist Projects
http://science.nasa.gov /citizen-scientists

Science for Citizens @ sci4Cits
http://www.scienceforcitizens .net

ISTE STANDARDS

NETS.S 3
Research and Information Fluency

21st CENTURY SKILLS

C21 INTERDISCIPLINARY THEME:
Environmental Literacy

C21 LIFE AND CAREER SKILLS:
Productivity and Accountability

FLAT CLASSROOM™ FRAMEWORK

NAME OF PROJECT: Shout Learning Tree Banding Project

WEBSITE URL: http://shoutlearning.org/treebanding.html

LOCATION: Local scientific measurements; global data analysis

COMMUNICATION: Interpersonal skills

GENERATION: Contemporaries; older generation

INFORMATION: Student observations; subject matter experts

LEARNING LEGACY: Put data into a project that becomes a permanent part of science

with assessments and teacher opinions? Citizen scientist projects can transform learning through having teachers, students, and administrators participate in all types of research that haven't been considered yet. Massive data collection and anecdotal observations are now possible to the researcher who can break free from the paradigms of the past. If citizen science is being used widely in environmental sciences, it can also be used in educational best practices research.

DIGITAL CITIZENSHIP AREA OF UNDERSTANDING

Habits of Learning

OBSTACLES OF CURRENT RESEARCH PRACTICES

It has been a profound struggle to include researchers in our projects because the ethical review board process is so extended. Potential researchers have sometimes had to "start over" because our projects run every 3 to 4 months with a new set of countries and students. "Blanket" research agreements wouldn't work with most institutions of higher education because each institution wants every student, parent, and teacher to sign his or her own form.

Could teachers establish approval for ongoing research relations with research approvals retained in initial permission forms? Can research tools be coordinated to include data collection for several research questions on the same pre- and post-project instruments? Is it possible to deposit data in some sort of cloud for blind research? Does the lack of social media savvy exclude some researchers?

Most global collaborative projects would welcome researchers. But research must evolve to be cooperative between institutions and projects to create ongoing relationships that protect research and participant integrity while easing administration for the already busy teachers managing the projects. Global collaboration has the potential to transform every room for the better: from classroom to boardroom, science laboratory, and lecture hall.

A LOOK AT RECENT RESEARCH RELATING TO THIS BOOK

It is our goal for research to become embedded into everything we do and achieve with Flat Classroom projects. It is through this research and analysis that we can learn how to improve the projects and how to update pedagogy to best support learning with technology and in a flattened world. We conduct our own reflections and surveys, but in order to share and be transparent, it is important to open up to research from those outside the project. After discussing constructivism and connectivism theories of learning, we will review two research studies relating to the work in this book. More are emerging as we speak, and we encourage you to share those with the #flatclass community on Twitter and other educational networks.

CONSTRUCTIVISM

Constructivist theory of knowledge is based on the premise that we construct knowledge rather than acquire it.[7] Formulated by Piaget, this theory argues that each learner is an individual with unique needs and background. Social constructivism emphasizes the importance of the learner's being active in the learning process and forming meaning influenced by cultural elements such as language and background. It also considers the teacher to be more effective as a facilitator than as a didactic lecturer. In terms of curriculum, constructivism emphasizes hands-on problem solving and the elimination of standardized curriculum.

As you read about the global collaborative projects in this book, you will see many constructivist principles represented, although certainly just about any form of learning is represented in online spaces.

CONNECTIVISM

In the age of digital communication connectivism is based on the use of networks and nodes to create connections and develop a personal learning network. According to George Siemens,[8] connectivism principles include that learning and knowledge are contextual and new information is constantly being acquired that users prioritize to feed into decision making. The individual is the starting point of connectivism, with the cycle of knowledge (personal to network to organization) allowing learners to update and remain current.

With many global collaborative projects requiring research and the acquisition of information, the required literacy skills link strongly with connectivist theories. Additionally, the learning pathway discussed in this book (introduced in Chapter 3) will help you create a well-rounded group of information sources to keep yourself well informed and current.

ETHNOCENTRISM AND GLOBAL COLLABORATION

Many teachers and students who collaborate have reported a shift in student views of other countries on a global basis. Based on this anecdotal evidence, researcher Dr. Craig Union has evaluated the evidence and shares his findings in a story here with the full case study available online.[9]

In this instance, Dr. Union was intrigued by teacher reports that the worldview of their students was changing. As he participated in the Flat Classroom project as a judge and expert advisor, teachers started sharing this question with him, and Dr.

Union formed a research question: Did students become less ethnocentric as a result of these global collaborations? He studied the topic of student **ethnocentrism** for his doctoral dissertation and found:

> The use of Web 2.0 technologies during the Net Generation Education and Horizon projects was successful in the fight against ethnocentrism in this cross cultural learning environment mainly because ethnocentrism was reduced to and/or maintained at a minimal level after only a few weeks of project participation.

Read a longer summary and the full research dissertation at http://tinyurl.com /fcbookresearch1

RESEARCH SUMMARY ON THE NET GENERATION EDUCATION 2009 AND 2010 AND HORIZON 2008 PROJECTS

Ethnocentrism is a problem because it can perpetuate prejudice and stereotypes against certain students in a classroom or become a form of discrimination directed against certain students on the basis of their ethnic group and background. Therefore, my research examined the working relationships of students, and whether the use of digital technologies (i.e., Web 2.0 technologies) by digital natives can help reduce the level of ethnocentrism in cross-cultural classrooms during the Net Generation Education 2009 and 2010 and Horizon 2008 projects.

The conceptual framework for this study drew on Levinson's concept of ethnocentrism,[10] which highlighted dominant in-groups and how in-groups react negatively and hostile toward out-groups; on Papert's constructionism,[11] which recognized that people learn more effectively when they engage in constructing personally meaningful artifacts when using technology; and on Friedman's concept of the world's being flat,[12] which referred to equalizing by using flattening forces to empower people with more tools to connect, compete, and collaborate.

The research used a qualitative method of inquiry, the case study approach (timeframe: March 1, 2008, to June 2, 2010), and the analytic induction method as the data analysis strategy. The data sources were interviews from the coordinators of classrooms with students located in Canada, Korea, Pakistan, Qatar, and the United States; responses to predetermined questions created by the project coordinators/creators from students located in multiple countries; and a review of the online wiki discussions from the participating students and teachers located in multiple countries.

The following research questions guided this study:

1. What factors in the Net Generation Education/Horizon Project encourage and impede the level of ethnocentrism?
2. What patterns related to ethnocentrism develop in working relationships among students when using Web 2.0 technologies during the Net Generation Education/Horizon Project?

The researcher concluded that the use of Web 2.0 technologies during the Net Generation Education and Horizon projects were successful in the fight against ethnocentrism in this cross-cultural learning environment, mainly because ethnocentrism was reduced to and/or maintained at a minimal level after only a few weeks of project participation.[13]

CHARACTERISTICS OF EFFECTIVE ONLINE COLLABORATIONS

Heidi Everett-Cacopardo interviewed several teachers from both Flat Classroom projects and many other global collaborative projects and shared findings that support the content of this book. Her findings, shared here, emphasize the importance of planning, a diversity of tools, and the showcasing of student work as some essential common best practices for successful online collaborations.

ONLINE INTERNATIONAL COLLABORATION STUDY SUMMARY (HEIDI EVERETT-CACOPARDO)

HEIDI EVERETT-CACOPARDO
@haever81

This study investigates the effective literacy and learning practices associated with online, collaborative projects between classrooms in different countries. It explored two questions: (1) From a teacher's perspective, what are effective literacy and learning practices associated with successful online, collaborative projects between classrooms in different countries? and (2) What challenges do teachers face when implementing online, collaborative projects between classrooms in different countries?

The descriptive results indicate that several instructional practices were considered effective by the teachers in this sample:

1. Joining a teacher more experienced in online projects for the first several online collaborative projects between classrooms in different countries
2. Planning projects sufficiently far in advance to permit all partners to prepare
3. Ensuring commitments from project partners
4. Communicating regularly between teachers
5. Having clear time lines in advance
6. Using multiple communication tools, in addition to email, such as wikis, blogs, and video conferencing
7. Using a project website to showcase student work and help to engage others classrooms in collaboration.

Social bookmarking
tag for research:
flatclassroom_research

FINDING MORE RESEARCH

These are just two research studies. If you use your social bookmarking service and find research on global collaboration, tag it #flatclassroom (on Twitter) or flatclassroom_research (in other places) and share with others.[14]

SUMMARY

The voices of change echo forth from classrooms that are connecting globally. Educators and students express the value of the approach. The social-media nature of global collaboration brings a new set of challenges to the educational researcher, forcing researchers to tap into online conversations. The fact that global collaboration includes an increasing use of technology causes questions of isolating the correlations with increased student improvements in learning. The opportunities to monitor student and teacher behaviors in these online spaces as a true observer beckon researchers to join in projects and delve into the potential of having students and educators serve as citizen scientists in their own learning.

ESSENTIAL QUESTIONS

- Do you know someone who has already collaborated on a global basis? What does the person say about his or her experience?
- What are the risks to a global collaborative curriculum that does not evolve?
- In what ways can flattening your classroom positively impact on learning for all?
- How can constructivism and/or connectivism influence and support curriculum and pedagogy in a flattened learning mode?
- What is ethnocentrism? How does it impact society?

Join in the discussion about these topics at http://tinyurl.com/flatclass-ch2 ▶

THE FLAT CLASSROOM™ DIARIES

Diary Entry 3

JULIE LINDSAY, E-LEARNING JOURNEYS— COLLABORATION: CONCEPT, POWER AND MAGIC

Concept. The ability to connect, communicate, and collaborate with educators and students in all parts of the world using common online tools has changed the way I teach in the classroom, as well as changed the way I work as an administrator. A 21st century educator is connected, communicates in a reliable and responsible way, and "flattens" the walls of [his or her] classroom in appropriate ways to enhance the educational learning experience of all. Therefore, every topic, every unit of work, every opportunity needs to be reviewed in terms of how it can be made relevant through external contact and collaboration.

Gone are the days where it was too difficult to bring the world into the room. You, the teacher, are only limited by your imagination! With tools such as Skype, wikis, blogs, and Blackboard Collaborate (Elluminate) there is no excuse for not staging a real-time or asynchronous link-up to support your curriculum objectives. There is also no excuse any more for not participating in a global project, a more deliberated, designed, planned and executed approach to collaboration via the Internet.

Power and Practice. I equate practice with power. If you are practicing collaboration you have the power to change the world, one classroom at a time. The power of learning in a social and extended context, yet in a safe and supportive environment is achievable. I think sometimes schools and teachers give up too easily, put this in the "too hard" basket too readily.

Magic. The magic of collaboration comes from seeing students and teachers find their own voice and take charge of their own learning. It comes from being given choices and ownership and empowerment of their learning path.

Read the rest of this Flat Classroom Diary entry online.

http://tinyurl.com /flat-magic

Diary Entry 4

TEACHERPRENEURS AND FLAT CLASSROOM KICKOFF

VICKI DAVIS, Cool Cat Teacher™ Blog.
The first day of the first Flat Classroom Project, November 2006

I was chatting with Craig in Greece today and I asked him what Flat Classroom meant to him—he said this:

"No walls."

Today is the kickoff of the Flat Classroom Project. This is on my mind because today was Day 1 of the Flat Classroom collaborative project between Julie Lindsay's classroom in Dhaka, Bangladesh, and my computer science classroom in Camilla, Georgia. . . .

Caveats to this project

There is a fine line between information exchange and privacy that we walk daily and in our introductions that we recorded to one another; we've had to complete several edits for my students. We also have time issues so we have exchanged Skype IDs. This is truly as asynchronous of a project as it comes! Julie and I communicate each morning and evening because during mid-day one of us is usually sleeping (because it is the middle of the night).

My students have already learned so much about Bangladesh on the first day!

Read the rest of this Flat Classroom Diary entry online.

http://tinyurl.com /teacherpreneur

DIGITAL CITIZENSHIP AREA OF UNDERSTANDING

Safety, Privacy, Copyright, and Legal

CASE EXAMPLES OF GLOBAL COLLABORATION

Case Study 3

Casey Cox, Westwood Schools, Camilla, Georgia, USA
Flat Classroom Project 2006, Flat Classroom Conference 2009

PDToolkit for *Flattening Classrooms, Engaging Minds*

Read full Case Studies in PDToolkit online.

WEBSITES

Flat Classroom Conference http://www.flatclassroom conference.com

As a sophomore in high school, I could have never imagined the way that this project would create opportunities for me in the future. I know that regardless of what career path I choose, I can move back to southwest Georgia and still reach a global community using modern technology and the communication skills I learned from this collaboration between classrooms.

No student would probably ever admit to enjoying homework or assignments, but that is why the Flat Classroom Project was so immensely effective. It was not merely an end-of-semester project; it was a joint effort with students from another country—and another lifestyle. What truly set this project apart from all the others, aside from all of the new technology and communication that we utilized, was its innovation. Implementing creative projects nurtures a student's motivation to participate in the project as well as giving the teacher new approaches to basic educational methods. Projects such as this are imperative to both stimulate students creatively and academically and foster a collaborative mindset among peers.

Growing up in rural southwest Georgia, global collaboration is a hard concept to grasp. Before Flat Classroom, I never imagined working with fellow students from countries as diverse as Bangladesh, Oman, and Qatar. Originally planned as a conference that focused on diversifying education, we quickly discovered the diversity among ourselves. Prior to the conference, our perceptions of each other were colored by our respective media outlets. All of the students were timid initially, yet as we began to mingle, all of our preconceived notions were dispelled.

We learned lessons that only experience can teach. As we discussed issues such as discrimination, poverty, conservation, and education, I learned that every person, regardless of nationality, wants to positively impact the world. Crossing these cultural barriers, we banded together as a group with a common purpose. How easily we worked together is indicative of the readiness in which we all wanted to accept one another. After this trip, I decided to form my opinions based on personal experience only, rather than generic typecasts. The common fascination we all share with each other is something valuable and very attainable with an open mind.

Case Study 4

Cannelle Cuvelier,
International School Dhaka, Bangladesh
Flat Classroom Project 2006

PDToolkit
for
*Flattening Classrooms,
Engaging Minds*
Read full Case Studies
in PDToolkit online.

The Flat Classroom Project ensured that I reflected upon the effectiveness of technology, in its ability to offer students situated in different parts of the world to communicate together, using different tools, and being able to create something out of that connection. This project was not only necessary in me manifesting a profound interest in the tools that my partner and I had to use, such as virtual communication and open sourcing, but it also provided an occasion for me to explore a wide range of new ways to use them, in order to complement the understanding of this project.

Perhaps, what struck me most about the project, and what I surely will remember most, was the easiness with which my partner and I communicated, in spite of the miles that separated us, the time difference, and the technical difficulties that we encountered. After all, this was how this project changed my view about the use of technology. School work and communication with friends and family using technology wasn't new, but using technology with another student across the world, and communicating to create a wiki page, that surely was, and it is my hope that this type of project continues, as it is very enriching. It is not an aspect that springs to the mind so quickly, perhaps, when thinking of Thomas Friedman's *The World Is Flat,* but Friedman mentioned that the world is not flat, but rather flattening. It is thus my belief that a further increase of technology, as well as technological progress will enable students to collaborate together, in order to fulfill themselves as creative, unique individuals according to their potentialities and within the limit of technology.

Step 1
Connection

The pressures for change are real, but they cannot, and should not be used as an excuse for careening from one change to another, no matter how sound the new direction seems to be in the abstract. We do not live in the abstract. Adaptation to new realities requires change, but not all change will get you there. What to change, how to change it, when to change it, and at what cost are all critically important considerations.

D. M. HEROLD AND D. B. FEDOR[1]

We'd like to begin this first step by having you connect to other teachers as they share why they connect and collaborate. Connecting yourself is the first step on your journey. As Wendy Melnick, a Flat Classroom Certified Teacher from Hamilton, Ontario, Canada, says:

> Collaboration is an essential element of everyone who holds a job today. But, in the future, where will we be without collaboration—active communication? This transcends borders; this will ensure the future of the world.

Honor Moorman, another Flat Classroom Certified Teacher, brings students into the collaboration conversation:

 **WENDY MELNICK**
@WestdaleMedia
Website: http://digitizeme.ca

CHAPTER 3 WEB RESOURCES
http://www.flatclassroombook.com
/connection.html

SHARE IT

Twitter hashtag for this book:
#flatclass

In his TEDxNYED talk, Michael Wesch asserts the necessity for students to be "more open, caring, daring, creative, collaborative, self-motivated, and voracious as learners." Global collaboration gives students the unprecedented opportunity to practice and develop these skills and habits of mind in an authentic and meaningful way.

Fred Haas, a Flat Classroom Certified Teacher from Hopkinton High School, MA, USA, continues the discussion of skills development:

Nothing my students have ever done in school is as ambitious, calling on so many different skills. The Flat Classroom Project is something intellectually challenging, conceptually deep, exceedingly current, and forces them to develop or hone a host of skills that schools typically don't demand.

These are some Flat Classroom teachers. But what do other teachers doing other projects say?

As educators, we know the skills that students need to develop in order to succeed in an interconnected world. In the 21st century, communications go well beyond reading, writing, and speaking. Our kids need to be *Networked*. They'll need an "outboard brain," more collaborative, more globally aware, more active, more connected to their communities, to their environments, to the world.

> MARTA LAVISTA, ICT Coordinator
> ALEJANDRA QUAGLIA, Y6 Language Arts Teacher
> St. Andrew's Scots School in Buenos Aires, Argentina

On a personal note, I found the tools extremely helpful when—mid-project—my father died. From another city, I was able to check my students' progress online and use Skype to connect with them. Heather even Skyped into my class, teaching my students the next step. It was all pretty amazing, now that I think back. Our project embodied the true use of online tools—the ability to connect and communicate wherever and whenever.

FLAT CLASSROOM™ FRAMEWORK

NAME OF PROJECT: Global Learning

WEBSITE URL: https://sites.google.com/a/sanandres.esc.edu.ar/global-projects

LOCATION: Buenos Aires, Argentina

COMMUNICATION: Asynchronous through Voicethread, Google Docs, Glogster

GENERATION: Contemporaries (ages 11–13), previous generation (for hero project)

INFORMATION: Connecting to books for book club; peers for cyberbullying information

TIME: May/June through December (*Note:* Many southern hemisphere schools have school years different from those in North America.)

LEARNING LEGACY: Voicethreads about heroes, documents about books, cyberbullying posters on Glogster

FLAT CLASSROOM™ FRAMEWORK

NAME OF PROJECT: Social Justice

WEBSITE URL: http://heatherdurnin.com/2010/06/19
learning-in-a-global-collaborative-classroom-project-with-scmorgan

LOCATION: Virginia, USA, and Ontario, Canada

COMMUNICATION: Synchronous via Skype; asynchronous via Voicethread and Google Docs

GENERATION: Peers

INFORMATION: Social justice background from *To Kill a Mockingbird* and review of *The Universal Declaration of Human Rights*.

TIME: 2 to 3 months during North American school year

LEARNING LEGACY: Voicethread Research Results

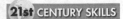

> Though Heather and I often "chatted" in the evenings to check in on the project, we soon found the students doing the same—and learning about each other in the process.
>
> SUSAN CARTER MORGAN, Virginia, USA, about her collaborative project
> with HEATHER DURNIN, Ontario, Canada, Grade 7–8 teacher

There are teachers doing this now! How will your students compare to theirs? What if you could interact with them and their students? You can! Can't you feel the enthusiasm and excitement in their voices over something new and invigorating that has come to their classroom? Don't you want that? Let's learn how and do it! It all starts with you.

OVERVIEW OF CONNECTION

Effective global collaborators transcend time and space to learn, connect, and create. Today, the boundaries of learning exist only between the known and unknown. Think about it! The knowledge of the existence of an unfamiliar word or term is the transit token to embark on a new journey of discovery. Learning is no longer a matter of being located near a "think tank"; instead, it is about being located near a search engine or network of colleagues when you hear about something new. When you know how to connect effectively, you have the power to learn.

It all starts with you. The teacher sets the tone for learning by being a willing participant in the learning process. In this chapter's "Self" section, you will learn how to connect yourself and develop healthy habits of a lifelong learner with efficient strategies that will "pull" information to you. Time-saving pull technologies are taught as ways to supercharge your learning in small chunks of time during the week. We'll finish up with a self-assessment so you can set personal learning goals.

In the "School" section, you'll learn what it means to be a **teacherpreneur** in a way that won't frighten your administrators or colleagues. We'll give you guidelines that will help you create safe learning environments for your students. How do you integrate global collaboration into the curriculum in a way that is agile and manageable? How can you get support from the administration and other faculty as well as backing from the local media? How can local administrators foster an environment of innovation in their teachers? Connect with your school before the project begins to lay the groundwork before collaborating globally with students.

As we look at connecting students in global collaborative environments in the "Students" section, we'll share how to create a strategy using our connection planning tool and the taxonomies of global connections: a simple way to understand the five basic ways classrooms connect.

Remember the Flat Classroom™ diaries and case studies at the end of this chapter. This is also the chapter where we begin our Flat Classroom Fifteen challenges that we introduced in the Preface.

 SELF: Connect Yourself and Build a Learning Pathway

HEALTHY HABITS OF LIFELONG LEARNERS

ISTE STANDARDS

NETS.T 3
Model Digital-Age Work and Learning

The world is changing so quickly that we all have to learn and relearn as information changes in our profession. Behind students engaged in learning is a teacher who is engaged in a personal learning journey. Students will model what they see you do. Is it OK to make mistakes? Are you talking about something you learned today? More than content purveyors, teachers are learning process relayers modeled in flesh and bone.

tweetable

More than content purveyors, teachers are learning process relayers modeled in flesh and bone. #flatclass

Surround Yourself with the Best C. S. Lewis said, "The next best thing to being wise oneself is to live in a circle of those who are."[2] The great men and women of the ages would look at us with envy as we now have the greatest opportunity in human history to immerse ourselves in the circle of the wise. Using the technology at your fingertips you can now surround yourself with the leaders in your field and even become one yourself.

You become like who you are around. You are not just what you eat; you are also what you think. Think on good, accurate things—it has more influence on you than you realize. For example, researchers van Dellen (University of Georgia) and Hoyle (Duke University) had volunteers make two lists of their friends and family: those with self-control and those without. They then had the volunteers take a computerized test to measure self-control. The name of a person from one of the lists flashed on the screen for 10 milliseconds. This was enough time to go into the volunteers' subliminal minds but too fast to be read.

ISTE STANDARDS

NETS.T 5
Engage in Professional Growth and Leadership

21st CENTURY SKILLS

C21 PROFESSIONAL DEVELOPMENT

Researchers found that those who saw the name of a person with more self-control in their subconscious mind showed more self-control in the test. Those who saw the name of a person with less self-control had less self-control in the test.[3] To take this further, Giacomo Rizzolatti proved in 1996 that mirror neurons exist that cause us to mirror the actions and behaviors of those we observe.[4] Self-control is contagious! Positive and negative behaviors move through social networks. Embed your learning with excellent thinkers, writers, and motivators, and you will become more excellent in your own performance.

Embed Professional Development. Embedding professional development in our weekly routine makes so much more sense than sitting in a course for 10 hours and then trying to do all the things you learned back in your classroom. Go ahead, set an appointment with yourself. Pencil in two 15-minute sessions this week when you will connect yourself and apply what is in this chapter. This is your personal research and development. Make it an appointment that you keep every week.

This is why programs like the Twenty-Three Things (and now the Flat Classroom Fifteen) that have educators research and do learning activities relating to new technology tools are so incredibly transformational.[5] Professional learning community participation is shown to optimize professional development.[6]

Consistency and Efficiency. Ninety-five percent of what you accomplish is due to your habits.[7] You become what you do consistently. Think about it. Each of us starts off with the same 24 hours in the day and the same basic abilities to function in this world. The lifetime learner will make learning a priority and use the efficient strategies we teach in this chapter to integrate learning into routines.

EFFICIENT LEARNING STRATEGIES FOR THE 21ST-CENTURY TEACHER

There are two basic types of technology-enabled ways of gathering information: push and pull. *Push technologies* typically require you to push a button like on a search engine or search query. Just about everyone knows how to push.

Pull technologies can bring information to you. What webpage do you see when you open the Internet? Lives have changed because of a **serendipitous** item pulled onto a well-constructed start page. Starting up on an empty search engine page is wasting an opportunity to learn. Your Internet start page is one of the single most important decisions you make in your professional career! Efficient 21st century teachers need a mastery of both push and pull technologies.

Push Learning. Although many people describe "push" as the older method of learning that "treat people as passive consumers,"[8] in this case, we're talking about the type of learning that happens when you have to push yourself out onto the Internet by creating a query on a search engine or other resource. You are pushing a button to open a doorway to learning. To learn effectively with push technologies you need to know how and where to search, whether you are on the web or a handheld device, and the information literacies involved.

Know How to Search and Vet Sources of Information. It is important to be familiar with effective searching strategies and search operators (like quotation marks and wildcard "*") so that you can find information quickly. Most search engines have an "Advanced Search" or "Search Tips" button on their start page that will educate you about how to get information quickly.

You should also know how to search on your mobile device. This is pretty easy in most countries if you have a smartphone, especially if you do search engine queries using text messaging.

The Flat Classroom Fifteen
http://www.flatclassroombook
.com/flat-classroom-15.html

Twenty-Three Things
http://plcmcl2-things.blogspot
.com

DIGITAL CITIZENSHIP AREA OF UNDERSTANDING

Habits of Learning

ISTE STANDARDS

NETS.T 3
Model Digital-Age Work and Learning

21st CENTURY SKILLS

C21 INFORMATION, MEDIA AND TECHNOLOGY SKILLS:
Information Literacy

DIGITAL CITIZENSHIP AREA OF UNDERSTANDING

Literacy and Fluency

Google Mobile
http://m.google.com

Google SMS Searching
http://www.google.com/mobile
/sms

You should also know how to read QR codes. We introduced QR codes in the Preface and have placed them throughout this book to allow you to easily retrieve information. QR codes are the search queries of the mobile phone era and will allow you to go to websites simply by taking a picture.

After you search, you should understand how to vet the sources on the web. A vital clue is "**dead text**" in a document where you should see citations or hyperlinks. For example, if a source states the results of research, it should hyperlink or quote that research using a hyperlink. (If you write, you should also know how to insert appropriate contextual links to give your writing authority.) Contextual hyperlinking is a very basic, entry-level skill that still has many people stumped.

Vetting information should be a daily classroom practice. If your students have access to the Internet, you can use search-engine–enabled **Socratic teaching,** where the teacher asks questions and allows students to search and share their answers with the class. This puts searching in the context of securing accurate information, vetting sources, and digging deeper. It provides for contextual real-world learning.

Know Where to Search. Public search engines are not enough. To ignore **deep web** resources is to leave academic pursuits to the whims of the public search engines, which sometimes change their rankings, based on advertising and social media and not necessarily on relevance or accuracy.

Some experts estimate that the deep web has 50 times the data than what are available on the surface web.[9] Some deep web indexing services include the IPL2, Infomine, and the World Wide Web Virtual Library, but there are many more. Lifelong learners know where to go to find these deep web resources and build relationships with media specialists who curate and provide use of these services.

Pull Learning. Whereas push technologies require you to push a button, pull technologies pull information to you. Well-constructed pull technologies help you siphon manageable sips of meaningful, useful information from the torrent of information that could drown you. According to authors Hagel, Brown, and Davison in their book *The Power of Pull,* "Pull is the ability to attract people and resources to you that are relevant and valuable, even if you were not even aware before that they existed. . . . The first and simplest level of pull is all about flexible access—the ability to fluidly find and get to the people and resources when and where we need them."[10]

In order to embed your professional development, it must be as easy as glancing at the page that starts up when you open your web browser or turning on your eBook. By using pull tactics, you can take advantage of bits of time—such as the moments your browser starts, those 15 minutes at break, or even time under the hair dryer at the beauty shop. That is what pull technologies are about: pulling useful information to you effortlessly.

Most people do not yet fully harness the power and convenient learning that can happen when they plan their pull technologies. Let's look at eight emerging pull technologies:

Pull Tech 1: The RSS Reader. RSS ("Really Simple Syndication" or "Really Simple Subscription") is a virtual paperboy tossing items of interest into an RSS reader that combines the items into a simple, easy-to-read format. It is like a personal newspaper.

RSS readers come in several forms:

- Portal-based RSS readers show on one webpage with customized boxes or "widgets." Examples: iGoogle, Netvibes.
- Web-based feed readers turn feeds into a newspaper-style format and include advanced features such as integration with mobile apps. Example: Google Reader.
- Desktop-based RSS feed readers install on your computer. Example: Microsoft Outlook's RSS Reader.
- Browser bookmark-based RSS feeds have been put into the bookmarking features of many popular web browsers to let information be delivered to your browser. Examples: Internet Explorer and Firefox.
- Tablet or Smartphone RSS readers can serve as a standalone RSS reader or interact with web-based services such as Google Reader or Instapaper. Examples: Flipboard, Zite.

Because students and teachers are so mobile, the portal-based and web-based feed readers are often the tools of choice for educators unless they own a tablet device.[11] Those with a tablet often choose to use Google Reader online with an app such as Goodreader or Flipboard to read on the go.

Whatever you choose, most RSS readers can separate your information much like the dividers in a notebook. This valuable tool for educators is being used to build personal learning networks (PLNs), to monitor public classroom activity (**classroom monitoring portal; CMP**) and to monitor web activity around a brand name or school's name (**brand monitoring portal; BMP**).

RSS as a Personal Learning Network (PLN). A well-constructed PLN is like a well-planned workout for an elite athlete. As an elite learner, you will directly reap the results of consistent interaction with a deliberate system designed to meet your individual needs. Time spent understanding your own learning goals and designing a system that works for you will aid your professional career. Take time to set up your PLN. Every three to six months you should reevaluate and redesign it based on your current learning goals.

Most RSS readers will automatically find the RSS on a website (newspapers, blogs) after you have set them up, but sometimes you have to click the button that says RSS to activate your readers' subscription process. One of the best ways to use RSS is to set up a search query. For example, you can search the news for *classroom +* *"best practices"* to find current news about best practices in the classroom. Look for the RSS button and subscribe to have news delivered to you. Google will literally re-run the search for you throughout the day and deliver the new results to your reader(s)! You can also subscribe to parts of your favorite news media websites such as the education section of the *New York Times* as shown in Table 3.1.

Other things—for instance, calendars and to-do lists—can be added to many portal-based RSS readers as a "widget." Apply **Pareto's Principle** and look in your web browser's history to determine the 20 percent of the websites that you go to 80 percent of the time and put them in a bookmark widget to save time typing. Look for to-do list managers and widgets that interact with your Smartphone or tablet that can sync and also appear on this page.

This standard button on websites using RSS is called a "chiclet."

NETS.T 5
Engage in Professional Growth and Leadership

C21 PROFESSSIONAL DEVELOPMENT

TABLE 3.1 Powerful Places to Find RSS

Source	URL	Description	Example
Google News	http://news.google.com	Search for news about a topic. Look for the RSS button at the bottom.	Search for news about your hometown or school "Camilla, Georgia" or "Westwood Schools" The quotes mean both words should be found in a search.
Google Blog Search	http://blogsearch.google.com	Search current blogs and subscribe to the search through the RSS button.	To search for blogs about a topic of interest, type: free, iPad app education. (This will give you information on blogs about free apps for the iPad.)
Twitter Search	http://search.twitter.com	If you do not want to get on Twitter but want to search for a topic or hashtag, you can do that here and subscribe.	Follow conversations about this book #flatclass Follow educational technology #edchat #edtech.
RSS Search Engine	http://ctrlq.org	If you want to find an RSS feed about a topic or on a website, this is the easiest place to go.	Education site:nytimes.com will help you find all the RSS feeds from the *New York Times* about education.

So, you can make one webpage on a topic that will scrape relevant information off the Internet and your personal networks into one place. With the ability to summarize an entire learning pathway on one webpage, RSS readers used for building a PLN are the powerhouse of pull technologies. Figure 3.1 shows Vicki's current iGoogle page. (She also uses Google Reader.)

RSS as a Classroom Monitoring Portal (CMP). Taking students onto public online spaces scares many teachers. There is no need to worry; RSS can be used to monitor anything with a public RSS feed. This is only available for public projects, so teachers

FIGURE 3.1 PLN Screenshot

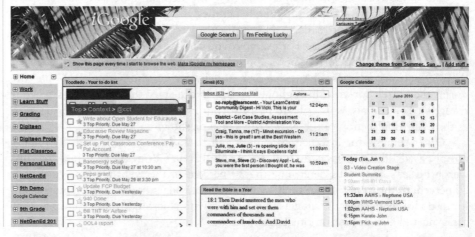

of younger children in private websites would monitor in a different way. There is more discussion on this, along with a screenshot, in Chapter 4.

RSS as a Brand Monitoring Portal.   Wary of YouTube videos and other items posted online about their school or organizations that could go viral, savvy administrators use RSS to construct platforms that will scour the Internet for any mention of their school or organization.[12] Additionally, professional bloggers or those who manage projects often create brand monitoring portals to monitor the Internet for what is said and respond. (More information on this topic appears in Chapter 10.)

Pull Tech 2: eBook Readers and Tablet Devices.   **EBook readers,** such as the Amazon Kindle, and **tablet devices** such as the iPad, bring hundreds of books and resources to people's pocketbooks and briefcases.

Mark Hurst, in his book *Bit Literacy,* says we should use these tools and take time to decide on our **media diet,** which he defines as "a constantly pruned set of publications (digital, print, and other media) that keeps us informed about what matters most to us professionally and personally. . . . In this environment of abundant information and scarce time, our job is to say 'no' early and often and to say 'yes' rarely."[13]

An RSS reader may have hundreds of sources of information, but it is helpful to have a small group of resources that you pay attention to daily. EBook readers can focus your time because they are often single-task devices that keep you concentrated on one thing: reading and learning about your topic of interest. You can also use free **apps** such as Flipboard or Zite, to scan your online reader and news sources while on the go.

Most eBook readers also have the added benefit of allowing text to speech and can increase reading comprehension through **dual encoding.**[14] If you are selecting an eBook reader for those with **accessibility** needs, consider if it allows voice-enabled navigation. As of this writing, the iPad was the only eBook-enabled device allowing voice-enabled navigation, but this is sure to change.[15]

Pull Tech 3: Handheld Devices and Mobile Phones.   Note that many of the apps available for handheld devices and mobile phones include the ability to create personal learning networks or to interact with the portals you've created online. Some of these apps are full-fledged RSS readers or a version of another reader such as the Kindle.

If you don't have a Smartphone, there are many options to empower a phone using **standard messaging service (SMS).** Services such as 4Info.net allow you to subscribe to text messages on topics of interest, weather, game scores, and even news alerts. Engaging the power of your handheld as part of your pull technology will help super-charge your learning.

Pull Tech 4: Social Bookmarking.   Social bookmarking services such as Delicious and Diigo let you bookmark and share. By tagging your bookmarks, you can see patterns emerge in your research. For example, the educators' group on Diigo uses a standard set of tags called a tag dictionary to group common bookmarks together. So, a math teacher can join the group and click on the "math" tag and find hundreds of bookmarks related to teaching math that have been vetted by other educators.

Many professors and teachers set up bookmark-sharing groups with standard tags and let the students build course content from current information on their topics of study.

NETS.T 2
Design and Develop Digital-Age Learning Experiences and Assessments

NETS.T 4
Promote and Model Digital Citizenship and Responsibility

NETS.T 3
Model Digital-Age Work and Learning

4Info.net
http://www.4info.net

NETS.S 3
Research and Information Fluency

21st CENTURY SKILLS

C21 INFORMATION, MEDIA AND TECHNOLOGY SKILLS
Information Literacy, ICT Literacy

ISTE STANDARDS

NETS.T 5
Engage in Professional Growth
and Leadership

21st CENTURY SKILLS

C21 LEARNING ENVIRONMENTS

WEBSITES

K12 Online Conference
http://k12onlineconference.org

Global Education Conference
http://globaleducation.ning.com

Flat Classroom Conference
http://www.flatclassroom
conference.com

**International Society of
Technology Educators (ISTE)**
http://www.iste.org

SHARE IT

Twitter hashtag for the weekly
Edchat: #edchat

Twitter hashtag for Educational
Technology: #edtech

Listing of popular Twitter
hashtags: http://www.november
learning.com/hashtags

Pull Tech 5: Joining Online Webinars, Conferences, and Twitter.   At a party, it is rude to walk up to strangers and interrupt their conversations. However, online, there are many spaces where this is not only acceptable but also encouraged.

When joining many webinars and webcasts, you can listen in and ask questions in the chat box. Places like Edtechtalk and Classroom 2.0 have become hubs for this type of activity where people talk and meet.

Additionally, online conferences such as the K12 Online Conference and Global Education Conference (online conferences); the Flat Classroom conference (a face-to-face conference with a virtual component); and even massive conferences such as ISTE often have virtual aspects where you can connect. Many people "meet" potential partners in global collaboration through these spaces.

Twitter is an essential tool for conference-goers. Before you go to a conference, find out the hashtag and follow it on Twitter or in your RSS reader. As people share where they are and what they are doing, you'll be part of the "action" and see where to go to learn and connect even if you are at the conference alone. Conferences often have "tweet ups" where people who follow the hashtag meet and people wear their "Twitter handle" on their nametags to put names with faces.

The effective use of Twitter is an essential pull strategy that will not only help you find people but also find answers and product recommendations before you make a purchase. Sometimes if you tweet about something, you'll get an answer faster than if you called on the phone! (You can even get a response from the manufacturer.)

There are ongoing conversations that have evolved in education around certain hashtags such as #edchat, a weekly discussion of topics voted on by those who use this tag. Find the hashtag for your field, follow it, and you will learn something. Additionally, many professors now use hashtags to facilitate course discussions. Also, this book uses #flatclass to facilitate discussion about the book.

Emerging social media tools such as Tumblr, the simple social-blogging service, use hashtags for sharing, and this looks to be a part of social media sharing.

Pull Tech 6: Engage with Networking Organizations.   According to Brown, Davison, and Hagel,

> Social networks can provide us with unparalleled opportunity to achieve our potential by allowing us to access resources and attract people who can help us while we help them. We construct our own personal ecosystems, an interesting blend of local relationships and global relationships, and mutual leveraging occurs.[16]

Face-to-face conferences are leveraging online and face-to-face relationships in this way. In Michigan, the MI Champions program begins with an intense learning experience at one year's conference where teachers are assigned mentors from a the previous class that is concluding their year of intense study at the very same conference.[17] During the year, they keep up with their mentors in online spaces and through email. Effective conferences are no longer just about delivering training but about leveraging connections that are made during the rest of the year. Annual face-to-face meetings are natural starting or ending points for online interactions held throughout the year. It is time to blend the conference!

Networking organizations such as Google Teacher Academy, Apple Distinguished Educators, Discovery STAR educators, Adobe Education Leaders, Microsoft Innovative Educator Forums, Flat Classroom, and eTwinnings create massive communities for networking where all teachers are launched with a common learning experience, are able to connect throughout the year in online spaces, and are provided with additional face-to-face learning experiences where they can meet those they have encountered in their community networking online.

Pull Tech 7: Location Based Apps. Global positioning satellites (GPS) coordinates have transformed driving and are beginning to transform the way we use the web. Location-based services allow you to use smartphones and other GPS devices to "check in" at a location. Services such as Foursquare and Gowalla will give you tips or information about a certain location. Indispensible for travelers in strange airports and locations, these services will be coming into the educational space soon and allow educators to be able to geotag information about a location for future learning.

Geotagging and geolocation services carry significant privacy risks because the latitude and longitude are embedded in the service. For example, many cameras include geotagging; when uploaded, the picture itself identifies the latitude and longitude where the picture was taken. Educators must be careful to turn off location-based services unless significant privacy protection features are in place.

These services will also allow future **augmented reality** applications that will provide powerful learning opportunities. Imagine looking through the camera of your Smartphone at a local historical site and seeing a computer-generated overlay telling you about the history of the place! Expect powerful pull technologies with privacy features to emerge in the future. A link between the physical world and online resources is a called a **hardlink** and is part of location based apps, QR codes, and the key concept behind augmented reality.

BUILDING YOUR LEARNING PATHWAY

Now that we've discussed the many ways to put together architecture for learning, we're ready to consider how to build a learning pathway for our students and ourselves. Previously, information sat in books on shelves or in the heads of teachers; thus, education had a textbook-/teacher-centric approach to "delivering" content. A good pathway will have a variety of sources of information (see Figure 3.2), including learning resources, peers, subject matter experts, learning communities, and media. The savvy learner understands how to connect with each of these sources of information.

Parts of a Learning Pathway
Teachers. Teachers aren't just a source of information; they are also co-travelers and coaches on the learning journey. They can be face-to-face or in another physical location. Learning is no longer "delivered" in this environment but facilitated and guided. Teachers are no longer singular entities but teaching in the "cloud" happens when groups of teachers work with a group of students.

Learning Resources. Learning resources or learning objects include the textbook, electronic websites, and all types of information typically shown on a course syllabus. Informally, sources of information such as Wikipedia and Spark Notes have become

DIGITAL CITIZENSHIP AREA OF UNDERSTANDING
Safety, Privacy, Copyright, and Legal

NETS.T 4
Promote and Model Digital Citizenship and Responsibility
NETS.S 5
Digital Citizenship

NETS.T 3
Model Digital-Age Work and Learning

C21 LEARNING ENVIRONMENTS

FIGURE 3.2   Building the Pathway of Learning

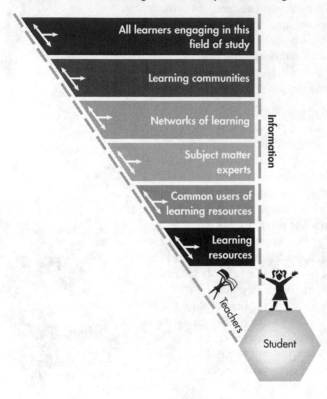

C21 LEARNING ENVIRONMENTS

part of most students' learning resources (whether the teacher likes it or not).

Common Users of Learning Resources.   The effective modern learning resource allows *two-way* communication between learners. When learners can comment on, add to, share, modify, and contribute to content that is shared with other learners, valuable learning relationships emerge. Learners can leave a legacy for other learners on the path.

Subject Matter Experts.   Subject matter experts such as book authors and researchers can link with learners in many ways. Increasingly, an official "connection" with authors of texts used in courses will become part of the package offered by savvy publishing companies who will no longer deliver only content but will also facilitate connections. Currently, however, much of this content often has to be found by students and teachers. Interesting conversations emerge through Twitter, Facebook fan pages, and other social media as students contact experts directly (see Figure 3.2).

Networks of Learning.   Some of the most exciting parts of the effective learning pathway include places where learners network. Networks of learning can emerge through formal networks such as those created by textbook companies, professional associations, or districts. Private email lists are often the tools of choice for district information technology experts. These networks typically require "joining" and approval by a network administrator.

Learning Communities.   Informal learning communities also exist in a loose-knit way around popular sites like Facebook, Twitter, and Second Life, or even within video games such as World of Warcraft and Xbox Live. Interestingly, these informal learning communities often find previously unidentified subject matter experts who distinguish themselves through knowledgeable sharing in the informal networks. People can easily move in and out of these networks and are distinguished by their ability to participate and contribute.

All Learners Engaging in This Field of Study.   Eventually, the learning pathway includes all learners engaging in this field of study because one may learn a great deal from casual conversation with a next-door neighbor or a guide at a museum.

The Well-Rounded Learning Pathway.   Although most people may lean heavily on one aspect of the learning pathway, the effective modern learner uses all areas in her or his information gathering and learning process. When a new field of study emerges into a learner's repertoire, then it is time to build a new learning pathway. Because this connection is such a vital part of learning, it requires many literacies and competencies that are discussed at great length in Chapter 5.

SELF-ASSESSMENT SURVEYS

PDToolkit
for
*Flattening Classrooms,
Engaging Minds*
See the survey results in the
online PDToolkit before moving
on to the next section.

Before moving to the next part of this chapter, take this self-assessment survey. Take it a step further and set personal learning goals as you discuss these questions with colleagues, including your wider learning network, to determine your current level of confidence and ability with connection strategies.

1. **When searching, I am comfortable with search operators and can usually find what I'm looking for in:**
   a. Less than a minute.
   c. 5 minutes or more.
   b. 1 to 5 minutes.
   d. I rarely can find what I need on my own. Somehow it just doesn't work.

2. **When I am researching a topic, I can usually:**
   a. Find the Wikipedia page on the topic.
   b. Find (a) and verify the accuracy of the information there.
   c. Find a website or two about the topic, and all of the above.
   d. Find out who some of the leading experts are on the topic and all of the above.
   e. Find and join learning networks discussing the topic and all of the above.

3. **Every week I am learning about the following:**
   a. The subjects that I teach (my content)
   b. The profession of teaching
   c. The subjects I teach and how best to teach them
   d. I just have time for my hobbies and personal interests.
   e. I don't really have time to learn anything.

4. **Which of the following best describes how you learn?**
   a. I don't usually have time do anything but teach and work.
   b. I usually pick up a newspaper or magazine once a week for a few minutes.
   c. I have a few websites I read every week in the area I teach.
   d. I have several technologies I use to bring information to me (e.g., RSS reader, Twitter, eBook reader, etc.).

5. **Check every technology from the following list that you use at least once a week to learn something:**
   a. RSS reader
   b. eBook reader or tablet sized touch screen device
   c. Handheld device such as an iPod or cell phone
   d. Social bookmarking website
   e. Online conversations such as webinars, conferences, Facebook, and Twitter
   f. A location-based app such as Foursquare or Gowalla

6. **How many new tools or websites a month do you try out or "play with"?**
   a. None
   b. One
   c. Two
   d. Three
   e. Four or more

SCHOOL: Gain Support and Empowerment

TEACHERPRENEURSHIP: BOOST LEARNING IN THE CLASSROOM

ISTE STANDARDS

NETS.T 1
Facilitate and Inspire Student
Learning and Creativity

21st CENTURY SKILLS

**C21 LEARNING AND
INNOVATION SKILLS:**
Creativity and Innovation

C21 LIFE AND CAREER SKILLS:
Productivity and Accountability,
Flexibility and Adaptability,
Initiative and Self-Direction

A recent study by the Organization for Economic Co-operation and Development (OECD) determined that students in Finland were among the highest achievers in the world. However, when they examined how Finnish teachers taught, the OECD found that the teachers had a lot of independence to "pick books and customize lessons" while ensuring that student learning met national standards. The teachers are described as "entrepreneurs."[18] The teachers were *teacherpreneurs!*

Teacherpreneur is a portmanteau of "teacher" and "entrepreneur." An *entrepreneur,* by definition, is a person who takes initiative and risks in business affairs. So, a *teacherpreneur* is a teacher who sees an opportunity to make a profitable learning experience for students through the forging of partnerships with other classrooms with common curricular goals and expectations. The teacherpreneur accepts the responsibility and risks for the endeavor and is accountable for the outcome.

In today's level playing field, the greatest educational opportunities are not necessarily happening where the most money is being spent, but where the best teacherpreneurs are attracted and empowered. A successful teacherpreneur makes rich learning experiences for his or her students through innovation and customization by meeting the specific learning needs of the students. Like successful entrepreneurs, the most successful teacherpreneurs often receive great accolades but can also, conversely, be those who sometimes "rock the boat" as they innovate and move ahead.

Teacherpreneurs enjoy autonomy and empowerment, and sometimes the working environment attracts them as much as the financial incentives. As a good entrepreneur abhors unprofitable ventures, likewise, teacherpreneurs resist lose-lose situations where they are forced into methodologies that are not reaching their students or curriculum that doesn't meet their high standards. Teacherpreneurs want to see students engaged and learning.

21st CENTURY SKILLS

**C21 STANDARDS AND
ASSESSMENT**

**C21 CURRICULUM AND
INSTRUCTION**

Can Teacherpreneurs and Standards Coexist? Those who standardize learning outcomes must realize that every classroom is a unique ecosystem comprised of the students, teachers, curricular resources, and even the location of the classroom. For example, a classroom with a loud air conditioner may be a very poor place to create podcasts and movies. If all classrooms in the school are required to make movies and podcasts, that particular classroom will experience frustration and disenchantment with the process. One can standardize learning outcomes without standardizing the process: look at Finland.

Empowering Teacherpreneurs. Teacherpreneurs are accountable for what they are doing in the classroom. Accountability without authority is a recipe for teacher classroom dysfunction. It is important for teacherpreneurs to have a wide variety of tools, but also to be allowed to select those that fit their situation and teaching style the best.

GUIDELINES AND WORK HABITS THAT SUPPORT AND HOLD ACCOUNTABLE

Good teacherpreneurs aren't renegades; they are connectors. They connect curricular objectives to customized learning processes. They also connect with their administrators and curriculum advisors to keep everyone moving forward together. As the teacher, it is your job to work in positive ways in your school.

Review the Context of Your Environment.   Before you can build a bridge across the world, you have to build a bridge with your own administration. Every educator has a unique context within which to work. It is the responsibility of educators to assess their local environment and act appropriately. Evaluate your unique situation, including:

- Local school policies and procedures
- Laws governing your school
- Relationships with administrators and curriculum directors for instructional implementation of new projects
- Methods for having sites unblocked
- Communications with parents and appropriate permissions
- Past experiences with global collaboration
- Local mentors or advocates for global collaboration
- Trust relationships among you, administration, and the IT department
- How long you've been at your school
- Local standards and requirements for your course

For example, the authors of this book, Vicki and Julie, each had a very different environment for the first Flat Classroom project: one with administrative and curriculum approval required before implementing the project and another with empowerment to control instruction in the classroom, within a given framework. Never assume that because a teacher "down the street" or even "down the hall" can do it, you can, too.

Agree on Core and Optional Outcomes with Stakeholders.   Global collaboration is a balancing act between group-required outcomes and the individual needs of the classroom. Teachers must balance both in order to be good classroom teachers and colleagues who can be trusted by those in their network around the world. Tables 3.2 and 3.3 show examples of global collaborative projects along with their required and optional core outcomes. When teachers join a project, they are agreeing to participate in the required outcomes of the project. Without this connection, a project cannot exist: It is the thread holding the project together.

Sharing Learning Goals with Your School.   After you understand the required elements of a project, you can determine if it is a good fit for the course. Craft an overview of the project, as it will look in the classroom, including required components from project organizers and optional components with the project as well as anything extra you'll be adding to meet your local standards. Align the standards and communicate if any special calendaring arrangements will need to be made locally to ensure your participation.

NETS.T 2
Design and Develop Digital-
Age Learning Experiences and
Assessments

**C21 CURRICULUM AND
INSTRUCTION**

TABLE 3.2   Core Outcomes of Flat Classroom Projects

Project	Core Outcomes
Flat Classroom Project This project is typically for grades 9–12; studying leading technology trends and producing video artifacts and includes peer review classrooms down to grade 5 and expert advisor and judges from the educational community at large. Multiple times per year. http://www.flatclassroomproject.net	Required: • Collaboratively edited wiki • Digital storytelling artifact with outsourced clip Optional: • Preproject and postproject blogging • Forum discussions and responses to keynotes • Student summit presentations in Blackboard Collaborate • Diigo social bookmarking and research
Digiteen Project This project is for students ages 11 and up studying digital citizenship with partners around the world and culminating in a local-school digital citizenship action project. Multiple times per year. http://www.digiteen.org	Required: • Collaboratively edited wiki • Local school offline action projects • Action wiki reporting outcomes with documentation Optional: • Reflective posts from project introductory videos • Postproject reflections • Diigo social bookmarking and research • Unique projects assigned by the teacher as part of the action project based on curricular objectives
Eracism Project This project is a middle school debate project using Voicethread. http://www.eracismproject.org	Required: • Student debates using Voicethread Optional: • Debate lesson plans and classroom debates • Virtual World introduction • Blogging reflections on private classroom spaces
NetGenEd Project This project envisions the future of education through wiki writing and video with author Don Tapscott. Held once a year. http://www.netgened.org (with Don Tapscott)	Required: • Collaboratively edited wiki • Digital storytelling artifact with outsourced clip • Student project management for students nominated by local teachers Optional: • Preproject and postproject blogging • Forum discussions with Don Tapscott, author • Responses to keynotes • Student summit presentations in Blackboard Collaborate • Diigo social bookmarking and research

21st CENTURY SKILLS

C21 LIFE AND CAREER SKILLS:
Productivity and Accountability

Word of Caution.   Just as global collaborations often have students confront their stereotypes, these same stereotypes of other countries often emerge when trying to gain approval for projects. Share examples of what is already happening in global collaboration to assuage fears. Help administrators understand how you will monitor the online activities, and invite them to join if you wish.

TABLE 3.3   Core Outcomes of Other Global Collaborations

Project	Core Outcomes
Lucky Ladybug Project Organized by Dr. Sarah McPherson and Susan Silverman, this project is a collaborative Internet project for K–5 students that can be used to teach science, the scientific method, writing, and technology, depending on local needs. http://kids-learn.org/ladybugs	Required: Research Question: Why are ladybugs considered to be good luck? • Teachers must use UDL (Universal Design for Learning) in their lesson plans for this project. • Teachers must submit a maximum of seven graphics per class with a short narrative of the learning experience and how it meets the criteria for UDL. Optional: • Classes may create their choice of drawings, videos, podcasts, pictures, audios, music, models, and maps.
My Hero This website is more a place to communicate; however, teachers can collaborate with projects and participate in the film festivals and other competitions on this website, which has classrooms of students create artifacts about their heroes. http://www.myhero.com	Required: • Students will reflect on what a hero is and who is a hero in their lives. Optional: • Create a webpage about your hero. • Upload art about your hero. • Comment in the forum. • Create a video about your hero.
Pumpkin Seed Count This PreK–3rd grade project has students counting the seeds in a pumpkin and charting and comparing the results. It is run by Jennifer Wagner. http://www.jenuinetech.com/calendar.htm	Required: • Count pumpkin seeds, chart, and turn in results. Optional: • Do just about anything the teacher can determine, including charting and spreadsheet software.
Life 'Round Here The goal of this project is to help students around the world understand what school is like for others. This is a desire of mine to help students understand the differences and similarities between their own cultures and the cultures that are foreign to them. http://liferoundhere.pbworks.com	Required: • It must involve students from 8 to 15 years old. • Your class/school/group must be able to publish at least one video. • The stories must be in English or have subtitles in English. • Stories must be published and "watchable" by a set date.

Remember that it is your responsibility as a teacher to monitor spaces. Help administrators understand what you will do, and be prepared to back up your words with action. Your enthusiasm for the work, and ultimately your colleague's trust relationship with you, will go a long way to make this connection. Administrators will likely approve your first project on trust, but your subsequent global collaborations will be approved by your ongoing professional behavior and diligence. You can break down stereotypes with your actions and by sharing your own story and letting your students tell theirs.

CURRICULUM AGILITY AND STABILITY

DIGITAL CITIZENSHIP AREA OF UNDERSTANDING
Literacy and Fluency

NETS.T 4
Promote and Model Digital Citizenship and Responsibility

NETS.S 5
Digital Citizenship

NETS.S 6
Technology Operations and Concepts

NETS.S 6
Technology Operations and Concepts

NETS.T 1
Facilitate and Inspire Student Learning and Creativity

NETS.T 2
Design and Develop Digital-Age Learning Experiences and Assessments

The Hidden Curriculum.   The digital divide has injected a **hidden curriculum** in society. Such a curriculum may be opened by those with access to technology and unopened by those without access. The MacArthur report, *Confronting the Challenges of Participatory Culture,* highlights how access or no access to the hidden curriculum helps shape which youth will succeed or be left behind in school or the workplace.[19]

Although privacy and safety must be considered, we are beginning to see proof of the harm caused to students who have no Internet access. Without access at home or at school, students are impoverished by the lack of rich technology experiences that would enhance their social lives and ability to network. Students with access to Facebook and other social media at home are learning valuable online social skills that they will use in the workplace. It is this hidden curriculum identified that must be brought into schools.

Curriculum Agility.   Curriculum agility is the ability to detect *hidden and known* curriculum opportunities and bring them into widespread use to promote effective learning. Innovation should be an agile part of curriculum revision at schools, with room for innovative technologies built into the curriculum scaffolding.

Many states in the United States and in other regions of the world produce technology standards. As of the writing of this book, many of the standards reviewed by authors still included teaching about floppy disks, although computers do not now ship with that option. A streamlined, agile method should be developed to allow teachers to integrate a certain amount of current technology into their teaching without having to wait for standards to be updated.

Technology Ecology.   When planning the connection of classrooms, effective curriculum decisions look at technology use at the school as a whole to promote synergies. When used efficiently by a school, technologies operate in an ecosystem with one another both culturally and systematically.[20] For example, if there is limited access to cameras, and students are surveyed and found to have cameras and memory cards in their mobile devices, with parental permission, these could be used to augment camera equipment at the school to allow for projects to happen that require digital photography with no extra cost to the school or parents.

Students who are learning advanced photography could teach younger students who are just learning the skills. Cooperative groups, including vertically streamed classes or learners of different ages, can be established to share equipment and resources. And older students could film a play written and acted out by younger students. Programming and web design students can serve as administrators for the systems put in place for younger learners.

By paying attention to the technology ecology, natural symbiotic learning relationships can emerge that can also save money and promote efficiencies for the local school system (as long as educators realize that students will probably make more mistakes than a professional in such spaces.) For example, Vicki's students assist in administering the school's Ning and Facebook fan page as part of their coursework.

Learning Capital.   When you implement a new technology or project, you spend more than money—you spend the learning experience on someone. Capital can be defined as a resource that has value. Learning capital is the valuable learning opportunity created during the implementation of new technology or programs.

The most successful among us have usually had learning capital invested in our lives by others who commissioned us to create, implement, and manage projects. Deciding who is going to be involved in a project is as important as the project itself. You spend learning capital on people as they:

- Evaluate alternatives
- Present recommendations
- Select vendors and compare features
- Unpack the boxes
- Install hardware and software
- Conduct professional development
- Share best practices
- Reflect

Learning capital is a lot like a purchase order that requires two signatures. In order for learning capital to be spent, someone in authority has to include a person in the process and the person included has to decide to spend his or her time learning and participating. Delegating a new project entirely to the IT department may make sense, but excluding everyone else may kill the use of the technology in the long run. If your goal is successful adoption of the technology, it may be more logical to take the slower route that involves teachers and students. You can't have a grassroots movement to use technology by involving only the "trees" (administrative staff); rather, you must involve people at all levels of the organization. Let students, teachers, administrators, and IT departments be part of the process of selecting technology and implementing it in the classroom.

Students are some of the best places to spend learning capital. As leaders in pilot and project implementations, students learn project management and leadership skills as well as troubleshooting and technology skills. They also can be great advocates and learn real-world skills to apply in their future careers. Administrators should remember that when they are spending money on new technology to spend the learning experience on the stakeholders who will need to use the technology by involving them in the process.

Mapping the Future.   Many schools are forming lasting, long-term relationships and partnerships with schools in other parts of the world. Some are doing this through their formal organizations (such as the **International Baccalaureate; IB**) because of similar fit to the curriculum, and this is certainly an excellent thing to do. But, in order to give students a broad experience, curriculum leaders and teacherpreneurs should seek out a breadth of experience for their students: public schools, private schools, international schools of all kinds, and more should be a mapped part of the curriculum if students are going to be equipped and knowledgeable about a diversity of cultures. Understanding diverse cultures comes from diversity of connection.

The 21st century curriculum leader will literally have a world map on his or her wall with pushpins marking the ongoing collaborations at every grade level that is

ISTE STANDARDS

NETS.S 4
Critical Thinking, Problem Solving, and Decision Making

21st CENTURY SKILLS

C21 LEARNING AND INNOVATION SKILLS:
Critical Thinking and Problem Solving

C21 INTERDISCIPLINARY THEME:
Financial, Economic, Business, and Entrepreneurial Literacy

C21 LIFE AND CAREER SKILLS:
Leadership and Responsibility

21st CENTURY SKILLS

C21 CURRICULUM AND INSTRUCTION

a permanent part of the curriculum. This curriculum director intentionally looks at locations on a map to make sure his or her curriculum is representative of diverse areas of the world. Ongoing relationships to empower peer learning between diverse locations will become part of the curriculum landscape.

It is feasible that a school could set as a goal that students will have "met" and conversed with students from every inhabited continent before leaving their elementary school. Some teacherpreneurs, such as Cherrie MacInnes (profiled at the end of this chapter in Case Study 6) from Brewer Community School in Brewer, Maine, are doing it themselves. Here is the letter she sent out to schools around the USA:

> Dear Administrators and Third Grade Teachers,
>
> The 3rd graders at Washington Street School in Brewer, Maine, are on a quest to Google chat with a third grade classroom from every state in our country. Students from W.S.S. would share interesting facts about Maine and your students would reciprocate with some interesting facts about your state. The conference would be a one-time lesson lasting between 20 to 30 minutes. My class will record the date of our video-conference facts on a large map of the United States and keep a journal as well. We will learn a lot about the USA and meet a lot of great 3rd graders along the way! All that is needed is . . . . We look forward to hearing from you.[21]

CHERRIE MACINNES
@MacInnes3
https://sites.google.com/site
/chattingacrosstheusa

Cherrie inspired the creation of Class Chats (a site that District IT's Mark Jenkins, Barry Maherg, and Teresa Door created on their personal time to help Cherrie realize her dream), a website to help other teachers connect with classrooms that wanted to chat. She is an excellent teacherpreneur.

It is time for schools to map global connections. Administrators should ask for curriculum plans that include not only standards and objectives but also world maps with specifically noted schools and locations that will be collaborative partners in the long term.

FLAT CLASSROOM™ FRAMEWORK

NAME OF PROJECT: Class Chats

WEBSITE URL: http://www.classchats.com/connections

LOCATION: National—United States

COMMUNICATION: Synchronous; Technopersonal

GENERATION: Contemporaries (ages 7 to 9)

INFORMATION: Other learners in a network of learning.

TIME: A 20- to 30-minute Skype chat for each classroom; yearlong project for the classroom

LEARNING LEGACY: Teacher writes a blog. Stories shared on http://www.classchats.com

STUDENTS: Connect and Empower

**ISTE STANDARDS**

NETS.T 2
Design and Develop Digital-
Age Learning Experiences and
Assessments

21st CENTURY SKILLS

**C21 CURRICULUM
AND INSTRUCTION**

CREATING A CONNECTION STRATEGY

As you plan collaborative experiences, look at the types of connections. The connection planning tool shown in Figure 3.3 will help you provide a diversity of experiences for students. This framework allows teachers, curriculum directors, and administrators to understand the true nature of the collaborative project. When you plan a connection, you should consider five parts: information, location, generation, communication, and time.

Information.   We've talked about building your own learning pathway. Students need this valuable skill. At younger ages, educators may construct these for students using a tool such as PortaPortal or Netvibes. When students are older, they will want to construct their own PLN using an RSS reader.

FIGURE 3.3   Connection Planning Tool

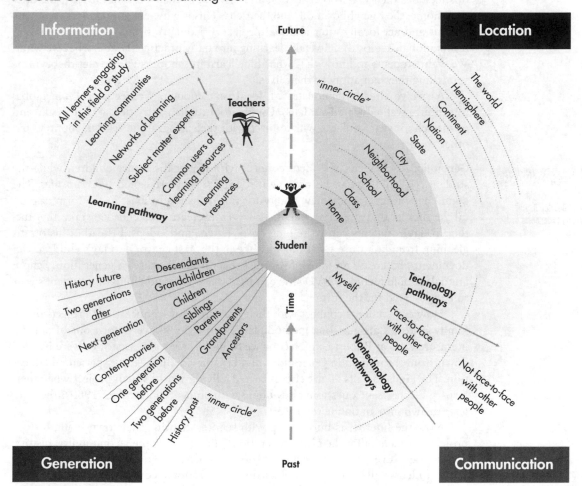

However, it is more than just constructing a PLN, for truly, a PLN is just a super-efficient learning pathway that can bring all of these sources of information into an easy launch pad for students. The bigger question is: How will students acquire and vet sources in their learning pathway? All types of information should be reviewed and planned into the project to allow for learning. How will students share their sources with other students (e.g., bookmarks, notebooks, wikis)?

What subject matter experts will be in their learning? Will they join learning networks? Are there appropriate communities for learning? Are they encouraged to link with other learners to talk about this project? What hashtags have emerged relating to this topic? Teachers should work to make sure every bucket on the learning pathway is filled to complete the journey and that they are co-learners on the path with their students.

Location. Some have criticized global collaborations because they think students must connect locally before they connect globally. Of course students need local connections. They also need close ties with their "Inner Circle" as depicted on the location part of the connection planning tool (Figure 3.3). In the academic context, this includes their classroom, school, and district. In their personal lives, it includes their home, their neighborhood, and their city. This is why it is good to have students present and act locally after a global project. Friedman's principle of glocalization (think global, act local) helps take learning into daily practice. That is what we want. We want students to know that what they learn in school isn't abstract theory; it is something they can apply to their lives.

As we've already demonstrated, local isn't enough. We need local *and* global to produce well-educated students. Use the tool to plan activities so that by the end of the school year students will connect with their geographic region, country, and other countries.

Generation. How can a student connect with her or his future children while the student is a child? We've been doing it for years; they are called *time capsules*. The digital age brings a whole new ability for time capsules to exist in the form of digital yearbooks that preserve videos; however, a creative teacher can take this further. Today's students can write blog posts, letters, and videos. Instead of historians gleaning from literature what life was like in the 21st century, today's children can document and create an online historical record that captures a generation. School annuals should include a DVD sleeve to hold the videos and efolio of a student's year to be preserved for the future.

How can students connect with their grandparents or ancestors? Projects doing family histories are just one method. The Foxfire books were born out of a 1966 literature class at Rabun Gap Nacoochee School in Georgia, as stories were handed down from the mountain generations and became a hallmark in experiential education. The Hudson Falls High School created a living World War II project when their history teacher sent questionnaires home with students in the late 1980s; the data have grown into an online repository.

Now the Internet is burgeoning with schools creating their own living history projects. Students film the older generation talking about their community, history, and heritage. Every second more people of the oldest generation die; as time passes, fewer students will have grandparents alive. Generational connections at the younger

ISTE STANDARDS
NETS.T 2
Design and Develop Digital Age Learning Experiences and Assessments

FLAT CLASSROOM™ FRAMEWORK

NAME OF PROJECT: Foxfire

WEBSITE URL: http://www.ericdigests.org/1999-3/foxfire.htm

LOCATION: Inner circle, local

COMMUNICATION: Synchronous; face-to-face—Interpersonal skills; asynchronous, through writing; Intrapersonal

GENERATION: History—past and older generations

INFORMATION: Subject matter experts and all learners engaging in a field of study

TIME: Books produced on a rotating schedule

LEARNING LEGACY: Magazines and books shared with an authentic audience

ages will truly become learning resources that can pass down a family heritage or historical perspective to be preserved. Again, using students to document history is important but it is more than history: This is their life.

Intergenerational learning experiences are vital because schools, by nature, are primarily populated with the young. Students need to understand the importance and validity of including multiple generational perspectives when learning.

Communication. Communication will be discussed in greater detail at the beginning of Chapter 4, Step 2: Communication. As one plans, it is important to include both technological and nontechnological pathways of communication as one connects to oneself (intrapersonal) and others (interpersonal.) It isn't all about technology; interpersonal skills and understanding who you are as a person is important. Netiquette, manners, and digital citizenship are part of what we must consider.

Time. Time passes. Each project should specify the time and workflow for that project, but also a student's own learning legacy is part of this component. Old

FLAT CLASSROOM™ FRAMEWORK

NAME OF PROJECT: The Hudson Falls High School World War II Living History Project

WEBSITE URL: http://www.hfcsd.org/ww2

LOCATION: Inner Circle, local, and the world—Past history

COMMUNICATION: Synchronous, face-to-face

GENERATION: Oldest generation alive

INFORMATION: Subject matter experts—Those who experienced World War II

TIME: Each year additional videos were added

LEARNING LEGACY: Recorded videos archived on the website watercolor paintings may fade, but digital scrapbooks have the potential to be kept ad infinitum. The road in the middle of the *Connection Planning Tool* shows the student's past and the student's future because these are also connections that a student needs to have.

By creating digital diaries, students can journal their lives and provide a way to connect with their future selves. Digital media gives us compact, simple ways to share in this way without the clutter of saving every shred of paper we've ever collected. This is why the digital portfolio is so important. Being able to connect with your future and past self helps you see your progress in life's journey. (Coauthor Vicki Davis often picks up her journal from when she was 12 years old, where she first penciled that she wanted to be an author. What a gift if every student could do that!)

Are There Other Diversities to Care About?   Some are concerned that today's students spend too much time inside buildings instead of outside. So, you may want to add a level of diversity to plan some activities to be outside as part of a project.

Or, you may be concerned and want a student to understand and relate to people from a broad range of cultures and religions. But be careful, often when you put a thing such as religion or race or culture as the main reason for connecting, it is more challenging to find commonalities than if you're studying a less controversial, more common subject such as math, languages, or technology. Those diversities will come out as the project proceeds, but we think it is helpful not to put them as the sole reason or cooperation. Some have done this well, but it is a fine balance.

How to Use the Connection-Planning Tool.   Use a blank copy of the tool and give each project you are planning a letter. Mark all the areas targeted by each project you've planned that year with their letter. Look for areas you are missing in your connection and work to redesign or find new projects to reach that segment.

By planning in this way for a year, a teacher and curriculum director can provide students with a wealth of experience. A balanced approach can help prevent criticisms such as "You're collaborating with the world and forgetting our local community." Glocalize: Think globally, act locally!

TAXONOMY OF GLOBAL CONNECTION

The most successful global collaborative classrooms are those where the teacher has prepared students ahead of time. Before you connect globally, connect inside your classroom.

Sometimes when a teacher is a veteran collaborator he or she can quickly bring students into a highly engaged public participatory environment. However, at the present time this kind of teacher is rare indeed. The taxonomy of global connection (Figure 3.4) is designed help you plan to help student's progress from your classroom to the world. If global collaboration were easy, we wouldn't have to teach it.

Level 1: Intraconnection (within Your Own Classroom).   Connect the students in your classroom to each other first. Often, teachers start by having students sit next to one another to edit a wiki or collaborative document.

tweetable

If global collaboration were easy, we wouldn't have to teach it. #flatclass

FIGURE 3.4 Taxonomy of Global Connection

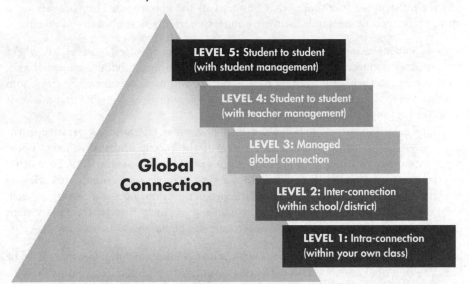

Global Connection

LEVEL 5: Student to student (with student management)

LEVEL 4: Student to student (with teacher management)

LEVEL 3: Managed global connection

LEVEL 2: Inter-connection (within school/district)

LEVEL 1: Intra-connection (within your own class)

Then, the teacher assigns students to work together across the room from each other with limited face-to-face interaction. This gradual movement in physical proximity prepares students for working with partners who will not coexist in the same classroom at the same time, but lets the teachable moments happen while both students can voice frustrations in front of the class about issues. Note that this is the "Inner Circle" on the location part of the connection-planning tool.

Level 2: Interconnection (with the School or Geographic Area).   Next, students connect within the same school or district. The teacher with several sections of a course may create a project where three students, one from each class, collaborate. Because they are not in class at the same time, they must increasingly depend on the discussion tab of the wiki or through the commenting system of the online word processor. Again, this allows teachers to coach students to further distance in proximity of both physical space and time.

Communication online can be synchronous (live meetings or chat), asynchronous (blogs, wikis), or may be a blended form with characteristics of both (social networks.) We go into more detail in Chapter 4 about the types of communication.

Interestingly, once a student is collaborating with another student outside of their own classrooms (where they will never be face-to-face) it usually "feels" global to students because it is asynchronous (not at the same time.) Because students are working with a profile and a face on a page, this is a good point to help students understand collaboration and digital footprints. For administrators nervous about global collaboration, if students can collaborate within their district and teachers can monitor the system, global collaboration tends to be easier in the future. You are still part of the "inner circle" of location at this level.

Level 3: Managed Global Connections.   In managed global connections, schools join existing projects. There are often detailed lesson plans and learning resources to

ISTE STANDARDS

NETS.S 2
Communication and Collaboration

21st CENTURY SKILLS

C21 INTERDISCIPLINARY THEME:
Global Awareness

C21 LEARNING AND INNOVATION SKILLS:
Communication and Collaboration

download. Typically, students are not connected directly to one another. Often, the teacher must upload or share what happens in the classroom. The students have moved past their "inner circle" and are connecting to others at a variety of distances.

Level 4: Student-to-Student Connections (with Teacher Management).   Level 4 is where true student connection and collaboration begins on an individual student basis. Students connect with one another to collaborate and work together. The classroom is leveled in that each student may have a distinct, unique learning goal that does not match others in the local classroom.

This environment is much like the **jigsaw** activities taught in cooperative learning in that each student researches a piece of the puzzle and the students come together to share learning through oral quizzes or class discussions. Topics are often interrelated so that mutually beneficial discussions happen when topics are reviewed in class. Teachers remain the leaders in the project, facilitating but directing as well. Oral quizzes and presentations complete learning as students share their piece with the others, creating powerful peer-to-peer learning experiences.

Level 5: Student-to-Student Connections (with Student Management).   The most level or flat type of global collaborative project has students working together directly with and for one another. This environment is much like an athletic team where the coach, or teacher, is on the sidelines encouraging and coaching the students in the project (on the playing field.) The project, or "game," is very much determined by the student "players" in the project "field." They have captains (project managers [PMs] and assistant project managers [APMs]) who lead them as they work on the project. This level of collaboration prepares students best for the participatory, collaborative environment in today's work environment and will provide students with real world marketable, beneficial online leadership skills.

Teachers typically intervene only on individual, private-basis matters concerning digital citizenship, cultural disconnects, or nonparticipation, but even then, the teacher is very much the coach. Project managers and students are taught leadership and interpersonal skills, and public teacher intervention is rare.

NETS.S 4
Critical Thinking, Problem Solving, and Decision Making

C21 LIFE AND CAREER SKILLS:
Leadership and Responsibility

SUMMARY

"If it is to be, it is up to me."[22] In today's world, where information zips past our eyes faster than a sports car, if we are to be lifelong learners it is our personal responsibility to laser-focus our learning in efficient ways and make it part of our weekly routine. Learning in the classroom starts with the teacher. Engaged students happen after you engage with your own learning first. You can do it easily by using the pull technologies we've learned in this chapter. You should have set personal learning goals to further the text based on the self-assessment.

In a world of standardization, you've been challenged to customize and personalize learning to the unique nature of your classroom by being a teacherpreneur. Teacherpreneurs can customize learning while connecting with administrators and curriculum directors to create an agile curriculum that respects the unique technology ecology of the school and brings the hidden curriculum of participatory media into the classroom. Every project has a few required outcomes as the thread that holds the project together. Teachers communicate and connect projects to their local standards and curriculum, whereas curriculum directors may choose to map global connections and create ongoing relationships with other schools around the world.

Two essential planning tools will help you map the connections for your students. First, the connection-planning tool helps you plan the information, location, generation, communication, and timing for projects so that you can help a student be well rounded, yet leave a legacy of learning to tap into in the future.

A steady methodology for taking students from connecting within your classroom to connecting with the world will help you get there. You can do this. Others are doing it, and you can too.

ESSENTIAL QUESTIONS

- Describe your learning pathway for this course of study.
- What are pull technologies? Do you have an example of a serendipitous learning experience to share?
- Can teacherpreneurs and standards coexist? How?
- Review a project using the connection planning tool and the mandatory and optional outcomes framework and be able to share. Which level of global collaboration is this project reaching?

Join the online conversation and share your answers at http://tinyurl.com/flatclass-ch3 ▶

FLAT CLASSROOM™ (15) CHALLENGES

If you missed it, the Flat Classroom Fifteen were introduced in the Preface and are also shown in the PDToolkit and online at http://www.flatclassroombook.com.

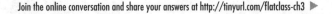

CHALLENGE 1: SET UP YOUR RSS READER

Do: Set up your personal learning network (PLN) using the RSS reader of your choice. Set an appointment with yourself for at least 15 minutes three times during the next week to learn from your PLN.

 SHARE: Comment on at least three blogs or sites in your PLN with your reflections on what they are saying. **The tag for this challenge is fcc1_pln. Use this when you blog or share with your group.**

(Note: If you are blogging or tweeting as part of your course assignment, this tag will serve as the "assignment tag"—if you are doing this on the Flat Classroom Ning, we will follow this tag to keep up with those who have completed the first challenge. You can also tweet that you've done it and it will go to the webpage for this challenge.)

Share what you did with your challenge at http://tinyurl.com/flat15-1 ▶

ISTE STANDARDS
NETS.T 3
Model Digital-Age Work and Learning

CHALLENGE 2: SET UP YOUR BLOG

Do: Set a time to talk to colleagues and/or administrators about what you are learning. Discuss blogging with them and what you have learned. Find out about the expectations for authoring a professional blog in your school or educational community. Set up your blog with appropriate

ISTE STANDARDS
NETS.T 5
Engage in Professional Growth and Leadership

privacy and permission settings. As an alternative to a personal blog, we invite you to join our Flat Classroom educational network and have your blog there. (http://flatclassrooms.ning.com)

 SHARE: Email the link to your blog to someone in your learning community. **The tag for this challenge is fcc2_blog.**

◀ Share what you did with your challenge at http://tinyurl.com/flat15-2

 **ISTE STANDARDS**

NETS.T 5
Engage in Professional Growth and Leadership

CHALLENGE 3: CONNECT AND REFLECT

Do: Research one or two of the connecting organizations mentioned in this section. (Join if you wish).

 SHARE: Reflect on your blog what you have learned and comment on at least two other blogs about this topic. Make sure that you tag your post! **The tag for this challenge is fcc3_join.**

◀ Share what you did with your challenge at http://tinyurl.com/flat15-3

THE FLAT CLASSROOM™ DIARIES

Diary Entry 5

"ARE YOU REALLY THERE??"[23] EXCERPTS FROM JULIE'S BLOG POST, MAY 12, 2008

 **21st CENTURY SKILLS**

C21 LIFE AND CAREER SKILLS:
Productivity and Accountability

Read the rest of this Flat Classroom Diary online.
http://tinyurl.com /fcp-ruthere

I am trembling as I write this. I am reading carefully chosen words and sentences that have powerful meanings. I am reading online conversations and interactions and opinions that come from teachers and students. I want to reach out and make everything right in the world, make people get on with each other, make people realize there are other people out there and that the world does not revolve around them. I want to cut through complacency and excuses, cut through boredom and inactivity, slice through selfish attitudes. I want to demand engagement and higher-order involvement of people I have never met, students I will never have in my class. I want to tell everyone that life is too short to be making excuses, life is too short to do nothing and life is too short to be invisible. . . .

Why are some participants more engaged than others? Is it technical ability, or lack of? Is it an unwillingness to be part of an online learning community? Is it just sheer confusion, an inability to understand the requirements and a feeling of being overwhelmed? Is the project too hard? Is it that they just don't care about grades, team members, and the challenge?? . . . . . If anyone had any doubts about the benefits of project-based learning, global collaboration, and relevance to real-world scenarios, you need look no further than this project. Students and teachers who are committed in value and time, and students such as Jonathan who *do* get it *are visible*. . . .

Vicki talks about the "currency of reputation," and addresses student complacency with this: "What would your currency of reputation be? Although now, in high school, you can take on this project and literally goof off—take the C or F and move on with your life. Very soon, you'll develop a reputation as a nonexistent person who cannot be counted on."

How can we change this? How can we change the world? Is our current education system(s) promoting effective global communication and collaboration? Are these skills valued enough to be part of what we do in schools on a regular basis?

Diary Entry 6

VICKI DAVIS, ABOUT IMMERSIVE "VICARIOUS" LEARNING

When we traveled to India for the Flat Classroom Workshop in 2010, the students in grades 3 through 8 immersed themselves in what we called the "India Immersion Project," which the students nicknamed "Cat India." My tenth-grade computer science students led the teams for blogging, Voicethread, Skype connections, the wiki, and video documentation. They did such a great job, they were invited to present at the Valdosta State Librarian Technology Conference and received exceptional reviews. Immersion learning never ends and often leads to more authentic projects that can be used for teaching.

21st CENTURY SKILLS

C21 LIFE AND CAREER SKILLS:
Leadership and Responsibility

Review the student presentations at http://digiteenatvsu.wikispaces.com

On the last day of school, students stated that the best learning experience of the year was the Cat India project. They said they not only learned about technology but a lot about project management and working with others. We will improve a lot the next time we run our immersion (when we go to China for Flat Classroom 2011), however, the learning capital was well spent because students learned a lot in a very short period of time.

CASE EXAMPLES OF GLOBAL COLLABORATION

Case Study 5

SALIM AL BUSAIDI, Flat Classroom 2008, 2010–present, Osama Bin Zaid School, Oman

Our story with Flat Classroom Project (FCP) started when Julie Lindsay and Vicki Davis invited me and my students to take the challenge to join FCP 2008. I chose four students for that project and they were working with me on an environmental project. The chosen students were from three different schools and Al-Yaqzan was from Muscat, the capital of Oman, which is about 120 miles from Adam town (where I live).

The first step I started with was informing the students' parents who supported me in that project and then I moved to my school administration who assured me that I would be able to use the school facilities. Since my students were in three different schools, I decided to depend on virtual communication with them with by having weekly evening classes at Osama Bin Zaid School. The school administration and technical staff provided us with the computer lab and learning resources center. We did not have a reliable Internet connection at our school, so we attended some of the project online meetings and summits at my house.

ISTE STANDARDS

NETS.T 1
Facilitate and Inspire Student Learning and Creativity

ADD FRIEND

SALIM AL BUSAIDI
@salim_albusaidi
http://omaneco.ning.com

During our participation in the project, I informed our Education Directorate of our participation and our plan to attend Flat Classroom Project Conference in Qatar 2009. They asked me to write a detailed report about the project, explaining the project's idea and its educational benefits to our students. After our successful participation in the project, we moved to work on our participation in the Flat Classroom Conference in Qatar. We had a short time to finish the trip arrangement starting from the Ministry of Education's permission and finding a sponsor.

PDToolkit
for
Flattening Classrooms, Engaging Minds
Read full Case Studies in PDToolkit online.

See Salim present on Omani TV about the Flat Classroom Project (in Arabic) http://tinyurl.com/salim-fcp

The project organizers were of great help and the parents assured me that they would pay for their children to attend that conference. As a last chance to get a permission to participate, I went to the Ministry of Education and we had a meeting with some educational experts who liked the project and supported us to attend the conference. We were told that the Minister of Education liked the project because he was familiar with Thomas Friedman, the author of *The World is Flat,* and that made my students and me proud of what we did.

Omani students reflect on the Flat Classroom Conference and the globalization of education (in English) http://tinyurl.com/oman-flat-classroom ▶

Case Study 6

A Global Collaborative Case Study — Class Chats

✓ ISTE STANDARDS

NETS.T 5
Engage in Professional Growth and Leadership

PDToolkit
for
Flattening Classrooms,
Engaging Minds
Read full Case Studies in PDToolkit online.

Cherrie MacInnes from Washington Street School in Brewer, Maine, used the website Class Chats to connect her third-grade classroom with another classroom in every state. This project was coordinated asynchronously with the goal of connecting with classrooms synchronously. When asked about the founding of the project, Cherrie says:

My classroom did a web conference project with a third-grade classroom in Minnesota. The interest level was so high and there was such a positive energy that I didn't want it to end. So I came up with the idea of trying to chat with a third-grade classroom in every state.

I didn't know if teachers would be receptive to doing this but their enthusiasm and interest has been so exciting.

I know there are other teachers in our country using web conferencing to enhance learning but it was very interesting that not one teacher in all 50 states who responded had ever done this before. Their tech people have been helping them; some schools have gone out and purchased web cams so that teachers could participate.

I'm hoping that people will join and eventually have an accessible place to connect with educators around the world.[24]

Find out more about this project at http://www .classchats.com

Case Study 7

Chrissy Hellyer and Global Connections

👥 ADD FRIEND

CHRISSY HELLYER
@nzchrissy
teachingsagittarian.com

PDToolkit
for
Flattening Classrooms,
Engaging Minds
Read full Case Studies in PDToolkit online.

Two things happened fairly close to each other about five years ago. I joined a group called OnlineProjects4teachers and I subscribed to a blog called Cool Cat Teacher.

Being part of OnlineProjects4teachers put me in contact with Kim Cofino, who at the time was a Middle School

✓ ISTE STANDARDS

NETS.S 2
Communication and Collaboration

technology teacher at M't Kiara School in Kuala Lumpur, Malaysia. I was an Intermediate schoolteacher in Napier, New

FLAT CLASSROOM™ FRAMEWORK

NAME OF PROJECT: Project Feel Good

WEBSITE URL: http://projectfeelgood.wikispaces.com

LOCATION: Malaysia and New Zealand

COMMUNICATION: Asynchronous—Wiki, Class blogs; Synchronous—Skype, YackPack

GENERATION: Ages 10 to 12

INFORMATION: Learning community with other students

TIME: 2 to 3 months

LEARNING LEGACY: Movies, class blogs, the wiki

Read the student sounding board work at http://tinyurl.com/horizon-peer

Zealand. We were both keen to use wikis in the classroom but weren't sure how to go about it. We were also put in contact with two other educators but because of time/work commitments and other things out of their control, the other two educators pulled out of our group.

Kim and I were still really keen to get a handle on this "wiki" thing so we decided that we would carry on with a project anyway. And so, ProjectFeelGood was born and so was a connection between two educators that has developed into a wonderful personal friendship. At the same time, subscribing to Cool Cat Teacher's blog was the best blog I could have ever started with. By subscribing to the RSS feed of this blog, the chance to become involved in the Horizon Project 2007 appeared.

My group of Year 7 (Grade 6) students and I became a sounding board peer review for the Horizon project.[25] This was an amazing opportunity for us and it was a privilege to be part of this project. My students were blown away at times with the information they were reading and watching and learning about. These students got to review multimedia presentations and wikis completed by students that, they themselves, will one day become. I had no doubt that being involved in this project seriously raised their level of multimedia and wiki presentation.[26]

In the meantime, Kim and I had concluded our first project together, and connected a number of times via Skype with our changing classes perfecting the Skype communication tips and tricks that we still use today.[27]

Later, we became involved again, in the sounding board peer review role, for the Flat Classroom Project 2007.[28] Finally, in Mumbai, India, at the ASB Unplugged Conference 2010, I had the opportunity to be involved in the Flat Classroom project once more. To be involved in a process where you actually get to see the effect that your feedback has on student work was humbling to say the least.[29]

Connecting online has changed the course of my life in a very profound way.

Step 2
Communication

Schools and after school programs must devote more attention to fostering what we call the new media literacies: a set of competencies and social skills that young people need in the new media landscape.[1]

HAROLD JENKINS
Confronting the Challenges of Participatory Media

Taking Those First Steps to Communicate

To begin our journey into communication, we share the stories of two countries, two teachers, and two third-grade classrooms that were part of our Flat Classroom™ 2010 Elementary Project, 'A Week in the Life…'"

Wow, I was completely impressed with how easily my students (grade 3) logged on to Edmodo, changed their icons, and began writing about themselves. They wrote without a first draft, and some needed reminders about capitals and periods and there were many questions about what is "personal information."

During the introduction, I forgot the lecture "that this is not Facebook"—that the students need to post and respond thoughtfully—so we had to stop and talk about that. What struck me the most is that this is real-time, relevant learning.

They are posting (protected) public comments and are learning what is too personal, taking the time to express themselves in writing at their best and how to thoughtfully respond to another person. In essence, [they are learning] how to communicate effectively. And this was just the first day to log on to Edmodo![2]

NANCY VON WAHLDE,
Prague, Czech Republic,
Elementary Flat Classroom Project 2010

I discovered Skype and the possibility of linking my classroom with others around the country on a snowy day in February. In the 3½ months between that day and the end of our school year, my third-grade students and I Skyped with 17 different states, 3 countries, and 3 times with authors. It was an incredible learning experience for both me and the students!

We learned firsthand about experiences that others had with tornadoes, earthquakes, hurricanes, and monsoons. We talked with schools who had 800 students and schools that had only 38 students. We learned about famous people and famous places from each new area that we met.

What was eye-opening for my students was not only the differences between us but also the many similarities. The other students liked the same foods, movies, video games, and books. Skype also taught my students how to speak in front of a group of peers. All of our sessions were exciting to me, but my very favorite was when we traveled around the world on Skype to meet Mr. B's classroom in New Zealand. My students had to come into school at night because of the time difference so I invited parents to observe. I'm not sure who was more excited, the adults or the children!

We loved to hear the differences in the speech of the New Zealand third-graders. They were telling us about the sport of rugby and they mentioned their famous team, what sounded to us like the "Ooblecks." The next day I googled their rugby team in order to put the correct spelling onto our blog. To my surprise, I found that they were called the "All Blacks." Now that my classroom is "flat" I don't think I could ever go back!

I am very excited this year to have discovered the Elementary Flat Classroom Project. This project can take my students and me to the next level—global collaboration.[3]

TINA SCHMIDT,
Grade 3 Teacher,
St. Ignatius of Antioch School, Yardley, PA.

NANCY VON WAHLDE
@nancyvonw
http://learningmosaic.wordpress
.com

**DIGITAL CITIZENSHIP AREA
OF UNDERSTANDING**
Safety, Privacy, Copyright, and Legal

ISTE STANDARDS

NETS.S 2
Communication and Collaboration

NETS.S 5
Digital Citizenship

21st CENTURY SKILLS

C21 INTERDISCIPLINARY THEME:
Global Awareness

C21 LIFE AND CAREER SKILLS:
Social and Cross-Cultural Skills

TINA SCHMIDT
@mrsschmidtb4
http://mrstinaschmidt.edublogs
.org/

OVERVIEW OF COMMUNICATION

"If you are reading this right now, I thank you, because no one seems to understand the concept of communication,"[4] begins Jonathan Choi, student project manager on the Horizon Project 2008, in his appropriately titled blog post "Desperation." The number-one complaint we hear from those trying to collaborate globally is that they contact someone and communication doesn't happen.

Communication in the 21st century is different. We still have to relate to ourselves as individuals and to relate to others face-to-face, but a whole complex world of technopersonal skills and digital citizenship has arisen that we don't really understand. There are many opportunities to communicate, but time zones, culture, and geography challenge us. The fact is that teachers can't get up every night at 2:00 am to meet with their friend in Beijing or Budapest. The first section of this chapter, titled "Self," aims to simplify and make sense of the complexity of communicating online.

In the "School" section of this chapter, we alleviate the worries of managing a project that runs 24/7 by introducing the concept of teachersourcing and how to set yourself up for success the moment you start a project. The methods of running productive teacher meetings conclude this section.

We end by focusing on student communications in the section referred to as "Students," with how to start your student interactions strong with a good project handshake. We also give you tips for how to maintain momentum in the project with simple routines for starting and ending class that you can adapt for your situation.

 SELF   Sustainable Global Communication Practices

COMMUNICATIONS IN THE 21ST CENTURY

21st CENTURY SKILLS

C21 INFORMATION, MEDIA, AND TECHNOLOGY SKILLS:
ICT Literacy

According to communications theorist, Harold Lasswell, communication is "who says what to whom in what channel with what effect."[5] When you talk to yourself (as we all do), that is **intrapersonal** relations. **Interpersonal** relations are between people. But, in today's technology-infused society, we now have a new type of communications that uses technology as the channel: We call this **technopersonal communications**. Technically, this is a subset of interpersonal skills; it is communications between people using technology as the channel (see Figure 4.1). You also saw this in the last chapter in the connection-planning tool.

Intrapersonal Skills.   Although some say that a person who talks to himself is "crazy," "self-talk" researchers say that "almost everybody talks to themselves"[6] because every person daydreams and has internal monologue. "Self-suggestion makes you master of yourself," says Clement W. Stone.[7]

FIGURE 4.1   Types of Communication

Intrapersonal	Interpersonal (face-to-face)	Interpersonal (not face-to-face)
Without Technology		
With Technology		

Past the motivational hoopla, intrapersonal intelligence has been discussed not just as a form of communication but as a form of intelligence. Gardner's theory of multiple intelligences defines people with intrapersonal intelligence as those who are "good at being aware of their own emotional states, feelings and motivations. They tend to enjoy self-reflection and analysis, including day-dreaming, exploring relationships with others and assessing their personal strengths."[8] Intrapersonal skills are an important part of communications.

Internal dialog is often considered a basis of self-esteem and one's ability to tackle difficult subjects.[9] The beginning of 21st century problem solving is the Stone Age self-reliance our ancestors felt when they went after a mammoth with spears and a belief that they could kill the beast and eat that winter. Students need to believe in themselves, and teachers need to believe that their students can do it!

Interpersonal Skills.   Perhaps the most often discussed communications are those of interpersonal skills, where a person is relating to another person. Books such as *How to Win Friends and Influence People* by Dale Carnegie teach us how to interact positively with others.[10]

Howard Gardner also considers this area a form of intelligence. Interpersonal intelligence is shown by those with a "good understanding [of]. . . interacting with other people. These individuals are skilled at assessing the emotions, motivations, desires and intentions of those around them."[11] We need to be able to interact with people! Interpersonal skills determine how we get along with others.

Technopersonal Skills.   If one reviews the aforementioned definitions, it is easy to wonder what happens when technology is involved. Harold Jenkins, in his MacArthur report, *Confronting the Challenges of Participatory Media,* says participatory media includes social skills:

"The new literacies almost all involve social skills developed through collaboration and networking." Further, he defines these skills as "play, performance, simulation, appropriation, multitasking, distributed cognition, collective intelligence, judgment, transmedia navigation, networking, and negotiation"[12] and asserts that students will not be successful without these skills.

What we are seeing is a new way to communicate between humans empowered by technology. Although a student may have great interpersonal skills in a face-to-face environment, if that student is from an impoverished home or poor school district without progressive access to technology tools, her or his lack of technopersonal skills can harm the natural interpersonal ability of that student when using technology. A student without web access has no opportunity to develop the technopersonal skills essential for success in today's world.

Context and Emotion in Technological Communications.   It is said that the words we say are only 7 percent of communication, with face, voice, and body language the other part.[13] So, in effect, it could be argued that if a student understands how to type and spell-check, he or she has only 7 percent of the skills needed to communicate online, as there are whole languages of emoticons, netiquette, and even an understanding of the variety of spellings as he or she communicates with others around the world through technology.

C21 LIFE AND CAREER SKILLS:
Initiative and Self-Direction

C21 LIFE AND CAREER SKILLS:
Social and Cross-Cultural Skills

NETS.S 2
Communication and Collaboration

21st CENTURY SKILLS

C21 LEARNING AND INNOVATION SKILLS:
Communication and Collaboration

C21 INFORMATION, MEDIA, AND TECHNOLOGY SKILLS:
ICT Literacy

tweetable
A student without web access has no opportunity to develop the technopersonal skills essential for success. #flatclass

NETS.S 5
Digital Citizenship

FIGURE 4.2 Context in Communications

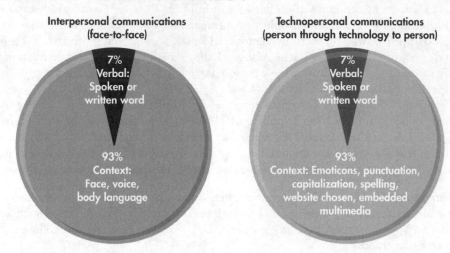

As shown in Figure 4.2, sometimes the technology that empowers communication also adds meaning to the communication—such as a voice inflection adds meaning to the punch line of a joke. Unfortunately, technologies can also create "glitches." Those without technopersonal skills can often jump to conclusions without realizing what has really happened.

For example, in the second Flat Classroom project, Ning was free but funded by **Google AdSense**. Because of an AdSense glitch, the students in Qatar started receiving advertising to "Click here to see sexy women in Qatar." Understanding how Google AdSense worked and that these ads were not coming from Vicki's classroom in Camilla, Georgia, Julie and Vicki quickly contacted leaders at Ning. Because of the AdSense glitch, Ning removed the ads for all educational spaces anywhere in the world for three years to prevent such embarrassing impediments to global collaboration. In this case, the computers, algorithms, and advertising robots added context to the communication that was not welcome. This is a big reason that educational spaces for K–12 should be ad-free.

So, as one can see, although technopersonal skills are a subset of interpersonal skills, they are different. Communications-savvy people are our best inoculation against the disease of inadvertent misunderstandings caused by technology glitches and nuances.

Profiles Are People. Students can dehumanize their partners in other parts of the world before really "getting to know" the person. In "video game" cultures it can be difficult to comprehend that a living, breathing person is on the other side of the world communicating with them. Consequently, people say things in online spaces that they would never say face-to-face. They might make fun of names or not understand why someone cannot post their photograph. In the real world, this has had dire consequences. Just ask Brian Chase, former operations manager of Rush Delivery, who lost his job after stating on Wikipedia that John Seigenthaler Jr. was a suspect in the Kennedy assassinations.[14] What started off as a joke turned into Brian Chase losing

his job and people beginning to doubt Wikipedia's accuracy. Ultimately, as a result of this incident, Wikipedia changed their editing policies.[15] Online behavior has offline consequences! Profiles represent people.

Some People Are Posers! Although on a class project, students should know that other participants are verified, students should also understand the flip side of the coin. Yes, most profiles are created by honest people but sometimes people make up their profiles in online spaces and pose to be someone they are not. This teaches students to check their sources and learn to verify the backgrounds of those they quote.

New Communication Literacies Include Habits. Technopersonal skills or "media literacies" are skills and habits that allow a person to communicate effectively with technology. The first of the American Library Association's Nine Information Literacy Standards for Student Learning covers the importance of students' being literate in the process of gathering information in a way that is efficient and effective.[16]

Part of being effective is having habits. Being able to access information efficiently and effectively isn't just about ability but about stability. Having a stable routine is vital to digital-age work and learning; otherwise, a person just flits from distraction to distraction, unable to focus.

We see this in our projects. Teachers begin projects and "drop out" when they don't check their email and miss deadlines for enrolling their students. Stability allows ability to shine in the online world. Teachers must have consistent habits of logging into communication portals and working with others.

Trustworthy, steady people excel consistently in online collaboration because they are there day in and day out—in their inbox, on the website. They are consistent. For this reason the prescreening of Flat Classroom projects is designed to remove the inconsistent, unconnected teacher and keep those with stable habits involved. The consistent habit of connecting online is a prerequisite to the teachersourcing discussed in the next section.

OPPORTUNITIES AND CHALLENGES OF COMMUNICATIONS

Communication online can be synchronous (live meetings or chat), asynchronous (blogs, wikis), or a blended form with characteristics of both (social networks). Each form presents opportunities and weaknesses that are important to understand as one selects communication tools.

Synchronous Communications. To best understand **synchronous communications**, consider synchronized swimmers. They work together to synchronize their motions to happen at the same time. Likewise, there are many technologies that allow you to talk, see each other via video, chat, and work in common spaces often while recording video and audio.

Opportunities. It is often these synchronous experiences where students "talk" that captivate the news media. Who can blame them? Many people want to see kids around the world interacting.

For example, when talking to sisters Hussainatu and Hassanatu Blake from Focal Point Global about their U.S.–Namibia HIV/Aids Education Initiative, you are

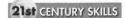

C21 INFORMATION, MEDIA, AND TECHNOLOGY SKILLS: Information Literacy, Media Literacy, ICT Literacy

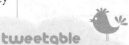

NETS.T 3
Model Digital-Age Work and Learning

DIGITAL CITIZENSHIP AREA OF UNDERSTANDING

Habits of Learning

tweetable

[Students must learn that] online behavior has off-line consequences! #flatclass

21st CENTURY SKILLS

C21 INTERDISCIPLINARY THEME: Health Literacy

FLAT CLASSROOM™ FRAMEWORK

NAME OF PROJECT: Focal Point Global

WEBSITE URL: http://www.focalpointglobal.org

LOCATION: Namibia, southern Africa and Baltimore, Maryland

COMMUNICATION: Asynchronous—local projects promoting HIV/AIDS awareness documented and shared with other participants. Synchronous—Skype conversations between the students.

GENERATION: Peers (14- to 17-year-olds); older generation (resources, facilitators); younger generation (receive information through local project)

INFORMATION: Reliable printed health resources provided to students prior to conversations. Each other. Facilitators.

TIME: Three days of research, presentations to one another via Skype, and idea sharing. Entire school year for resulting action project promoting HIV/AIDS awareness in local community.

LEARNING LEGACY: Videos and documentation shared on website.

NETS.T 2
Design and Develop Digital-Age Learning Experiences and Assessments

understandably touched as you think of inner-city students talking to the students in Namibia about the devastating impact that AIDS has had on that country.[17] The U.S. students come in on the weekend and talk on Skype because their school doesn't have the flexibility for such interactions "during school time." This form of communication often helps "humanize" those on the other side of the technology and can help broaden the worldview of students with just one interaction.

Synchronous meetings are essential for project organizers and teachers to communicate about the project and keep the project focused. Synchronous editing of documents can assist in workflow between teams and allow documents to stay current. For the teacher, synchronous face-to-face environments mean that the teacher can physically ensure the student's presence in the classroom. Teachers can notice physical cues from the student as to his or her attention and participation levels.

Challenges.   The reality of time zones, holidays, and the school day means that classrooms are often not in session at the same time. In order to allow the linkup between Namibia and Baltimore, students in the United States had to come in on a Saturday, as did the students in Namibia. In the other direction, China is 13 hours ahead of the U.S. East Coast time zone (12 hours during the summer), so synchronous class activity is impossible unless an evening or very early morning meet-up is organized.

Time zones are a challenge but another comes from the differences in hemispheres. Northern hemisphere countries typically have summer vacation in June through August, whereas some southern hemisphere countries have summer vacation in December through February, but every country is different and there are exceptions to these guidelines.

Additionally, many educators expect that their workday be from 7:30 am until 3:30 pm and are unwilling to meet outside of the normal school day. This is an issue, particularly in North America, where time zones are soaked up in the waters of the Atlantic and Pacific Oceans causing U.S. students to generally be in school while their peers around the world are asleep or at extracurricular events.

Understandably, teachers who commit to synchronous communications as their exclusive method of communication report exhaustion and burnout from coordinating the odd meeting times against busy school happenings and opening up their classrooms sometimes at very late or early hours.

Another drawback happens when students use tools such as Skype or Facebook chat. It is often difficult for teachers to tell who is participating and contributing in a project group without replaying a recording or reading a chat log. When these communications are verbal, most students do not record the conversations. Using only synchronous communications can make group assessment more difficult, as the individual contribution of each student to the project is harder to ascertain. When used at the wrong time in a project, live chat can be a distraction and an excuse students use to get off task. There have been times we've started a project with a live chat and removed it as the need for the live chat lessened.

Asynchronous Communications. **Asynchronous communication** methods are those that do not happen at the same time. Like Facebook, Ning, and many other websites, information in various forms is posted for others to view and interact with at a later time. Blogs, wikis, podcasts, video sharing, and most forms of online communications where one is posting to a website are asynchronous. Additionally, email remains the most popular mode of asynchronous communications among adults[18] with "social networking sites" as the most popular asynchronous daily activity among teens.[19]

Opportunities. Many tools like blogs and wikis require less bandwidth and include more schools. When a person is notified immediately of a change on the website, asynchronous communications can be a gateway to unplanned synchronous communications that happen because two people "figure out" they are online at the same time. Many tools like Google Docs and Ning now include a live chat feature that lets you see and chat with others who are online at the same time. Sometimes spontaneous synchronous interactions are better than planned ones.

With asynchronous tools, each student has his or her own username. This allows for collaborative work to be done while still allowing for individual assessment. (Try that with a poster or diorama.) This is a cooperative learning dream! In the early days of cooperative learning, many teachers gave all of the students in a group the same grade regardless of the quantity of input from each team member. Fairness has a face in online learning—it's called the **userid!**

Challenges. "Leaving a message" can seem not as satisfying as connecting directly. It is for that reason that many schools, not understanding the true nature of global

ISTE STANDARDS

NETS.T 3
Model Digital-Age Work and
Learning

Read the Children's Online
Privacy Protection Act of 1998
at http://www.ftc.gov/ogc
/coppa1.htm.

collaboration, choose not to pursue asynchronous collaboration methods. They think it is all about direct, live connections and are limiting what they can do.

There should still be some common timelines involved, however. For example, when a project happens and students are editing a wiki, they should be editing the wiki within the same period of time so that they understand collaboration. In the ideal classroom, if a student leaves a message, his or her partner would leave a message by the time the first student returns to class the next day.

When a project is too asynchronous, the project ceases to be a project and the webpage is just a webpage that people happen to occasionally edit. To have a project of significance, some form of synchronicity is desired in order to provide the collaborative environment required to teach online global collaboration.

It is also good for students to understand the different work weeks around the world. Many Western countries have a Monday to Friday work week, but in the Middle East the working week is typically Sunday to Thursday.

Sometimes, vacations, holidays, and special events, as well as conflicting priorities of local administrators, can usurp the ability of classroom teachers to keep to agreed time lines and actions. (Pulling kids from an "elective" class to attend an assembly or special event without notice is a common problem.) It is easy for administrators and teachers to "forget" that a real person is on the other end of a project and waiting for a response. The person at your desk or on the intercom easily takes priority over the passive nonpresence of project participants half a world away. So, collaborative projects require educators with integrity who adhere to time lines and advocate for adequate time for a project. This requires coordination and support from local administration.

When embarking on global collaboration, administrators must understand the reality that other classrooms depend on the classroom in their school. Their school is no longer an island. When their decisions result in broken communication and broken trust, it may impede future collaborations. Some administrators treat technology-related courses as unimportant places from which students can be excused without impunity. This sends the wrong messages to students who must understand collaboration and be led by example. Class time for global collaboration should be respected particularly when deadlines are looming. The modern administrator must model digital citizenship and respect global collaboration timeframes by planning special events ahead of time to allow teachers to plan accordingly.

ISTE STANDARDS

NETS.T 2
Design and Develop Digital-Age Learning Experiences and Assessments

Flattening Communications: Blending Both.   Quick, name a number from 1 to 24. As we all know, there is a place in the world right now where the clocks say that hour. So many of our students don't realize this fact in a real way!

To be successful in a 24-hour world, students must master both methods of communication: asynchronous and synchronous. Just as steel is an alloy that becomes stronger than the original elements, when synchronous and asynchronous are mixed effectively, a resilient, healthy communication structure emerges for participants and organizers.

For example, Facebook and Ning have added the ability to have live chats. Conversely, Skype, a free live video and audio voice over the Internet (VOIP) service, has recording capabilities for voice, video, and computer screens.

Furthermore, an essential requirement of all Flat Classroom projects is a teacher meeting that is recorded and shared via video and audio to those teachers who cannot be present. Just as coaches view game film to improve performance, so teachers and organizers can view this "game film" from teacher meetings to improve learning and efficiency!

True global collaborators "flatten" and level their synchronous experiences by always recording and sharing with other participants (see Table 4.1). This also gives researchers an opportunity to review live interactions without exerting undue influence with their presence. (See Chapter 2 for information on the "flat world" researcher.)

Challenging Education's Time Paradigm. The global collaborating educator must work with administrators to redefine class time for their students and planning time for themselves.

TABLE 4.1 Blending Synchronous and Asynchronous Communications for Resilient, Healthy Communication Networks

Technology	Synchronous Aspects "At the same time"	Asynchronous Aspects "Not at the same time"
VOIP (voice over IP) and Skype	**Talk, video, and voice, and text chat at the same time**	*Record conversations. Record can be archived and retrieved*
Videoconferencing and Web Conferencing (like Blackboard Collaborate and Web Ex)	**Talk, video, voice, text chat, share whiteboard, collaboratively edit, screen share**	*Record the session and post as video or audio*
Blogging	*A live chat box, "Skype me," or online status can be added, live blog statistics like those provided by Chartbeat can be used to show how many are on the site at that moment*	**Post writing, embed video and audio, RSS feeds, embed the "feed" in other websites**
Wikis	*Same widgets are available as those for blogs.*	**Post writing, embed video and audio. Collaborative editing on a wiki is by definition asynchronous**
Videos	*Can be recorded live and posted simultaneously through some live video sites. Can also include a live chat and be password protected.*	**Post video and receive comments**
Google Docs	**Synchronous editing and commenting**	**Asynchronous editing and commenting, publishing as a webpage updated live when changes are made**

Bolded items represent the original, primary use of the technology. Those in italics represent a blended element for enhancing communications.

DIGITAL CITIZENSHIP AREA
OF UNDERSTANDING

Etiquette and Respect

NETS.T 4
Promote and Model Digital
Citizenship and Responsibility

For example, a U.S. course focusing on Middle East studies might decide to come in early in the morning or later in the evening. This would let them watch live news reports and interact with people in that region during their daytime. We need to get creative about class times as we begin to collaborate—businesses do!

Planning times must also evolve. Teachers who collaborate globally meet at odd times, often very early or late. Progressive administrators will work with teachers to have flexible planning hours in such cases.

When teacher meetings do happen during a school day, some teachers report that colleagues rudely interrupt or come in and talk loudly during the meeting. (This is why knowing how to use the mute button is essential!) A teacher with a headset in an online meeting should be respected like a teacher sitting down with three people in a room. Another teacher would not interrupt a face-to-face meeting that another teacher was having. Perhaps this is ignorance, but it is time for savvy schools to create an awareness of respecting online meetings. Maybe we need to make signs to put on our computers when we are in a meeting and cannot be disturbed.

Education's time paradigm must evolve to allow for nontraditional meeting times for students and teachers and also provide respect for those immersed in global collaboration planning meetings.

Realistically Evaluate the Time You Have. In order to prepare for effective communication, be honest with yourself about the time you have to connect and work with other teachers. We've designed this communications inventory to help you find balance, not burnout, in your global collaborative future.

S E L F - A S S E S S M E N T   S U R V E Y

COMMUNICATION

for
*Flattening Classrooms,
Engaging Minds*

See the survey results in the
online PDToolkit before moving
on to the next section.

After taking this survey, discuss these questions with colleagues and your wider learning network, to determine your current level of confidence and ability with communication strategies.

NETS.T 5
Engage in Professional Growth
and Leadership

1. **Am I willing to meet with teachers outside my regular school day?**

   a. Yes.

   b. No.

   c. Maybe.

2. **Am I willing to reach out to administration for an exception in my class time at least once during this collaboration to allow a meeting at a different time in order to meet with another classroom?**

   a. Yes.

   b. No.

   c. Maybe.

3. **Do I check email daily?**

   a.   Yes.

   b.   No.

   c.   Maybe.

4. **Do I have Internet access at home?**

   a.   Yes, broadband.

   b.   Yes, but it is slow.

   c.   No.

5. **Can I access one email account from home and school?**

   a.   Yes.

   b.   No.

   c.   I would have to work on this.

PREVENTING BURNOUT

After assessing your ability to communicate, consider preventing burnout before it happens. Have creative discussions relating to time scheduling with administrators before you are tired and it becomes an issue. Although global collaboration is still somewhat in its infancy, there are already teachers who have experienced burnout.

This is nothing new in the workforce. In the paper *World-Wide Work Stress: Multi-Case Study of the Stress-Coping Process in Distributed Work,* Nina Nurmi states, "Coordinating across time zones added job demands in . . . global teams . . . usually, they ended up working long hours and compromising their personal time off work. This resulted in overload, work-leisure imbalance, and strain from which the team members did not adequately recover between work days."[20]

This burnout happens with highly engaged, energetic teachers who believe that synchronous interactions, because of their power, are the "only" way to collaborate globally. These teachers might have their students in at odd hours to meet with other classes. Often, after the novelty of the experience "wears off," they find themselves unable or unwilling to continue with collaboration because of the sacrifice of personal time.

If you have more than eight hours of time (length of the average school day) difference between your time zones and that of other teachers, work to create asynchronous interaction spaces and head off burnout before it happens. Teachers need a personal life and should be fair to themselves by limiting synchronous interactions at odd hours. We predict that visionary schools will work with teachers keen to collaborate globally to create win-win scenarios for everyone with some sort of flexible time arrangements.

ISTE STANDARDS

NETS.T 3
Model Digital-Age Work and Learning

On a personal note, as parents of teenagers, as of the writing of this book, we often cover for one another as we attend jazz concerts, football games, or family vacations. Pitching in to preserve personal time for teachers and organizers is part of the community of practice of Flat Classroom projects as our teachers are in it for the long term but want rich, meaningful memories in their personal lives as well. With cooperation you can have the best of both worlds while you make a better world!

COMMUNICATION HABITS FOR LONG-TERM SUCCESS

Online collaborative projects are not a reproducible that a teacher can copy, hand out to her class, and sit back while they "do" it. Diane Hammond, co-founder of *Yes I Can! Science* in Canada, shares that "the engaged teacher" was the top factor in engaging students in their online science projects.[21] The stability of consistent engagement amplifies the teacher's ability and literacy. Although *Yes I Can! Science* dissolved in April 2011 (and thus no profile is listed), it had some incredible projects, including collaborations between students and scientists on the Space Station that need to be replicated and pursued in the future.

Effective global collaborative teachers should check their email, engage with students face-to-face, share their stories with other teachers, participate or listen to weekly meetings, monitor spaces through a class monitoring portal (CMP), and participate in discussions on the wiki. The teachers with the best results often do things a little early on the time line and do not procrastinate as they lead by example. We have found that teachers who are effective in the global collaborative environment share the following six characteristics discussed here.

Be Empowered to Act and Teach Everyone.   The teacher who finds a problem should be the one who handles the problem initially. Whether it is a major offense and needs a screenshot with communication to the student and the teachers or a minor tip such as the use of IMSpeak!—teachers should be highly engaged in teachable moments. All teachers should "own" all students and be part of the circle of educators working with students on a project. See more on problem resolution in Chapter 5, titled Step 3: Citizenship.

Engage with Other Teachers.   Each project will include a few tools that teachers use to communicate. Teachers should check their email or the teacher communications portal every day before holding class with the students in order to facilitate effective partnership with other classrooms, as discussed in Chapter 6, titled Step 4: Contribute and Collaborate.

Actively Monitor Classroom Activity.   The classroom should be monitored closely, particularly when content is posted live without pre-moderation. Public posting can easily be monitored through the construction of a classroom monitoring portal (CMP) using RSS and an RSS reader (discussed in Chapter 3). A classroom monitoring portal should be built by project organizers to manage the entire project. (We call it the Project CMP). It is built on a portal-based RSS reader such as Netvibes or Pageflakes that allows publishing of the link to the page. (As of the writing of this book iGoogle allowed the sharing of a page via email but not publication of a page by creating a webpage). Individual teachers sometimes build their own portal to focus in on their

students, especially if it is a large project with several hundred students. (We call this the Teacher CMP because it just has the students of one teacher in the feed. This is why we have a tag assigned to each school so teachers can extract their student information more easily.)

Brian Mannix, social studies teacher at Great Neck South Middle School in New York, says, "The classroom monitoring portal serves as a huge sigh of relief in a world where information overload can easily overcome both student and teacher in the connected classroom. Finally, a simple way to have all of the fluid classroom websites and updated assignment pages accessible in one easy-to-navigate place."[22] There will be further discussion on this in the section named "Students" that ends this chapter.

Be Willing to Learn and Teach. Many new tools and practices may be introduced and shared in a project. In a flattened learning environment everyone is learning something. Teachers should model a willingness to say, "I don't know, let me find out" and "Wow, you've taught me something new, I'm so excited."

Be Cognizant of the Teachable Moment. Teachers should resist the desire to achieve the perfect project. Many teachable moments emerge, with each student often having a unique experience and learning outcome. Problems are teachable moments. Good teachers in this environment are coaches.

Be Considerate of Those with Less Bandwidth. Internet bandwidth varies greatly around the world. In some countries such as Bangladesh and Pakistan, rolling power outages are used to remediate limited energy supplies. Teachers who send or post files should be aware that they may take a long time for others to download. Additionally, **video compression** should be used when uploading videos for a project. A large video may take a long time to load or download for a classroom with less bandwidth. Teachers should watch and coach students to be aware of the bandwidth abilities of others on a project.

 SCHOOL Building Relationships and Planning

PLAN AHEAD FOR GOOD COMMUNICATION

Communication doesn't just happen. If you want to work with someone at your school, you plan times to meet, talk, and work together. The same is true in online spaces, except communication must be blended in ways that suit the collaborators' work flow and habits.

Set Up Communication Conduits. A conduit is a channel or trough through which things flow. Each project has its own set of standard tools often based on the preferences of organizers. We call these **communication conduits**. Make sure the functions mentioned below are covered by your selected conduits.

Email Discussion Groups. Discussion groups linked to email accounts should be established to facilitate communication between all participants. By reading a

message and replying to the message, a response is sent to everyone in the group. This often allows teachers to get answers from each other within an hour that may take longer for project organizers to respond to.

Instant Messaging Group: "The Backchannel Chat."   Just in time *professional development* is becoming an important buzzword in professional development (PD) circles and rightly so. When teachers have problems and are working to solve them, they often have a tiny window of opportunity during their planning time or after school. In order to facilitate immediate help, most Flat Classroom projects have an instant messaging group. By adding everyone to the group, the others can see who is online. By chatting to the group, a person who is available can help the group or a student right then. The **backchannel** is available whenever someone is online and signed in.

This procedure shouldn't be counted on to provide answers 100 percent of the time, but it is often the "go-to" method of discussing student behavior issues when one teacher would like a second opinion. It also helps teachers get to know one another. This can also be done through chat rooms linked to educational networks like Ning, Gchat, or another tool of choice. Get the answer! Don't wait!

A Strong Email Connection between Teachers.   Ideally, the listserv or email group should be immediately delivered to teachers' inboxes instead of once a day in a digest. So, if student issues occur, the teacher who sees it should be the first to initiate appropriate action.

In a teachersourced environment students share all of the teachers and vice versa. Our policy of "ban first, ask questions afterward" has prevented the infrequent issues from escalating. Most of our projects are public and we do not premoderate student content. We want to build a network of trust and accountability.

When issues arise, the student receives a private message about why they are being banned and information on the review process and a screenshot of the issue is shared privately with the other teachers to build consensus if further action should happen or the student should be reinstated. The student's teacher is the only person who can ask for reinstatement. The backchannel should be a positive environment of support and understanding, as every teacher has students who make mistakes. **Screenshots** should be taken before any content is removed. The process should be transparent and students should feel comfortable reporting content to administrators through an anonymous process.

Appointment Groups.   Setting appointments can be one of the biggest challenges of multiple time zones. Although some projects use a website like Doodle, many sites require participants to convert the time zone manually.

An appointment secretary website that integrates with calendar programs like Google Calendar and Outlook and converts time zones is not just convenient but has boosted our meeting attendance from around one-third of the participants to over half at most meetings. After making up a group, the appointment secretary website (we use Timebridge) sends everyone an invitation for five potential times to meet. If it finds a time when everyone can meet, it automatically schedules the meeting; if it can't find an agreed on time, then the organizers select a time. Other sites serve as appointment secretaries; find and use them—doing so is the key to maximizing meeting attendance.

In extremely large projects such as NetGenEd™, we divide the world into "zones" and often have weekly meetings in both Zones 1 and 2. For us, Zone 1 is "the Americas" and Zone 2 is Asia through Eastern Europe. Care must be made not to set appointments solely on those who can attend, or a U.S.-heavy project will exclude those in other parts of the world. Although convenient, unless there is a set time every week when everyone can meet, project organizers should avoid having the same meeting time every week, as it will skew participation in the project to those who find the time more convenient and exclude those who may be busy or asleep during the weekly meeting.

Online Meeting Spaces. The synchronous meeting room that you select should allow recording, playback, and conversion to podcast and should be used for teacher and for student meetings. Put meeting recordings in the same place and if possible, convert to video and audio so participants can listen in the platform of their choice. Teachers who participate in online projects should attend meetings in person or listen in later. They are important and should be held for a reason.

Shared Calendars. Two types of calendars are useful for global collaborative projects: (1) a project calendar and (2) a calendar of class times. The project calendar includes all of the dates and phases of the project, including deliverables and group meetings. The calendar of class times allows every teacher to put her or his time into the calendar to determine when common times for potential class meet ups may happen. On Flat Classroom projects, we use Google Calendars for this function, but other calendaring systems may be used, so long as each participant can enter his or her time and confirm his or her time zone.

These calendars should be embedded throughout the project websites. Note that it is best keep these two types of calendars separate, or the project calendar will become so cluttered that no one will look at it!

Project Monitoring Portal. The project monitoring portal (see Figure 4.3) is the same thing as a class monitoring portal (CMP) (see Figure 4.4) except that it is established

FIGURE 4.3 Project Monitoring Portal

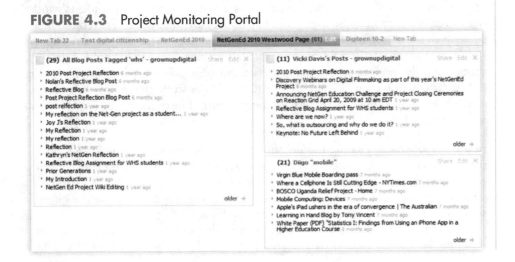

FIGURE 4.4 Sample Class Monitoring Portal

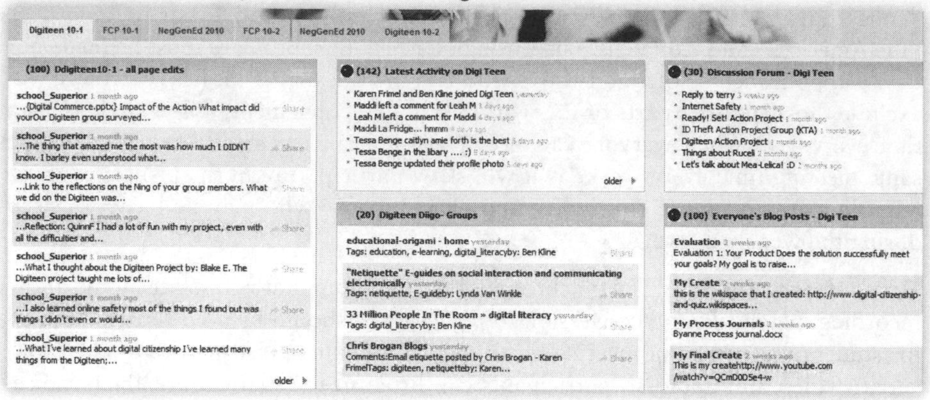

on a projectwide basis. As discussed earlier, project organizers should set this up for public projects, as some teachers may still find RSS daunting. Teachers should understand that all teachers should monitor content through the public areas as part of the community of practice habits. Plan ahead and communicate how projects should be monitored.

Items Included on the Project CMP. RSS feeds from all activities should be on the portal. This may include videos, photos, blog posts, and forum discussions on the educational network and wiki edits and discussions on the wiki as well as bookmarks from the social bookmarking group. Any place where students share publicly that has an RSS feed should be included. Every teacher should spend 5 to 10 minutes per class period, or one planning period, reviewing current content and providing comments on their student work. The calendar for the projects and links to all important websites should be there as well as links to the feed for the online meetings.

Items Included on the Teacher CMP. Similar to the way children know which presents belong to them by the tag on the box, teachers are able to grab their students' work out of very large projects by using tags. For this reason, many teachers require their students to tag all wikis, blogs, and photographs for assessment and monitoring.

Project organizers should organize and assign tags for each school before students begin the project and to make assessment easy. Some teachers have a strict policy, "If you don't tag it, I don't grade it," to demonstrate the importance of this skill. Others discuss the concept of **taxonomy** as part of introducing the standard tag for their school.[23]

Find Times to Meet. Finding mutual times to meet is particularly important when planning a new project. Teachers should compare their self-assessment surveys done earlier this chapter and also review the times that they will be able to collaborate with one another. This can be done informally or by using something like the spreadsheet synchronous time planning tool shown in Figure 4.5.

Times to meet can be found by using Timebridge, but it can be helpful to understand the big picture first. Have each teacher write down the 24 hours in their day

FIGURE 4.5   Synchronous Time Planning Tool

Synchronous Time Planning Tool

My Time Zone	Eastern									
GMT Difference		−5								

My Personal Time Tracker.

Step 1: Mark all times you are available for synchronous interactions. 0=not available, 1=possible, 2=good, 3=best.

Step 2: Go to a website like 222.greenwichmeantime.com and convert the time zones - Type the corresponding GMT time into the columns in step 2.

Step 3: Use the GMT comparison to find the times that you can most likely meet synchronously. The less synchronous times available the more likely you'll need asynchronous tools.

Person #1				Person #2				GMT Comparison		
Step 1		Step 2		Step 1		Step 2		GMT Time	Person 1	Person 2
Personal Time Tracker		Convert to GMT		Personal Time Tracker		Convert to GMT		Automatic Look Up		
Name: Davis, weekdays EST (−5)		Manual Paste!		Lindsay, weekdays (+8)		Manual Paste!				
5:00 AM	1	10:00 AM		5:00 AM	1	9:00 PM		5:00 AM	0	3
5:15 AM	1	10:15 AM		5:15 AM	1	9:15 PM		5:15 AM	0	2
5:30 AM	2	10:30 AM		5:30 AM	2	9:30 PM		5:30 AM	0	0
5:45 AM	2	10:45 AM		5:45 AM	1	9:45 PM		5:45 AM	0	0
6:00 AM	2	11:00 AM		6:00 AM	0	10:00 PM		6:00 AM	0	0
6:15 AM	2	11:15 AM		6:15 AM	0	10:15 PM		6:15 AM	0	2
6:30 AM	0	11:30 AM		6:30 AM	0	10:30 PM		6:30 AM	0	3
6:45 AM	0	11:45 AM		6:45 AM	0	10:45 PM		6:45 AM	0	3
7:00 AM	0	2:00 P...		7:0...	0	11:00 PM		7:00 A...	0	

and note their time zone as it relates to Greenwich Mean Time (GMT). Then, they should note all times during the day that they are willing and able to meet, with 3 representing the best time to meet, 2 good times, 1 not preferred but possible, and 0 impossible times to meet.

When all of the teachers in a project do this, then one can convert the times of all teachers into GMT to see if there are times that will be easy for the teachers to meet, as shown in the graphic in Figure 4.5 mapping the times Julie and Vicki are available, first in their own time zone and then converted to Greenwich Mean Time. Though tricky at first, once a person learns this skill it becomes easier. This is most manageable with a smaller group of teachers; however, with larger groups a tool like Timebridge may be best.

Effective Teacher Handshakes.   The first phase of the project starts before the project truly begins. We call this the **handshake** phase. Although some countries do not use the physical handshake, the term *handshake* originates from how people in Western countries meet and greet one another by grasping hands.

Just as a face to face handshake establishes a professional relationship and communication between two people it is also how online relationships start. In effect, a handshake is a beginning. Our Flat Classroom experience has taught us that the faster teachers and students connect when a project starts (during the project handshake phase discussed here), the better the initial connection and the better the final outcome. Typically, the online project handshake should happen within 10 to 14 days, but 7 or fewer days is ideal.

PDToolkit
for
Flattening Classrooms,
Engaging Minds

See a full synchronous time planning tool online at PDToolkit.

During the teacher handshake, teachers should join all of the teacher communication conduits for that project, and then actively begin using the three Rs of global collaboration (as discussed at length in Chapter 6, titled Step 4: Contribution and Collaboration)—Receive, Read, and Respond—as they check messages and respond to the other organizers.

TOP-NOTCH TEACHERSOURCING

Crowdsourcing has been called the "biggest paradigm shift since the Industrial Revolution."[24] Companies like Eli Lilly use crowdsourcing portals like InnoCentive to "connect with brainpower outside the company."[25] By tapping into the power of crowds, the website Threadless has people create T-shirt designs and others vote the designs into existence.

A relative of crowdsourcing, **teachersourcing** is an essential paradigm shift in the move to integrate sustainable global collaboration into the classroom. In practice, teachersourcing means that groups of teachers can be used for tasks such as managing large groups of students, creating global project designs, innovating new ways to do a task in projects, or any number of functions. It can provide almost round-the-clock monitoring that no one could afford if it was outsourced to a company. The quality of monitoring and participation is better too because teachers teach as they interact with students. Teachers provide the currency of attention paid for by their commitment to join the group in monitoring and participation. Many of the most vibrant projects in existence remain fresh, innovative, and relevant in this way. Good teachers are involved in their projects.

It's no surprise that a code of conduct and **community of practice** (CoP) emerges on projects. Teachers should understand what they need to do to make sure that projects run smoothly, and much of it is the habits of the teachers themselves. Building documentation, promoting the project, disseminating materials, planning, and communicating directly with teachers to ensure that they are going to engage and that emails go through are all activities that happen and become norms of behaviors for teachers in projects like Flat Classroom.

Preplanning.   Over half the time spent on a global collaborative project by teachers typically happens before the project begins. Project organizers should set the standard by respecting the time of others, keeping appointments, and keeping promises, and teachers should do the same. Everyone pitches in to help prepare and test websites to simulate ways students will use the site before they get there. Sometimes this can be done with a wide variety of people such as preservice teachers or classrooms that sign on early to "beta test" the project. Let people know when they are **beta testers** to set expectations that problems should be noted and reported. Companies like Google have been doing this for year—Gmail had the "beta" logo for several years, even after launch.

WorkFlow Software.   When multiple project organizers are involved, workflow software such as Basecamp can be used to manage incoming email and route issues to be handled.

As of the writing of this book, the Flat Classroom projects are using a workflow website intended for software called Fogbugz. This system checks the email boxes for each project and routes the email to the current project organizer(s). A ticket is opened for each inquiry, and emails may be sent as the tickets are updated.

We have found that when our projects moved past 10 classrooms and 100 students, the volume of email and issues to track became cumbersome. Ideally, one project organizer should be able to go on vacation without the project coming to a stop. Centralizing workflow is essential to project scalability. There are many free open source alternatives and free trials of software available for educational groups. Currently, workflow software for educational projects is virtually nonexistent but we expect this to change. Tasks and communication should be shared and, ideally, should flow around the world with the tide of students who are awake and engaged with project tasks.

Help Files.   If a picture is worth a thousand words, a video can often be worth ten thousand! The use of screen capture programs such as Camtasia, CamStudio, Jing Project, or the screen recording feature in Blackboard Collaborate allow organizers and teachers to record problems and share solutions easily. We maintain one place for all projects because of the overlap in best practices between projects. Make sure that help files are current and updated. Teach the teachers to update a central source of help documentation as part of teachersourcing. If they help one child, they have helped just one, but if they use that child's question to create an answer that can be used by others, they have helped everyone and saved time.

Batching Activities.   Piecemeal work is the anathema of the online project organizer. Establish regular intervals to set up users, approve those joining spaces, and update websites. Teachers should learn if they do things within the appropriate window of time that they will receive a faster response and set up than if they procrastinate.

Outsourcing.   Project organizers do not have to do everything. While working to create transcription meetings for this book, we outsourced some of the work on Elance and found affordable solutions for under $10 an hour.

We hope that firms specializing in educational online projects will emerge so that educators can outsource approvals, copyright review, and technical support for just a few dollars an hour. Although confidential student information must be protected, there are routine, lower-level tasks on just about every project that could be outsourced.[26]

Project Monitoring.   As part of teachersourcing it is important for all teachers to make a habit of checking the sites and the project-monitoring portal, and to deal with issues as they happen. For more information, see Chapter 5, Step 3: Citizenship.

Post Project Surveys.   Just as the effective teacher surveys and polls students at the end of a course, the effective project organizer surveys all participants to get feedback. We use SurveyShare to administer student and teacher surveys but many use Google Forms (part of Google Docs). Sometimes teachers feel more comfortable providing anonymous feedback to organizers because they have a relationship with the organizer and do not wish to hurt his or her feelings. Anonymous surveys are an important part of ongoing quality improvement.

WEBSITES

Current help wiki for Flat Classroom projects
http://helps.flatclassroomproject.org

Elance
http://www.elance.com

PRODUCTIVE ONLINE MEETING PRACTICES

There are several characteristics of an effective teacher meeting. These are discussed next.

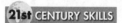

A Stable, Accessible Meeting Room.   As discussed in the previous section on communication conduits, the online web space should include a whiteboard, chat space, audio, video, and screen-sharing features, and allow recording, along with the ability to convert meetings to audio or video. Attendees should also be able to save and export the whiteboard and chat area.

Some online meeting sites allow telephone participants to dial into a special number so that they can participate. However, this is often an additional charge and not available in all countries, but it can increase participation rates. Teachers who have not learned the web conference facilities should be instructed to arrive early for a tutorial so that valuable meeting time with all participants is not used for tutorials for those who are beginners

Additionally, many conferencing services such as Blackboard Collaborate have accessibility features built in that allow teachers and students with accessibility issues to be full participants. One does not have to see or hear to participate in online meetings. Plan ahead if there are accessibility issues to test and ensure features are enabled, as this is still an emerging field of practice.

tweetable

If there is no reason to meet, there should
not be a meeting.
#flatclass

A Reason to Meet.   Every meeting should have a purpose. If there is no reason to meet, there should not be a meeting. Project organizers should be a model of efficiency in this practice.

Agenda.   Every meeting should have an agenda that participants have ahead of time. They should be told what preparation, if any, they need to have and the content of the meeting. The agenda for most projects is:

- *Room Set Up:* Twenty or thirty minutes before participants arrive, the moderator should set up the whiteboard and test their microphone. This can be delegated, but someone should be assigned to do this so the meeting will start on time. The organizer sets the stage.
- *Orientation:* Ten minutes before an official meeting start time, the facilitator leads teachers in understanding the use of the meeting room. After all teachers on a project are trained, the orientation is no longer needed.
- *Testing:* Participants should arrive a few minutes early and test their microphone and speakers. If they do not have a microphone, they should let organizers know in the chat.
- *Handshake and/or Round Robin Reporting:* Early meetings always begin with a "handshake" activity that varies depending on the phase of the project. Early in the project, teachers post pictures on the whiteboard and share why they are participating. Later on, teachers report where they are on the project by typing in the chat or sharing on mike. This should be fun if possible! Putting stars on a map where one is from, or a photo of oneself, helps teachers feel connected.
- *Review of milestones and problem solving:* Organizers talk about activities that should already be done, current student activities, and a review of what

to expect the next three to four weeks. Questions are taken from the chat with care to ensure that individual issues are handled as quickly as possible. It helps to have several organizers attend meetings so that one can facilitate and the other can troubleshoot and fix technical issues as teachers request it in the meeting. For example, a teacher might say that he or she has not been promoted to "teacher" status on Ning or granted administrative rights on the wiki; this can be handled quickly while still in the meeting and thus reinforces the benefits of attending meetings to get problems solved.

- *Tutorials:* Conclude with review of a tool via screen sharing with one of the leading project-experts on that tool. This is converted to video and posted as part of the help wiki for the project, thereby ensuring up-to-date videos that answer the pertinent questions of teachers. Veteran teachers may opt out of attending the tutorial part of a meeting so all business should happen before this. If veteran teachers stay, invite them to go on mike or share in the chat their tips for using the tool. If they share it in the chat, make sure to mention the tip using your voice to put it on the recording. (Chat windows are typically not captured in the recording of online spaces.)

Starting and Ending on Time.   Meetings should begin and end promptly. If latecomers come in, encourage them to listen to the recording if something they ask about has already been discussed. Remember that participants in online meetings have the ultimate freedom to walk away from the computer. The best way to prevent this behavior is to avoid repetition, which punishes those who have been online for the entire time. Those who feel their time is wasted in your meeting will soon stop wasting their time by coming!

If you wish to help latecomers, declare the meeting officially over and say that you will stay afterwards to help anyone with issues. If possible, end the general meeting 5 to 10 minutes early—it is greatly appreciated. Never run over!

Skilled Facilitation.   Facilitators should be familiar with how to help people with issues as well as how to remove speaking privileges and coach newcomers. It is helpful to have a lead facilitator and a technical expert who can troubleshoot problems in the room if they occur. Facilitators should be comfortable, and keep the meeting moving on task, and productive, and be unselfish with the microphone. If a facilitator sees that participants are suffering from "information overload," they should wisely refocus and schedule another meeting to tackle remaining issues at a later time.

Recording.   The fact is that many teachers will be unable to attend the meeting. Typically, most Flat Classroom project meetings have between 40 and 60 percent of teachers present, although sometimes this may go down to 25 percent, depending on the time of year. Therefore, postmeeting follow-up is as important as the meeting itself.

Syndication.   A link to the meeting recording and an email with a brief summary should be sent out immediately after the meeting to the whole group. Teachers who do not attend in person should listen to the meeting and respond with their questions and reports to the group. You can also podcast the meeting so that participants may listen while in commute.

DIGITAL CITIZENSHIP AREA OF UNDERSTANDING

Etiquette and Respect

C21 LIFE AND CAREER SKILLS: Productivity and Accountability

 STUDENTS Building Structures and Habits for Learning

We can usually tell how well a school is going to do in a project by how strong they start. Just like a race, most strong finishers start well. Schools that start a project well are usually those who continue with the project to completion. To ensure participation, project organizers and administrators should closely monitor the student handshake process to make sure that students join websites in a timely manner and complete essential tasks.

START STRONG WITH A GOOD HANDSHAKE

When an effective handshake takes place, we have found that the following seven essential components exist.

1. Students join all websites
2. Students join teams
3. "Meet and greet" partners
4. Understand time and place
5. Understand communication ground rules
6. Open the lines of communication
7. Establish routines that work

Students Join All Websites. This should be timed to occur as close as possible in time to "simulate" a synchronous experience, build momentum, and create excitement through the social connections. Often, teachers and students have delayed joining in a project for a few weeks, only to join and find themselves behind, lost, and overwhelmed.

Students Join Teams. Students are assigned to their teams and, if possible, are given some choice on their topics. Teams are split geographically to ensure diversity. This should be done as early as possible. Teachers are continually asked, "Who is my partner?" as curious, excited students engage with the project. Take advantage of that enthusiasm and momentum!

"Meet and Greet" Partners. Partners do not seem to "exist" until there is a digital footprint of their existence on the website. Typically, "meeting" partners can take several forms:

- *Preproject Reflection:* A preproject reflection can include how the student "feels" about the project. This helps students connect on a human level and can assuage the natural nervousness that students feel when moving into a new, strange environment.
- *Personal Greeting:* The best "handshake" experience is a greeting from students to their partners as a message on their profile page or in a common space for team members to work, such as on a wiki discussion tab. When such a greeting receives a response, we have observed impressive engagement levels in the students involved.

- *Synchronous Classroom Handshakes:* Classes enter their class times on the Google calendar. Teachers look for matches when they are in class at the same time. As discussed previously, because of the emotional impact of synchronous communication, this is great to do at least once per project.
- *Synchronous Student Handshakes:* Sometimes students establish a strong relationship from the beginning of the project and want to communicate via Skype or even Facebook. Eventually, student "offices" that record and archive meetings will facilitate personal connections between students. As with all student-to-student contact, teachers must maintain effective oversight and students should keep teachers informed if they wish to work directly.

UNDERSTAND TIME AND PLACE

The location and time zones of all classrooms should be posted in a prominent place to allow students to understand time and place.

Time Zones.   Students are taught about time zones but often do not truly understand the implications until they are working with another student who is really there.

Students commonly ask during a handshake, "What time is it where you are?" Although they may be older their eyes become large when they realize that although they are in class at 8:15 am, their partner is cozy in bed at 2:15 am. Then, the student will often comment, "Well, how am I going to work with her when she's asleep?" Such conversations about time zone help students understand the role of asynchronous communications in their lives.

Placing a clock in a prominent place on the project homepage with the time and date clearly listed beside the school name and location is a powerful practice.[27] Let each teacher post his or her own clock time so the numerous time zones and constraints around the world do not cause mistakes.

Geography.   Like time zones, which are taught at a young age, seasons and the tilt of the earth's axis are also in the early elementary curriculum. Somehow, however, the different seasons just are not real to students until they experience it. Often in December, students in the northern hemisphere are incredulous that their friends in Australia are getting out for summer break and heading to the beach! By working with people in the southern hemisphere, students truly begin to understand the geography and seasons. More importantly, they understand challenges they will face in a global workforce.

Holidays.   Classrooms are asked to put holidays on the class calendar and these times are noted by other participants. Once a student in the Middle East explained Ramadan, a significant Muslim holiday, to a student in the United States. He said, "Well, our Ramadan is like your Christmas to you." Understanding and respecting holidays of other classrooms is the doorway to respecting culture and religion.

Time.   Because of time zones, holidays, and class schedules, often very small windows of opportunity of collaboration emerge. Respecting deadlines and keeping promises

should be part of the student community of practice. See more in later chapters about encouraging student engagement.

UNDERSTAND COMMUNICATION GROUND RULES

To prepare the students for project expectations, teachers should discuss the use of appropriate language and the nuances they can expect. Also, writing is a vital skill and students are shown to be "motivated to write when they can select topics that are relevant to their lives and interests" and by "writing for an audience."[28] Both of these items are provided by online collaborative writing environments and rich projects that allow students to select areas of interest in which to work. That being said, students need to understand two specific communication ground rules to facilitate global communication concerning IM speak and standard language.

ISTE STANDARDS

NETS.S 5
Digital Citizenship

IMSpeak!   Instant messaging speak (called "IM speak" not to be confused with the software of the same name) litters social networks where teens congregate. With 85 percent of teens in the United States ages 12 to 17 engaging at least occasionally in some form of electronic communication, and 64 percent of teens admitting that they "incorporate some informal styles from their text based communications into their writing at school,"[29] IM speak in online communications is a major issue with student writing. Lack of punctuation, poor capitalization, and abbreviations speckle the writing of many students like ink spots on a white page.

21st CENTURY SKILLS

C21 LIFE AND CAREER SKILLS:
Social and Cross-Cultural Skills

Lest one think, however, that technology and IM speak has caused an overall lowering in writing standards, a comprehensive comparison of exam papers of the last 25 years was conducted by Alf Massey at Cambridge University. Massey found that today's teenagers "are using far more complex sentence structures, a wider vocabulary, and a more accurate use of capital letters, punctuation and spelling."[30] What was the one weakness? "Today's teens are ten times more likely to use nonstandard English in written exams than in 1980, using colloquial words, informal phrases and text messaging shorthand."[31] This is a measured shortcoming of today's students. As educators, we believe it is an imperative for us to discourage IM speak in academic language because it is exclusionary and unprofessional.

Exclusionary.   IM speak creates a barrier of understanding for those who speak the project's primary language as a second language. (IM speak can be in any language.) If the text of someone using IM speak is pasted into Google Translate, it is not translatable. It is a semantic dead end.

Unprofessional.   Certain behaviors are acceptable in social circumstances that are inappropriate at school. Schools are preparing students for life in the business world or academia where IM speak is not acceptable. Helping students understand context is important. A person talks differently to a friend than to a teacher or job interviewer and understanding context online is the same. Just because it is online does not mean it is social—it depends on the context of with whom one is communicating.

Academic Weakness.   IM speak laden language is becoming a major area of weakness for students. We believe that the students who make the most errors often are those who have never been allowed to write online in a school environment. It is time to teach students about context and that professional writing does not include IM speak.

Language. Two kinds of students are often on projects: native language speakers who are participating for content reasons and nonnative speakers who are participating to learn language with content as a secondary benefit.

Disclosure of Translation Service Use. For consistency, all Flat Classroom project research and collaborative documents are created in some form of English. However, in personal communications and reflections, students use the language of their choice. Eager student partners often copy this into Google Translate to understand their partners in other countries and will type messages in Google Translate to send back to the other students. Students are taught to disclose fully the use of a translation service and for both students to be cognizant that such translations can be filled with errors. If all students are taught this up front, it prevents misunderstandings.

Differences in Standard Language. Sir George Bernard Shaw said, "England and America are two countries separated by the same language." Flat Classroom projects that use wikis have students select the form of English and specify as: American English or British English. Students are taught that there are variances between the related types of English.[32] Much of the differences center around the use of *s*'s and *z*'s: (e.g., *analyze* vs. *analyse*) and the addition of *u* after an *o* in many words (e.g., *color* vs. *colour*).

Pronunciations differ too. It is an interesting activity to look up differences in language and discuss them. For example, in the United States, the last letter of the alphabet is pronounced "zee" and in the United Kingdom, it is "zed."[33] Julie always wondered why Americans say "aluminum" until she realized that it is spelled differently in Australia ("aluminium"). Many people around the world are not aware of these differences. Understanding the nuances of language prevents wiki wars and increases understanding that barriers in language can exist among different dialects of the same language.[34]

OPEN THE LINES OF COMMUNICATION

Students should understand they are part of a community and that each one of them has the responsibility to contribute.

Make It "Cool to Care." In Todd Whitaker's book, *What Great Teachers Do Differently,* he says:

> I wanted it to be "cool to care" in my room and in my school . . . the best teachers are able to achieve this in their classrooms. The students care, and they care deeply. They care about learning, they care about the teacher, and they care about each other. Once it is cool to care, anything becomes possible.[35]

The best teachers foster this environment of caring online too! They help students understand the common themes of all humanity (family, culture, religion) and help the students understand that living, breathing humans exist on the other side of the computer in their projects.

Caring teachers convey expectations that in social environments, each person has a personal responsibility to set the norms of behavior and to report inappropriate

tweetable

If you analyse English you will realise that each country has a favourite way of spelling colour. #flatclass

actions or concerns in positive ways. They show with their words and deeds a respect for the other participants and set expectations that 100 percent of their class is expected to engage. These teachers coach students through problem resolution without intervention (unless it is required) so that students can learn effective technopersonal skills through the problems that they solve.

Inoculation against the Bystander Effect.   John Darley and Bibb Latane first proved the "bystander effect" in which individuals will not offer help in an emergency situation when other people are present.[36] When Vicki discusses the bystander effect with her students, she shares the story of Kitty Genovese,[37] who was stabbed to death while many watched from their apartment windows. Although some say the Genovese story has been exaggerated,[38] it is the most widely known example of the bystander effect.

Cyberbullying and other instances where many people observe inappropriate online behaviors that go unreported show that the bystander effect has moved online. By discussing the responsibility of each person to act, students begin to understand that communities are made up of individuals and tend to contribute and communicate issues as they arise. This reinforces the student community of practice of reporting issues and self-moderating. We've seen engaged students converge and self-correct problems in Ning.

Communication with the Classroom Teacher.   The most important relationship in global projects is that between the local student and her or his in-room classroom teacher(s). Interestingly, Flat Classroom teachers have found that students who are not willing to "tell on" their peers in the immediate classroom are often more than willing to "tell on" their peers in other classrooms around the world. This could be due to depersonalization or ethnocentrism, but at this time, further research is required to understand this anecdotal observation.

Communication with Project Organizers.   Sometimes a student's classroom teacher is unavailable; in this case, students should have easy links to project organizers. Project organizers should communicate with everyone and let participants know who they are and how they may help. Communication is truly "flat" with access to everyone on the project. It helps to have a "human face" to project leadership.

Just be aware that if your school requires the use of a sign of respect such as "Mr." or "Ms." in front of teachers' last names, sometimes students of other cultures don't realize that you are a teacher because the profile photos can be small and non-existent in the chat. To those students, you are just "one of them" and sometimes it is necessary to let them know you are a teacher. Every project has students say things in front of a teacher in an online space because the students didn't know "who you were." This too teaches a lesson that one does not truly "know" who others are on a website and must always be on best behavior.

Communicating with Student Leaders.   When a project has students collaborating and leading groups, it is important to open a direct line to project organizers through consistent, private reporting mechanisms, such as asking for a Weekly Activity Report as we do in the NetGen Ed™ Project. All teachers should read these reports (while omitting the names of the students who wrote the report) and should recognize those students by giving positive mention to promote positive behaviors.

ESTABLISH ROUTINES THAT WORK

ISTE STANDARDS

NETS.S 3
Research and Information Fluency

When faced with a large project, it is easy to get lost. The reason many students and adults have trouble is that they don't know how to break a large project into small steps. Help students understand how to use their time every day, including the use of an RSS reader to construct her or his PLN as a launchpad for the day's work and routines to start and end class that will make them an effective communicator.

Construction of Student Personal Learning Networks.   Creating an effective PLN (see Figure 4.6) is an essential 21st century pull technology for students (as discussed in Chapter 3, titled Step 1: Connection). Although some teachers omit this step because it is a challenging concept to grasp, students who use this tool are better able to stay on top of projects. We believe that students need the challenge and that the construction of a PLN requires higher-order thinking. This is exactly where you need to be in your classroom.

21st CENTURY SKILLS

C21 INFORMATION, MEDIA, AND TECHNOLOGY SKILLS:
Information Literacy, ICT Literacy

There are seven basic types of information we currently pull into our student PLNs for our public projects:

tweetable

Creating an effective PLN is an essential 21st-century pull technology for students. #flatclass

1.   *The Teacher's Blog:* Students should subscribe to their teacher's blog to receive announcements and instruction.

2.   *Blogs of Student Leaders:* If students are managing the project, then the other students should monitor what student leaders say.

3.   *The RSS Feed for Collaborative Spaces:* The edits and discussion tab of wikis help students monitor their team's progress. Although students don't have to look at every edit, they should closely follow the discussions so they can respond, especially when someone asks for help.

4.   *The RSS Feed for Assigned Bookmark Tags:* Standard tags are discussed more extensively in Chapter 6, but when they are used, students should subscribe to the RSS feed to receive information from other researchers and students using this tag. For example, students studying mobile computing in the Flat Classroom project subscribe to the RSS feed for the tag "mobile" in the Diigo bookmark sharing group.

FIGURE 4.6 Student PLN Example

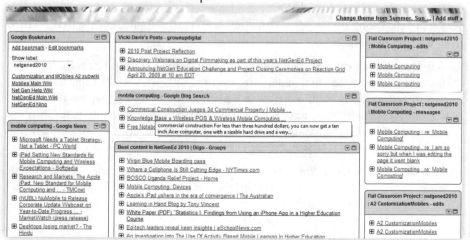

WEBSITES

Google News
http://news.google.com

They will receive links to leading research within moments of it being bookmarked! Talk about staying current!

5. *News Feeds on the Topic:* Crafting an effective search of the news takes work. By going to Google news, one can massage the search terms until good results emerge. This often requires the use of quotations (" ") or "+" or "–" as operators to limit searches.

In the example of item 4 above, most students follow "mobile computing" or "mobile technology" or "mobile technology" +innovation on Google news, to get current news on mobile technology. Students are encouraged to subscribe to various sources of news and videos on their topic, which may include YouTube, Twitter, and Google News. Any search engine or news source that has the ability to produce an RSS feed from the search is a potential source of information.

6. *Links to Project Sites:* Many students say this is the most useful widget on their RSS reader. With four or five websites used for each project, adding these hyperlinks on their PLN "dashboards" saves time. Everything is right there.

7. *Project Calendar:* Add the project calendar (not the class time calendar) to the RSS reader to ensure monitoring of deadlines. If the teacher has a class calendar for due dates, a student may prefer to subscribe to that instead.

21st CENTURY SKILLS

C21 LIFE AND CAREER SKILLS:
Productivity and Accountability

Beginning Class Routines.   It is easy with so many websites and tasks for participants to get lost. Student habits shape student outcomes, so teachers should carefully plan class habits from the "bell ringer" to the end of class. Here are several things students should do when their class begins to promote global collaborative excellence. Remember, do the most important things *first*. People should always be more important than places.

Check the Personal Learning Network.   Scan for important new information. Look at the "people" aspects of the PLN first, including wiki discussions. Have students make their PLN for the project to be their start page and when their browser opens, they are ready to start work.

Respond to Discussions.   Make sure those who have spoken in a meaningful way get a meaningful response. An answer of "yes" or "no" just isn't enough. Use strategies outlined in Chapter 6. Recall the bystander effect mentioned earlier? If a student sees someone asking for help it is that student's job to respond, even if to echo their question. No bystanders!

ISTE STANDARDS

NETS.S 3
Research and Information Fluency

Review Incoming Information and Share Important Items.   During research, take 5 to 10 minutes to review incoming links and current news related to the topic. Bookmark important information with a shared synopsis to the shared group so that others will benefit from what you have found. Don't make other students read all of an article—it should understandable from the summary. If something is of monumental importance, perhaps it is worth sharing on the discussion tab of the wiki.

Make a List of Work for Today.   Review upcoming deadlines on the project Google Calendar and look at the rubric. Sometimes it is helpful to guide student to make a list of work and how much time will be spent on each. Online projects are an opportunity to teach project management. If necessary, use an online timer to keep on task. Encourage students to spend time with the teacher if he or she feels stuck.

Ending Class.   When a student ends class, they have an opportunity to leave breadcrumbs for others to understand what work happened that day. When participants report to one another through status updates, they realize the other person is working, because sometimes wiki edits are hard to see. Therefore, at the end of class, students should review their work for the day, report what they've done, and request help in areas that need it.

Review and Report.   Just as animal prints in the woods are evidence that the animals are there, so status updates are evidence that one is engaging with a project. During the research phase, make sure that students finish work at least 5 minutes early to return to the wiki or Ning to update partners on what has been done today. With micro blogging added to Ning, the update can be a quick 140-character update on the profile page, but we encourage this to happen on the wiki discussion tab in our projects because some classes are not allowed to use social networks in their schools. This lets partners understand what has been done and builds trust. This review of the day's work is useful for teachers to know what a student did that day.

C21 LIFE AND CAREER SKILLS:
Productivity and Accountability

Second, after giving partners an update, students should give them an idea of where they can pick up work. Often a simple note like, "tomorrow I'm going to continue to work on the section about education, could someone else do the government section?" will help other students know where to contribute and also help the student know where they need to pick up work tomorrow.

Finally, the student should let their partners know if they are going offline or are done with their part of the project, as long as it is handled in a positive way. We've seen students leave a message like, "I'm sorry but we have to leave early so we can go on vacation. Hope you guys get this finished." That is not respectful to the team in that it could make them feel down or disheartened, especially if the student leaves with no warning.

It would be better to say something like, "Thank you all for everything. In our country, we go on summer break in November, so we have concluded our part of the project. You all are doing a great job and it has been great." The second example is more positive and respectful of the team.

Request.   After a student reviews and reports to their peers, they should let the teacher of any outstanding issues or concerns. Requesting help is a strength and students should know they are expected to do this every day. The teacher can let students know if it is preferred through a private conversation, note, email, or comment on his or her profile page. Teach students to ask for help ahead of time.

Reasonable Expectations for Work Outside of Class.   Some students, after beginning to collaborate globally, become highly engaged and eager to participate. However, some of these students may not have technology at home or may have slow connections. Obviously, the teacher should work with these students to help them use time efficiently in class, but some teachers will create time after or before school that students may come in to work on projects.

During the first year of Flat Classroom both authors opened our computer labs on the weekend and bought pizza for the students who were working frantically to get their videos complete. It was a joy to see the students so eager to be excellent! Many of our teachers see this same thing happen.

Students in a one-to-one laptop environment may want Internet access if it's not available at home, and this can be done by having work sessions near Wi-Fi hotspots.

Teachers must understand that when awards programs are used and students engage with the technologies, it can be a beautiful, exciting thing for students to clamor to learn and work at school. Be appropriate and fair, but expect that good projects will have students appealing for more computer time. Be sensitive and use your best judgment.

tweetable

Great teachers who ignite the fires of interest will find that students want to spend extra time learning. #flatclass

Also be aware that other teachers at your school may be concerned that you are giving an assignment that is too challenging and/or time consuming in comparison to other classes. (Why else would the students *want* to come to school?) Be careful to communicate with school leaders so they understand what is happening. But know this: When students choose to come to school on the weekend, *people will talk!* Great teachers who ignite fires of interest will find that students want to spend extra time learning—this is exciting and the highest compliment for a teacher.

SUMMARY

In addition to face-to-face intrapersonal and interpersonal skills, technopersonal skills have humans conversing with technology as the medium. With technology as the communications channel, emoticons are the new body language of the online world. Websites and apps can interject context into the communication and means that people need a whole new set of communication literacies, including understanding synchronous and asynchronous communications methods and their effective use in online spaces.

Online educational projects require preplanning as teachers introduce themselves, plan outcomes, and compare the times that they are available to meet. Teacher communication infrastructure is created to facilitate daily communication, scheduling, meeting, tracking time deliverables, and student work. Additionally, the practice of teachersourcing has teachers pooling their time and students in order to facilitate student work that happens 24/7.

Through development of a teachers' community of practice, work effectively flows around the world as students work both at school and at home.

As student projects begin, an effective "handshake" has students joining websites and teams, and interacting with partners in significant ways as the student community of practice emerges to foster effective communication and engagement with partners. Then, during online projects, students construct personal learning networks to track their work and pull research in rather than just searching ("push research"). Students need valuable project management skills and their teachers should coach them on productivity habits that will help them in a project-based world.

At all levels, functioning communities of practice and appropriate communication tool selection are vital to fostering an effective online project.

ESSENTIAL QUESTIONS

- What are the characteristics of teachers who are able to collaborate globally over an extended period of time? What are some common mistakes that teachers make when beginning to collaborate?
- How does teachersourcing compare to crowdsourcing? Why is it important for projects?
- How can teachers facilitate development of student communities of practice that help a project succeed?

Join the online conversation and share your answers at http://tinyurl.com/flatclass-ch4 ▶

FLAT CLASSROOM™ 15 CHALLENGES

CHALLENGE 4: COMMUNICATE WITH NEW TOOLS

DO: Select an asynchronous tool and a synchronous tool discussed in this section and use each of them (preferably with a partner). If possible, use one tool in both ways.

 SHARE: Reflect on it on your blog and include a hyperlink to the tool. **The tag for this challenge is fcc4_tool.** Use this when you blog or share with your group.

Share what you did with your challenge at http://tinyurl.com/flat15-4 ▶

BONUS CHALLENGE 4: SET UP A COLLABORATIVE CALENDAR

DO: Set up and test an online appointment scheduling service for you.

SHARE: Link with at least one other educator in another time zone. Those who use Google Calendar may link to their account if the service provides that feature. **The tag for this challenge is fcc4b_cal.** Use this when you blog or share with your group.

Share what you did with your challenge at http://tinyurl.com/flat15-4b ▶

CHALLENGE 5: GO MOBILE!

DO: Using your own mobile device, find at least one educational way it may be used.

SHARE: Using the text or multimedia of your choice, share on your blog how this may be done and your thoughts on using it with students (the age of your choice). **The tag for this challenge is fcc5_mobile.** Use this when you blog or share with your group.

Share what you did with your challenge at http://tinyurl.com/flat15-5 ▶

BONUS CHALLENGE 5: STUDENT PLN CONSTRUCTION

DO: *Older students (age 13+ in the United States):* Assist students in creating a PLN for a current project for one of their classes and encourage the use of the portal at the beginning of each class. *Younger students (age 12 and under in the United States):* Create a portal for students using the RSS portal creator of your choice for use with the project. Introduce the concept of a PLN.

 SHARE: On your blog, share a screenshot of a sample portal and your tips to other teachers covering this concept. **The tag for this challenge is fcc5b_studentpln.** Use this when you blog or share with your group.

◀ Share what you did with your challenge at http://tinyurl.com/flat15-5b

---

THE FLAT CLASSROOM™ DIARIES

Diary Entry 7

HORIZON PROJECT MANAGER BLOG POST

JONATHAN C.,
Student, Assistant Project Manager, Computing in Three Dimensions, Blog post May 11, 2008,
during the Horizon Project 2008, Glenbrook Academy. "Day 57: Desperation."[39]

21st CENTURY SKILLS

C21 LEARNING AND INNOVATION SKILLS:
Critical Thinking and Problem Solving, Communication and Collaboration

C21 LIFE AND CAREER SKILLS:
Initiative and Self-Direction, Productivity and Accountability

C21 INFORMATION, MEDIA, AND TECHNOLOGY SKILLS:
ICT Literacy

If you are reading this right now, I thank you, because no one seems to understand the concept of communication. We have all these problems regarding completion, because people are wondering what they are supposed to be doing. Well, if you don't check the discussion on the wiki pages, or if you don't check your group, well, then it is awfully hard to know much of anything, now isn't it?

Because people are not taking the time to look into what they are supposed to be doing, or they are not taking time to contact their project managers, there is a little bit of a problem, in terms of Horizon Project completion. Project managers and assistant project managers can only do so much. Subgroups need to be taking the initiative, and they need to start working together to solve problems. No matter how much cyber urging the PM does, if you do not check your discussion on the wiki, or if you do not check your main page, than the group is doomed to failure.

Another problem that I am seeing across the board is a problem with activity and motivation. A few students are working because their grade depends on this assignment. Others are contributing because they feel it is their duty, not to let others down. Others aren't contributing because they don't know what to do. Others aren't contributing because they don't have the tech, or do not have the grasp of English. *Others simply aren't.*

There is not much that someone can do to urge someone who has no interest in the project. You can't yell at them in person, you can't plead with them, you can't do anything. They simply disappear. They see that email notification of a post on their Ning, but they won't check it. They will see that there was a comment on a discussion board, but they won't check it. Follow-up is key to the survival of this project, and the fact that people are in la la land, is not helping.

So now that I have talked about the problems that i (sic) have observed . . . what do other people see? . . . Is there anyone out there who will answer this question?

Diary Entry 8

MEETING NOTES FOR A FLAT CLASSROOM PROJECT KICKOFF

JULIE LINDSAY's email to the Flat Classroom Google Group and posting on the project teacher wiki page,
January 14, 2010, during the Flat Classroom Project 10-1

Reflection: This is a typical summary communiqué to teachers during the handshake phase. Notice that this communication to teachers includes several items: (1) Link to meeting recording that was held for teachers in the online classroom, (2) Link to current teacher information wiki page, (3) Summary of current tasks for teachers with hyperlinks so it can be acted on within the email, and (4) Introduction of other people who may be involved in the project.

Teacher Meeting January 14, 2010

Review of Phase S1: Handshake

- Make sure all students are entered into the Team Grid. This must be finalized by the end of the week.
- All students are to join the Ning. Encourage them to write a blog post introducing themselves. Also encourage them to write comments to other students' blog posts.

- As a teacher you can have elevated permission on the Ning; please remind Kim or me to do that for you. Create a class group on the Ning and invite your students to join. Also encourage all participants to join the FCP10-1 Ning group.
- You are encouraged to share an introduction to your school on the wiki—a picture and paragraph of text, maybe a short video. Ask a student to create this for you!
- On the Home Page, please add your *name* as well as school so that we can get to know you and where you come from.
- Make sure you are a member of the Google calendar for Flat Classroom and then add your class times and holidays as soon as possible so that we can see when you are in session. This will also help with our planning and connecting for synchronous meetings between classrooms.

WEBSITES

Full notes from January 14, 2010, can be found at http://tinyurl.com/fcpteachernotes.

Teacher Handshake Meeting recording [will launch Blackboard Collaborate] http://tinyurl.com/fcp-handshake

---

CASE EXAMPLES OF GLOBAL COLLABORATION

Case Study 8

Simulated Synchronous: A Look at Asynchronous Global Debates Designed to Feel Synchronous, by VICKI DAVIS

PDToolkit

for
Flattening Classrooms, Engaging Minds
Read full Case Studies in PDToolkit online.

When creating the global collaborative debate project, Eracism, the challenge was to make the project look and "feel" like a debate, and debates are by definition live events. The organizers worked to create a "simulated synchronous" environment. By this, it means that organizers worked to make the debate "feel" synchronous.

Using Voicethread, students would leave their debate using a voice recording. Within the next 48 hours (the exception was weekends where sometimes it would take 72 hours), the other classroom would listen to the first student's debate argument and with two minutes of preparation (as with a regular debate) would

immediately respond. The debate passed back and forth in this way. As a teacher in the classroom, this felt pretty real; however, every teacher had to agree to an honor code to make this work.

Additional preparatory time for debate would have been unfair, so for this competition simulated synchronous was most appropriate. It needed to "feel" as close to a live debate as possible while still using asynchronous tools.

Other methods of helping students "feel" like they are interacting will create opportunities to have the advantages of the feeling of synchronous experiences while still being asynchronous. More information: www.eracismproject.org

Case Study 9

ANNE MIRTSCHIN, Teacher, Hawkesdale P12 College, Hawkesdale, Victoria, Australia, Horizon Project 2007, Flat Classroom Project 2008–present

ANNE MIRTSCHIN
@murcha
www.murcha.wordpress.com

PDToolkit
for
Flattening Classrooms,
Engaging Minds
Read full Case Studies in
PDToolkit online.

Whilst on Twitter one night, a tweet called out for interested educationalists/students to be part of the Flat Horizon Project to participate as moderators for current projects. Always searching for real projects and being an advocate for project based learning, I immediately enrolled my year 12 IT class, as they were studying "Virtual Teams" as part of their Victorian Certificate of Education course.

That was a "hook" for me and my classes. Soon after, when the final Flat Classroom Project for 2008 was advertised, I enrolled seven interested students who completed the project as part of their year 9 Information Technology elective subject. My principal and leadership team were very much in favour of the project as students within our school are isolated both geographically and culturally.

The prep to year 12 school of just 250 students is set in rural farming land in south east Australia. Class and year level numbers are small. However, the Flat Classroom projects gave them a social network including students from other countries, cultures and religions, a challenge to succeed, a trigger for motivation, standards to strive to and an entrance into the latest technology for educational purposes that the internet can give. Since then, whole classes of students have been involved

in three Flat Classroom projects, two NetGen Ed projects and Digiteen. One student has just completed her fifth project.

Some of the issues faced included problems with heavy filtering of our computer network. Technicians were approached to unblock a number of sites and were able to do so, especially the Ning for social networking. Students have learn[ed] that certain images and language can offend. Many teachable moments have arisen and these lessons are rarely forgotten as students experience what many just learn as theory.

When students receive an honourable mention or formal placing for their movies (final outcomes) judged by global judges, the pride displayed and the ongoing motivation engendered are immeasurable, but highly evident. Student work has an authentic and global audience. They have willingly joined the Elluminate virtual classroom to work with their virtual class mates in real time, from home at night time, with their proud parents watching on. Over the last two years, students still maintain contact with the network they have developed through the Flat Classroom projects.

Students have since travelled overseas to the Flat Classroom Conference in Qatar and Mumbai, allowing them to meet and work with their virtual class mates in the real classroom.

Step 3
Citizenship

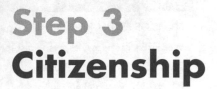

"I'm just beginning to rediscover what digital citizenship means. I know it needs to cover more than safety issues, literacy, and etiquette. I know it is not just about our rights as online citizens. It needs to concern itself much more with social responsibility and social learning than is currently being addressed."[1]

DR. ALEC COUROS, Education blogger, Professor of Educational Technology and Media at the Faculty of Education, University of Regina

ADD FRIEND   **DR. ALEC COUROS**
@courosa
http://www.couros.ca

SUPER SOCIAL SAFETY DIGITEEN ACTION

In 2009 a group of students at Westwood schools were concerned that their little brothers and sisters were playing in virtual worlds like Club Penguin, Webkinz, and others but that no adults were reviewing and understanding if these virtual worlds were age appropriate. Their research for the Digiteen™ project showed that many children were using these worlds in their leisure time.

So, for their action project, they banded together in a group and called themselves the "Super Social Safety" group. They created a Twitter account and a blog and began to scour the Internet for virtual worlds targeted to children age 12 and under.

CHAPTER 5 WEB RESOURCES
http://www.flatclassroombook.com
/citizenship.html

SHARE IT

Twitter hashtag for this book:
#flatclass

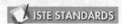

NETS.S 3
Research and Information Fluency

NETS.S 4
Critical Thinking, Problem Solving, and Decision Making

C21 LIFE AND CAREER SKILLS:
Leadership and Responsibility

View this video at http://
tinyurl.com/digiteen
-socialsafety.

A copy of the script
http://tinyurl.com
/socialsafety-script

FLAT CLASSROOM™ FRAMEWORK

NAME OF PROJECT: Super Social Safety

WEBSITE URL: http://supersocialsafety.blogspot.com

TWITTER NAME: @socialsafety

LOCATION: Researched globally on Digiteen, Local Action with custom project

COMMUNICATION: Asynchronous—wiki, Ning; Synchronous—online presentation, face-to-face presentations for younger children at the school

GENERATION: Peers (ages 12 to 14), younger generation (ages 6 to 10), older generation (adults at K12 online conference)

INFORMATION: Research to find websites recommended and marketed to children, direct experience through a method of evaluating websites

TIME: Digiteen (4 to 6 weeks), action project (1½ weeks)

LEARNING LEGACY: Recording of Digiteen

What they uncovered shocked them. Although around 90 percent of the sites they tested seemed to be safe, a fraction of the sites marketed to children sent inappropriate messages. (One allowed kids to take steroids to make their avatars muscular, and another had solicitations for sexual-related conversation from the first log on.) For more on this, see the Case Study at the end of this chapter.

They went to Vicki and asked how they could share their findings and signed on as student presenters at the K12 Online Conference 2009. Their work attracted the interest of Internet safety expert, Anne Collier, who joined them as a co-presenter in their presentation. In this example, students used digital citizenship to action to improve their world while learning valuable networking, communication, collaboration, and marketing skills. They also learned that they could research and produce findings that impact the world as they know it.

OVERVIEW OF CITIZENSHIP

We need a global and rational approach to working with and learning with digital technologies. Our future as a planet relies on our ability to use incredible technological advances for good and that begins with being able to relate to one another and prevent cultural disconnects from happening. The first two steps focused heavily on the technologies of connecting and communicating but citizenship is all about people.

In the first section, called "Self," we define an approach to understanding digital citizenship through the five areas of awareness and four core competency areas. These are discussed at length and with examples. We give several options for educators to mold their personal digital citizenship decisions and become more comfortable and capable in the classroom in this area.

In the section titled "School," we discuss approaches to digital citizenship in the classroom and provide strategies that prepare teachers and administrators. Any time students congregate, whether online or in the hall, issues will happen. Be ready for anything with these tips.

Finally, in the section referred to as "Students," we look at how to construct effective digital citizenship learning experiences. We give you examples of curriculum development and projects, including a review of the methods used in the Digiteen™ project.

 SELF Awareness of Digital Citizenship

The greatest changes of our future will not be the technology, but the power of people as they connect. Harold Rheingold, education futurist, says in his book *Smart Mobs*,

> The killer "apps" of tomorrow's mobile info-com industry won't be hardware devices or software programs but social practices. The most far-reaching changes will come, as they often do, from the kinds of relationships, enterprises, communities and markets that the infrastructure makes possible.[2]

Understanding the spectrum of digital citizenship decision making, many schools are grappling with some vital issues:

- What is digital citizenship? Should we teach it?
- How do we teach students to be responsible and reliable online learners?
- How can we use mobile devices and technologies effectively without compromising the privacy, costing parents money or promoting academic dishonesty?
- How can we promote digital citizenship within our school and community?

Digital citizenship encompasses many aspects of life with technology and cannot be limited to a definition that includes the word *computer*. As discussed in Chapter 4, technopersonal skills are communication skills where technology is the channel of communication. Although technology is used in communication, digital citizenship is still squarely about relating to people.

To help students and teachers understand digital citizenship and as a result of four years of the Digiteen project, we've developed a model called Enlightened Digital Citizenship shown in Figure 5.1.

Notice that digital citizenship begins with access. Every digital citizen must have access to technology before he or she can become a digital citizen. Technology access can no longer be exclusive to the affluent and is a primary function of being well educated. Schools take center stage in providing this access so this learning can happen.

Technology is changing so fast and people are so different, so how can teachers and students analyze the many variations of problems that they confront online? So, as students and teachers approach online situations, they should frame their analysis in five areas of awareness: technology, individual, social, cultural, and global. To make good decisions, a digital citizen should have heightened knowledge in four

 ISTE STANDARDS

NETS.T 4.
Promote and Model Digital Citizenship and Responsibility

NETS.S 5
Digital Citizenship

21st CENTURY SKILLS

C21 INFORMATION, MEDIA AND TECHNOLOGY SKILLS:
Media Literacy

FIGURE 5.1   Enlightened Digital Citizenship

key "rays" of understanding: Safety, Privacy, Copyright, and Legal; Etiquette and Respect; Habits of Learning; and Literacy and Fluency. Let's learn more.

TECHNOLOGY ACCESS

Before a person can become part of the digital society, she or he must have access to it. Students need access to hardware, software and networks (both online and offline). This is the beginning. Those without access are said to be separated from society by the **digital divide**.

FIVE AREAS OF AWARENESS

There are five underlying areas that permeate every area of digital citizenship. Intentionally consider these five areas of awareness as a lens for viewing digital citizenship choices: technical awareness, individual awareness, social awareness, cultural awareness, and global awareness.

Technical Awareness.   If you don't know how to put on shoes, having them will do you no good. Likewise, technology access is not enough. You have to know how to use a technology. We see this all the time in schools. A teacher is given the latest interactive whiteboard technology and uses it as an expensive dry-erase board.

Digital citizens are aware of the features and the functions of a tool, and have a basic competency with the hardware and software and know how to access networks before moving further. Technical awareness is the core awareness that enables a person to be a digital citizen. It lets you put on your "shoes" and run into the 21st century.

ISTE STANDARDS

NETS.S 6
Technology Operations and Concepts

21st CENTURY SKILLS

C21 INFORMATION, MEDIA AND
TECHNOLOGY SKILLS:
ICT Literacy

Individual Awareness.   As a digital citizen, you decide how you will set up your profiles, interact with others, and behave online. Ultimately, as you understand the big picture, it comes down to how you want to behave online and if you will go online at all. Healthy lifestyle choices, balance, and a person's individual goals factor into their individual awareness. Life is not lived by default. To blindly accept a website's default privacy settings is to hand over your digital destiny.

21st CENTURY SKILLS

C21 LIFE AND CAREER SKILLS:
Initiative and Self-Direction

C21 INTERDISCIPLINARY THEME:
Health Literacy

Social Awareness.   Some think that face-to-face society is suffering from too many people not paying attention. Distracted driving, distracted parents, loud technology noises: A good digital citizen is aware of social situations both online and face-to-face. Social awareness allows the digital citizen to interpret situations and retain interpersonal skills with friends and colleagues whether they are face-to-face or online. Social awareness helps a person understand the norms of behavior in social spaces. The novelty and addictiveness of technology can hurt our productivity and relationships unless we take control.

tweetable

To blindly accept a website's default privacy settings is to hand over your digital destiny. #flatclass

Cultural Awareness.   Much of the world lives in a homogeneous environment. Don't take the word *homogeneous* to mean just of one race or religion. Imagine the shock of a person used to diversity when interacting with a society without diversity. Oddly, living in a diverse society is homogeneous in a way.

In some ways, understanding what we have in common is a key to unlocking cultural awareness. Knowing that other people have families, favorite sports teams, favorite music, and hobbies makes a different culture less threatening. If you can see a person behind the culture, you will be ready to understand the culture. It builds trust. A person who is culturally aware is alert for differences in cultures and knows how to build trust relationships so the communication of those differences can flow.

21st CENTURY SKILLS

C21 LIFE AND CAREER SKILLS:
Social and Cross-Cultural Skills

tweetable

The novelty and addictiveness of technology can hurt our productivity and relationships unless we take control. #flatclass

Global Awareness.   Understanding geography, politics, and local bandwidth concerns makes one a complete and effective digital citizen. Nationality transcends culture because most nations are made up of many different cultures.

For example, some countries have "taboo" subjects that are part of their legal system. On a forum post in a project, a student asked a question to compare views on abortion of different countries. The teacher in Pakistan emailed the teachers urgently with a message that such a discussion would get her school banned from the project by local authorities. Because the project was not about abortion as the essential question, the student posting the conversation was alerted and everyone involved chose to close the discussion to keep the Pakistani students involved.

21st CENTURY SKILLS

C21 INTERDISCIPLINARY THEME:
Global Awareness

All Five Areas Are Important.   Being aware of these five areas is the beginning. They are our lenses or filters to interpret circumstances and determine appropriate behavior in different situations. These fundamental competencies of a person living and learning in the 21st century foster better understanding of the world and support life-long learning.

"RAYS" OF UNDERSTANDING

A huge majority of students know what it means to be online. They are, after all, known as the "Net Generation" according to Don Tapscott, who states in his book *Grown Up Digital,* "Young people have a natural affinity for technology that seems uncanny. They instinctively turn first to the Net to communicate, understand, learn, find, and do many things."[3] Most young people have certain technology fluencies, including being comfortable with multitasking and exploring new software and online spaces.

Babies are not born with the capability to know how to walk. They have legs, but they have not yet matured. When babies mature, learning to walk is an often-painful process of skinned knees and parental guidance to help the process along. Eventually, it becomes automatic.

Likewise, humans are not born understanding digital citizenship. These behaviors can be taught and it is our responsibility as educators to support this through effective teaching and exposure to positive experiences in online learning. The rays of understanding key aspects of digital decision making must permeate the understanding of both students and teachers. It is sometimes through "living the story" that students and teachers are best able to learn about the process of becoming an effective digital citizen.

DIGITAL CITIZENSHIP AREA OF UNDERSTANDING

Safety, Privacy, Copyright, and Legal

Safety, Privacy, Copyright, Fair Use, and Legal Compliance.   For legal reasons, legal compliance often been the starting point for schools looking into digital citizenship as it concerns intellectual property and student safety. Risky behaviors on school networks could cause legal issues for schools and those that operate online projects. As a result, many schools aggressively block all social media tools and do not allow teachers to request that specific sites be unblocked.

Filtering in many schools is rampant. The fact, however, is this: no filter is perfect, and the best filter created is between the ears of the person using the computer. Students should be educated to protect themselves in preparation for the day that a filter is not there blocking harmful content and malicious viruses. Teachers should be involved in online spaces and watchful just as they are watching in the hallways on campus.

Some are reticent to cover such topics because they seem insurmountable and ever changing. The biggest reason people become victims of Internet crime is because they are uneducated clickers. The Internet Crime Complaint Center's list of "Internet Crime Prevention Tips" shows that most of the crimes listed happen when a person clicks or responds to the perpetrator.[4]

The fact is that **identity thieves**, cyberbullies, **cyberstalkers**, computer **virus** writers, sexual exploiters, and **intellectual property** thieves are people who lay virtual minefields for digital citizens throughout the Internet. They trick the naive to click and allow harmful software like **spyware**, **malware**, and viruses to come onto their computers through **phishing**, **pharming**, or other means. Educated digital citizens are an army prepared to protect themselves from the vagrants who want to steal their future.

tweetable

Educated digital citizens are an army prepared to protect themselves from the vagrants who want to steal their future. #flatclass

Much like driver education teachers, teachers covering these topics should know that statistically there *will* be students in their courses who are victims of Internet crime. Cybercriminals look for the innocent, naive, uneducated, often technically incompetent person who clicks and reveals information.

It is fair to say that the enemies of cybercrime are educators who arm their students with knowledge of the common electronic crime issues of the day and teach them the steps to take if suspicious activity is noticed or if offenses occur. It is beyond the scope of this book to cover all issues concerning this core area of safety, privacy, copyright, and fair use; however, some overarching concepts are discussed in Table 5.1.

TABLE 5.1 Enlightening the Areas of Awareness by Understanding Safety, Privacy, and Copyright, Fair Use, and Legal Compliance

Area of Awareness	"Rays" of Understanding: Example Topics
1. Technology Awareness	• *Safety:* Do I know how to take screenshots, block people who treat me without respect, and report abuse to a website? • *Privacy:* How do I take a privacy inventory of my profile on a website, change my privacy settings, and find terms and conditions? • *Copyright:* Do I know how to access creativecommons.org to generate a license and embed media? • *Fair Use:* Do I know how to find the license on material and determine if fair use applies? • *Legal:* Do I know how report criminal activity and deal with infringement of the copyright on my intellectual property?
2. Individual Awareness	• *Safety:* How can I be a self-confident advocate for myself and others when safety is of concern? Am I aware of geo-tagging in my photographs and if it compromises my safety and that of others? • *Privacy:* Do I understand the long-term implications of inappropriate photos and have I made a decision about the type of photos that are acceptable in my online spaces. Do I know how to safely purchase online? • *Copyright:* Do I know the kind of licensing I prefer for my work depending on where it is being used? • *Fair Use:* Will I adhere to fair use? • *Legal:* Can I self-confidently resist peer pressure to pirate music or videos? Am I able to resist texting while driving?
3. Social Awareness	• *Safety:* Do I know when the behaviors of my "friends" may compromise the safety of others? Do I have the technopersonal skills to deal with issues in a way that is positive and not condemning? • *Privacy:* Do I notice when behaviors of others compromise the privacy decisions of others in the group? Do I understand what information, if divulged, can lead to identity theft? Do I know how to validate friend requests and build networks of friends in safe ways? Is having a lot of friends more important to me than being safe? • *Copyright:* Do I realize when sharing between friends becomes piracy and do I have the ethics to resist infringing on the copyright of others? • *Fair Use:* When I am not in an educational setting, does my use of media reflect an absence of fair use? Am I able to advocate and use media in appropriate ways with friends in online social environments? • *Legal:* Do I understand the legal risks of sharing? Do I understand the legal ramifications of cyberbullying behavior and not reporting criminal activity?

TABLE 5.1   (Continued)

Area of Awareness	"Rays" of Understanding: Example Topics
4. Cultural Awareness	• *Safety:* Do I know that discussion of certain taboo subjects according to a person's culture can cause personal ramifications to the person in the other country? • *Privacy:* Do I know about cultural differences in modesty and dress? Am I aware that people of certain societies may not be permitted to discuss nonacademic topics with a person of the opposite sex, including plans for the weekend or hobbies? • *Copyright:* Am I aware of varying degrees of enforcement of copyright between countries and am I able to discern that although others may behave in a certain way, it may not be legal in my country? • *Fair Use:* Do I realize that some people have in their belief system that using the work of another is wrong even if it could be claimed as fair use? • *Legal:* Am I aware that people in other countries must follow their laws and that certain online behavior, although legal for one person, could cause problems for another?
5. Global Awareness	• *Safety:* Am I aware of varying degrees of safety in other countries and do I know to be sensitive to a person's unwillingness to discuss certain sensitive political issues that may be censored in a country and could cause repercussions on the person or their family? • *Privacy:* Am I aware that certain personal subjects relating to family are taboo subjects with strangers? • *Copyright:* Copyright laws vary from country to country as does enforcement. Do I realize that by having a person in another country purchase or transmit something that is legal in their country back to another person, the receiver could be breaking the laws in their own country of residence? • *Fair Use:* Am I aware that Fair Use is a "United States" term and may not apply in other countries? • *Legal:* Am I aware that the "country of origin" of a website determines acceptable behaviors on a website and that one can be banned from a site for not following the laws of the country where the website is hosted?

Safety.   Students must be taught how to be safe online. Additionally, they should know how to protect themselves if they are made to feel uncomfortable by others. Students also should realize that pictures that show street signs or car tags or include location (geo) tags can actually impinge on their own privacy. When others reveal private information, students should have the confidence to delete the content or ask for its removal. In addition, they must understand never to meet a person from online unless they are in a public place with their parents (unless they are older and then with friends).

When having issues online, they should follow this five-step guideline developed by co-author Vicki Davis in her Internet safety poster series[5]:

1. *Stop:* Stop what you're doing. Don't keep clicking.
2. *Screenshot:* Take a screenshot. Save a copy and print a copy.
3. *Block:* Anyone offensive should be blocked and removed as a friend if he or she is on your friends list.
4. *Tell:* Tell your teacher or network administrator (or your parents if you are at home) about the situation and give them a copy of the screenshot. When you

have a problem, do not stop speaking out until you find someone who can help you.

5. *Share:* After talking to your parents and/or teacher, if the incident is appropriate to discuss, share it with others to promote Internet safety.

Privacy. Students should understand how to find and interpret the terms and conditions as well as the privacy policies of websites and how to view their profile as the "public" sees it. They should peruse the Internet intermittently for information that may have been posted about them and guard against identity theft. By reviewing case studies of those who did not protect their privacy, the students should understand the importance of protecting their own privacy and that information that is not posted cannot be used against them.

Copyright and Fair Use. It is important for students to know how to find content and to license their own. They should understand when fair use applies (at school for schoolwork) and when it does not (in their social lives and at home). For example, they should know the difference between free music and owning the copyright to music—just because music is free does not mean that students have the right to copy or use it in their multimedia creations. It is amazing how many students insist that because they bought a song on iTunes and have it on their iPod, they should have the right to use the music in a movie. "It is mine!" they say. "It is yours to listen to, not to republish," we answer.

Legal Compliance with Country of Origin. Digital citizenship includes students complying with local laws as well as laws of the country of origin of websites and artifacts used by their school in projects. Although the Internet is global, it is governed by a mélange of inconsistent and often conflicting legislation in the countries where it is used. For example, a student in a country where copyright laws are not encompassing or fully enforced may take the advantage and use or repurpose copyrighted material on YouTube or the Internet, without penalties.

However, if the student uploads that content to Ning (a U.S.-based company), the website is bound by the **Digital Millennium Copyright Act** in the United States, and the student may be suspended as a user, or the user's entire Ning site itself may be removed for violation of the Terms of Service, even if the user is in a country with freer intellectual property laws. This happened to us on the Digiteen project! A student had uploaded some music to share with others on the Ning and we were issued a takedown notice and a time to respond. If we had not responded, our entire Ning site would have been removed! If a website complies with DMCA then every participant is required to comply as well, even if their country has freer copyright laws. The user agreement of a website typically defines the rights of the user to be in line with the local laws governing that website.

Project organizers must make all participants aware of the user agreement and hold participants accountable to adhere with the copyright rules. Teachers and schools should review the **Terms of Service** and **Privacy Policy** of websites that they use, and project organizers should post these visibly. There is no reason to lose a project website because of copyright noncompliance. Expect students to upload their "favorite" music or photos from Google Images. Most of them just don't know

DIGITAL CITIZENSHIP AREA
OF UNDERSTANDING

Etiquette and Respect

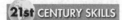 **CENTURY SKILLS**

C21 INFORMATION, MEDIA, AND TECHNOLOGY SKILLS: Information Literacy, Media Literacy, ICT Literacy

C21 LIFE AND CAREER SKILLS: Productivity and Accountability, Leadership and Responsibility

that it is illegal. Make them aware! It is important to teach them about Creative Commons and the types of works they can reuse.

Etiquette and Respect.   Good manners respect the intrinsic worth of others (see Table 5.2). Respectful digital citizens promote and support participation in learning and sharing, as well as advocate for respectful treatment of everyone in online spaces. Most often the term *cultural disconnect* is used relating to the cultural norms of good manners in a society. If you have respect for the other person, then you will open up communications to share cultural norms and remain open even if an offense has occurred. Often offenses occur in the expectations for affection, familiarity, male/female relationships, appropriate covering of the body, and even the use of terms such as *sir* and *ma'am*. (Interestingly, some cultures see the term "sir" when used by a teen as disrespectful, and others think it is disrespectful not to use the term.)

TABLE 5.2   Enlightening the Areas of Awareness by Etiquette and Respect

Area of Awareness	"Rays" of Understanding: Example Topics
1. Technology Awareness	• *Etiquette:* Am I willing to limit my own access to technology in public places when the use could be considered offensive to others in their face-to-face environment? • *Respect:* Am I helpful to beginners and sharing of new insights and tips for using technology? Do I respect parents and companies by not making unauthorized use that would cause an excessive bill?
2. Individual Awareness	• *Etiquette:* Do I have a personal code of conduct of how others will be treated? Am I tuned in to my own emotional state before sending emails or communications that may be regretted later? • *Respect:* Do I respect my need to be offline and disconnected from technology in order to recover and rest?
3. Social Awareness	• *Etiquette:* Am I aware of the appropriate use of certain technologies in different social contexts? Am I polite to others present when answering a mobile phone call in public? Do I understand that ALL CAPS is considered shouting in online communications? Am I careful with sarcasm and humor online? • *Respect:* Am I willing to focus on face-to-face people and put down technology at appropriate times to facilitate bonding with others?
4. Cultural Awareness	• *Etiquette:* Am I aware that certain taboo subjects can be offensive to others? • *Respect:* Do I know how to respond respectfully when a taboo subject has been broached? Do I convey respect in word and action with the culture of others?
5. Global Awareness	• *Etiquette:* Do I realize that fundamental differences exist in personal closeness and information that should be shared in public spaces? • *Respect:* Am I sensitive to notice when disconnects are occurring? Do I understand that national pride is often called into question if volatile political issues are broached?

Habits of Learning: Responsible, Reliable Management of Online Activity. What are appropriate habits of learning in the digital age? Being responsible means having a professional approach to the use of all things digital. Students can be professional! Their online behavior in academic spaces should reflect an understanding of appropriate behavior and that it is different from how they will interact socially online. Students must also know how to maintain age-appropriate personal privacy boundaries and how to learn safely among the minefield of resources the Internet provides (see Table 5.3).

Reliability is shown by having an online presence, often called "digital footprint," that is proliferated through sensible actions and responses while using digital tools. Students are reliable contributors and collaborators in online spaces.

Literacy and Fluency. Language, including spelling and colloquialisms, differs globally. One culture or region does not always have to dominate (see Table 5.4). (*Note:* Language denomination in a collaborative wiki environment has prompted many global discussions with teachers and students during Flat Classroom projects. On some wikis we ask the students to decide which English is being used [U.S. or British] and then appoint an editor to maintain that consistency.)

DIGITAL CITIZENSHIP AREA OF UNDERSTANDING

Habits of Learning

DIGITAL CITIZENSHIP AREA OF UNDERSTANDING

Literacy and Fluency

TABLE 5.3 Enlightening the Areas of Awareness by Focusing on Habits of Learning: Reliable, Responsible Management of Online Activity

Awareness Area	Consideration
1. Technology Access and Awareness	• Do I know how to learn about new technology and find information online about it? • Do I know options for accessing technology? • Do I understand how to build a PLN? • Do I understand the difference between free and open source and the alternatives for finding software? • Do I know open source alternatives exist for educational materials and how to take advantage of them?
2. Individual Awareness	• Do I have personal habits that facilitate lifelong learning? • Do I share with others and understand their own value of education?
3. Social Awareness	• Do I know how to connect with networks of people to expand their PLN and how to join in the conversation effectively? • Do I know how to build networks of people and resources to accomplish the tasks in their lives?
4. Cultural Awareness	• Do I work toward understanding cultures and resist tendencies toward ethnocentric behavior?
5. Global Awareness	• Have I considered the geographic strengths of certain areas of the world to bring appropriate people and resources from those areas into their PLN? • Do I realize how to outsource activities and to value the potential for building global partnerships? • Do I understand time zones and how to easily facilitate time-zone meetings?

TABLE 5.4   Enlightening the Areas of Awareness by Understanding Literacy and Fluency

Area	"Rays" of Understanding: Example Topics
1. Technology Access and Awareness	• *Literacy:* Do I know the functions of software? Do I know how to access tools, software, and resources to accomplish tasks? • *Fluency:* Am I fluent in the major aspects of the creation of digital media: word processing, spreadsheets, databases, audio, video, and photography? Do I know how to publish on the Internet in various media?
2. Individual Awareness	• *Literacy:* Do I appreciate personal preferences for software and tools based on budgetary concerns and personal access? • *Fluency:* Do I have an accurate self-awareness of my own ability and where gaps may exist in fluencies? Do I have self-confidence to problem solve?
3. Social Awareness	• *Literacy:* Am I literate in interpreting emoticons and the behavior of others in online websites? • *Fluency:* Do I understand how to build networks of friends and am I fluent in finding assistance from others to achieve goals?
4. Cultural Awareness	• *Literacy:* Do I know the timeframes of various holidays in different cultures and consider workflows with those who live in those areas? Am I understanding and respectful of the holidays of others as valid and important in their lives? Do I understand the difference between culture and geographic location and that they are not necessarily interconnected? • *Fluency:* Am I fluent in cultural understanding and aware of major issues within different cultures?
5. Global Awareness	• *Literacy:* Am I literate in time-zone bridging behaviors and appropriate technologies to collaborate with people in other locations? • *Fluency:* Am I fluent in methods that allow the bridging of language barriers?

 **ISTE STANDARDS**

NETS.T 4
Promote and Model Digital
Citizenship and Responsibility

DIGITAL CITIZENSHIP DECISIONS FOR EDUCATORS

Digital citizenship teachers are connected to digital citizenship resources and create engaging learning environments to help their students form educated opinions and behaviors for on-line safety. Students who care about digital citizenship need a teacher who cares. We encourage teachers to become better education practitioners and digital citizens, to empower digital citizenship education in class, and to develop confidence to embrace an action-based approach to digital citizenship in the classroom. Informed digital citizens make more educated decisions. We will now describe how you can become an effective digital citizenship educator.

Research the Technology—Lead the Way.   Connecting students to other classrooms requires teachers to have a good understanding of how the technology works, especially collaborative Web 2.0 tools, such as wikis, educational networks, blogging platforms, RSS, and social bookmarking. Use the connections you made in Chapter 3 to research new technology. You don't have to know a lot, just be willing to learn. By being a person who learns and shares, you encourage that behavior in your students. Let them see you learn.

Also allow students to take leadership and become collaborative learners with you as the teacher in the classroom as well as with others externally (e.g., peers, expert advisors) in a flattened mode. The aim is to set up collaborative and networking experiences for success in learning.

Monitor and Be Engaged.   Using an educational network to support learning in a classroom is not the same as using a social network to connect with friends and family. We stress to our students and to the participants in our Flat Classroom projects that an educational network is a professional group of people coming together for the purpose of sharing experiences in a focused and monitored environment. All students and teachers should conduct themselves in a professional and culturally sensitive manner. This includes the types of avatars they choose, the styles of language they use, and the quality of material they upload.

ISTE STANDARDS

NETS.T 3
Model Digital-Age Work and Learning

Sometimes participants in online learning and in global projects slip into a social-network mode of communicating. Perhaps they will use text-speak or even inappropriate language, or they might upload pictures that are not acceptable in all global classrooms. (Some countries do not allow women to show their arms.) This is where teachers must monitor in an engaged manner and watch for disconnects.

When misunderstandings happen, teachers should coach students about responsibility and sensitivity. Teachers must also be active members of the same community and model a regular digital presence. This engagement has a win–win quality. Not only are students supported in their digital adventures but, as a teacher, through regular reading and reviewing of online material (blogs, discussions, multimedia, etc.), you will benefit from getting to know your students' thoughts, abilities, and skills. For example, the quiet students who do not speak up in class can often surprise you by being avid bloggers.

Avoid the Fear Factor—Make a Difference.   Fear-based education is ineffective in changing student behaviors. When you start out, realize that you are not alone. Others have navigated the waters of connecting their classrooms and immersed their students in authentic digital citizenship experiences. Learn from them. They can show you the way to go and alert you to the pitfalls. You can do it!

Model Legal Wisdom: Choose Your Own Copyright.   Be aware of the different ways original work can be and is licensed online. The Creative Commons[6] site provides clear and comprehensive details for all types of work, and prides itself in "maximizing digital creativity, sharing and innovation." The "choose your own license"[7] feature walks users through questions that shape the license choice, such as if you will allow modifications to your work, if you will allow your work to be used commercially, and so on. You should explicitly choose a copyright and guide your students to select a copyright unless your school specifies the copyright of student work for them. Every video and website should clearly define the copyright of the work there.

SELF-ASSESSMENT SURVEY

PDToolkit

for
Flattening Classrooms, Engaging Minds

See the survey results in the online PDToolkit before moving on to the next section.

Before moving to the next part of this chapter, we invite you to take this self-assessment survey. Discuss these questions with colleagues, including your wider learning network, to determine your current level of confidence and ability with citizenship strategies.

1. **Am I willing to research a new technology and try something new with my students?**

    a. Yes, but only if I know everything there is to know and have a manual.

    b. Yes, if I feel comfortable and have recommendations from friends.

    c. Yes, I'll try anything.

    d. No. I have no room for anything new in my classroom.

2. **I have published something online and selected a copyright from Creative Commons.**

    a. No, but I'm willing to try.

    b. Yes, I've already done this.

    c. No, I will never post anything online, even in a private place.

3. **I am willing to let students discuss etiquette and respect as it relates to digital citizenship without dominating the conversation.**

    a. Yes, I am happy to let the students discuss and interject thoughts without dominating.

    b. Yes, I am willing to try but it is hard for me not to lecture.

    c. No, I have to lecture in order to teach.

4. **I monitor my student work and develop appropriate ways to interact with them online.**

    a. Yes, I read their work, make comments and interact in online spaces.

    b. No, I don't have time for that.

    c. Maybe, I just wish I had more time.

5. **If I find an inappropriate action or artifact, I usually ban the student from participating in the online work with no chance of return.**

    a. Yes, I have zero tolerance and expect all students to know how to behave the first time.

    b. Yes, I will ban them but will possibly restore them to online work if I feel it was a lack of education or they have learned from their mistake.

    c. Yes, I will ban them, but I will also stop all online activities for all of my students. I cannot risk any problems online.

 SCHOOL **Proactive Digital Citizenship Practices**

PREPARING FOR ONLINE AND BLENDED LEARNING

Develop an Attitude for Learning. Many governments, communities, schools, and parents around the world have taken and continue to opt for a restricted approach to digital access instead of educating learners to be responsible for their own learning environment. The fear of the unknown, the fear of reprisal, and the mistrust in students being able to manage their own online identity and activity is a reality from Asia to the Arab world and across major western countries. It crosses religious and cultural boundaries and is grounded in the belief that safety and privacy is assured through imposed measures. The respect for self-determined use of emerging technologies and realization of digital/global citizenship through best-practice use is often missing or is not balanced.

A typical teacher today may not be fluent with new technologies and how to embed them into everyday practice. Responsible learning continues to be within a very controlled classroom environment where "reliable" methods that can further restrict access to digital tools are used. Respect for student ability to manage and improve their digital citizenship is not always present, sometimes due to an inability of the teacher to manage and understand his or her own online and digital life in a rapidly changing world.

Digital citizenship is far more than digital literacy—just as 21st century skills encompass much more than simply "skills." Digital citizenship is not about creating a list of things to do or a stagnant curriculum that you can use for the next 10 years. It's about transforming yourself into a professional who can effectively empower student-centered learning to create vibrant, exciting learning projects.

There are also tools such as mobile phones and other mobile devices that are viewed as "disruptive" by many to the normal flow of the classroom. Instead of holding students accountable to stay on task, many schools opt for a complete ban on all mobile devices. Today's mobile devices have more computer power and faster Internet access than the computers most schools were paying thousands of dollars for just 10 years ago.

In a modern world where schools are often cash-strapped, some are starting to realize that a lot of learning can happen with mobile devices. Let's talk more about how to turn problems into positives as we consider being open-minded about access to mobile devices and student involvement. This isn't about harmful, unsafe practices; there are many schools using social media, mobiles, and other progressive technologies without the perceived problems that keep many schools "locked down."

Acceptable Use Agreements.   Schools must determine the appropriate use of their network. Because legal actions are concerns for schools, the Acceptable Use Agreement is often cited as something that restricts schools from being proactive. You can craft creative AUAs. For example, Andrew Churches at Educational Origami shares Digital Citizenship **Acceptable Use Agreements (AUAs)** for different school levels or sections.[8] Every school must make its own decisions about how technology will be used in the classroom, and there are many alternatives.

PRACTICES FOR DOCUMENTATION AND CORRECTION

Overview.   When students and classrooms collaborate in common online spaces it is inevitable that some problems will occur. In Flat Classroom projects, teachers strictly moderate all online collaborative and networking sites for membership and content. When students step over the line, all teachers understand the process to deal with it.

NETS.T 2
Design and Develop Digital-Age Learning Experiences and Assessments

C21 LEARNING ENVIRONMENTS

ISTE STANDARDS
NETS.T 1
Facilitate and Inspire Student Learning and Creativity

Read more about AUAs at http://tinyurl.com/aua-samples.

ANDREW CHURCHES
@achurches
http://edorigami.edublogs.org

The person who discovers the offensive material, such as a picture or comment, makes a screenshot of the item and shares it with the student's classroom teacher, and then reports it to space administrators, who remove it. The classroom teacher decides the appropriate action, which may include asking the student to apologize to the educational network or, in some cases, suspending or even banning the student from the network.

One of the advantages of working as a global team on these projects is that the networks are monitored 24 hours a day and RSS feeds (including classroom monitoring portals) make it easy to see new content as soon as it's posted. It is very rare that a student deliberately or maliciously sets out to be offensive when collaborating online as part of a project. In fact, we've permanently suspended or banned fewer than 10 out of thousands of students in over five years.

Essential Practices.   The practices discussed earlier in this chapter—"Stop, Screenshot, Block, Tell, and Share"—apply here as well. If a teacher notices or is informed of inappropriate behavior, the teacher should *stop* and immediately review it. The teacher then should take a *screenshot* documenting what has happened. Next, the teacher should *block* the current behavior from being viewed by deleting the content and, depending on the severity of the offense, blocking the offender from the site.

After blocking, the teacher should *tell*. First, the teacher should inform the offender what he or she has done via a message that the teacher also screenshots to share with other teachers. Second, the teacher should send all screenshots through the private teacher group so that other teachers may reflect and the teacher of the student may determine the appropriate course of action.

In our projects, we require that the student who is banned may be reinstated only by her or his teacher. If the student is reinstated and repeats the offense, then the school where the student is from risks being removed from the project and not be allowed to participate in future projects. Schools and students must understand the accountability required for operating in an online environment. Some may say this is severe, but it has been the only way to prevent and minimize problems in a forum where the public can see everything posted. Everyone on a project must know and understand that online behavior has offline consequences. It is an underlying principle of all online activities.

After a problem has been resolved, teachers share the teachable moment with students in an appropriate way that protects the privacy of those concerned. Problems are the field from which we harvest the greatest yield of digital citizenship learning experiences.

tweetable

Problems are the field from which we harvest the greatest yield of digital citizenship learning experiences. #flatclass

TURNING PROBLEMS INTO POSITIVE LEARNING EXPERIENCES

Here are some examples of things that have happened and how they were handled following the five-step *Stop, Screenshot, Block, Tell, and Share* method.

- *Cultural Disconnects, Including Copyright Infringement.* Some cultures think nothing of pirating photographs, videos, and books. It is literally part of their culture. When this happens, it is important to educate students in all the classrooms as to the cultural disconnect happening and come to a common agreement in order to be fair on final outcomes.

For Flat Classroom projects this means adherence to the Digital Millennium Copyright Act because files are hosted on servers in the United States, where the law was passed (see earlier notes on country of origin). Teachers should agree up front on this or there will be concerns from some students who cannot use popular music and those who can. Some also feel it biases the judging process (videos with popular music tend to score better naturally because people like the music).

In an early project, Vicki had her U.S. students angry to "lose" the video competition to students who used copyrighted music because Vicki made them remove the music from their video. "My video would have won if I could have used the 'good' music, it isn't fair," said one student. Since then, steps have been taken to make sure consistent copyright standards are used. We've also seen students take entire video clips from popular sitcoms and cartoons and this practice is also discouraged. Can you turn in a three-minute video as yours when over 2 minutes was created by another author? Is that fair?

- *Cultural Taboos.* One student in Qatar had no idea that the pretty picture he had posted as his avatar could be offensive. The image of brightly labeled bottles looked attractive and festive, but the word *cerveza*[9] caught the teacher's eye and he was called over for a discussion. As an international student learning in the Middle East, didn't fit in the culture yet and had not contemplated the impact an image representing alcohol could have in the immediate community. The image was replaced without further problem.

- *Language Disconnects.* As mentioned earlier, there are different spellings. When wiki wars emerged because of spelling, it was resolved by having one student volunteer to edit in the language of his or her choice ("British English" or "American English," for example). Before this was put in place, we'd have students battling over the proper spelling of "analyze" (with the American "z" or British "s").

- *IM Speak or Characters Representing Profanity.* The gray area between social networking and professional educational networking is like a no-man's land for some students. They are torn between wanting to do the right thing, not quite understanding yet what the right thing is and being already firmly entrenched in social modes of online communication.

  One girl added a widget to her Ning profile that allowed her to IM and share short messages. Unfortunately, her enthusiasm for sharing her immediate thoughts crossed back over the line to include a written expletive with "*" for some letters—but expletives nonetheless.

- *Private Jokes.* This is rare, but when it happens it can be a shock for the teacher, and often for other students if they get to see it. What some consider normal teenage banter on Facebook is misconstrued horribly in front of a global audience. We've seen students call their good friends bad names or joke about how "bad" another person is. These students are usually in the same room with each other, are friends, and are laughing. They don't realize that other participants can only see their words and have no idea what is going on.

It is shocking! This is a prime reason why teachers must be monitoring online work to avoid inappropriate language and behavior that could be construed as cyberbullying. Tell students, "If in doubt, leave it out."

- *Impersonation.* The problem of impersonation occurred on the Digiteen educational network—fortunately, it was noticed and removed quickly. It is *extremely* rare, but we have also seen a student try to "frame" another student by posting something malicious on their wall, when they stepped away from the computer without logging off the Ning. Interestingly, the partner was in Vicki's classroom and said, "I know that my partner would not write this, it doesn't sound like him—see what happened so he doesn't get in trouble." She was right! Students know each other, even online!

  Teachers should teach students that they never share a password and to log off computers when walking away for an extended period. This has a kernel of identity theft and should be dealt with severely by teachers to send the message that passwords are to be kept private and identities never "stolen." It is not funny.

- *The Unengaged Partner.* When a student refuses to contribute, it is often something that she or he does while "pretending to work," and the local teacher doesn't realize the student is unengaged. We've seen students add and delete punctuation or go on the Ning and use the chat facility or message friends and not work on the task at hand. This is one reason that good teachers rarely sit, even when their students are doing work online.

  As a backup, our teachers have students list the names of those they "haven't heard from" or are not responding. Then, by listing the names in the teacher email group, other teachers have a "heads up" to reach out to those students. Sometimes there is a good reason—such as a personal problem or illness—the lapse has occurred, but students still need to know to keep their partners apprised so they are not missed. Teachers should be able to coach their classes into 100 percent participation, but it takes effort.

- *Inappropriate Pictures.* More clothing worn and less skin shown is always the best approach when choosing an icon or static avatar for an online profile. That profile picture will remain for a long time—in fact, it can be longer than when the user may decide to take it down, as images often get copied and distributed across the Internet.

  There are many examples where students have innocently displayed photos of themselves in skimpy summer clothing, not realizing that in many countries around the world it is offensive and highly inappropriate. On our projects, students do not show their upper arms as a general guideline. Some schools do not allow photographs of their students to be posted at all.

 STUDENTS Digital Citizenship in the Classroom

Our challenge as educators is to introduce digital citizenship into our schools and learning communities. Creative curriculum design and embedding digital citizenship competencies across the curriculum through immersion or hands-on opportunities that go beyond use of Facebook or Twitter as social connection tools is a great way to teach digital citizenship. There are many options and websites out there, including our own, to help you on your journey.

DEVELOPING A POWERFUL DIGITAL CITIZENSHIP CURRICULUM

Ignorance is not bliss in the online world. Ignorance is danger. Online trends are evolving so quickly, it is vital to integrate the latest happenings into any digital citizenship curriculum. A new security threat can spread through the Internet in a matter of weeks—much faster than even an online curriculum can be updated. The digital citizenship curriculum must be agile.

tweetable

Ignorance is not bliss in the online world. Ignorance is danger. #flatclass

Why Stagnant Digital Citizenship Curriculum Doesn't Work and What to Do.
Whatever curriculum is chosen, flexibility must be included to incorporate today's headlines. Students will want to talk about what is happening today and how it relates to the content. If the content on digital citizenship is prepackaged and delivered via lecture, with no room for discussion, students will often respond negatively and tune out the speaker. Therefore, whether you select an action project such as Digiteen or another curriculum, students should be involved as part of the research and discussion in a way that discusses topics openly without interjecting false fear that is not backed up by research (i.e., strangers online are going to harm you).

Essential Construction Strategies.   The Digiteen project, as with other Flat Classroom projects, through a hands-on as opposed to a locked-down approach to technology use, promotes digital citizenship competencies in all the areas of awareness. Many schools will review this model and want to establish their own project-based action project. These two strategies should be considered.

Project-Based Learning.   Having students research and produce collaboratively edited documents about current trends, in essence, produces a document that can be used throughout a school and community to reference up-to-date information. When students create such documents, they not only learn by being immersed in the project but they also serve their community by becoming experts in the topics at hand.

Service Learning Projects.   After each student researches an aspect of digital citizenship, groups come back together to brainstorm and determine appropriate action projects. Students learn how to brainstorm and often take over the process. After voting, students then sign up for the action that they wish to undertake.

Some classes have one large project; others have smaller groups with action for different audiences. By providing a service, students become powerful advocates and also learn presentation skills and leadership as they work to improve the digital citizenship knowledge of parents, students, peers, and teachers. Students with coaching and advisement from teachers create the service learning projects, so they are customized to the local situation in a powerful, salient way with more meaning than a transplanted approach or curriculum could typically impart.

Additionally, some research has shown that the use of service learning with technology, as shown in the EAST case study example at the end of this chapter, actually

21st CENTURY SKILLS

C21 INTERDISCIPLINARY THEME:
Civic Literacy

C21 LEARNING AND INNOVATION SKILLS:
Critical Thinking and Problem Solving

"attracts students into STEM (Science, Technology, Engineering, and Math) who might not otherwise gain critical STEM skills."[12] Service learning and technology are a powerful combination for improving schools and improving test scores.

Use Authentic Research to Keep Content Current.   The problem with digital citizenship is that as soon as a curriculum is printed, it is outdated! The Digiteen project was developed to empower students as researchers on current digital citizenship topics. After researching trends and writing a wiki report, the project transforms into a service learning project where students propose and conduct an action project in their local school to teach and promote awareness about the digital citizenship topics that are most important in their local district.

Have a Reliable Digital Citizenship Model to Frame Research.   The Digiteen project has used two frameworks; the first six Digiteen projects used Mike Ribble and Gerald Bailey's nine aspects of digital citizenship.[10] We used student and teacher feedback to design what we consider to be a model with less overlap between the topics, and in Digiteen 10-3 we began using the Enlightened Digital Citizenship model outlined in this chapter.

It is helpful to use credible sources of information as the backbone of your project. We use PBS Kids, the Growing Up Online series, our content, and information from other sources such as Common Sense Media. Common Sense Media[11] is a newly developed free curriculum for digital citizenship growth within a learning community. It provides videos and worksheets and reading material for students, teachers, and parents with a staged approach.

You can take just about any reputable digital citizenship framework as long as it is adapted to create small enough groups to facilitate editing and collaboration. When students research and produce recommendations for behavior by age group they put their learning into practice with actionable recommendations. It forces them to propose and advocate behaviors and internalize those recommendations.

Once recommendations have been formalized, students are ready to take action (like above). This process, however, not only teaches digital citizenship as the content but it also teaches technology fluencies of editing collaboratively and authentic research skills.

Learning by Doing.   In the Digiteen project and effective digital citizenship programs, learning by doing should be the aim. It puts trust and responsibility into the hands of the students to become reliable and responsible and respectful when using digital tools. The mere practice of researching, reviewing current case studies, and engaging in dialog about digital citizenship issues gives students a framework for making decisions in the future. Effective project-based digital citizenship initiatives are about inviting students to lead the way and model best-practice online community building and learning.

PikiFriends[13] is an interesting way to bring young people into the realm of creating an online identity, interacting with others and blogging. The PikiFriends interface allows membership to a facility where students can find friends in a safe learning environment. This example was developed in Japan and has a global outreach.

WEBSITES

Common Sense Media
http://www.commonsensemedia
.org/educators

FLAT CLASSROOM™ FRAMEWORK

NAME OF PROJECT: Pikifriends

WEBSITE URL: http://www.pikifriends.net

LOCATION: Worldwide

COMMUNICATION: Asynchronous—posting information

GENERATION: Ages 11 to18 (junior and senior high school)

INFORMATION: In Japanese and English, this website has powerful privacy features and teacher-monitoring capabilities that make student interactions easily seen

TIME: Year around; can join at any time

LEARNING LEGACY: A friendship

Recent developments include a curriculum with a teacher guidebook, student textbook, and student worksheets.

Focus on Digital Citizenship Content.   Through careful design, a digital citizenship project shouldn't be about "social" networking for the sake of being online and sharing likes or dislikes; rather, it is about teaching students how to connect, communicate, and collaborate in a professional manner.

Collaboration and Peer Mentoring.   For many students digital citizenship projects are their very first experience in a professional online learning environment, including their first blogging adventure. Peer mentoring plays a significant role here, where students monitor each other's activity to inform, encourage, and support new friends and team members. In the Digiteen project, students are grouped into smaller teams, then move to a wiki platform where they research an aspect of digital citizenship and collaborate on a wiki page. Authentic research is shared using social bookmarking, and discussions about the research and final wiki presentation take place on the discussion tab.

ISTE STANDARDS

NETS.S 2
Communication and Collaboration

Experiential Learning.   As students take responsibility for what they do as online learners, they acquire a set of tools and skills to protect themselves from the dangers they might encounter. In addition they learn valuable lessons that move beyond the classroom into further education and social situations. Importantly, they learn through personal experience, not merely through reading about it in a book, how to work across time zones in mixed-culture teams asynchronously to create a final product. These skills are invaluable for future employment and global citizenship.

Service Learning through an Action Project.   As a culmination to the Digiteen project each class focuses back on its own community and designs an Action Project that, when implemented, will raise awareness of digital citizenship and the topics studied during Digiteen. Action Projects are based on the needs of each student's immediate community. Some participate in whole school activities, such as a school assembly or "Digital Citizenship Day." Others include preparing lessons for younger students or talking to parent gatherings. It is through this action that students become empowered to make a difference.

SAMPLE DIGITAL CITIZENSHIP LESSONS

Recommendation by Collaborative Writing. Writing collaboratively to produce recommendations for students and adults produces powerful discussions and useful recommendations (see Table 5.5). Anecdotal evidence of online tragedies may get students talking but it does little to produce specific behaviors. By writing recommendations collaboratively, students internalize as a group what behaviors can prevent the problems and anecdotes they find in their research.

tweetable

A well-placed sentence from a peer can often have more effect than a one-hour lecture from a teacher. #flatclass

Recommendation by Personal Reflection. Students should also be challenged to write in first person about their feelings and specific recommendations (see Table 5.6). When personalizing their words in their own voice, it becomes owned by the student and also serves as a reinforcement of behaviors when other students read the words of their peers. A well-placed sentence from a peer can often have more effect than a one-hour lecture from a teacher.

Westwood Schools: Virtual World Digital Citizenship. Students used a virtual world, Google Lively (now defunct), to role-play. Some students operated avatars from the library to play the role of the "friendly stranger." They were friends but used role-playing to see whether students would share inappropriate information. The students said:

> We picked the seventh grade as the class that we would teach digital citizenship to because we felt like they were the class that needed it the most. Our first session went amazingly. In this session, we introduced them to Lively and showed them one of our virtual rooms, Digiteen World, which Tyler R. had created. The seventh-graders really enjoyed the room and even though it was just our introductory lessons they learned a lot. In fact, many of them were very eager to create their own avatars and play in the virtual world.[14]

Digiteen Community Coffeehouse. In New Brunswick, Canada, a group of St. Stephen students organized a coffeehouse-style event for discussion.

> The students at St. Stephen High decided to host a "Political Coffeehouse" which was held on Tuesday, June 8th, 2010. The organizing members were Alexx A, Gena B, Kirk A, and Taylor C.
> Students designed and distributed posters in the school and generated a Facebook "Event" to publicize the Coffeehouse. There was no entrance fee and the students provided snacks/treats for those in attendance. The committee set a goal for each class member to bring at least 5 people to the event. There were roughly 120 people seated in the St. Stephen High School

TABLE 5.5 Sample Student Collaboratively Written Recommendations

Student Reflection	Aspects of Note
Recommendations for Providing People with Access Written on the Digiteen Wiki for Digiteen 09-3 "In countries that do not have the internet and other technologies available, children's education is suffering, uneducated people and societies are also suffering. The solution? An inexpensive, solar charged laptop! the <u>OLPC XO-1,</u> is a small green and white laptop(picture at the top of the page) that will be used to teach kids knowledge that was impossible before this invention. The United Nations is aiming to raise awareness of the divide during the World Information Society Day. Other solutions to this are that the Dictators/ Leaders of the areas allow their community members to participate in global access to the Internet. If you can't afford the High speed internet then I think that the government should allow public Access to the Internet as well computers. However if they do not allow them to then there is other ways."	• This was collaboratively edited between the students. • This paragraph shows a wide variety of sources of information and a hyperlink. • On the negative, this wiki page moved from third person to first person. Typically first-person voice is used in blog posts and a third person, journalistic tone is used on wikis.
Students in Digiteen 2008 Review of Social Ethical Aspects for Middle and High School Aged Students "Middle Schools students with too much free time spent surfing the internet affects a family and a community. For example, let's take the case of thirteen year old Alisha. She lied about her age on a public page in order to have sexual intimacy. Legally, this is reported as a rape, but Alisha lied about her age, provoking this to happen. So now, Alisha is mentally affected and her life will never be the same. Her family's profit may decrease because of the money used in court. Now the family does not have very much money and sustaining themselves is a struggle. This family affects the community because now they are not paying taxes, or contributing to the economy. So because of a simple digital law being broken, an entire population is affected in a negative way. A community may be affected in a very little positive way, although for some it can also be negative. If a student in a class sends all his classmates the newest movie both positive and negative events occur. It is positive because now the movie is very popular. A lot of people know it, and it could even win awards. All the students would be able to watch it and this would enrich their minds for free. It also has a negative impact in the sense that the authors or actors from the movie are not getting the money they deserve because their movie is being illegally distributed. This means that their salary decreases not allowing them to live better after all the work and hours dedicated to this movie. A community is affected in a bigger way if a movie or software is illegally distributed. So the negative impact is greater; this means that there must be a stop to the illegal leaks."	• These students show both sides of issues and reflect on how online behaviors affect the families of those who make mistakes. • Students are reflecting on piracy and both sides of that topic. • This is written in third person but still possesses a narrative format that is interesting to read.

Source: Security and Safety Group, D. (November 24, 2009). Security and Safety. Retrieved June 15, 2011, from http://digiteen09-3.flatclassroomproject.org/ Security_and_Safety and Group, D. D. L. (November 20, 2008). Digital Law. Retrieved June 15, 2011, from http://digiteen2008.wikispaces.com/Digital+Law

Theatre (which is a large number for a small town). The audience included fellow students, parents, siblings, and relatives.

The students introduced and broadcast the film *Bowling for Columbine* (by Michael Moore) to the audience for the first portion of the event. Later, the students presented the topic of Bullying and Cyberbullying to the crowd. They talked about the telltale signs to look for that would indicate that your

TABLE 5.6 Sample Student Personal Reflections about Digital Citizenship: Student Blogs

Student Reflection	Aspects of Note
"I strongly encourage that digital citizenship be taught in schools today. Children should not feel overwhelmed by the ability of the Internet, so these classes would aid them in gaining Internet skills. In my opinion, I think that grades third through eighth should be taught digital citizenship skills. The skills I find to be most important are how to handle cyberbullying, how to tell if you are cyber-bullying, what information and pictures are appropriate to post on the web, "netiquette," and how to tell if a website is legitimate." by Ashley, Westwood Schools, Digiteen 09-3	• Student recommendation to schools with specifics. • When students share what is most useful, teachers can see the concerns of their students reflected in their words.
"Digital literacy is the idea of everyone being smart when using technology. Being digitally literate means that you are able to be safe on the internet. It also means that you can be very intelligent while using technology. A literate person will know how to express their feeling while using technology in an efficient way. Being digitally literate is very important." Uzair, 9D, Qatar Academy Response to teacher question "What Is Digital Literacy?" http://digiteen.ning.com/forum/topics/what-is-digital-literacy?commentid=1990934%3acomment%3a26293	• This student relates digital literacy to the idea of being smart. • This student talks about intelligence and the use of technology and could have supported their argument with links to research

Source: WHS Digiteen Reflective Blog Post. (2009). Retrieved June 15, 2011, from http://digiteen.ning.com/profiles/blogs/whs-digiteen-reflective-blog-2; and Uzair 9D (April 13, 2009). Reply to "What Is Digital Literacy?" by Terry Freedman. Retrieved September 11, 2011, from http://digiteen.ning.com/forum/topics/what-is-digital-literacy?commentid=1990934%3acomment%3a26293.

child is being bullied as well as various ideas for dealing with the problem from the perspective of the home, school, and RCMP (Royal Canadian Mounted Police). The students ended the evening with a question/answer session, with the students fielding varied questions about the movie and the topic of Bullying/Cyberbullying. The response from the event was very positive! A donation bucket was passed around and all funds donated went directly to the school's "Bully Blocker" committee.[15]

SUMMARY

Some schools will not venture out of their "walled garden" and inner circle of their classroom, school, and district because they are afraid of student behavior online in spaces with other students. Understanding the areas of awareness—Technology, Individual, Social, Cultural, Global—can help teachers educate students in the areas they need to understand and make decisions to be aware of all aspects of the decisions they are making. The four competency areas we call "rays of understanding" identify the competencies that students should have in order to

be successful online digital citizens: Safety, privacy, copyright and legal; Etiquette and respect; Habits of learning; Literacy and fluency. Several important decisions—including how to research technology, monitor student actions, overcome, and select copyright are discussed with teachers in the section of text titled "Self." Understand it so you can teach it by using the digital citizenship model introduced in this chapter.

In the "School" section of the text, acceptable use agreements and documentation aspects of handling online behavior and common problems such as culture, copyright infringement, and inappropriate pictures were discussed to give a framework for looking at problems.

Finally, in the section called "Students," how to construct effective digital citizenship learning experiences that build on student engagement rather than fear were discussed.

ESSENTIAL QUESTIONS

- How do the areas of awareness impact digital citizenship decisions?
- Review each area of awareness as it relates to a case study taken from current events.
- What are some common digital citizenship issues in collaborative projects? How should teachers handle problems when they happen?

Join the online conversation and share your answers at http://tinyurl.com/flatclass-ch05 ▶

THE FLAT CLASSROOM™ 15 CHALLENGES

CHALLENGE 6: CREATE A CLASSROOM MONITORING PORTAL

Do: Using the RSS reader of your choice (that allows publishing), create a CMP (classroom monitoring portal) for your classroom (*Note:* RSS must be public) or for a sample project (you can find sample projects on our social network). Your CMP should include (1) wiki edits for the site, (2) wiki discussions, (3) blog posts from your students on your social network, (4) at least one live research feed on the project topic, and (5) other research of your choice.

(Note: If you do not have a current project, visit the website page for this challenge for some links to construct a sample CMP.)

 Share: Publish it and share it with another teacher or on your blog. The tag for this challenge is **fcc6_cmp.** Use this when you blog or share with your group.

Share what you did with your challenge at http://tinyurl.com/flat15-6 ▶

CHALLENGE 7: EMPOWER DIGITAL CITIZENSHIP ACTION

Do: *For those in a school now.* Discuss the possibilities of student-empowered digital citizenship with your administration and/or colleagues. Plan and determine how you will use "reverse mentoring" opportunities to stay abreast of digital citizenship and how this can be shared through your organization.

For those not in a school. Select a popular social media that students are now using. Educate yourself on the proper use. Interview a student who is currently using the tool and ask her or him about the problems or issues she or he has observed.

Share: Reflect on what you have learned and blog your ideas using text or the multimedia of your choice. Ensure that you do not post full names of minors without prior permission. The tag for this challenge is **fcc7_empower.** Use this when you blog or share with your group.

◀ Share what you did with your challenge at http://tinyurl.com/flat15-7

THE FLAT CLASSROOM™ DIARIES

Diary Entry 9

JULIE'S DIARY

October 3, 2007, during the Flat Classroom Project 2007

It is so good to see the students coming onto the Ning and posting their audio introductions. My students were very keen today to know who was in their group. I am fast-tracking this for my group as I only see them twice in class in the next 2 and a bit weeks!!! Already some of them have sent messages to team members. This "first contact" is so important and can set the scene or the mood for the entire project for some students. If contact is made and not responded to, it becomes disappointing for the initiator. We discussed this in class and my students know they need to be proactive in communication. However, they asked me some strange questions today. Things like: "What if we do not like our partners?" "What if they say something bad about us—can we say something bad about them?" One boy said, "My father told me to respond to bad words with bad words" (I am paraphrasing here). A couple of children said, "What if they think we are all terrorists?"!!! I was a little surprised by this statement, but maybe they are right, maybe some students in the other countries think that Muslims living in the Middle East are terrorists. Maybe this project will help to dispel these myths. I am always the optimist!"

Julie's postreflection: Muslim students speaking frankly about their nervousness as they embark on a global project. In many respects their fears are similar to those of students anywhere in the world, just a different and more emotive topic of the era. Students in Australia could just as easily have said, "What if they think we all ride kangaroos?"

Diary Entry 10

EXCERPTS FROM THE SUPER SOCIAL SAFETY PRESENTATION AT THE K12 ONLINE CONFERENCE 2009

VICKI DAVIS

Erin: Hello, and welcome to SuperSocialSafety's presentation. I'm Erin, the Project Manager, and this is Riley (say hey), the assistant project manager. We are a group of teens working under the Digiteen project that has set out to review sites targeted at kids ages 12 and under. We rate these sites then blog and tweet about our results. We hope teachers and parents whose children are spending time online will view our blog or follow us on twitter and see our ratings. Our reviews are based on educational value, appropriateness, and, of course, fun. We rate each site based on this and it can receive up to 10 stars. We also tested to see if the safety policies of the site were enforced.

(We tried to be the most annoying, stubborn, and naughty little brother we could imagine—you get the picture.) We have put together a list of our best and worst sites, and first on the best list is Moshi Monsters..."

Hannah: Hello everybody. My name is Hannah and I reviewed the site Habbo. Many people have recommended this site, saying it's very good. I wanted to find out what the age recommendation was, and I found that it was aimed at teens. . . . When I first went into the site, I was immediately shocked by the names of the rooms and some of the conversations that people were having. They were disgusting and inappropriate for kids at a young age. . . .

The whole time I was in a room people were asking each other if they were single and asking for private information. While I was there for five minutes I had been asked if I was single five times. I was also asked if I had MSN and if I had a webcam so we could " talk." I was offended and disgusted the whole time I was on the site. I do not think that people realized how bad this site was, and they did not know that their children were on this site.

Maybe the next time someone recommends a site that they think will be good, they should go and check it out first. Thank you for listening for what I thought about the site Habbo..."[16]

CASE EXAMPLES OF GLOBAL COLLABORATION

Case Study 10

Digiteen Project—
International School of Vienna, Austria

Barbara Stefanics
@bstefanics

for
*Flattening Classrooms,
Engaging Minds*

Read full Case Studies
in PDToolkit online.

This classroom was one of the three that participated in the first Digiteen project in 2007. After researching their topic, the students decided to have a Digiteen Action Day. In their words, they took school action by:

1. Seeking all 600+ students in grades 6 through 11 to agree to responsible, ethical and legal uses of digital technologies (see poster [Figure 5.2]).
2. Raising parent awareness through the school newspaper and parent newsletter.
3. Using their Digiteen logo for all digital citizenship activities (i.e., posters, badges, advertising).[17]

The students designed the Digiteen logo and the Digiteen call-to-action poster as shown in Figures 5.2 and 5.3.

Teacher, Barbara Stefanics, on the Digiteen Action Project

Teenagers are keen users of the Internet and social networking tools, but they are often unaware of issues related to the responsible, ethical, and legal uses of the Internet. The Digiteen project provided a platform for students to collaboratively research and investigate what it means to be a good "digital citizen" based

on the work of Dr. Mike Ribble of Kansas State University. During the Digiteen project, students in each of the schools involved were required to collaboratively research what it means to be a digital citizen and to develop a plan of action to make other students aware and committed to "digital citizenship."

The classroom was completely transformed from a traditional classroom to a beehive of activity where students were taking responsibility for their own investigations, research, and learning. Students not only helped one another in mastering skills in using the Web 2.0 tools required to complete activities but they also often used the interactive whiteboard to present their findings to the class and to demonstrate how to use specific tools. Students eagerly entered the classroom for every lesson and were enthusiastically engaged in the next stages in the project.

When it came to the Action Project, the students decided that their action would be to create digital citizenship rules for students to follow (i.e., rules by students for students). The grade 8 students planned and implemented their "Day of Action" where they attempted to give the digital citizenship rules to and get the signature from every student in grades 6 through 11. The students were asked to read the rules and then if they agreed, they were asked to sign. After signing they received a "Digiteen" badge.

FIGURE 5.2   Digiteen Pledge
Students developed this action poster to have their fellow students sign as part of their Digital Citizenship Action Day.

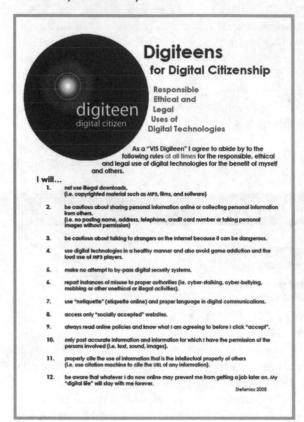

FIGURE 5.3   Digiteen Call-to-Action Poster
Poster Developed by Students in Austria for Digiteen Project

The Digiteen project is an invaluable experience for students, and it places digital citizenship in a real context within a school. It is certainly my highest recommendation that any school that is serious about promoting "digital citizenship" in their school get involved in Digiteen project.

Case Study 11

The East Program, by MATT DOZIER

PDToolkit
for
***Flattening Classrooms,
Engaging Minds***
Read full Case Studies
in PDToolkit online.

The EAST initiative, a nonprofit organization that provides new ways of learning for modern students,[18] began in Arkansas, where students began by identifying needs of their school and/or community. They select projects based on their own specific interests and/or skills. Sample projects include an award-winning robotics team from Eureka Springs,[19] Sylvan Hills' Anti-Texting While Driving PSA Initiative,[20] and Mountain Pine Students Documenting the Gulf Oil Spill,[21] to name a few.

What does the research say? Several research studies have been conducted on this program and have found that:

- EAST attracts students who might not otherwise gain critical STEM skills into STEM learning environments.
- Interpersonal skills, intrapersonal skills, lifelong learning skills, and college transition skills are learned concomitantly in the EAST classroom and are transferred to other classes and situations, motivating more responsibility by the students in their academic lives and better preparing them for college study.

- EAST has a positive impact in problem-solving domains such as defining the characteristics of a problem, assessing the outcomes of a solution, and revising strategies in response to the assessment of outcomes, as well as in motivation for school derived from accomplishment and self-directed learning style. These domains are widely recognized as being important for both academic and career success.
- EAST students perform better on benchmark exams than non-EAST students, and EAST students who started their EAST experience in the middle grades outperform students who do not start EAST until high school.[22]

These results show the power of service action projects and technology. As schools grapple with facilitating problem-solving skills, it may be as close as using technology to solve problems that will improve the schools and communities in which students live.

FLAT CLASSROOM™ FRAMEWORK

NAME OF PROJECT: East Initiative

WEBSITE URL: http://www.eastinitiative.org

LOCATION: Arkansas in local classrooms

COMMUNICATION: Asynchronous—videos and items are documented and shared; synchronous—in the classroom daily

GENERATION: Peers (ages 12 to 18); community projects may involve all ages

INFORMATION: Community assessment to determine a need and meet it using technology

TIME: Projects run through the school year

LEARNING LEGACY: Documentation of what was done and also the results of a service project left behind in the local community

Step 4
Contribution and Collaboration

"Individually we are one drop. Together, we are an ocean."

RYUNOSUKE SATORO[1]

A Story of Friendship and Collaboration in a Flat World

Casey and Cannelle, the self-proclaimed "Two C's," are a success story about making global collaboration work from opposite sides of the flat world. These two girls, Casey from the state of Georgia, and Cannelle from Bangladesh (an international student originally from Belgium), connected and bonded early in the inaugural Flat Classroom™ Project of 2006.

Assigned to work on a wiki together, the first thing they did (without being asked) was record a video introducing themselves. Cannelle, in her white tiled bathroom in Bangladesh, and Casey, in the white living room of her antebellum southern home in the United States, together brought different perspectives and backgrounds into a coherent message about how technology is changing the world. They lived it and did it.

> "If you want to know more about VOIP's such as Skype, instant messaging such as MSN messaging, desktop sharing, and video conferencing, this is the page for you! Casey and I have created this page . . ." begins their introductory video.[2]

Their thorough research and engagement attracted the attention of the teachers and Thomas Friedman, author of *The World Is Flat*. Without any encouragement, they collaborated over

CHAPTER 6 WEB RESOURCES
http://www.flatclassroombook.com/collaboration.html

SHARE IT

Twitter hashtag for this book:
#flatclass

and above project requirements. Casey traveled to Qatar in 2009 for the first Flat Classroom Conference and ultimately gained acceptance into the honors program at the University of Florida due to her excellent academic credentials and her well-spoken understanding of the trends concerning the globalization of society.

True stories of engaged global collaboration are not always evident, but these two C's show the power and potential of the two C's of global learning. Contribution and collaboration is what we want for all students.

OVERVIEW OF CONTRIBUTION AND COLLABORATION

Collaborative contribution has been identified as a "first class collaborative element" by Meta Collab's collaborative research in its quest to develop a general theory of collaboration.[3] Defined as "a creative contribution . . . made by a collaborative participant which leads to the emergence of shared understandings and contributes explicitly or implicitly to the collaborative output,"[4] it is important enough to be one of the five ISTE NETS.S standards for students and a C21 standard.

In this chapter you will learn how to develop and foster good contribution and collaboration skills so you can be a better global project leader and participant.

In the Self section of this chapter, we review the three R's (receive, read, and respond) of effective collaboration and how to become involved in the wider global community as an active contributor.

In the School section there is a review of effective contribution strategies, further discussion on how to establish an online learning community, and an overview of the challenges to collaborative learning. We share nontraditional roles for classrooms and opportunities for educators to lead through "flattened" involvement in collaborative experiences.

The Students section of this chapter covers tools, strategies, and challenges to learning when embarking on a project that is collaborative in nature. We share extended learning modes for all community members and reflect on the changing definition of teachers as contributors and collaborative learners. Through real examples from Flat Classroom projects, we share solutions for students that can be implemented into curriculum and assessment design for success.

 **ISTE STANDARDS**

NETS.S 2
Communication and Collaboration

21st CENTURY SKILLS

C21 LEARNING AND INNOVATION SKILLS:
Communication and Collaboration

 SELF   Contribute and Collaborate: Putting You into the Picture

Collaborative learning starts with reliable and responsible contribution. To collaborate effectively, you must be "visible" online while contributing meaningful content in conjunction with others around the world. You put yourself into the picture through this contribution. Visible contribution online is one of the most difficult objectives for educators and students to grasp, and yet in a traditional classroom this is one of the most obvious to observe and record. Lurking is not an option in global

ISTE STANDARDS

NETS.S 2
Communication and Collaboration

NETS.T 4.d
Promote and Model Digital
Citizenship and Responsibility

collaboration because collaboration is an activity requiring participation from all involved: You can't collaborate alone!

In a meaningful global collaboration, contribution goes beyond sending or receiving an email. Contribution starts at the first connection and includes communicating successfully, exhibiting good digital citizenship attitudes and habits, and collaborating. You also have to recognize differences and similarities between people around the world. To be online and learn online is not the same as being "tech savvy"; rather, it is about being an active contributor.

A participant in a collaborative project can become "invisible" if he or she is uninvolved or will not communicate. A formula for online social networking communities called the *90-9-1 principle* reveals that 90 percent of community members watch and do not actively participate, 9 percent show some activity, and only 1 percent of any online community creates or contributes content.[5] To have a vibrant learning community, every student should contribute. Education must break away from the typical 90-9-1 inactivity happening in social networks and hold educational networks to a higher standard. Our goal should be 100% participation. In Flat Classroom projects, all participants are required to contribute, collaborate, and be visible online. The metrics and learning analytics we use in our educational networks should help us measure and move toward this goal.

ISTE STANDARDS

NETS.T 4.d
Promote and Model Digital
Citizenship and Responsibility

THE THREE R'S OF GLOBAL COLLABORATION: RECEIVE, READ, AND RESPOND

tweetable

The three R's of global collaboration: receive, read, and respond. Become a visible participant in educational spaces. #flatclass

Whether it is an email, blog post, or wiki comment, when students and teachers practice the habits of receiving, reading, and responding, it will cement relationships and build trust.

Often students complain that they have messaged their partner and their partners are not reading their messages. When the teacher is involved and speaks to these nonresponsive partners, the teacher is often met with a defensive "I have read every message and am doing _____." What the defensive students fail to understand is that they often have not even one time responded. As shown in the cartoon, Figure 6.1, if one doesn't respond or is not present online, this is viewed as not existing at all! Let's break this down and address obstacles preventing successful completion of the three R's.

ISTE STANDARDS

NETS.T 3
Model Digital-Age Work and
Learning

Receive. As of November 2010, approximately 86.4 percent of all email is unwanted bulk email or spam.[6] With 1 in almost 300 emails being viruses and 1 in about 600 emails being a phishing scam, aggressive email scanners have been put in place by schools, colleges, and other educational institutions. We often joke at the beginning of a Flat Classroom project that "Barracuda hates me," referencing the Barracuda firewalls employed in so many U.S. schools that won't let messages get to teachers. To diminish this problem we purchased our own domain name.

It is essential at the beginning of a project that all participants actively *look* for the emails to make sure they are being received. Sometimes this means asking the IT department to make sure that organizer's emails are whitelisted or unblocked in the anti-spam software. Make sure you exchange other contact details such as Skype and phone numbers as a backup to make sure communication can happen if email isn't

FIGURE 6.1 Online Existence

replied to. Give the intended recipient the "benefit of the doubt," especially when starting a project. During our early projects, we often talked of participants who "fell off the face of the earth" only to find out later that they had not been receiving our emails. (In fact, they thought we had "fallen off the face of the earth.")

Read. This is a challenging daily habit for many. The habit of reading electronic correspondence as part of daily work routines is important to being able to collaborate and contribute effectively.

During a global collaboration teachers should read messages relating to the project on a daily basis. There are ways to help this email "rise to the top" of a flooded inbox by using tools such as Gmail's priority inbox, marking the project participants as important senders , or using a service like Away Find.

Respond. Reading a message is not enough, especially early in a project. Other participants do not "know you are there" unless you respond. We call this the *handshake* in Chapter 4. To respond to the handshake, place your hand firmly back in the hand of the organizers and let them know you are there by verbally responding to important emails. You may read every message, but the lack of response is often perceived as a lack of involvement.

We encourage weekly activity reports from all project teachers to go out to everyone so that we all definitively *know* that others are out there doing the work (as well as learn what they are doing). Even a one-line email like "We are on track currently and I have no questions! Good luck everyone!" has the powerful impact of telling organizers and the other teachers that you are present, reading emails, and

actively participating. Later in a project, when many emails are being sent, it becomes less important to respond to *every* email.

As shown in the following examples, a response to a message elicits responses from others and prompts more student engagement. By boosting response rates, you are encouraging the engagement that comes from the partial reinforcement of being responded to at least some of the time. Remember, this is not just about email but also about all electronic communications including forum discussions and blog posts. This is a better way of teaching. A recent study on student engagement in high school classrooms[7] found that participants were more engaged in individual and group work than in lectures. So let's encourage better ways to respond and engage more learners in the process.

The Digiteen Project invites student discussion almost immediately after one joins the learning community.[8] The forums, blogs, and groups provide countless opportunities to contribute to task-related discussions and to start their own. One example of this is "Will Technology Be the Key to the Future or the End" started by Sadie W.[9] Another is the discussion started by expert advisor Terry Freedman, "What Is Digital Literacy?," which to date has received over 200 responses from around the world.[10]

COLLABORATION: ENCOURAGING HIGH-QUALITY CONTRIBUTION

In his book *Wikinomics*, Don Tapscott talks about the growing strength of peer production, which allows us to "harness human skill, ingenuity, and intelligence more effectively."[11] Collaboration in learning is a relatively new concept supported by constructivist principles and more recently supported by Web 2.0 tools such as a wiki.

Collaboration requires working together with others to achieve a common goal. In Chapter 1, we discussed the concept of Global Collaboration 3.0, where co-creation of information and artifacts is the aim. Co-creation isn't a co-operative "create and share" model, but represents the true collaboration we need in modern society.

Working together to successfully create such things as the content on a wiki page, in a quality Wikipedia style, involves higher-order thinking skills. By learning to co-create in the K–12 environment, students will be ready to collaborate to solve larger world issues as they mature.

Establish Your Community. Establishing a sense of purpose and belonging within an online learning community—and in fact creating a **community of practice (CoP)** of people who learn how to do something better as they interact regularly—takes time and effort. A community of practice has three crucial characteristics: a shared domain of interest, a community of joint activities and shared information, and a shared practice and repertoire of resources.[12] An effective global collaborative project develops a student-centered community that brings together cross-class teams and involves the wider community in the learning, as shown in the Community Creation Chart, Figure 6.2.

It is important to allow participants in a learning community to feel comfortable and willing to contribute to the community. In Flat Classroom projects we encourage

FIGURE 6.2 Community Creation Chart

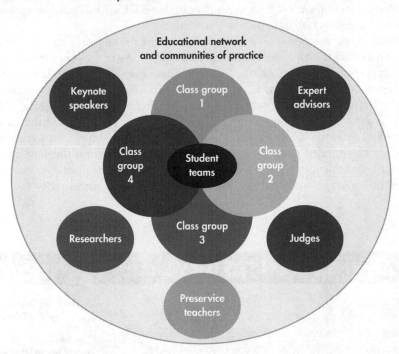

students and teachers to "friend" others in their immediate team grid and leave messages of introduction and welcome via the network. Schools are asked to create a group specifically to include their classroom members and to create a group within the larger community. There is a place, and often more than one, for every member of the learning community to join and become an active member as she or he needs and wants, or as the expectation of the joint activity dictates.

Engage in Dialog. When a participant is part of a community, it is expected that interactions will occur. Disappointment on the part of some teachers and students occurs when they reach out to others and receive no response from their friend request or "wall" comment. It can be hard work finding a niche in an online community or network, but reaching out and actively posting and responding starts this process.

INVOLVING THE GLOBAL COMMUNITY

Community building for a global project embraces wider involvement from outside people. To encourage the global community to contribute while enticing experts and educators to spend their free time interacting with global project collaborative learning communities, you must get the message out about your project. And you must convey that through giving you also receive. Being a Flat Classroom project judge, for example, is one of the best ways to evaluate the project and determine

21st CENTURY SKILLS

C21 LIFE AND CAREER SKILLS:
Social and Cross-Cultural Skills

NETS.T 3
Model Digital-Age Work and Learning

It is important to allow participants in a learning community to feel comfortable and willing to contribute to the community. #flatclass

suitability for your own class. Being an expert advisor provides the opportunity to hone in on communication skills and better understand student misconceptions and issues with construction of collective knowledge.

Methods we use across all projects to broadcast to the world and invite sign up and contribution from a wider community include a Twitter account for each project, a project website blog, the use of educational networks such as flatclassrooms.ning .com, Facebook, and our Flat Classroom databank. We'll discuss these networks in Chapter 10, when we focus on managing and marketing a global project.

As another form of community building, in a more private sense than a public educational network, a Google group, or other message board is an excellent way to collect like-minded people together for discussion. Working through an online interface that feeds into regular email (according to preference settings), we use this to send out messages and alerts to project participants (not students).

Flat Classroom Database of Global Projects
http://projects.flatclassroom project.org

✓ SELF-ASSESSMENT SURVEY

PDToolkit
for
Flattening Classrooms, Engaging Minds

See the survey results in the online PDToolkit before moving on to the next section.

Before moving to the next part of this chapter, we invite you to take this self-assessment survey. Discuss these questions with colleagues, including your wider learning network, to determine your current level of confidence and ability with contribution and collaboration strategies.

1. **Am I comfortable working with Web 2.0 tools, including wikis, blogs, and social bookmarking?**

   a. Yes   b. No   c. Maybe

2. **Am I willing to contribute regularly to online spaces for a project, including starting and responding to blog posts and discussions?**

   a. Yes   b. No   c. Maybe

3. **Do I encourage my students to contribute to global project online spaces outside of class time in order to broaden the collaboration?**

   a. Yes   b. No   c. Maybe

4. **Am I embedding opportunities for collaboration and related assessment into curriculum design?**

   a. Yes   b. No   c. Maybe

5. **Am I willing to be a collaborative learner in the global classroom and encourage and monitor all students, not just my classroom, including developing strategies for nonresponders and lurkers and those with language or cultural disconnects?**

   a. Yes   b. No   c. Maybe

6. **Am I taking the opportunity to involve me and/or my class in nontraditional roles in global projects, such as providing expert advice, judging multimedia, and being a sounding board?**

   a. Yes   b. No   c. Maybe

SCHOOL Creating Leadership and Encouraging Contribution and Collaboration

Learning does not take place in isolation. An important role of the classroom teacher and the school is to invite others into the classroom in order to support knowledge acquisition while encouraging discussion and problem solving. This is a philosophy that drives Flat Classroom projects and undergirds everything we do in the classroom and beyond.

JUMPSTARTING CONTRIBUTION

If you want effective contribution from students, you must put in place the tools, expectations, digital footprint expectations, and the online learning community infrastructure. This is a process and does not automatically happen. Expecting a student, or even a teacher, to automatically know how to present himself or herself in an online learning environment without prior practice is unrealistic. We teach this because contribution skills are not intuitive.

Establish the Toolbox. Careful selection of the collaborative media[13] that will compose your "classroom toolbox" will jump-start success. Choose tools that allow individual customization and provide simple ways to connect and communicate. In a classroom setting, we also need collaborative tools that allow tracking and documentation of contribution.

In the Web 2.0 world we have a lot of tools to choose from. Do not avoid a tool because of having to pay for basic or advanced features. The trend is for well-developed collaborative tools to be user-pays.[14] In some **freemium** models, you can try a basic service for free but when extended features or a lot of users are needed, you may be asked to pay. Collaborative and community building tools used in Flat Classroom projects include an educational network (Ning or Edmodo), a collaborative authoring tool (such as Wikispaces), real-time virtual meeting space (such as Blackboard Collaborate), and other tools for sharing research, authorship, or organization (such as Diigo, Google Groups, Google Docs, Timebridge, or Google Calendar). These tools essentially provide access to an online community network for meeting and greeting and interaction; collaborative learning spaces for co-creation; a real-time virtual classroom for meeting and celebrating (presenting); and workflow mechanisms for research sharing and additional communication.

Educational Networks Are for Community Building and Collaboration. An online educational network brings together disparate community members, who, in a global collaboration, are usually geographically distanced, for the purpose of sharing common ideas, goals, and needs. The features of this online community include using technology to serve through providing simple and user-friendly access.[15]

In an ideal situation, an online learning community is **transparent**. Members are able to maintain some privacy of data, but blog posts and discussions and forums, including uploaded multimedia, are usually available for the community to share and

 ISTE STANDARDS
NETS.T 2
Design and Develop Digital-Age Learning Experiences and Assessments

21st CENTURY SKILLS
C21 LEARNING ENVIRONMENTS

ISTE STANDARDS
NETS.S 2
Communication and Collaboration

 **21st** CENTURY SKILLS
C21 LEARNING AND INNOVATION SKILLS:
Communication and Collaboration

learn from. An online learning community takes advantage of social-based learning, allowing students to use communication and collaboration tools to create personalized networks.[16]

Setting up an educational network is the first step in developing a collaborative global project and a community that learns from its members as the main source of knowledge in a task-driven environment.

With younger students, a tool such as Edmodo provides a secure place for community building, once again through avatar development, "friending," posting comments, and replying to others. In addition, Edmodo allows for specific subgroups to be set up, thus allowing for smaller teamwork and communication. The ability to embed multimedia into posts as well as upload to a file repository makes this a distinctly unique learning environment for this project.

Wikis Are for Disruption and Collaboration. A wiki allows for sharing of ideas and collaborative authoring; therefore, having a team of users working asynchronously on the one wiki page contributing to content is possible. A wiki is also disruptive, as it has challenged our thinking and practice on how students and teachers engage and relate with the world. Used wisely and creatively, a wiki is a platform that supports collaboration and co-creation that can ultimately transform society. Tapscott calls wikis "weapons of mass collaboration"[17] and their robust capabilities allow them to live up to this assertion easily.

Traditionally, only one person can edit a wiki page at once, which is different from a Google doc, which many users can be editing simultaneously. A phenomena we affectionately call **wiki wars** can occur in a wiki when more than one person is editing at once. Eventually, a pop-up box will alert each user that he or she is not alone and, after saving, another alert will inform whose work will be lost or saved. It takes a little experience to understand how to work in this situation. Now on Wikispaces you can embed small wiki pages in a larger page, which lessens this problem and allows more students to edit the same page, one section at a time. Other wiki features for sharing contribution include tags; comments, which can be used to indicate what was edited when saving a page; notifications via RSS; as well as a range of widgets.

The wiki provides recovery for technical glitches by giving users a choice when going into edit mode to save or discard the previous draft of the page. On Wikispaces, discard is always advised unless the same user has just had a technical glitch and needs to save the automatic draft of the page. In a single classroom situation, verbal communication to inform who is working on which wiki can help avoid wiki wars. However, in a global collaboration it is not clear always if other classrooms or individuals are editing at the same time, hence the disruptive nature of this environment. Problems aren't a problem—in fact, they make the collaborative work more realistic. In the business world collaborative technology doesn't work flawlessly either.

Set Expectations After you've selected tools, clearly set expectations at the start of collaboration—how often to contribute, where to contribute, and what format the contribution should take. Combine this with the decisive expectation for participants (teachers and students) to be online and visible. Have a clear time line or workflow structure for a project with milestones for contribution. Some teachers create checklists and calendars with dates for their classroom.

As Julie advised her students at Qatar Academy, "Do not be a non-contributor and lurk somewhere in the darkness. Come out and be part of the construction."[18] This makes it clear that the expectation is to be a visible part of the knowledge construction through regular contribution.

Many collaborative tools, such as a wiki, allow for viewing and editing permissions to be "protected." This means anyone in the world can view, but only members can edit the content. For older students, protected rather than private permissions on tools provide a link to the real world, allowing their contributions to be "out there" and visible by all, not stuck behind a virtual closed door or **walled garden** while keeping unwanted editors out.

For younger students, tools such as Edmodo provide the freedom to contribute in a more private environment, where only members can view and/or edit, while digital citizenship expectations are practiced and reviewed.

CHALLENGES TO COLLABORATIVE LEARNING

Teachers who want to thrive in a collaborative environment must:

- Be willing to adopt and adapt Web 2.0 tools such as blogs, wikis, social bookmarking, and RSS, and become skilled and comfortable using such tools with the students.
- Be able to foster an online learning community or community of practice, where the walls of one's classroom are lowered and where an open relationship exists between the teacher and the class members.
- Be able to set aside a chunk of classroom time to be intensely involved on the actual project with time before to prepare and after to evaluate.
- Have an imaginative and risk-taking nature and supportive school.
- Be able to work toward and meet deadlines as a respect for other members of the project.
- Be flexible and patient when connections and tools do not always work.

Many of the challenges or threats to global collaborative project success are solved through better understanding of the needs of the project, and also through experience. Often, teachers taking on Flat Classroom projects are unaware of the demands and the need for a shared understanding of contribution and engagement. They will sometimes comment in the second or third time of taking a class through a full project how they are finally "getting" it. This next section addresses some common challenges to collaborative learning that we have experienced.

The "Noncontributor" or "Lurker." Lack of participation could be a reflection of not understanding online learning, or it could be difficulties in other areas such as language or irregular Internet access. Whatever the reason, the noncontributing participant, both teacher and student, is a problem during a global project.

When this happens, we suggest a classroom conversation stressing the importance of being part of the learning through effective contribution. Sometimes it is best to sit beside the student to understand the knowledge gaps that are causing the lack of participation. Require contribution in your assessment methods and accept no excuses. Students who are used to not contributing to group projects will resist

ISTE STANDARDS

NETS.S 2
Communication and Collaboration

21st CENTURY SKILLS

C21 STANDARDS AND ASSESSMENT

being a part because they have to work. (Vicki had a student once exclaim during a project, "Mrs. Vicki, why can't we just do a worksheet today? I don't want to think.") Regular online teacher meetings and invitations to contribute to project development and the learning community can help encourage the "lurking" teacher to contribute as well.

The "Nonresponder." Participants should respond and contribute on almost a daily basis in most projects. When students complain that they have not heard from their team members, there are usually two main reasons for this (given an absence of technical issues): teacher inability to stress how important being connected and responding is; and student inability to see how, in a professional learning community, responses are the glue that holds the relationships together.

NETS.T 4
Promote and Model Digital
Citizenship and Responsibility

Language Disconnects. Despite the many language translation tools now available, language differences will continue to impede collaboration. Projects that are primarily in one language require a suitable level of that language for students to feel comfortable contributing. In Flat Classroom projects, students are challenged by the differences in U.S. English compared with British English as well as colloquial versions of English.

Cultural Taboos and Disconnects. How do you talk to someone from a different culture? How do you move past your stereotypes and establish a working, collaborative relationship that is based on trust? Are some cultures naturally more collaborative than others? Encouraging true collaboration via Web 2.0, a wiki, or other medium elicits a variety of responses.

Recently a class in a Digiteen project displayed disconnected behavior, partly due to lack of confidence with language, and partly because they worked on getting their contributions "right" first. They preferred to share their work as distinct paragraphs rather than collaborative writing. In addition, rather than posting directly to the wiki, they used a word processor for their writing and pasted into the wiki, which erased the work of others, but also frustrated those classmates who were attempting to collaborate. They also signed their name after the work. We had to work through this and encourage the reticent classroom to collaborate and co-create and to help them realize that the wiki user ID tracks their contribution. Unless prompted to do so, signing your name beside a wiki contribution is an acknowledgement that you don't understand the functionality and purpose of the collaborative process.

DIGITAL CITIZENSHIP AREA OF UNDERSTANDING

Literacy and Fluency

Poor Technopersonal Skills. When classrooms come together from around the world, the students will naturally have differences in access to hardware and software and differences in abilities to use these tools. If a class has never used a wiki before, the understanding of editing wiki pages and discussion comments is a steep learning curve.

Do not let the lack of technology skills be an inhibitor or a confidence destroyer. In some projects the expectation to belong to a Ning network, a wiki, and a social bookmarking tool, as well as set up an RSS reader, can be a lot to achieve in a short time. This problem can be solved through exploring tools before the project begins. The wiki in particular has certain idiosyncrasies that all users struggle with at first when editing and saving. Developing **digital fluency** is paramount to success.

The Culture of Learning: Social versus Educational.   Where do you draw the line between "social" and "educational" performance in a global educational project? How do we encourage students to maintain a professional persona while connecting and communicating as well as rise above daily chit-chat to actually discuss real issues and topics?

Apart from being a challenge for every teacher across the globe in a traditional classroom, in a virtual classroom, this poses new problems. For example, in 2010, we enabled live chat rooms on our project Nings as a backchannel (discussed in Chapter 4). At first, it promoted connection. Some students started using IM speak and eventually, it was obvious that the chat was being used as a distractor from editing film and working on research. When teachers felt the chat was a distraction, the chat was disabled.

As teachers have learned the skills of backchannel facilitation, this has become less of a problem, but it was the right decision at the time. In Edmodo, we have a group for each project called "recess for conversations." This group is more social in nature rather than a discussion of the core topic of the project. Even in the recess group, though, we encourage students to do more than the usual social chit-chat and text-speak to the level of engaged discussion and sensible interaction. This is not a question of student maturity; it is a matter of expectation from the learning community and the teachers involved. Finding a group of students happily exchanging "silly" comments on the chat, one strategy is for any teacher to interact and move the conversation to more meaningful content. Students need to learn appropriate behavior for academic spaces. Context is key. Students must face the facts—every online space is not Facebook and social behavior is not appropriate everywhere.

It is interesting to see how, with teacher contributions and involvement, students can be better communicators using this medium. No teacher should stand back and watch time wasting and distractive behavior; they must get in there and facilitate and be part of the best-practice example of how to use this unique technology. Teachers should influence the behavioral norms of appropriate use of learning communities in projects.

Copyright and Plagiarism.   The challenge in any online project is promoting originality and better understanding rather than allowing copy and paste techniques. When plagiarism occurs, peer as well as teacher pressure comes into play, with the passage ultimately being rewritten with attribution or deleted from the wiki or blog either by the student or the teacher. Recently, we've begun to notice students of newer projects copying from previous project wikis, so it helps when teachers watch for large chunks of text that are pasted into the wiki when reviewing recent edits.

Team Dynamics.   Why are some collaborative teams more successful than others? How can we scaffold this approach to learning to achieve success for all? In the real world, a person may work better with some co-workers than others and may like one boss and not another. All human beings have likes and dislikes. A student may

ISTE STANDARDS

NETS.T 3
Model Digital-Age Work and
Learning

ISTE STANDARDS

NETS.T 4
Promote and Model Digital
Citizenship and Responsibility

**DIGITAL CITIZENSHIP AREA
OF UNDERSTANDING**

Safety, Privacy, Copyright, and Legal

be with a partner or two that she or he does not "connect" with on a personal basis. It happens. However, students must learn how to work together.

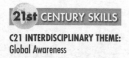

21st CENTURY SKILLS

C21 INTERDISCIPLINARY THEME:
Global Awareness

Some students will run to their teacher for intervention or asked to be removed from a team if they don't "like" the other person. (Surprisingly, it is often due to what is perceived to be an odd profile picture or wall post.) Teachers must resist the urge to intervene unless it is significant. Real-world teachable moments about team dynamics and the importance of knowing how to work with all types of people emerge from these discussions and can positively impact the entire class. Post-project discussions about misinformed stereotypes commonly grow out of this. Other students may not understand the impact a bizarre profile picture has on their ability to connect with others.

Time-Zone and Calendar Differences. Share school times and holidays via an online calendar so it is clear when students are in session. Understand time lines and commitments that are different for each individual classroom and work together to minimize miscommunications to make the project successful.

While a 24-hour turnaround is ideal, 48 hours is more realistic. Anything more than that, unless it is over the weekend, shows lack of engagement and collaboration from the participant.

Help students understand seasons, holidays, and the traditional work week (Monday through Friday for many countries, or Sunday through Thursday for many Middle East countries) to prevent misunderstandings.

EDUCATOR LEADERSHIP ROLES

ISTE STANDARDS

NETS.T 5
Engage in Professional Growth
and Leadership

Flat Classroom projects of all types encourage and support leadership among educators. This leadership and higher-level involvement can take a variety of forms.

Project Management. The Australian Flexible Learning Framework notes that effective facilitation is a major factor in the success of an online community.[19] Lead projects by establishing, planning, and solving technical and other issues. Be an active member of the community and lead by example rather than direction. Read more about project management in Chapter 10.

Keynotes. The role of a keynote is to provide a catalyst for further reflection and research and intellectual discussion beyond what the immediate teacher or school community can provide. Keynote speakers for Flat Classroom projects have come from diverse areas but all have challenged and shared ideology in education, been fun and funny, and provided that extended vision for a better world. By providing an uploaded video (or podcast in the case of our first keynote, Karl Fisch), project participants can watch in their own time and respond and interact around the content material (see Table 6.1).

Keynoters have included David Warlick from a cornfield in Iowa talking about the meaning of the flat world;[20] Terry Freedman in a coffee shop in the U.K. talking about a new age of collaboration;[21] Dr. Curt Bonk from a television studio with a humorous sidekick talking about leading innovations in the history of computing that were opening up education;[22] student-generated media, as in the students from Peggy Sheehy's school with "No Future Left Behind" filmed partially in their island on the virtual world platform Second Life where kids flew, spun on their heads, and ran through classrooms;[23] and Suzie Nestico's students from Mount Carmel who sat in the library and discussed how their inner-city world changed as they collaborated, and (for some) some even traveled to India.[24]

TABLE 6.1   Table of Sample Keynote Presentations

Description	QR Code	URL
David Warlick FCP 10-3	http://flatclassroomproject.ning.com/video /david-warlick-flat-classroom	http://tinyurl.com/fcp-warlick
Terry Freedman FCP 2008	http://flatclassroomproject2008.wikispaces.com /Keynote	http://tinyurl.com /fcp-freedman
Dr. Curt Bonk FCP 2009	http://www.youtube.com/watch?v=G3hvFR5Cz9M	http://tinyurl.com/fcp-bonk
Dean Shareski FCP 2007 Original Keynote and a response to the student request asking how to green screen which launched many students into doing green screen without their teachers knowing how first!	http://flatclassroomproject.wikispaces.com /Keynote	http://tinyurl.com/fcp-shareski

TABLE 6.1   (continued)

Description	QR Code	URL
Students at Suffern Middle School (under Tutelage of Peggy Sheehy and Marianne Malmstrom) NetGen Ed™ 2009	http://www.youtube.com/watch?v =kra_z9vMnHo	http://tinyurl.com/fcp-suffern
Mt. Carmel Area High School FCP 10-2 Suzie Nestico	http://www.youtube.com/watch?v =IKCvYLbizdw	http://tinyurl.com/fcp-nestico
Don Tapscott NetGen Ed™	http://grownupdigital.ning.com/forum /topics/is-this-the-dumbest-generation	http://tinyurl.com /netgen-tapscott

ISTE STANDARDS

NETS.T 5
Engage in Professional Growth and Leadership

21st CENTURY SKILLS

C21 PROFESSIONAL DEVELOPMENT

Expert Advisors.   Many Flat Classroom projects involve expert advisors who take on the role of reading topic wikis and providing regular feedback and encouragement to the students. Sometimes they are true experts in their field; other times they are classroom teachers from other schools who have volunteered a little time to interact with students via this global project and who also want to understand the project better through this interaction. Many are preservice teachers with professors coaching about how to teach in online collaborative environments.

For students to have comments made about their work from people who are not their teacher is a leveling experience. This example by Salim Al Busaidi (Oman)[25] (see Figure 6.3) shows a thoughtful response to a student-created collaborative wiki, as formative review to their work. Every teacher—in fact, every interested adult learner—has the potential to be an expert advisor. Every student (young or old) appreciates the care and commitment shown in a response that indicates analysis and synthesis through time. This practice can take place within a school, teacher to teacher, or globally. The principle is the same: extending the classroom walls and bringing the outside world in to support learning and broaden the learning community.

FIGURE 6.3   Salim's Response

```
Dear students,

I would like first to thank you all for your hard working on this wiki.

Here is my feedback:

1. Overview: You gave good definitions of some important concepts. Very good! What do
you think of writing a short introduction of your topic?

2. Current news: Well written!
I think the first 3 lines can be put in the Overview part as introduction.
You might want to add a good picture.

3. I liked your examples and the way you stated them!
You just need to hyperlink where necessary and add a good picture.
I think there is no need to rewrite the title Wireless Connectivity (Education).

4. Government, Politics, and Employment
I liked your example of Government. Very good!
You might add more examples and information with a relevant picture!

5. Arts, Entertainment, and Leisure: You mentioned a good example (Lans) Very good!
You might hyperlink where necessary and add a relevant picture.

6. This part is empty. You might help each other to finish this part.
Generally you need to work on the language editing and page layout (font, space, etc.)
and don't forget to delete the instructions.

I wish you all the best.

Mr. Salim Al-Busaidi
OBZ School
```

Judging and Feedback. In the case of the Flat Classroom Project and the NetGen Ed™ Project, a set of external judges is engaged to review the multimedia artifact and recommend the best products overall from the project. Once again, these are other educators, preservice educators, or interested experts, some of whom are not familiar with the project but want a chance to see an end product and understand the process of creation through observing and reporting through the criteria. Still others who are evaluating digital storytelling for their school participate to become aware of assessment possibilities of multimedia artifacts and to get a wide view on what students around the world are doing.

In recent Flat Classroom projects an experienced meta-judge has been invited to take the top videos from each of the 11 topics and come up with the top three videos for the entire project. Review comments from the meta-judge provide valuable feedback to students and the other educators who initially vetted the films. All students need to know why the top videos are the top. Numbers don't accurately tell the story. For example, from Barbara Stefanics (Austria), meta-judge in 2009:

Images, video clips and other multimedia seemed to be edited to improve the impact of the artifact. However, where interviews were used, students need to be more selective and not allow longer interviews to dominate their video. The interview content needs to be effectively integrated into the video.[26]

And, from Torsten Otto (Germany), also a meta-judge in 2009:

Dear FCP09-2 participants,

thank you all very much for providing me with such a difficult and yet enjoyable task. As to be expected for a Flat Classroom Project, you covered a wide range of topics using a wide range of formats from still images to news shows involving a cast of many. I judged the stories themselves, not their connection to the wiki texts which left something to be desired for. The movies clearly were the product of careful planning and for the most part skillful video work.[27]

The addition of preservice teachers to be contributors and collaborators opens up a whole new world for learning and connecting. It is a great opportunity to learn with the very students they will be teaching, and a great way to learn techniques for applying pedagogy with Web 2.0 before being full time in the classroom. Perceptive teacher educators such as Dr. Leigh Zeitz (University of Northern Iowa) and Dr. Eric Brunsell (University of Wisconsin–Oshkosh) recognize the value in this learning experience and have integrated it into their courses for their college students in teacher education programs.

NONTRADITIONAL ROLES FOR CLASSROOMS AS COLLABORATORS

Mutually beneficial, symbiotic relationships can emerge in projects where creativity is used to bring in students of various ages and guide them in age-appropriate interactions. This provides students with audience and meaning in their work and should not be limited to the examples shown here as we work to provide meaning.

Sounding Board. Peer review is a powerful motivator for student engagement, on both sides of the process. Why should "work" only be seen and reviewed by the teacher? Collaborating on content and on multimedia in Flat Classroom-inspired projects means the work is available for others around the world to see and respond.

The practice of applying a **sounding board** class to review student work has benefits both for the reviewers and for the creators, and provides immediate feedback to the teacher. Direct editing of a student wiki by the reviewer is not allowed; however, the discussions tab on the wiki allows guest comments and posting of links to further blog or wiki reviews. The sounding board case study at the end of this chapter details more clearly the process and benefits. This is a suitable option for classrooms that may only have one or two days for a technological and/or collaborative experience. Some schools have reported a change in focus of their students and school after seeing the multimedia and editing work done by their peers.

Outsourced Partners. The practice of outsourcing in education is unfamiliar to many. In the actual Flat Classroom Project it is an integral part of the flattened learning

TORSTEN OTTO
@iTOtto

DR. LEIGH ZEITZ
@zeitz
http://drzreflects.com

NETS.T 2
Design and Develop Digital-Age Learning Experiences and Assessments

Peer review is a powerful motivator for student engagement, on both sides of the process. #flatclass

experience where students design a personal piece of multimedia as a communication piece in response to the topic they have studied. Part of the 5-minute video (about 30 to 40 seconds of it) is outsourced to a student in another classroom. This student or this classroom may be in the same project, and is most likely someone the first student has been communicating with throughout the project, but not necessarily.

Artifacts, ideas, and tasks can be easily outsourced to others to provide better workflow and an opportunity for real cultural diversity and co-creation. The outsourcing technique for Flat Classroom currently involves the educational network Ning as the medium for uploading and accessing the shared clips (ripped using a Firefox plug-in) as well as the final place for storing and sharing multimedia. Enhanced online tools such as Dropbox and Zamzar allow for seamless sharing and conversion of larger multimedia files. Typical of many Web 2.0 tools, including YouTube and Slideshare, Ning provides online commenting, the ability to embed videos back into the wiki, featuring, and "favoriting."

STUDENTS Contribution and Collaboration in the Classroom

Let's look at expectations and requirements for students when involved in a global collaborative project.

Create Effective Personal Profiles. In an online learning community, contribution starts with building a profile, choosing an avatar, and creating an introduction about you for the community. First impressions via a constructed online profile are just as important as the first impressions when you meet someone face-to-face. When joining a global project, students and educators are encouraged to share a little about themselves and to reach out to the community. For many this may be their first real attempt at setting up a digital profile and stamping their digital footprint.

Selection of the profile avatar is a personal choice. Some students and teachers are comfortable contributing a headshot; others prefer to use another icon. Users are encouraged to share their personality, culture, or environment through image choice; however, it is important to stress cultural sensitivity and appropriateness. Using a robust platform (such as a Ning network) allows for personalization, or customization, of a profile page, including theme selection, choices for sharing or hiding information such as birth date, and access to multimedia uploading tools. Each school should establish expectations for appropriate profile photographs before the project begins.

STUDENT ENGAGEMENT LEVELS

Students in a project are of three types: (1) those who are engaged and do the work in a timely manner, (2) those who procrastinate, and (3) those who are totally unengaged and do not join. Often those who procrastinate learn by experience in their first global collaboration that those who jumped in and did the work had engaging experiences and powerful stories to tell. Evidence of understanding the three types of

tweetable

First impressions via an online profile are just as important as first impressions when you meet someone face-to-face. #flatclass

DIGITAL CITIZENSHIP AREA OF UNDERSTANDING

Safety, Privacy, Copyright, and Legal

 **ISTE STANDARDS**

NETS.S 5
Digital Citizenship

DIGITAL CITIZENSHIP AREA OF UNDERSTANDING

Etiquette and Respect

student collaborators can be seen in Jonathan C's blog post "Day 57—Desperation" as shown in the Flat Classroom Diaries at the end of Chapter 4.

Engaged. Those who engage share powerful learning experiences, even if it is in observing the behavior of those who procrastinate or do not engage. This is powerful learning for collaboration and online leadership skills. Ultimately, the goal should be to increase the percentage of students in a class who truly engage in such projects.

In future projects, we have set as a goal to develop measures of engagement, including "edit rates" (percentage of students who edit the wiki), "submission rates" (percentages of students who submit videos), and "handshake rates" (percentages of students who exchange conversation with partners) by project and school. This will require working with vendors to provide the learning analytics we need for this to happen. Anecdotal evidence to date indicates that these are going to be important measures of global collaborative excellence.

Procrastinators. Procrastinators find themselves making excuses and end up having problems finding student partners to help them complete their project. However, when these students begin to understand the missed opportunity, such as receiving outsourced work from others and having assistance, they are faced with the fact that although they can turn work in late, it will be incomplete because of their own procrastination.

Often these students, if held accountable for their procrastination in the first project—and if given the opportunity to complete another project—will learn from their mistakes and engage much sooner in future projects. In Vicki's classroom at Westwood, students complete three global collaborative projects (Digiteen,™ Flat Classroom, and NetGen Ed™) before graduating from high school, and by the third project, all students who completed previous projects are successful at handshaking and turning work in on time. They learn to develop effective collaborative relationships. One project is not enough.

Unengaged. Some students pretend to be working. Imagine a teacher's shock when she or he realizes three or four weeks into the project, just before wiki editing is complete, that a student has yet to join the wiki! This is why it is important to verify student joining and to allow students to complete self-assessments on their work (verified by the teacher) early in the project. This is best addressed with one-on-one attention. Effective teachers keep a checklist of who has joined each site. Don't rely on students to acknowledge such problems, as you may not find out until it is too late.

STUDENT LEADERSHIP ROLES

ISTE STANDARDS

NETS.S 5.d
Digital Citizenship

Student leaders in global collaboration are usually self-selecting. However, teachers also play a role in supporting development of leadership skills. The first student to join the educational community and "friend" others and "post to walls" may be the best leader. That student may even lead the way with contribution and enhanced awareness of social media, but will need support from his or her teacher to actually lead a project section.

Project Management. An often-untapped resource when collaborating globally, student leaders can manage and organize, inspire and motivate, as well as make decisions about contribution and collaboration as a project develops. Never underestimate the power of peer review and the ability of students to effectively and efficiently take charge.

The NetGen Ed™ Project is a good example here, where each team has a project manager (PM) and assistant project manager (APM). These positions come with job descriptions[28] and the expectation that reports will be completed and shared with teachers. The PM and APM are also expected to create personal multimedia responses to their topic that may include some content from the various subgroups.

Our chart for Global Collaboration 3.0 in Chapter 1 records student leadership in a global collaborative project as a higher-order thinking skill to be encouraged and coveted. Asking students to take on surveyor, facilitator, director, and overall management roles within a project further levels the playing field in learning. Communication between student leaders and teachers is important and the use of weekly private surveys from students to teachers is helpful for staying on top of problems.

tweetable

Never underestimate peer review and the ability of students to effectively and efficiently take charge. #flatclass

Project Manager Job Description

- To take charge of primary editing of the team wiki page that knits the subgroups together for that trend/topic/team
- To make sure that the subgroups contribute content to their section of the wiki
- To make sure that there are links to the other projects and to facilitate discussions/meetings/conversations within the group as well as give peer feedback to the other teams
- To communicate regularly with the class teachers regarding progress, and to discuss problems and issues as they arise
- To create a personal multimedia artifact based on the team topic that may include some content from the subgroups for that team
- To ensure all work is completed within the essential time frame
- (for APM) To support these objectives as well and fill in where the project manager is absent
- (for both PM and APM) To fill in a regular (bi-weekly) report for organizers to review

Informal Leadership Roles. Students should be encouraged to take on roles that emerge as they work together. For example, Gregor from Germany (Flat Classroom Project 09-3) had a hobby of making film and shot green screen for the other students in his group from his home. Vicki often teaches her students about "Web 2.0 leadership" and encourages them to lead by example in communicating on the discussion board.[29] Many of these students take on an informal leadership role of facilitating discussion.

MODALITIES OF CONTRIBUTION

Once an online presence has been established, various modes of working can be explored to foster consistent contribution in different ways. The project requirements and whether an educational network, a wiki, or another tool is used will dictate methodology.

http://tinyurl.com
/fcp-9-3-intro

http://tinyurl.com
/dalian-intro

C21 LEARNING AND
INNOVATION SKILLS:
Communication and Collaboration

Introductions: Multimedia Choices. After students establish a viable online profile as mentioned earlier in this chapter (Jumpstarting Contribution), and as the students move into the handshake phase of the project as discussed in Chapter 3, it is often best to blog or post an introduction that includes further reference to life in general and life at school. This so-called ice breaker is often in the form of simple images that will add to helping others on the project get to know the person and the culture and country of origin.

Sometimes other Web 2.0 tools are used, including video and slideshow tools, to share facts or influences on daily life more fully. Using a tool such as Animoto[30] is a useful way to share, in 30 seconds, a lifestyle and situation and can be more accessible than text, or complement the text.

As well as personal or individual introductions it is always a good idea to share school introductions, once again via images and videos. The Flat Classroom Project 09-3 shows effective examples of how this looks.[31] This is often facilitated by the teacher and is usually done when time is limited or students are just beginning to grapple with multimedia skills. The opening video from Dalian School in China is another notable example.[32]

Sharing Blog Posts. The opportunity to blog as part of a global project is often a student's first entry into the practice of blogging. It is important to understand the difference between *forum contributions* and *blogging*. When starting a project, this is something that often confuses students. Blogging in a global project provides the opportunity for an individual student to share the process by discussing progress and also reflecting on new experiences associated with this. It also provides a place for evaluation of interpersonal as well as intrapersonal activity.

Commenting on blog posts is another skill that fosters constructive review and critical thinking in conjunction with language development. Discussing with students how they feel about comments they receive and noting examples of good comments will help promote effective conversation and commenting on projects, which will then help create a highly engaged group of students. If students aren't encouraged to comment, then teachers must model this. Encouraging or requiring students to create meaningful comments creates a valuable online conversation skill while simultaneously promoting engagement levels in the online learning community.

Wiki Netiquette: Editing and Discussing. Moving into a wiki-centric collaborative environment requires further understanding of online netiquette in order to contribute effectively using this tool.

Wiki membership for each student can be either teacher generated, and therefore not require a student profile or sharing of a personal email account, or student initiated via independent creation of an ID and profile. It is important to remember that each wiki page has a complete history of individual contribution by profile name. Thus, students should use names that will honor themselves and their schools. We've often had students set up a profile name and later realize that they need to change it because of the poor image that a hastily selected name can have.

As the wiki page is saved, contributors are encouraged to leave a comment to advise other users what they have just done, as shown in Figure 6.4. In order to get a qualitative rather than quantitative measurement and therefore a true indication of real contribution, the "compare" function of the history tab on the wiki reveals color-coded additions and deletions (see Figure 6.5).

Cross-commenting and active contribution via the discussion tab is another essential wiki netiquette responsibility. This is done to share what recent edits have been added and to discuss the collaborative work on the wiki.

In Figure 6.6 (from Flat Classroom Project 09-3), the Web 2.0 topic discussion tab shows 60 contributions, with many of these viewed often, but it is not the best example of plentiful replies or responses. More engaged communication and contribution is encouraged through regular replies and responses to keep the project moving and to allow all participants to feel their contributions are received and valued.

FIGURE 6.4 Wiki History

Date	Compare	Author	Comment
Oct 24, 2007 4:05 pm	select	sarawill	"added all the places connecting at the top."
Oct 24, 2007 3:57 pm	select	rockerchick2010	"RSS feeds"
Oct 24, 2007 3:52 pm	select	rockerchick2010	"working on RSS feeds"
Oct 24, 2007 3:50 pm	select	rockerchick2010	
Oct 24, 2007 3:49 pm	select	rockerchick2010	"added another RSS feed"
Oct 24, 2007 3:47 pm	select	sarawill	
Oct 24, 2007 3:43 pm	select	sarawill	
Oct 24, 2007 3:32 pm	select	rockerchick2010	"fixed feed"
Oct 24, 2007 3:30 pm	select	sarawill	
Oct 24, 2007 3:27 pm	select	rockerchick2010	"added peer to peer networks RSS feed"
Oct 23, 2007 4:33 pm	select	rockerchick2010	
Oct 23, 2007 4:32 pm	select	rockerchick2010	"added my name to 2007 editors"

Virtual Communication — page ▾ | discussion (50) | history | notify me

FIGURE 6.5 Wiki History 2

A) Overview   Additions =   Deletions =

There has been significant development in the mobile area. From the mobile devices like Cell phones, Ipods, Laptops and computers. It seems they get smaller but dramatically increase on in the amount of stuff information held on the device. I find this to be a very effective solution to technology because seeing as nobody wants to carry around a huge ipod or a huge cell phone like what they had in the past. past generations dealt with. You want it to be nice and slim and easy to use but also you need it to get the job done for you. Technology is going to keep increasing will continue to advance as the years go by because people keep think thinking of better and more innovative ideas.
The mobile connectivity with new devices allows business people to stay connected at all times allowing them to do there work on the go on a blackberry or other smartphones. Internet on your mobile device is really good because you can always be connected and it's just a good app to have because it saves you also allows individuals to save money because if you have an individual has a Smartphone you they don't necessarily need more than one more computer computer.

FIGURE 6.6 Discussion Tab

Subject	Author	Replies	Views	Last Message ▲
Web 2.0 wiki feed back	Initsche	0	39	Dec 1, 2009 11:20 pm by Initsche
Outsourced Video	KadenB	2	75	Dec 1, 2009 12:15 pm by KadenB
Work	KadenB	2	70	Dec 1, 2009 8:09 am by KadenB
Outsourced Video	DRounds	6	116	Nov 29, 2009 12:54 pm by darrenyum
Outsource Video	ptisawesome	1	53	Nov 25, 2009 1:19 am by KadenB
Hello	KadenB	0	27	Nov 24, 2009 2:59 am by KadenB
Hello	KadenB	0	27	Nov 24, 2009 2:51 am by KadenB
Introduction	jborgen	2	70	Nov 20, 2009 10:16 am by jborgen
Step back and let's read!	jborgen	0	38	Nov 20, 2009 10:14 am by jborgen
Outsourced Video?	12sg	0	49	Nov 15, 2009 9:16 pm by 12sg
hey	ptisawesome	0	36	Nov 12, 2009 3:25 am by ptisawesome
changes	DRounds	1	50	Nov 12, 2009 3:24 am by ptisawesome

The Web 2.0 page shows: discussion (60), history, notify me, + New Post, Search Posts

WEBSITES

Horizon Project
http://www.nmc.org/horizon
New Media Consortium
http://www.nmc.org
Educause
http://www.educause.edu

ISTE STANDARDS

NETS.S 3
Research and Information Fluency

Sharing Research Online.   One of the exciting facets of global collaboration is being able to share research online. The potential for this is huge and has already been tapped into by numerous initiatives. An excellent example of this, external to global project work, is the creation of the regular Horizon Report by the New Media Consortium and Educause, where research is shared and contributions help build a database of current examples that feed into determining what the trends are and predicting future pathways. These leading researchers in technology create a set of standard tags for their research. So, it makes sense that when students of the NetGen Ed™ project begin their research, the standard tags are adopted in the project, as they are using the Horizon Report as one of the key elements of the project's research. In this way, as Ph.D.s and thought leaders around the world bookmark, students are literally tapped into their work immediately as bookmarks go from the desks of Ivy League scholars into the classrooms of students around the world, and vice-versa.

Sharing research requires simple systems and shared understandings to be established prior to commencing. The two popular tools used in Flat Classroom projects for social bookmarking and networked research are Delicious and Diigo. The choice to use one or the other, or both, depends on geographic location[33] and teacher preference. Some classes prefer to start with Delicious as an introduction to social bookmarking and then move on to Diigo. It is also possible, through Diigo settings, to transfer bookmarks over to Delicious as well. The advantage of using Diigo in school projects is access to an educator account that ensures privacy settings for students, simple class registration, and appropriate advertising. Diigo also provides the ability to save a bookmark and notes to a group and access to a standard tag library when saving a resource.

Using social bookmarking effectively relies on contributions being added with a systematic approach to tagging. Agreeing upon tag taxonomy that can easily and reliably be found by the learning community facilitates sharing. For example, the Digiteen™ project uses a taxonomy that incorporates the Areas of Awareness as

TABLE 6.2 Digiteen™ Tagging Standards

	Term	Tag
Areas of Awareness	Technical Access and Awareness	digital_access
	Individual Awareness	individual
	Social Awareness	social
	Cultural Awareness	cultural
	Global Awareness	global
Core Competence Areas	Safety	digital_safety
	Privacy	digital_privacy
	Copyright, Fair Use, Legal Compliance	digital_law
	Etiquette and Respect	netiquette

well as Core Competency Areas,[34] such as digital_privacy or social_media. Users can search bookmarks via tags and find relevant information to their topic saved by team members. This can be combined with a folksonomy approach, where users add additional tags of their own choosing. **Folksonomy** is a valid way of recording research; however, in a collaborative project, or in a group situation, it is far more effective to use common tagging terms and develop a taxonomy standard such as the Digiteen™ Tagging Standards shown in Table 6.2.

Outsourced Material. An expectation in the Flat Classroom or NetGen Ed™ Project is that each student will contribute an original outsourced video clip or other multimedia to be included in another student's final video. This contribution is systematically organized via an online system of pitching a personal request for the multimedia, finding another request to complete, uploading the multimedia to the Ning, and communicating its existence back to the requester. Finally, the recipient downloads and converts completed requests ready to insert into his or her final work.

With so many steps and skills involved, including effective communication skills to pitch the initial idea clearly and technology skills to cope with the uploading and downloading, this is a challenge for all participants and teachers. However, when it works (and it does most of the time!), it is a delight to see how a simple clip videoed in one country can support cultural awareness and understanding in another. Additionally, it teaches the elusive knowledge of understanding the interdependence of teams. When students communicate effectively, teammates are appreciative and relationships are built. Conversely, when students do not communicate, it becomes a learning experience for everyone because most of the class will know it.

Effective workflow software that will allow online multiple student editors of a piece of multimedia does not yet exist as of the writing of this book; however, initial insight into some emerging software from companies such as Adobe, or tools such as

ISTE STANDARDS

NETS.S 4
Critical Thinking, Problem Solving, and Decision Making

Kaltura,[35] indicates that this software is just on the horizon. When these co-creation tools are here and schools can access them with their bandwidth abilities, global collaborative classrooms should move into this arena of co-creation with excitement, as this is where we want to go!

PRACTICES FOR MEASURING STUDENT CONTRIBUTION

NETS.T 2
Design and Develop Digital-Age Learning Experiences and Assessments

Strategies and tools combine to monitor and measure as well as account for student contribution both in quality and quantity. Remember: In a digital online world, everything is recorded and never lost unless deliberately destroyed or reverted. Most tools do not allow for deletion of another person's work, but in the case of a wiki, collaborative editing allows for changes of other's work.

Rubric: Wiki. Contributions to a wiki can be measured quantitatively using the wiki tool itself. A relatively new feature in Wikispaces allows a "by user" search for all edits and additions across the wiki.

A typical student will potentially have many edits and messages across a number of pages. This search function provides an efficient way to collect all of these per student, or per page. An early point in the Flat Classroom Project 10-3a is shown in Figure 6.7, where the student "baileyp5" between the dates of October 9 through October 24 is found to have edited the Virtual Communication wiki 4 times and posted 2 messages.

This knowledge of student contribution can inform rubric-based assessment such as the one used for the Flat Classroom Project 10-3, Criterion C: Online Interaction and Engagement with the Project. (See Appendix A, Flat Classroom™ Project Rubric Assessment.) The goals for this rubric are to collaborate and interact with classrooms around the world on the theme of the "flat world." We also want to students to use higher-order thinking skills by engaging in organization, peer review, and reflection activities; synthesizing ideas; analyzing and evaluating trends; and creating web pages and multimedia products.

FIGURE 6.7   Wiki Change Tab Example Filtered by User "baileyp5"

The descriptor for the top level for these criteria states: "Communication with team members and teachers was frequent. There is evidence of being a considerate partner, providing feedback and effectively communicating ideas to the project. The wiki page editing and multimedia artifact were completed by the deadline. High-level organization skills were demonstrated."[36]

Rubric: Student Participation. Another example of measuring student participation related to contribution is the rubric created collaboratively by Phil Macoun from Canada and Digiteen™ 2008 teachers.[37] Criteria for top marks include Criterion A: Finding and Understanding (Research); Criterion B: Analyzing and Evaluating (Content); Criterion C: Communicating and Using Web 2.0 Tools (Organization and Presentation); and Criterion D: Demonstration of Digital Citizenship (Conduct). There are marks for individual work as well as group work.

When asked about rubric construction, Phil, who has supported Flat Classroom through project participation, shared these thoughts:

> I will say that I am still really struggling with this one. I think the rubrics that I shared with you are a start but in my own practice I don't think they are enough. My thinking these days is that with skills like collaborative wiki work the onus is on the teacher to carefully scaffold and demonstrate the skills needed so that students can hang the rubrics on real life experience with the technology. Students need to have a chance to practice the skills in their own classrooms first with ample opportunity to reflect on the advantages and pitfalls of this kind of collaboration and the sorts of skills/roles that make it successful BEFORE trying to do it with students they haven't met.[38]

ASSIGNMENT EXAMPLES

Sample Assignment: Preproject Blog Post. Beyond introductions, blog posts during the project can take a number of forms. Typically, a preproject blog post introduces and shares lifestyle and front-loads material by having students reflect on videos or other concepts before the project begins.

Sample Assignment: Postproject Blog Post. Writing a postproject blog entry is a chance to contribute final multimedia and ideas in one place, and also to invite comments on completed work and self-evaluation of one's work ethic and product. Ideas are shared in this example for creating a reflective (also called a postproject, blog post[39]). In this case, the contributor is given the choice to communicate using text, video, or audio but is expected to discuss the topic and wiki editing process, talk about the multimedia creation, including information about the outsourced video experience, and share the final product with more explanatory and reflective comments. Samples are in the PDToolkit online.

Assessment for Success. One of the challenges of group work or teamwork in a project-based learning environment is determining who contributed and how much and therefore how each student can be individually assessed or acknowledged. In a traditional classroom, the less collaborative students are often the more academically

http://tinyurl.com
/digiteen08rubric

PHIL MACOUN
@pmacoun
http://macoun.edublogs.org

for
*Flattening Classrooms,
Engaging Minds*

See several preproject blog post
assignment examples in the
PDToolkit online.

able and have developed what could be called "defense mechanisms" for preserving their good standing. Being asked to work in a group with others who may reduce their overall mark or grade is not necessarily advantageous. At the same time, working with others who process material and respond or contribute at different rates and abilities can also be frustrating.

With global collaboration these frustrations can be compounded by not being in the same place at the same time as your team members; a feeling of isolation due to noncontribution from others; and a strong sense that no one else is doing any work (a common complaint from students as they first start editing wikis and partners are still coming online). Teachers must expect and require that every student contributes to the wiki. Accountability of each member of the project should be high, as is the focus on qualitative as well as quantitative contributions.

Building in assessment strategies for student success is an important key to success in global collaborative projects. Such strategies might include a combination of individual and group tasks; a structured progression of assessment pieces throughout the project, including choices for response; and a mandate to share the process as well as the outcomes, through blogging and network discussion contributions. Flat Classroom projects are not prescriptive in terms of assessment; rather, they encourage individual teachers to align assessment with their school and program needs. We will discuss this further later in this book.

SUMMARY

Contribution and collaboration do not happen by accident. There are three new R's in education that have to do with global collaboration: receive, read, and respond. There are also new tools and strategies that will support contribution and collaboration. The first and perhaps one of the most important contributions project participants make is creating their profile, which begins their digital footprint. A good profile with appropriate descriptive information (that also protects privacy) will lead to dialog.

Leadership and reliable collaborators are needed in successful learning communities. There are challenges, though.

Interestingly, there may be a new level of educational volunteerism emerging as classrooms and teachers serve as audience, teacher, and student of one another in meaningful symbiotic learning relationships between all ages and stages of life.

A variety of methods for assessing qualitative as well as quantitative contributions in online spaces will help the teacher encourage contribution. The biggest point is to reach out to nonresponders and inactive participants. An inactive participant is a nonparticipant: Don't pretend students are involved in a project when they are just wasting time. Good teachers address the problem as outlined in this chapter.

ESSENTIAL QUESTIONS

- What are the three R's of global collaboration?
- What are some ways that the global community could be involved in a student project?
- How can students be used to help manage a project? Why would this be beneficial for the students? For the teachers?

- How can different types of students be encouraged to participate in collaboration? What are some ways that students can contribute? How can they be assessed?
- How important is it to link authentic assessment models with collaborative projects?

Join the online conversation and share your answers at http://tinyurl.com/flatclasschapter6 ▷

FLAT CLASSROOM™ **15** **CHALLENGES**

CHALLENGE 8: COLLABORATE AND COMMUNICATE

DO: Participate in a collaborative wiki project with your class or in one of our online communities with a group of at least four people.

SHARE: Compare and contrast a collaborative wiki editing project with traditional in-class group work on your blog. What is the difference between cooperation and collaboration? How can collaboration be taught? **The tag for this challenge is fcc8_wiki. Use this when you blog or share with your group.**

Share what you did with your challenge at http://tinyurl.com/flat15-8 ▷

BONUS CHALLENGE 8: EDIT WIKIPEDIA

DO: Join Wikipedia and edit a topic about which you are knowledgeable. Before editing, familiarize yourself with the talk page and engage in discussions there. Note that some pages on Wikipedia require one to earn a certain "status" or trust level on Wikipedia, and information posted in error could cause you to be banned from the site as an editor. Follow the topic for several days.

SHARE: On your blog, reflect on editing Wikipedia. How can students be prepared to contribute in a world where increasingly those who edit and converse succeed and those who consume information without contributing can be left behind? **The tag for this challenge is fcc8b_wikipedia. Use this when you blog or share with your group.**

Share what you did with your challenge at http://tinyurl.com/flat15-8b ▷

CHALLENGE 9: ASSESS

DO: Use the Wiki Rubric, and/or the Peer Evaluation Criteria and Summary (both found in PDToolkit online) and/or another form of assessment created by you, to assess three students from the wiki project you completed in Challenge 8.

SHARE: Compare your assessment with a partner, the self-assessment of the students who participated, or with the sample completions online. Blog your thoughts on the assessment

process on your blog or in a group. If you share with a group, record your discussions via the multimedia of your choice and post. **The tag for this challenge is fcc9_assess. Use this when you blog or share with your group.**

◀ Share what you did with your challenge at http://tinyurl.com/flat15-9

BONUS CHALLENGE 9-1: JOIN AS A PEER REVIEW CLASSROOM

DO: If you are in a school, join an online project as a peer review classroom.

SHARE: Share information about the project, including a hyperlink, a review of the process, and some student observations on the process. Suggest options for using peer review in a project. **The tag for this challenge is fcc9b1_peer. Use this when you blog or share with your group.**

◀ Share what you did with your challenge at http://tinyurl.com/flat15-19b1

BONUS CHALLENGE 9-2: JOIN IN AS AN EXPERT ADVISOR OR JUDGE

DO: Join an online project (Flat Classroom project openings will be found at www.flatclassroom-project.net) as an expert advisor or judge.

SHARE: After completing the process, share with the project organizer what you have learned from this experience. Reflect on your blog ideas you have for educators to collaborate with online projects as mentors, coaches, and contributors. **The tag for this challenge is fcc9b2_advise. Use this when you blog or share with your group.**

◀ Share what you did with your challenge at http://tinyurl.com/flat15-9b2

THE FLAT CLASSROOM™ DIARIES

Diary Entry 11

FLAT CLASSROOM DIARIES: JULIE LINDSAY FROM QATAR ACADEMY, SEPTEMBER 2007 AND MARCH 2008

[2007:] I don't care what anyone says, the world really is flat. Today I invited the students from my previous school, International School Dhaka in Bangladesh, who did both the Flat Classroom Project and the Horizon Project, to participate in the new Flat Classroom Project this semester as student advisers. These young adults are now completing their final year of high school, the second year of the IB Diploma and have a lot on their plate. I would not suggest they actually do the project again but my idea is to have them interact with the other newcomers and act as peer supporters and help with the judging toward the end. I think we could even include a peer award where they could give their choices and awards.

Later that lesson I noticed Paul Fairbrother had just joined the Ning so in the midst of our blogging, audio experiments, and Ning work, I pointed out to the class that this new member was in fact the head of online learning for the IBO, based in Cardiff. Yes, the world is flat. I can collaborate with my ex-students from Bangladesh, who have become even more globally aware and attuned to the importance of sustaining online learning communities, while teaching in the Middle East, and also be part of a global project that has as its hub a Ning where we can all see who is online and monitor contributions.

[2008:] An interesting conversation between one of my project manager students and me today –

[Direct messages via the Ning: On May 3, 2008 at 9:56 PM, Julie Lindsay wrote:]

Karim, I have just browsed the wikis for your group and am quite concerned that not a lot has been done. I also do not see you in there in the discussion of each wiki encouraging and helping your teams. You must go into the discussion of each wiki and ask if they need help, make suggestions and check who is working or not. When you do your next PM report early this week I will expect you to have a list of who is not contributing and not discussing etc. Just that little bit of extra effort will make a lot of difference to your wiki pages.

Mrs. Lindsay

[Karim's response:]

Hi Mrs. Lindsay, after I got my grades today I was quite shocked and I was not happy with what I earned. So, I put up the blog about the Don Tapscott video on the Ning, and I also went to all the separate wiki pages and wrote on the discussion tab. I praised whoever did some work and tried to encourage the people who didn't to do some more work and editing.

[My response:]

"Karim, the expectation on you as a PM is higher in terms of being active on the wiki. I know this is the first project like this you have done so it is a shock to realize that nonactivity is not acceptable. I know you have been browsing the wiki pages and communicating on the Ning; however, you now need to be on the wikis and leaving messages and trying to support your teams. You will be OK, just be consistent in your efforts.

Diary Entry 12

DIGITEEN STORIES[40], PHIL MACOUN, ASPENGROVE SCHOOL, CANADA

Story 1—The Teacher and the Chat Room

I was the most nervous about involving my students in the Ning as I knew that it had potential to ring alarm bells with the parent community at my small private school on Vancouver Island (Washington state), and I took pains to do my due diligence in informing parents and having conversations with my students around the issues of personal and private information and digital etiquette stereotypes. I also made sure to check in on the Ning periodically to make sure everything was OK.

During one of these visits I stumbled upon the Ning chat room and realised that somewhere around the world there was a class of students on the Ning and in the chat room. Most of the chat seemed to be the students saying hello to each other in various ways, but a couple of the comments were quite inappropriate. So,

Read the full diary entry as a blog post, including comments, at http:/ /macoun.edublogs.org /2008/10/25/digi-teen -stories.

being an administrator on the Ning, I did what I thought was best and deleted the chat immediately.

But the comments kept coming and I was pretty sure that some of them were meant to be hurtful to others. So I decided to join the chat. Heart racing, I entered a comment something like, "Hey guys, I'm a teacher over here in Canada and I'm concerned that some of what you are typing isn't very appropriate. . . ." I knew it sounded pretty stuffy but I was at a loss to express myself properly in such a limited medium. As was expected, I got some quick replies along the lines of "We're just having a bit of fun." So I started typing away, trying to express myself, when I started getting replies of a much different nature. More apologetic and thoughtful.

CASE EXAMPLES OF GLOBAL COLLABORATION

Case Study 12

 Sounding Board Case Study by KIM COFINO and LISA DURFF

PDToolkit
for
Flattening Classrooms,
Engaging Minds
Read full Case Studies
in PDToolkit online.

The Sounding Board process involves younger students in the Flat Classroom Project. Younger students get an opportunity to preview high school student work, explore the various methods for collaboration and communication used during the project, and provide opinions on that work as well as suggestions for improvement.

Each classroom involved in peer review selects a specific topic (or several topics, depending on the size of the class) to review. The review process consists of sounding board students' peer reviewing wikis prepared by high school students. As a guideline, the Sounding Board classrooms utilize a simple rubric for evaluating the wikis, collaboration, and final written projects. This helps provide both a structure and consistency among all sounding board classrooms.

As their final feedback to the FC project pages, all Sounding Board classrooms provide specific, constructive feedback to the teams using the 3-2-1 method of feedback: three things learned, two things liked, and one thing that needs improvement. This structure allows both very young students (grades 4 and 5 have provided feedback as Sounding Boards) as well as more mature students to share their thoughts in an appropriate and approachable way.

As a Sounding Board classroom teacher for the past four years (and Sounding Board organizer), we have consistently been impressed with the way students respond to the experience. Not only are they exposed to exciting new methods of collaboration and communicate along with the opportunity to learn about new technological developments around the world but they also feel empowered and engaged in the whole project experience because of their ability to contribute to a global project. When asked what they learned during the experience, students shared the following . . . .

ADD FRIEND

KIM COFINO
@mscofino
http://www.kimcofino.com/blog
LISA DURFF
@durff
http://durffsblog.blogspot.com

Case Study 13

Reflection and Evaluation postproject blog entry from YARA (Student) in 2007[41]

Online interaction in this project was much more successful than I thought it would be. With both the Ning and the wiki for communication, I believe that one could contact a group member in numerous manners. I believe it was crucial to have both the Ning and the wiki during this project. When addressing issues, concerns, or my thoughts about the Wiki page, I would use the wiki discussion. This is because, the discussion tab is targeted for a larger amount of people and thus I can guarantee more feedback. Also, if I needed more opinions, or if my group were not responding, I would usually post a discussion on the wiki. However, when I was addressing one particular person in the group, I would use the Ning. This helps distinguish our needs and what we need from the group. For example, when I gave feedback about the wiki page, I started a discussion on the Ning, and gave my thoughts about the changes. On the other hand, I asked one of my group members for an outsourced clip via the Ning.

I think the only way that this can be solved for future projects is that there are regular teacher checks, and stricter deadlines placed especially when submitting outsourced clips.

I thought that the time difference between regions would be the biggest difficulty I would have to encounter in this project. However, I realized that the principal problem was the lack of response from some of the group members. It seemed like there were a number of students who did not seem to contribute much in this project and rarely communicated in the Ning and wiki. . . .

Step 5
Choice

"'Beefsteak or liver' quite took away Philip's power of choice. He begged for a glass of milk ..."

MARK TWAIN

Tim's New Horizon

Tim, diagnosed with a form of Asperger's syndrome, couldn't communicate. The teacher and students would wait painfully while he stuttered just to get out one sentence. Imagine the teacher's (Barbara Stefanics) surprise when she saw the video Tim created for the Horizon Project! Yes, that was Tim on the video, but it was a Tim that she did not know. This Tim was at home in the comfort of his own room acting in his own video without a stutter or stammer! He could do it!

ISTE STANDARDS | NETS.T 1
Facilitate and Inspire Student Learning and Creativity

At the end of the project, Tim needed to present in the student summit. Ready for the time it would take, Barbara and the technician helping her listened in awe as he presented fluently without a glitch via his microphone into the room. There was an incredibly intelligent student underneath the stutter waiting to get out and she had the proof she needed to aid in his diagnosis and for Tim to succeed. Technology was the key to unlock his potential.

The Horizon Project that year wasn't just a project for Tim; it was quite literally a new horizon of learning for him, particularly when he received a top award for his video. The world's classrooms are full of Tims waiting to be unearthed. If there is one story like this, there are more. Giving students choices is not only good teaching—it helps in reaching everyone. (Read this story in Barbara's words in the Flat Classroom™ diaries at the end of this chapter.)

CHAPTER 7 WEB RESOURCES
http://www.flatclassroombook.com/choice.html

SHARE IT

Twitter hashtag for this book:
#flatclass

OVERVIEW OF CHOICE

You can make a child sit at his or her desk, but only the child can decide to learn. Engaging a student's intrinsic motivation is the holy grail of academicians everywhere. This chapter talks about the principles of multisensory learning, how to create conducive environments for learning, and how to give students choices to increase their motivation.

In the section titled Self, we discuss how giving students choices in the classroom is a proven way to deliver effective instruction, engage students, promote critical thinking, and utilize the multisensory power of technology to reach every student. Whether it is called project-based learning (PBL), universal design for learning (UDL), multisensory learning, **learning styles**, inquiry-based learning, or differentiated instruction—all of these speak to the need for choice in the classroom.

Although many schools haven't changed in the last 100 years, there are progressive schools trying new things. Cushy couches and steaming hot mugs of coffee served on cold mornings foster conversation between colleagues and students in some schools. In the section titled School, you'll learn about Ewan McIntosh's Seven Spaces of Learning and the evolution of the library into a "Learning Commons." Everything from the places students meet both face-to-face and online and the faces that greet them at the door should be conducive to giving students choices to learn and share.

Finally, in the section called Students, students are encouraged to question, to be a part of constructing the spaces and places for learning, to connect with resources and other students around the world, and to learn in powerful ways with others. Contests and awards, and cool knowledge give students incentives for more than just getting a good mark and give them meaning as they build a footprint of learning that will span their whole lifetime. Content knowledge can be but for a day, but habits of learning are for a lifetime.

DIGITAL CITIZENSHIP AREA OF UNDERSTANDING
Habits of Learning

 SELF The Teacher's Choice That Unleashes Learning

Choice is important because it is part of what human beings want to do, the inherent freedom that we want to determine something in our lives, whether it is the color of our shoes or the book on our nightstand. We talk about choice in this chapter as part of the strategy of differentiating instruction, a powerful teaching method that underlies a lot of what we advocate.

DIFFERENTIATING INSTRUCTION IMPROVES LEARNING OUTCOMES

Giving students choices in their learning is important because:

- Current research points to the effective use of choice.
- Effective choices can increase student engagement.
- Today's students must have critical thinking skills that surpass memorization.
- Different modes of delivery and assessment are made possible by technology.

NETS.T 5
Engage in Professional Growth and Leadership

C21 PROFESSIONAL DEVELOPMENT

Research. Learning starts with the teacher who is leading the classroom. Teachers should understand the research behind effective classroom pedagogies. We (authors Julie Lindsay and Vicki Davis) are teachers, and consider the whole view of research as it points to best practice in the classroom rather than the debate of individual theories. In this case, there are several interrelated research-based best practices from which we draw. Although there may be disagreements about a particular theory or study, the research as a whole supports differentiated, multisensory approaches to learning.

ISTE STANDARDS

NETS.T 1
Facilitate and Inspire Student
Learning and Creativity

Differentiated Instruction. **Differentiated instruction** is "a teaching theory based on the premise that instructional approaches should vary and be adapted in relation to individual and diverse students in the classroom."[1] All of the theories and practices mentioned in this section allow the teacher to differentiate instruction. Incorporating multiple senses, giving students choices, adapting the teacher's relationship with the student based on her or his readiness level, and incorporating student interest into a project-based learning environment are all ways that differentiation is used in the classroom. One of the most prominent methods of creating lesson plans utilizing differentiated instruction is the universal design for learning (UDL) discussed in this section.

Project-Based Learning. In 1997, Jo Boaler studied two schools in the United Kingdom and demonstrated that the school using **project-based learning** for teaching math had three times as many top-scores scores as the traditional, direct instruction method school.[2]

Edutopia's article "PBL Research Summary: Studies Validate Project-Based Learning," stated, "A growing body of academic research supports the use of project-based learning in schools as a way to engage students, cut absenteeism, boost cooperative learning skills, and improve test scores. Those benefits are enhanced when technology is used in a meaningful way in projects."[3] This is closely related to **problem-based learning,** which uses similar pedagogies but is based on solving a particular problem.

Dual Encoding Theory. This theory[4] by Paivio demonstrates that recall/ recognition is improved by presenting information in both visual and verbal forms.[5] This was discussed at length in Chapter 3 relating to the use of eBooks. By using technology to incorporate multiple senses, learning increases. Although dual encoding is important for many students with learning disabilities, it can help everyone.

Multisensory Learning, VAK Modalities, and Learning Styles. Studies from the National Institutes of Child Health and Human Development demonstrate that children having problems learning to read benefit from the multisensory teaching method. These modalities are called VAK, an acronym for visual, auditory, and kinesthetic.[6] Some call this "learning styles," with visual learners learning through seeing; auditory learners learning through listening; and bodily kinesthetic learners learning through touching, moving, and doing. Engaging more senses creates a deeper learning experience.

Theory of Multiple Intelligences. Howard Gardner proposed the theory of multiple intelligences in 1983.[7] The intelligences now include spatial, linguistic, logical-mathematical, bodily-kinesthetic, musical, interpersonal, intrapersonal, naturalist, and existential/spiritual. We like to draw these in what we call the "learning pie," shown in Figure 7.1. (See also page 171 and later in this chapter to see this tool in action.)

Although some theorists debate whether empirical evidence validates the existence of these intelligences,[8] we use the intelligences in a "learning design pie"—a planning tool that allows a teacher to select tools and design projects to reach the many modalities of how humans function. Typically, existential intelligence is left off the planning pie, as it is the kind of intelligence "seeking out answers to the larger questions in life"[9] but you may choose to add this. Certainly choice is also about adding meaning to the learning process. Author Stacia Tauscher says, "We worry about what a child will become tomorrow, yet we forget he is someone today." Sometimes students do need to know why, and that can give meaning.

Universal Design for Learning (UDL). The National Center on Accessible Instructional Materials, under the research of Principal Investigator Dr. David Rose of Harvard's Graduate School of Education, has developed a method for planning lessons called universal design for learning (UDL). This method encourages teachers to present information and content in different ways, differentiate the ways that students can express what they know, and stimulate interest and motivation for learning.

Even if one theory mentioned above were disproved, the preponderance of evidence indicates that when students receive information in a variety of modalities, they learn better than just being lectured to. Although there is a time and place for lecture, it is never 100 percent of the time. Increased modalities in instructional

FIGURE 7.1 Blank Learning Design Pie Planning Tool

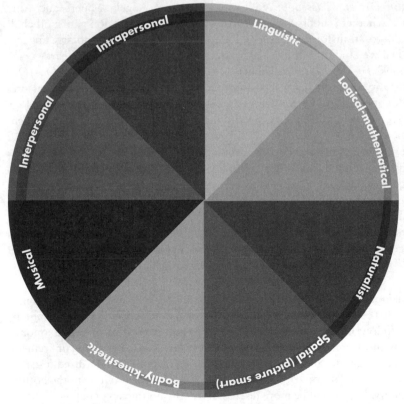

delivery equals more learning. Technology makes multisensory delivery easier than ever before.

Student Engagement.   A great cartoon of a little boy yelling back at his mom as she drops him off for the first day of school says, "You can make my body go to school, but my mind will be outside running through sprinklers." We can put a child's body in a desk, but only the child can put his or her heart into learning.

There is a learning method that has a step that says "Require learner participation." You can require a lot of things, but students do what they choose to do. Choice is about engaging children's interest; otherwise, their minds will be on Xbox or X-Men while they are putting x's on their worksheets.

In his 1987 book *Achievement Factors,* Vicki's college professor Dr. Eugene Griessman[10] interviewed hundreds of the most successful people of that generation and compiled their stories into common themes. From Isaac Asimov ("I guess the essence of life for me is finding something you enjoy doing that gives meaning to life"[11]) or Jack Lemmon (who, standing on stage as a 9-year-old student at Rivers Country Day School in Chestnut Hill, Massachusetts, decided "I think I like this"[12]) to author Vicki Davis (sitting in her dorm room researching Griessman's assigned paper and saying to herself, "I love writing and wish I could do this"), the common thread among these successful individuals was a passion for their work. We can all be that teacher who helps students find something they love to do; it is part of our mission.

Good teachers have a passion for helping students find their passion. In their book *Passion Driven Classroom,* educational authors Angela Maiers and Amy Sandvold ask whether schools have an "achievement gap or passion gap" and challenge teachers to "transform a learner's energy and passion into scholarly engagement."[13] When we tap into a child's passions, they fully engage and can learn.

In his book, *The World Is Flat,* Thomas Friedman has a formula: $CQ + PQ > IQ$.[14] It means curiosity quotient (CQ) + passion quotient (PQ) is greater than a person's intelligence quotient (IQ). When a student loves your subject area or the technology in your classroom, they will learn more than the naturally gifted student who is unengaged and bored.

DIGITAL CITIZENSHIP AREA OF UNDERSTANDING

Habits of Learning

But we would modify Friedman's formula further to be $IQ (CQ+PQ) + HQ = success$. This means intelligence (IQ) multiplied by curiosity (CQ) and passion (PQ) plus habit quality (HQ) equals personal success. We think that intelligence, curiosity, and passion are not enough. Without good work habits, such a student could wander aimlessly from topic to topic. The habit quality (HQ) includes good work habits such as persistence, organization, focus, and taking advice from mentors. Students with intelligence, curiosity, passion, and good work habits are destined to become an unstoppable force that will shape the world tomorrow.

Critical Thinking.   In Bloom's Revised Taxonomy of Higher-Order Thinking,[15] "remember" is the lowest form of thinking. "Understand, apply, analyze, evaluate, and create" follow in that order, with "create" being at the top of the taxonomy. Unfortunately, most standardized tests only measure lower-order thinking or "remember." If we allow our education system to be defined solely by standardized tests, we will have a lower standard of learning in all our schools as we gravitate to the bottom of the taxonomy. (There will be more discussion on this in the next chapter.)

Critical thinking is essential for students. In *The Skill Content of Recent Technological Change: An Empirical Exploration*, authors Autor, Levy, and Murnane found that a significant increase in "abstract tasks" is required of U.S. workers with a decline in routine and manual tasks.[16] It is not possible to memorize a chart or some dates and solve an abstract problem. Memorization can make you the king of the routine. But memorization without understanding makes one a pauper of problem solving. Problem solving requires critical thinking and creativity. (See the presentation linked to the QR code in the margin.)

"Technological Change and Job Polarization: Implications for Skill Demand and Wage Inequality," a presentation by David H. Autor

http://tinyurl.com /workforce-changes

Reaching Every Child.   If Helen Keller were in your school today, would she become the Helen Keller we know and admire? Helen Keller, blind and deaf but incredibly intelligent and talented, was reached by her teacher Anne Sullivan, who broke through the barriers to teach her to sign and write.

Keller said, "What a blind person needs is not a teacher but another self."[17] Technology can, in effect, give students "another self" like it did for Tim in the opening story. Technology has enabled genius Stephen Hawking to continue to communicate, although he has been unable to talk since a bout of pneumonia in 1985. Students who have dysgraphia (inability to write legibly) can record lectures on their mp3 player and transcribe using voice recognition software like Dragon Naturally Speaking.[18] Assistive technology has become a tremendous opportunity for people with many types of disabilities. In fact, pop musician Stevie Wonder, blind since just after birth, thanked Apple cofounder Steve Jobs (just prior to his death in October 2011) for his efforts to make iOs products accessible to everyone, "Because there's nothing on the iPhone or the iPad that you can do that I can't do."[19]

When most of us reflect on the most meaningful educational experiences of our lives, we typically don't name a test but rather the projects, interactions, and moving environments of learning that tested our character, creativity, and critical thinking ability. Choices in delivery, assessment, and learning environments help move learning away from the industrial age to the 21st century.

tweetable
Choices in delivery, assessment, and learning environments help move learning away from the industrial age. #flatclass

TEACHING IN THE CHOICE-RICH CLASSROOM

Isn't it interesting that when children "play school" that a child stands at the front, often with a long twig in hand, telling the other children lined up in rows to be quiet and listen. Why do we call this school?

And yet, many who practice this amazing form of choice-rich learning are still listening to the lies that say a teacher must lecture or a teacher is not teaching. Sometimes, project-based learning seems chaotic. It might feel like the teacher is abdicating some responsibility or perhaps even "losing control" of the class. We must quash the lie that the most legitimate form of teaching is lecture. Nothing could be further from the truth.

Teachers Should Be Filters, Not Fact Repositories.   Content is important but pedagogy is as important. Without effective pedagogies, content remains words on a page, never crossing the synapses of the student's mind.

"Teachers are the filters for the day-to-day reality of school. Whether we are aware of it or not, behavior sets the tone," says Todd Whitaker in *What Great Teachers Do Differently*.[20]

How is a teacher a filter? When Vicki was at the first Flat Classroom Conference in Qatar, she had her ninth-grade students working and learning in **Open Sim**, a virtual world. She would "meet" her students on the island each evening her time (during their class) to see their work. The students had "made friends" with Reaction Grid organizers (the host of their island), so while Vicki was gone, they used their personal learning network to surpass Vicki's knowledge.

After contacting the Reaction Grid organizers and learning her students were indeed ready for this skill, Vicki unlocked their ability to **terraform** and asked them to teach her terraforming techniques when she returned from the Middle East. In this case, Vicki filtered the activity (she knew what they would be doing and that it was safe) and knew it would surpass the objectives she had outlined for the week. Vicki was a filter for a powerful learning experience but removed herself from having to be the expert. She controlled the pedagogical pathway, not the content knowledge itself.

ISTE STANDARDS

NETS.T 1
Facilitate and Inspire Student Learning and Creativity

21st CENTURY SKILLS

C21 STANDARDS AND ASSESSMENT

C21 CURRICULUM AND INSTRUCTION

Teachers Should Be Pedagogical Customizers, Not Pedagogical Standardizers.   There is a difference between using content standards and pedagogical standards. Unfortunately, there are many in education who think that scripting teachers and having every classroom "on the same page" is the answer. We don't think this is always best.

The concepts of teacherpreneurship discussed in Chapter 3 are essential to delivering personalized learning to students. Empowering teacherpreneurs who are adept at constructing personalized learning opportunities is at the heart of a choice-rich classroom environment and quality learning experiences. Susan Israel, author of *Breakthroughs in Literacy,* says, "What we learn . . . is that teaching is more than giving students a choice . . . or linking instruction with learning styles. It is about personalized teaching for specific students, lessons, or skills."[21]

Personalized learning starts with a personal interest in students themselves. "Students who believe their teachers are interested in them as people are much more likely to behave than students who believe the opposite."[22] Customizing the learning process to reach all learning styles and engage the interests of the students starts with their teachers—who should repeat to themselves, "Meaning begins with me."

Teachers Should See Technology as Enabling, Not Replacing.   Some have predicted that computers will completely replace teachers.[23] However, computers cannot as yet look a child in the eye, realize that the child was awake all night, and have sensitivity to family circumstances. Computers cannot do everything.

Good teachers can become better with technology and make their own job easier! Think of it this way: A carpenter could build a whole house with a hammer and one screwdriver; however, specialized tools such as nail guns can help the carpenter make the house faster and stronger, as well as make better use of his or her time! Well-selected technology helps a teacher make better use of valuable time.

The journey into using technology is about making progress, not about using geeky words and reading user manuals! Some teachers start by using simple **document**

cameras, letting students record information on their cell phones, creating **web quests,** or having email pen pals from other countries.

The drive for technology integration isn't to rev up proud parents but to transport learners to a better education. It is never about the technology; rather, it is about what the technology lets us do. Focus on what you want to do and it will make it easier to select the technology.

Teachers Should Be Coaches, Not Lecturers. "Most people view didactic methods such as 'telling and testing' as the only expedient way to teach. It is expedient, for the teacher, but it is not effective for the student. This is not only an ineffectual method of teaching but it actually inhibits learning," says Jerry Goebel in his book *Reimagining Education*.[24] Some believe that lectures should be banned from schools,[25] but this makes no sense. Lecturing is part of learning, but it should be less a part of learning because it is typically passive.

In 2010, while Vicki observed her school's state winning football coaches, she had an epiphany: These coaches know football and have played it themselves. They have excellent content knowledge. But the measure of those coaches is not whether *they* know football, but whether they can *teach* football and *elicit* a masterful performance of football under stress from their players. Once a week for an hour they review film and analyze past performance. Their practices are spent doing learning and reinforcement, with a few minutes at the beginning and end of practice for setting the game plan, reviewing, and building *esprit de corps*. Kids with complementary field positions stay afterwards to help each other. Our classrooms should be like that!

ISTE STANDARDS

NETS.T 2
Design and Develop Digital-Age Learning Experiences and Assessments

Many teachers who use project-based learning open and end class in a similar fashion. The class opens with the game plan for the day. The class ends with a review, helping the students know that what they are doing has a purpose and meaning for their lives. Projects are reviewed afterwards to discuss performance and how it can be done better next time. Morale is an important part of classroom success. Students are a team and depend on each other for help and learning. If harnessing individual intrinsic motivation is the holy grail of education, unleashing group motivation ("You are 'Knights of the Round Table!'") helps more students find it.

Teachers Should Be Actively Engaged. As seen the Effective Web 2.0 Classroom, as shown in Figure 7.2, the engaged teacher underlies everything. He or she moves throughout the room listening, answering questions, but never trying to control the creative process.

ISTE STANDARDS

NETS.T 1
Facilitate and Inspire Student Learning and Creativity

21st CENTURY SKILLS

C21 LEARNING ENVIRONMENTS

As Mark Twain says, "We should be careful to get out of an experience only the wisdom that is in it—and stop there; lest we be like the cat that sits down on a hot stove lid. She will never sit on a hot stove lid again—and this is well; but also she will never sit down on a cold one anymore." Good teachers help students frame meaning into experience. For example, a student may have problems when another student pastes plagiarized work on their project wiki. The angry student could draw the conclusion that "people from that country just don't respect copyright—it is part of their culture." This student is making a "cat on a hot stove" generalization, an incorrect conclusion. Wise teachers help point out stereotypes. Generalizations like this are usually disproven with personal relationships. This is one of the most important outcomes of global collaborative experiences.

FIGURE 7.2   Pillars of the Effective Web 2.0 Classroom

Effective Web 2.0 Classroom

Web safety & privacy

Information literacy

Web citizenship

Web teamwork

International web activities

Accountability

The engaged teacher

Teachers Should Be Human, Not Perfect.   Look close enough and every teacher has something to improve. Allow students to see you learn. Admit mistakes when you make them. Laugh often, but continue to retain responsibility and accountability for the direction in your classroom.

While in class one day, one of Vicki's students came across a website that said "Microsoft Firefox 2007 can deliver online pornography at blazing fiery speeds." After verifying that over 1,700 **blogs** had linked to this site and never having seen a **parody website**, Vicki wrongly assumed this was legitimate and blogged about it.[26] It was embarrassing when commenters pointed out the site was a fake parody, someone's idea of humor.

Rather than "cover it up," she edited the blog post to share how even when someone verifies things that person can still be fooled and to share the meaning of a parody site. (Links do not mean authenticity.) Then, the next day the class dissected the website and discussed recommendations for "Mrs. Vicki to not be taken again." Openness meant a powerful lesson in digital citizenship. Mess-ups can be learning opportunities if the person will get up, fess up, and educate up on how to handle it differently next time.

Teachers Should Have Personality, Not Uniformity.   Some teachers are musicians; others are talented writers. So one teacher may begin integrating technology by using audio and podcasts, whereas another might use blogging. Others may be scared of technology, but have found a simple technology like Voicethread or a wiki that they want to use.

When teachers are allowed to begin using technologies that build on their individual strengths, they become more engaged and excited. Although there is a case to be made that all students should be exposed to a wide variety of technology tools, there is also the fact when teachers select tools within their strengths it will allow the teacher to be more engaged and comfortable.

For this reason, perhaps one teacher in each department could be the lead teacher for a certain technology, as teachers share learning spaces and teachersource participation. Every teacher shouldn't have to master every technology. For example, a teacher comfortable with GPS and Google Earth may lead a geography unit using Google Earth while another teacher with a fluency in debate may lead a Voicethread debate. We can standardize content without drubbing the meaning, vigor, and enthusiasm out of teachers and students by forcing the standardization of content delivery. Standardization of content delivery is often just another word for "boring" (for teachers *and* students.)

When a teacher is student-centric, the teacher is willing to learn new things and move past his or her comfort zone. Teacherpreneurship will see teachers start with technologies interesting to the teacher and move past that into technologies interesting to the students. The point is to start somewhere.

SELF-ASSESSMENT SURVEY

PDToolkit
for
***Flattening Classrooms,
Engaging Minds***
See the survey results in the online PDToolkit before moving on to the next section.

Before moving to the next part of this chapter, we invite you to take this self-assessment survey. We also suggest you discuss these questions with colleagues, including your wider learning network, to determine your current level of confidence and ability with choice strategies.

1. **If you are already in the classroom, what area do you think needs improvement?**

2. **What technology or learning method would you like to learn more about?**

3. **What are your hobbies and passions? Include ways you like to express yourself, including arts or any particular technologies you enjoy.**

4. **List any technologies that you are already "ready" to try or use.**

5. **If an administrator or other teacher walks into my classroom and the students are doing projects, I feel the need to apologize.**

   a. Yes   b. No   c. Maybe

6. **I feel like I should know everything about my subject and am uncomfortable if a student seems to know something I don't know.**

   a. Yes   b. No   c. Maybe

(continued)

Self-Assessment Survey *(continued)*

7. What is your teaching situation?

a. I teach a small number of students each week and therefore get to know all of them very well.

b. I teach fewer than 120 students each week and generally get to know them well.

c. I teach over 120 students each week and am challenged by knowing them in depth. Sometimes I cannot remember their names, and struggle to identify their learning needs in some cases.

d. I am a current teacher and none of the above describes me.

e. I am not a teacher.

8. How much do you lecture in your classroom?

a. 90 percent of instruction or more

b. 50 to 89 percent of instruction time

c. Less than 50 percent but more than 15 percent

d. 15 percent of the time or less

e. Lecture? What is a lecture? I never do this.

9. How often do you sit at your desk assessing work or doing work unrelated to the classroom while students are working? (*Note:* This does not include working in online spaces where the class may also be working.)

a. More than ¾ of the time

b. More than ½ of the time but less than ¾

c. More than ¼ of the time but less than ½

d. Less than ¼ of the time

e. Never. I am always up and working with students.

10. If I make a mistake of some kind in class, I typically respond by

a. Denying that I made a mistake

b. Ignoring it and hoping no one will notice

c. Admitting my mistake but being hugely embarrassed

d. Admitting my mistake, perhaps laughing about it, and using it as a teachable moment if necessary

21st CENTURY SKILLS

C21 LEARNING ENVIRONMENTS

SCHOOL **Creating a "Choice" Environment for Learning**

Learning environment has been researched since Halpin and Croft in 1963 created an instrument called the Organizational Climate Descriptive Questionnaire (OCDQ).[27] The learning environment for the purposes of this chapter includes the spaces inhabited by students, including learning centers, online spaces, and the materials, supplies, and resources available to them as well as the administrative effect on that environment. The learning climate is the tone or atmosphere of the teaching setting, and this is part of the environment. Other factors that are part of the learning environment, such as school safety and overall discipline, are beyond the scope of this book except as related to citizenship (see Chapter 5). It is helpful to review the Seven Spaces of

Learning as proposed by Ewan McIntosh when planning spaces based on the premises in this chapter.

THE SEVEN SPACES OF LEARNING, WRITTEN BY EWAN MCINTOSH[28]

 Matt Locke at the UK's Channel 4 Television Corporation first came up with the notion of six "spaces of social media," to which I've added a seventh. I also took these media spaces and sought what kind of learning might take place in each of them.

- *Secret spaces.* When we're engaged in secret spaces (sending text messages to one other person), as opposed to public publishing spaces (like a webpage or even sending a "text" to our hundreds of Twitter followers), our body language is totally different; therefore the consideration of physical space has to be made. Glasgow's Saltire Centre features inflatable igloos into which one can escape for a moment of learning intimacy with oneself. [*Note from authors:* This library has doubled its foot traffic with a dramatic redo.] Technology examples: SMS (texting), IM (instant messaging), email.
- *Group spaces.* Digital group spaces work because learners are engaged around the question of how we help people to find their friends and engage with them in sharing and conversation. In school, it seems like most spaces, indoors and out, are geared up to making this virtual "gathering around the fireside" hard or impossible to achieve. Technology examples: Facebook, MySpace, etc.

Comfortable bean bag chairs for reading dot the second floor of this library at St. Cyprians.

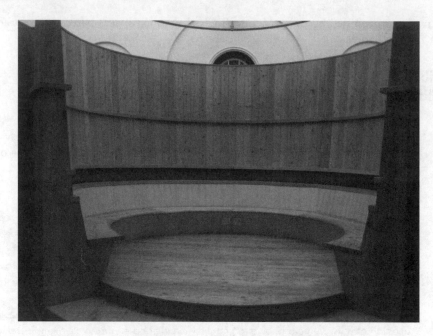

Here, you see one of the three story pods in the library of
St. Cyprian's in Capetown South Africa that allow a class to
gather and hear a story.

- *Publishing spaces.* Online, when we publish a blog post or put up a photo on Flickr, we're hoping that people might find it. We're publishing. In schools' physical spaces, we might start to think about how digital artifacts of learning can be shared through the building space, much like N Building in Tokyo, where Tweets from within a building are broadcast to its shell through a QR code painted large on the building exterior and viewed through mobile phones. Technology examples: Flickr, YouTube, blogs, etc.
- *Performing spaces.* Performing spaces allow people to be someone or something they are not. In buildings, these performing spaces are traditionally epic concert halls. I wonder what the opportunity is for transforming learning spaces into temporary universes where we can immerse ourselves in a "imagine if" environment. Technology example: MMORPGs (World of Warcraft).
- *Participation spaces.* When employees of IDEO, a global design consultancy firm, meet to solve a problem, it's not clear where the boundaries of certain space and employees' ownership of that space lie. And why are we not turning our schoolyards and grounds into Edible Schoolyards—the ultimate in participation spaces, surely, where we no longer pay for grounds men to mow immaculate lawns, but turn the entire space into a community garden that feeds the school and teaches us all about the sustainability issues of organic food? Technology examples: Meet up, Threadless, MySociety.
- *Data spaces.* Some schools such as Gullane in East Lothian have gone as far as showing the data of their energy consumption and production, but few if any have gone as far as creating a participation space where the community can actually use that data to change their actions.

- *Watching spaces.* These are the ones schools are probably most geared up to at the moment. However, if we change everything about the school from the norm being the front of the classroom to the norm being having no "front" in the classroom, then we have a wonderful opportunity to really celebrate the great lecture for what it is. TED Talks have proven the global appetite for superb, but short, lectures. By making the norm in schools one of collaboration and teacher as a guide, then we can afford to create genial spaces for lectures—spaces that thrill and delight and celebrate those occasional moments of lone insight that only a real, living, flesh and blood teacher or visitor or student could ever offer. Examples: television, cinema, sports, theatre, etc.

PLACES: CREATING A PHYSICAL ENVIRONMENT CONDUCIVE FOR LEARNING

Uniform rows of desks with school supply stock posters adorning the wall just don't have the magnetism of the local coffee shop with lush chairs, wireless access, computers, and spaces for conversation or reading. Some schools have responded by reinventing their schools into places for coffee and conversation. The adage "You attract more bees with honey than with vinegar" is true with schools' designing spaces full of furniture, fixtures, and technology to attract and retain learners for different learning experiences—both group and individual.

Libraries Are Being Replaced with the Learning Commons.   When a leading expert on library design, David Loertscher, considered revising his book *Taxonomies of the School Library Media Program*,[29] he realized, "I had pushed the traditional model

DAVID V. LOERTSCHER
@twitter
http://davidloertscher
.wordpress.com

This is a look into the student "pit" at the International School Dhaka in Bangladesh. Students go here to work, study, and communicate in this 1:1 laptop school.

Furniture can be used to create spaces for learning and talking with a class. Move away from desks to comfortable places that invite conversation, discussion, and collaboration.

See pictures of the transformation in Valerie Digg's slideshow at http://tinyurl.com/lib-commons

of school libraries about as far as it could go. We don't need a revision. We need a reinvention."[30] Thus, Loertscher and his colleagues coined the concept of the **Learning Commons,** defined as "the showcase for high-quality teaching and learning—a place to develop and demonstrate exemplary educational practices. It will serve as the professional development center for the entire school—a place to learn, experiment with, assess, and then widely adopt improved instructional programs."[31]

Previously, a library was judged by the books on the shelves. Overall, it was a read-only library, where students left books untarnished and pristine for the next reader. In the Learning Commons, what you can access is what you get (see Figure 7.3). In this read/write environment students may write, photograph, record, film, create, and collaborate. The standard resources of books, films, and audiotapes are augmented by text, pictures, videos, immersive experiences, ebook checkout, and guests.

In the Chelmsford High School Library's central information desk, where Valerie Diggs is the librarian, she has painted the words, "Ask, Ask, Ask" and in the café area the words "Think" and "Create."[32] One day a week students and faculty arrive early to converse and learn at the Java Room while local vendors serve coffee. For Listening Lunches, students bring their lunch or a treat to share while other students perform.

Using the Learning Design Pie Planning Tool shared earlier in this chapter, see how Valerie has designed an area that incorporates the different intelligences, as shown in Figure 7.3. She is differentiating her library! A Learning Commons may look many different ways, as shown in the photographs of various schools around the world.

School Design.   Before buildings are constructed Ewan McIntosh says that parents, students, and teachers should discuss what they would like to do in a new building

FIGURE 7.3 Learning Commons Design Using Pie Planning Tool

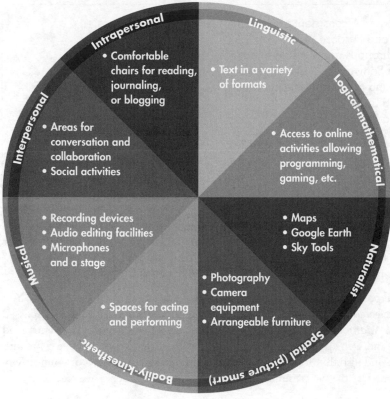

and "then design a flow between the right mixes of spaces for the projects they will undertake."[33] Learning and space design always starts with what you want to do. Effective learning spaces give teachers more choices beyond their own classroom and create an ecosystem for learning if well planned using the seven spaces proposed by Ewan earlier in this chapter.

SPACES: DESIGNING ELECTRONIC SPACES FOR CHOICE

Electronic spaces should be constructed with as much intention and purpose as the physical property of a school. Most schools consider electronic spaces as an afterthought and consequently they are often disjointed and require duplication of work. Others have older buildings and haven't constructed any spaces with the intention of technology-friendly work environments.

Building a Classroom Framework. When building an online classroom framework, there are several considerations, as shown in Figure 7.4.

Establish a Home Base. One of the first concepts of constructing a class framework is to establish a consistent **home base**. Also called a launching pad by some, students know where to start their learning process, and how to find teachers' assignments

ISTE STANDARDS

NETS.T 2
Design and Develop Digital-Age Learning Experiences and Assessments

21st CENTURY SKILLS

C21 LEARNING ENVIRONMENTS

FIGURE 7.4   Elements of a Classroom Framework

- Home Base: A consistent place to start learning experiences.
- Variety and Purpose
  - Synchronous and Asynchronous
  - Local Software and Web Apps
  - Learning Styles and Intelligences
- Learning Legacy
- Learning Portals
- Trusted Tools
- Trendy Tools with a Purpose
- Monitoring Plan
- Multisensory
- Content Syndication

and networking spaces. This can be a content management system like Moodle or Blackboard, a wiki, a PLN portal, or really just about any tool as long as it is consistent and part of students' habits, as discussed in Chapter 6.

Variety and Purpose.   These two ingredients are also important as you select tools. You need a well selected assortment of asynchronous and synchronous tools, as discussed in Chapter 4. *Additionally*, a mix of locally installed software (both proprietary and open source) and web apps are appropriate for ensuring that students have a breadth of experience and also that lessons can continue if Internet bandwidth or connectivity problems occur. Use the pie-planning tool to make sure all students are reached.

Learning Legacy.   Many students receive an annual with photos capturing the memory of their year. Why not include a DVD sleeve for students to archive a digital portfolio of their own work and photos?

Schools should have electronic portals of learning flourishing with the best student and teacher-created resources and places for conversation and rankings. For example, each year a teacher could have students build video games to study concepts. Next year's students can "play" the artifacts made by prior students and then create another set of video games for another concept. Every year the learning legacy grows with students producing content for future students. The audience of a learning legacy can be contemporaries, across geography, or across generations. Learning legacies are also created when students perform authentic research and take action in a way that can benefit society, like the DeforestACTION project sponsored by Taking IT Global.

Some schools require four-year portfolios as a requirement of graduation to document the proof of learning. Furthermore, one could argue that cheating is pretty easy on a standardized test, but cheating on an electronic portfolio would be extremely difficult. There can be future professional benefits of a good portfolio—Julie's student Atif was contacted after graduation and was able to sell his website he created as a student to share tourism facts about Bangladesh.

Customized Learning Portals.   Personal learning portals should be part of major projects and establish the concept of a personal learning network (PLN) discussed in Chapter 3. Development of a PLN can be done using an RSS reader for older students

21st CENTURY SKILLS

C21 INTERDISCIPLINARY THEME:
Financial, Economic, Business and Entrepreneurial Literacy; Environmental Literacy

ISTE STANDARDS

NETS.S 4
Critical Thinking, Problem Solving, and Decision Making

DIGITAL CITIZENSHIP AREA OF UNDERSTANDING

Habits of Learning

or a website like Portaportal or Netvibes. Students must get past the push technologies of typing a request in a search engine and learn the pull technologies that can make them efficient and competitive.

Trusted Tools.   Choose classroom tools with purpose, not just because they are trendy. Select technologies that build on principles you know are effective. For example, the wiki builds on proven cooperative learning strategies such as **think-pair-share** and the jigsaw (Chapter 3). By migrating proven cooperative learning strategies from face-to-face learning, it is easy to move cooperative learning onto a wiki.

Trendy Tools for a Purpose.   There is a place for the trendy. It is OK to "play" with something trendy that has been vetted and tested by the teacher for a lesson or two as part of having an agile curriculum (Chapter 3). Students learn to find mistakes, troubleshoot, and solve their own problems. Students can also compare and contrast tools in meaningful ways like the Venn diagram shown in Figure 7.5.

Trendy websites often fail, but you can learn anyway. When the virtual talking history site, Virsona, emerged, Vicki saw this as a way to have her students create talking icons from the history of computing. Unfortunately, Virsona allowed only five computers from one location to log in and edit at the same time. Although the Virsona didn't work as planned, after troubleshooting, the class had a valuable and needed lesson on the way computers are numbered on the Internet.

Other factors are there that students need to understand. In China, one day a tool is available through the **Great Firewall of China** and the next day it will be blocked (with no warning). Julie, as E-Learning Coordinator, bought a school Voicethread account at Beijing BISS International School,[34] ran workshops, and implemented the tool across the school. It was gaining momentum, and teachers and students were excited, but then it was suddenly blocked by the government![35]

tweetable

Choose classroom tools with purpose, not just because they are trendy #flatclass

ISTE STANDARDS

NETS.S 4
Critical Thinking, Problem Solving, and Decision Making

21st CENTURY SKILLS

C21 LEARNING AND
INNOVATION SKILLS:
Critical Thinking and Problem
  Solving

C21 INFORMATION, MEDIA,
AND TECHNOLOGY SKILLS:
ICT Literacy

**DIGITAL CITIZENSHIP AREA
OF UNDERSTANDING**

Safety, Privacy, Copyright, and
Legal

FLAT CLASSROOM™ FRAMEWORK

NAME OF PROJECT: DeforestACTION

WEBSITE URL: http://dfa.tigweb.org

LOCATION: Worldwide

COMMUNICATION: Asynchronous—Taking IT Global Network; Synchronous—Classrooms, Webinars

GENERATION: Current and future generations with a focus on K–12 students

INFORMATION: Online resources and authentic research

TIME: Any time during the year that the teacher determines

LEARNING LEGACY: The aim is for students to create local, national, and international entrepreneurial initiatives that protect and regrow endangered forests and to create local projects promoting awareness and action.

FIGURE 7.5   Venn Diagram Comparison of Word Processors

Google Docs

Many people can edit at one time
Can be made public or private
Toolbar can change with no notice
with an online upgrade

Internet
needed for
both
editors

All
three allow
you to type
and edit and
copy and
paste

Will let you
save a
document

No undo button
Hardest software
for typing
and editing

iNetWord Editor

Internet
not needed
Simple buttons
and toolbars

Microsoft Word

Google Docs and iNetWord Editor
are both free Internet services that
allow you to type and edit documents,
and Google Docs lets many people
edit at one time.

Microsoft Word software
allows you to type. Word
does not need Internet
connection, and you can
use many different things
such as clip art and word
art in it.

On the positive side, leading tech programs must be willing to experiment and beta test. After Twitter was well established, parents and former students of Vicki's remarked about how "cutting edge" the technology program was to have introduced them to this service and spotted the trend before the masses. Beta testing is a learning experience in itself. When Vicki's students beta tested IdeaFlight for Conde Naste, they documented bugs and feature suggestions and had a conference call with programmers. Lots of apps and programs release beta services to the public; this is something all classes can do.

Monitoring.   All public spaces where students are producing should be monitored with RSS, as discussed in earlier chapters. Evaluate the ability for students to message one another and assess whether it can be monitored. As of the writing of this book, many free tools do not allow oversight of student communications using messaging; however, if students are aware of how to document issues, this can be a nonissue for many schools.

The biggest question remains: how students will "hand work in" for assessment. For simplicity, many teachers use the home base or a **content management system** and have students post their work on the page where the assignment was given. Services like Edmodo aggregate these and make it simple to grade the assignments.

Another option is to use tags. **Tags** allow you to label digital artifacts to provide meaning and cataloging. Although tags were first used to provide meaning to the massive amounts of information on the web (folksonomy), they can now be used to help teachers find the work of students in their classroom (taxonomy.)

At the bottom of their artifact, students can usually label the item with a tag. Students may tag their work "turnin,"[36] for example, and the teacher follows that tag

ISTE STANDARDS

NETS.T 2
Design and Develop Digital-
Age Learning Experiences and
Assessments

21st CENTURY SKILLS

C21 LEARNING ENVIRONMENTS

to have work delivered via a virtual in-box the moment students tag and turn in the work. Either way is an efficient way so long as students know, when they are given the assignment, how they are expected to turn it in and teachers know how to find it.

Meaning can also emerge from documents through the use of **word clouds** or **tag clouds**. In Figure 7.6 the authors uploaded this chapter to Wordle and created a word cloud for this chapter. The more a word is used, the larger it is. You can see that this chapter is centered on student learning, teachers, classrooms, and technology with just a glance.

Tag clouds work the same way as a word cloud but ignore everything but the tags used. Many social media websites will automatically generate word clouds and tag clouds for you from students' work. This helps you spot the topics of conversation with just a glance. We think word clouds should be used more often in educational spaces to help teachers stay abreast of what is happening in an efficient way.

Multisensory. The mouse and keyboard just aren't enough! Microphones, cameras, and touch screens are important modes of input as well. Additionally, the motion controllers such as Kinect, Wii, and Microsoft Surface give opportunities for teaching because of the power of bodily-kinesthetic learning integrated into the process.

Tablet devices like the iPad have incredible multisensory apps. T. S. Eliot's masterpiece "The Waste Land" is available on the iPad as an immersive visual experience, including the text synchronized with Eliot's own reading, and manuscripts that show the evolution of the poem. A network of educators at I Education Apps Review (founded by Scott Meech) has emerged to write reviews of educational apps; it is worth joining no matter what the platform.

A fascinating set of augmented reality tools (mentioned in Chapter 3) are emerging around mobile phones and handheld devices. Augmented reality adds meaning on top of the real world surrounding us using GPS and/or barcodes. Australian

ISTE STANDARDS

NETS.T 3
Model Digital-Age Work and
Learning

21st CENTURY SKILLS

C21 LEARNING ENVIRONMENTS

SOCIAL NETWORK
iEducation Apps Review network
http://www.iear.org

SCOTT MEECH
@smeech
http://edreach.us

FIGURE 7.6 Word Cloud for Chapter 7

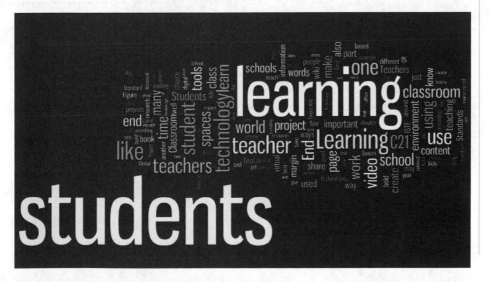

health teacher Jarrod Robinson puts QR codes on his class skeleton so that students may review the bones in the body and use the scanner on their mobile device to check their answers.

These tools are exciting because they incorporate bodily kinesthetic, spatial, nature, and logical mathematical intelligences. Other tools, such as **Claymation** animations and video game technologies, are important for these reasons as well. Harvard University has been testing their own augmented reality game designed to teach math and science literacy skills to middle school students.[37]

Multisensory learning helps all children but, because it engages the body with learning, it is a lifeline of learning for those with learning differences. Some technologies, such as touch screens and interactive white boards (when students can touch them), become even more beneficial when used to **cross the midline**. Crossing the midline happens when a person moves an object across their field of vision and body from one side of the body to the other. Some believe it helps connect the different sides of the brain.[38] Interacting with learning games and activities are great ways to incorporate multisensory learning.

Syndicated Content.   How can students retrieve content? This is becoming increasingly important as some classrooms experiment with the flipped classroom concept.

Sample Class Frameworks.   Artists select their media—the canvas and paints or sketchbook and charcoal—based on what they are trying to do as well as their budget. Likewise, teachers and schools must do the same, knowing that it is OK for teachers to have unique things used in only their classrooms that represent their strengths. It is also important to have systemwide tools such as assessment and course management systems. Here are some example frameworks selected for classrooms, including the framework for each of the authors of this book.

A framework can be simple; it can have one tool or it can have several tools. For example, in the Global Church Partnership Project shown in the case study at the end of this chapter, the schools chose to exhibit their videos as part of a Google Earth file to represent a pilgrimage of sorts into the lives of the priests profiled in the videos. Each school had different video editing programs. It did not matter, though, as long as the students could produce the final product: a video. Each school had a framework in place that allowed them to produce the required outcomes and they were linked on common outcomes but not common software programs.

Vicki's Classroom Framework.   Let's look into the classroom of one author, Vicki. In Figure 7.7, you can see how Vicki filled out the pie planning tool to examine the uses of various tools for her ninth-grade computer fundamentals course. When she started using this method, she realized that some items needed to be added to her framework to make sure all areas of the pie were represented and all intelligences are considered. Although this toolset may seem large, it didn't happen overnight. There is always something new to do and another way to improve! After students know how to use a tool, it is very simple to keep it going.

As shown in Figure 7.8, Vicki's classroom uses several tools and technologies during the course, introduced over a period of time. Let's look at each tool, the reason for selection, and some ways that the tools are introduced.

FIGURE 7.7 Planning Pie for Sample Computer Fundamentals Course

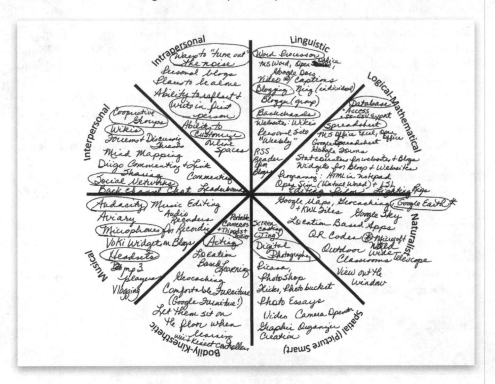

FIGURE 7.8 Sample Classroom Framework of Vicki Davis

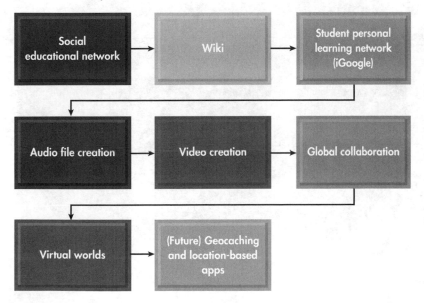

Part 1: Content Management System. Two tools are used for this purpose: Ning in eighth grade and the wiki from ninth grade on.

CMS Tool: Educational Network Larry Rosen, author of *Rewired*, lists five things social networks offer education: students are already using them, they are flexible and use multiple modalities, they allow collaboration, support cooperative learning, and are more immersive than a face to face classroom.[39]

After students have learned all of the letters on the keyboard in the grade 8 keyboarding course and have learned the MLA format for writing papers, they are immediately introduced to Ning as their social network for the class (see Figure 7.9). It looks a lot like Facebook; however, Vicki points that it is not a social network but rather an educational network.

When arriving on the Ning network, the students are asked to create their avatar and customize their profile page, friend those they want to, join the class group, and post a status update (called *micro blogging*). Students write a blog post in first person—they are asked to embed a YouTube video from a popular movie and pretend to be one of the characters in the scene. After two days of class, the students are now ready to use the Ning to share audio, video, and embedded items from other sources like classtools.net. The Ning is home base for their grade 8 year until students learn the wiki in grade 9.

FIGURE 7.9 Planning Pie for Ning Educational Network

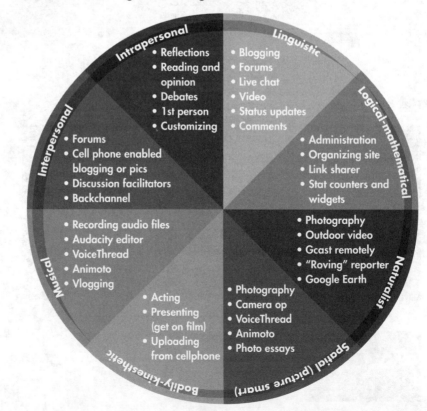

CMS Tool: Wiki The wiki is an envelope that can hold just about anything digital. The first day of grade 9, the wiki is introduced and students learn to collaboratively edit documents. Every change is tracked, providing a lot of control and flexibility. Because this technology underlies collaborative powerhouses such as Wikipedia, it is an important platform for understanding collaboration. This is now home base.

As soon as students go onto the wiki, all of them are asked to edit the same page. As they write over one another and experience the frustration of a poor use of the wiki, they are taught about wiki wars and introduced to the history tab and to how they can copy and revert from the history so that no one's information is ever lost.

One wiki is used for all classes, and lessons are shared on the wiki through using Google Calendar and assignments typed onto the wiki. When students create video games for reviewing for tests, they are embedded into the wiki for other students to play when they review for the exam. See the wiki planning pie in Figure 7.10 for other examples of how the wiki is used.

Part 2: Setting Up a Web 2.0 Personal Learning Environment. A variety of tools and competencies are required to allow students to create and share in this environment.

Student PLN Using iGoogle The RSS reader and student PLNs were discussed in Chapter 3. In Vicki's grade 9 course, students create an iGoogle page the first week

ISTE STANDARDS
NETS.S 2
Communication and Collaboration

21st CENTURY SKILLS
C21 LEARNING AND INNOVATION SKILLS:
Communication and Collaboration
C21 INFORMATION, MEDIA, AND TECHNOLOGY SKILLS:
ICT Literacy

ISTE STANDARDS
NETS.S 3
Research and Information Fluency

21st CENTURY SKILLS
C21 INFORMATION, MEDIA, AND TECHNOLOGY SKILLS:
ICT Literacy

FIGURE 7.10 Planning Pie for Wiki

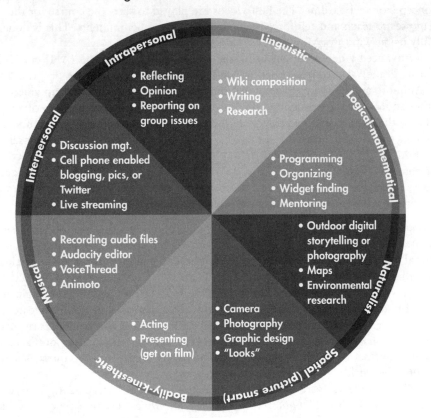

DIGITAL CITIZENSHIP AREA OF UNDERSTANDING

Safety, Privacy, Copyright, and Legal

ISTE STANDARDS

NETS.S 5
Digital Citizenship

NETS.S 6
Technology Operations and Concepts

21st CENTURY SKILLS

C21 INFORMATION, MEDIA, AND TECHNOLOGY SKILLS:
ICT Literacy

ISTE STANDARDS

NETS.S 1
Creativity and Innovation

See Virginia's original YouTube video http://tinyurl.com /youtube-virginia

See Edutopia's video profile of Virginia http://tinyurl.com /edutopia-virginia

ISTE STANDARDS

NETS.S 2
Communication and Collaboration

with links and feeds pertaining to the project at hand. Over the course of the next two years, students will have at least six class-related tabs and are encouraged to have tabs for their major hobbies or interests. The PLN is reinvented with every new topic of study. This portal is the browser start page. Game widgets are allowed only on their personal iGoogle tab and not for use on their iGoogle page used with their school Google apps account. See the extensive information on student PLNs in Chapter 4.

Ability to Create and Upload Photos   Students use the photography tool of their choice (often a cell phone) and learn to capture and upload. Creating screenshots on all devices is taught and used as students document learning and learn to stay safe online.

Ability to Create and Upload Audio   Recording audio is taught about three weeks after introducing the Ning network and is taught when the class uses Glogster to create a graphic blog (glog) about the students' interests. A microphone or handheld is used to record audio, and students are taught how to move the file onto the computer. Students are then taught how to record multiple tracks, edit, and **render** into a final file using Audacity. Students also learn how to render audio into an mp3 (the file type for mp3 players and the Internet) or .wav (the format on CDs) file and the fundamental differences between the two.

Ability to Create and Upload Video   Video is created during the grade 8 keyboarding course as a summative project (see Figure 7.11). Students film a video to teach the concepts of keyboarding. The best videos are played to start the course for the next semester to teach and reinforce the concepts to the other students. This is done initially using Windows Movie Maker or Photo Story.

Advanced video is taught using the American Film Institute (AFI) curriculum during grade 9 as students learn to use Pinnacle Studio and online programs such as Animoto and uStream. Eventually, students learn to use video and **rip** video from other sources (with permission, of course) during the outsourcing phase of projects such as the Flat Classroom Project or NetGen Ed.™ Students are taught to upload to various sources, including YouTube. This led to one student, Virginia, being selected by Edutopia to be part of their digital youth program. Many scholarship competitions now center on creating and uploading videos. When competitions happen, Vicki allows students to choose between current video projects and creating a video to enter in the competition instead. Students are given a choice.

Global Collaboration Competencies   Global collaboration is not a "tool" per se but an attitude of engagement and empowerment. As is discussed throughout this book, global collaboration can take many forms and can include linking between classes, into the community and throughout the world.

In Vicki's class, global collaboration is introduced when students begin blogging on topics of their choice. They learn to comment and communicate with experts. Next, during the Digiteen™ project in the ninth grade, students are encouraged to validate sources and to reach out to experts via Twitter or Facebook. Eventually they present in Blackboard Collaborate and answer questions from around the world.

When students were studying nanotechnology, they attracted the interest of Earl Boysen, author of *Nanotechnology for Dummies*. Using Skype, they video

FIGURE 7.11 Planning Pie for Digital Storytelling

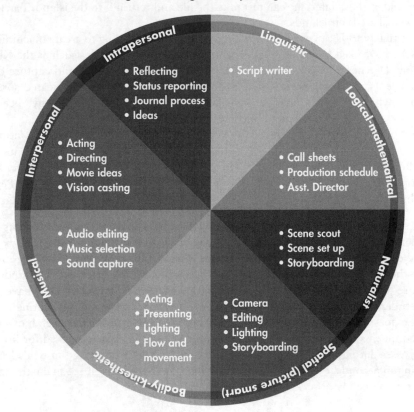

conferenced to learn more and to propose their "inventions" for how nanotechnology may be used in the future.

Virtual World Competencies Second Life, *World of Warcraft*, and *SimCity* are all widely known virtual worlds, but for various reasons they were deemed inappropriate for the use in Vicki's classroom. She wanted a world that was a *tabula rasa* (or "blank slate") that could be built, demolished, and rebuilt in private as students learned freely without a lot of expense. For this reason, Open Sim, hosted by Reaction Grid, is Vicki's virtual world platform, as was mentioned earlier in this chapter. She's also testing Jibe as a platform that is an even more flexible platform that lets students use the world with just a web browser.

Students are able to customize their avatar, create buildings, learn Linden Scripting Language to make things move and fly, and even learn basic physics as they use x, y, and z coordinates. They can terraform or shape land. This allows an incredible amount of teamwork to happen and deep learning as content knowledge is shared.

In Digiteen™ 2008, students created a virtual world called "Digiteen™ Island" to teach digital citizenship on Reaction Grid. In 2010, some students created the Seven Ancient Wonders of the World as a project designed to teach history. Because this is done in Open Sim, Vicki can make a copy of the island (called an **OAR** file, or

C21 INTERDISCIPLINARY THEME:
Global Awareness

C21 LEARNING AND INNOVATION SKILLS:
Communication and Collaboration

C21 INFORMATION, MEDIA, AND TECHNOLOGY SKILLS:
ICT Literacy

NETS.S 1
Creativity and Innovation

Open Archive Record) to use later and wipe it clean and start over. If she wants to use an older island later, she can just take the file and return it to the island. Teachers can even share their islands.

Virtual worlds can even be combined with video capturing to create machinima. Students have used OpenSim but very often use Gaming Consoles such as the Xbox 360 or 3D generators like Google Sketchup or Blender to record and capture dramatic events and plays acted out in virtual words to make a sophisticated sort of cartoon where every avatar is an actor. The NetGen Ed keynote by Peggy Sheehy's students mentioned in Chapter 6 includes machinima.

Chris Dede at Harvard University is showing positive results with the National Science Foundation funded River City virtual world project for teaching an understanding of the scientific method.[40] There are teachers still using Second Life, and this one special-ed teacher, whose story was shared on virtual world pioneer Peggy Sheehy's blog says,

> I must say . . . this Second Life experience is great! My special-ed students are learning this virtual world much quicker than I. Not only are they hands on, they are learning critical thinking skills, navigation, cooperation, among many other skills, and attendance is almost perfect (a big thing for us). The students are teaching me and the confidence that gives them is beyond great. I have one student with major speech issues. He has a very hard time communicating . . . so he doesn't. But in Second Life, this kid becomes alive! I've never seen him smile so much and get so excited about school. My whole class has asked for library passes during lunch. Who gives up lunch? Kids that are having fun while learning in Second Life!! All teachers should get their students in . . . make the time, it won't be lost.[41]

Understanding of Augmented Reality and Use of QR Codes   Augmented reality (as covered in Chapter 3) is a link between the physical world and online world. GPS (global positioning satellites) satellites circle the earth. Devices that use this service include the exact latitude and longitude as part of the file. Twitter and Facebook and the game Foursquare allow people to post their information tagged with GPS coordinates. Many cell phone cameras "geotag" the photo with GPS coordinates without a person realizing it is happening. Because of the safety concerns of tagging with one's exact location on the planet, it is important that students learn the safe use of this technology. We need private spaces for teachers and students. Vicki set up a Foursquare check in location at the school so her students could learn about the service.

Perhaps the best use of augmented reality has been the QR codes handed in with any printed material from the web. By attaching a QR code to a printed web document, Vicki can use her iPad or iPhone to check and assess the quality of the uploaded artifact. It saves time. By snapping a photo, her iPad is viewing the page on the web.

Cloud Storage   Students use a shared Dropbox and print files to PDF for Vicki to annotate in Adobe Acrobat Pro or using an app on her iPad. The students share a notebook using Microsoft One Note and Skydrive. With their Google App accounts, the class shares a Google Docs folder. All of these services used in tandem allow classes to be as paperless as possible.

Julie's Classroom Framework. Let's look at Julie's classroom based on her current classroom practice in grades 9, 10, and 11.[42]

Part 1: Content Management System. Working within the school- determined learning structure, Beijing (BISS) International School has Studywiz[43] as the content/learning management software. It is here that all assessment tasks and course objectives are shared with students and the wider community. It includes an email function, a basic chat room, multimedia sharing, assignment uploading and more. Julie uses this as the first point of call for all classes and to communicate with parents, but quickly moves students out into a Web 2.0 environment, including using Wikispaces as a digital portfolio platform and wiki-centric class collaboration tool.

Part 2: Setting up a Web 2.0 Personal Learning Environment

Social Bookmarking The tool Delicious provides a basis for research and starts the process of online storage as well as interaction and sharing rather than localized bookmarking. Students set up the browser toolbar, explore tagging, folksonomy, and tag clouds.

Wiki There are three parts to this. First, Julie runs a wiki-centric class portal.[44] Students are led from Study Wiz to this portal for further explanations, for collaborative group work and interactions. Second, all students have their own wiki portfolio using Wikispaces, and each student has the responsibility to develop this throughout the year, in conjunction with developing a digital footprint. BISS holds student-led conferences each April where digital portfolios (along with other hard-copy work [e.g., art, design technology]) are the center of discussion about learning between students and their parents.

The third part is belonging to other wikis as needed as part of collaborative projects (e.g., Digiteen™). The ability to work with a wiki is essential for all students: knowing how to edit, add images, embed widgets, design navigation, history, and effective use of discussion.

Educational Network Using Ning, students learn how to belong to a network and behave in a professional learning environment. Students customize profiles, communicate, and understand advanced sharing of multimedia. They can blog here as well.

Blogs Every student has a personal blog used as a process journal for her or his subject. With careful use of categories and tags, students maintain the same blog for all learning, rather than having a handful of blogs for each subject. Teaching in China, Julie has to make constant adjustments to have her students' blog: shifting from Blogger, to Edublogs, and then to an Edublog campus site, which is currently one of the few blogging tools she can use. Blogging via a wiki page has also been a viable option, although lacking authenticity of a real blogging platform.

RSS Reader RSS Reader is essential for all learners. Finding a workable tool in China is a challenge, but iGoogle has been the most (but not always) reliable.

Multimedia Tools and Storage As an Apple 1:1 school, BISS students carry Macbooks and connect via a robust wireless network. There are no computer labs anymore. More and more, it is a one-on-many environment, as iPads, iPhones, and other devices—usually owned by the student—are commonplace in the classroom and students make choices as to what to use when in their learning. These tools support

ISTE STANDARDS

NETS.T 2
Design and Develop Digital-Age Learning Experiences and Assessments

21st CENTURY SKILLS

C21 LEARNING ENVIRONMENTS

ISTE STANDARDS

NETS.S 6
Technology Operations and Concepts

NETS.S 4
Critical Thinking, Problem Solving, and Decision Making

21st CENTURY SKILLS

C21 INFORMATION, MEDIA, AND TECHNOLOGY SKILLS:
ICT Literacy

C21 LIFE AND CAREER SKILLS:
Productivity and Accountability

WEBSITES

Edublogs
http://edublogs.org

ISTE STANDARDS

NETS.S 3
Research and Information Fluency

NETS.S 1
Creativity and Innovation

NETS.S 2
Communication and Collaboration

the creation of audio and video material and enhance communication. In conjunction with mobile technology and multimedia creation students also use Dropbox or other forms of cloud storage.

With many media tools blocked in China, including YouTube and Vimeo, Julie's school relies on less-known media hosting tools, including very popular Chinese tools that work very well. Although the sites are in Chinese, they make uploading and embedding a video possible and quick. Working with wikis and Ning, media uploading is supported for most smaller file needs. Larger media files are problematic and in-house development of media storage that can be made accessible to outsiders via a web interface has been recently developed as a priority. Classrooms and students can now upload locally but also embed to Web 2.0 portals and share multimedia with others around the world.

Global Collaborative Tools In conjunction with all of what has been discussed, in order for students to collaborate globally (as they all do!) other tools are chosen and used to facilitate this. These are introduced either by the teacher or the student as the need arises, and if they become blocked in China, an alternative is sought. Both synchronous and asynchronous communication and sharing require different facility (e.g., Skype, Voicethread), and skill development with a basketful of tools is necessary.

FACES: SUPPORT FOR CHOICE IN THE CLASSROOM

Teachers are not autonomous. They are very interdependent on other teachers, IT support staff, and administrators. Although innovation can happen in one classroom and spread, ultimately schoolwide improvement requires a group of people—All looking ahead, learning and working together. The only nondebatable issue should be the mission: to educate and be student-centric in decision making.

Student-Centric Focus.   Good teachers focus on their students. If many students fail a test, the good teacher tends to blame himself and thinks he should have taught differently. When a good administrator has an entire department struggling, she will look at herself to determine what she can do better. If a teacher's content knowledge is strong, then it comes down to pedagogy. It isn't about "delivery" of content but really about "learning facilitation."

Administrative Leadership.   Poor leaders erect obstacles; good leaders remove them. When talking to Ed Hallisey, principal at Putnam Valley Middle School in 2010, he was in the fifth year of the school's one-to-one laptop project with breakage under 6 percent, no theft, and, according to Ed, a net cost to the district of *5 cents per laptop* after accounting for the grants and funding mechanisms. Every classroom had an interactive whiteboard and the entire campus was wireless with broadband access. What was his secret? "It really isn't me. I supported them [the teachers] until they felt cared for and understood. Now they are described as fearless users of technology."[45] Ed knew that effective technology change is people-centric.

Project Red, a study of technology use in more than 1,000 schools, found that "a strong principal and strong district leadership are among the most important variables when it comes to implementing education technology and transforming schools, which suggests that change management training is especially important for principals involved in large-scale technology implementations."[46]

Good administrators carefully look at how learning is evaluated to ensure that choice can happen. Data can help educators make good decisions (and save them from FEAR: False Evidence Appearing Real), but too much data can paralyze teachers and is the anathema for a differentiated environment.

Effective administrators look at data collected and the paperwork required of teachers and ask: Who is using this? How? Does the use justify the time spent? Is there another way to meet the requirement?

Effective administrators are visionary, but they don't let rapidly changing technology paralyze their decision making as they wait for the next "big thing." We don't know where technology will end up but when leaders educate themselves about best practice in education, it is often simple to see the next thing to do. Sometimes the best thing for a school to do is to do the next thing and not wait for the next "big thing." Given the hype of mass-marketing engines of today's companies, there's always another next big thing around the corner.

ISTE STANDARDS

NETS.T 2
Design and Develop Digital-Age Learning Experiences and Assessments

21st CENTURY SKILLS

C21 LEARNING ENVIRONMENTS

Choice Rich Challenges.   There are many books written on classroom management strategies such as those in *Classroom Management That Works* by Robert Marzano. This book is not intended to give answers to all the pedagogical challenges. However, as one plans for differentiation, it is helpful to be realistic about the challenges of the choice-rich environment, including noise and disruption, group dynamics, disruptive devices, teacher's discomfort with technology, poor use of time, misunderstandings, students who like tests, and lack of vision.

Potential for Noise Level and Disruption.   Some activities, particularly digital filmmaking, can require large unexpected noises. Teach students to give each other "Quiet on the set" orders to keep the noise level down. Also, remember that not everything can be filmed in the classroom.

Group Dynamics.   Many schools have not had their students truly work cooperatively; consequently, students (and teachers) are deficient in these skills. When first implementing cooperative learning strategies, there can be a learning curve.

Disruptive Devices.   Some schools see assistive devices such as mp3 players, iPads, and laptops as toys, and some students misuse the devices. Instead of focusing on best use, some teachers respond to off-task students by taking the item away from everyone instead of holding certain students accountable.

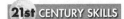

21st CENTURY SKILLS

C21 LIFE AND CAREER SKILLS:
Productivity and Accountability

Teacher Discomfort with Technology.   Change is hard! Start with technologies that teachers are interested in and move forward. Focus on why technology is important and the benefits. Like all people, teachers can get emotional and stubborn when they feel they are being forced.

ISTE STANDARDS

NETS.T 5
Engage in Professional Growth and Leadership

Poor Use of Time.   Technology should support the outcomes that are dictated by the content. It is easy for a weaker teacher to be sidetracked by a technology. Parkinson's Law says that the amount of time one has to perform a task is the amount of time it takes to complete the task.[47] Deadlines are essential. Realize that when students

21st CENTURY SKILLS

C21 LIFE AND CAREER SKILLS:
Initiative and Self-Direction

ISTE STANDARDS

NETS.T 5
Engage in Professional Growth
and Leadership

are enjoying a project (e.g., making videos) they will use every moment you give them.

Misunderstandings.   Some "old school" teachers think lecture is the only way and frown on the chaotic-looking noise-producing methods that happen in such contexts as those proposed here. Communication and professional development can help share the best practices for this type of teaching. Remember that anything in excess or implemented poorly can be dangerous. We need water to live, but give us too much water and we drown!

Some Students Like Tests.   Yes, there are some students doing incredibly well in the academic world. They test well and they learn very well in the academic environment, as it exists today. Some of these students are also extremely challenged when required to create, invent, and perform abstract thinking tasks required in many of the activities advocated in this book. Expect a bit of obstinacy from some of your top students (and their parents.) Some of the best students do not want to work with others and only want to take tests. Their parents may think their students don't have to work with others to be well educated. People are part of life and the well-educated person is well versed in people as well as content knowledge.

Lack of Vision.   Planning and vision are important. Some jump into technology without professional development or have no idea how it is going to be used. You can buy technology, but you can't buy vision into how it should be used to transform learning.

tweetable

You can buy technology
but you can't buy vision.
#flatclass

STUDENTS   The Choices That Increase Student Engagement

Curtis Bonk, author of *The World Is Open,* says,

> Perhaps above all other aspects of Web utilization, the power of choice is what sets the Web of Learning apart from other forms of learning. With opportunities to make personal decisions related to their explorations and potential online discoveries, learners develop a sense of ownership and self-directedness or self-determination.[48]

Putting choice into the classroom will naturally direct students toward their own interests and strengths. It can allow students to "shine" in unimaginable ways.

Curtis Bonk
@TravelinEdMan
http://travelinedman.blogspot
.com

TO QUESTION

Do you want students who blatantly accept what they read on every webpage? What happens if they accept the validity of a Wikipedia entry without proper citations or the blog post of someone who is not an expert on the topic? We need informed, literate people who can ask questions to help verify sources; otherwise, erroneous information can impact decision making.

The ability to form good questions is vital in our search-engine society of inquiry-based learning, and even more important when students construct their

ISTE STANDARDS

NETS.S 4
Critical Thinking, Problem Solving,
and Decision Making

PLNs. Wiggins and McTighe, in *Understanding by Design*, state that creating meaningful questions "render a unit more coherent and make the students' role more appropriately intellectual."[49] Authentic research projects where students do research, catalog, and share are powerful methods of teaching students how to ask and how to verify questions and their answers.

Assignments themselves can be questions. For example, in one class Vicki has students create a time line of the 10 most important events in the history of computing. After embedding them on the wiki for other students to review, the time-line students have to be prepared to defend their selections. Such an assignment requires questioning.

TO BUILD

Students have helped build Ning networks, wikis, and virtual worlds with their teachers. If students help build your technology ecosystem, they are already there. It isn't a matter of getting them engaged—they are engaged!

Let students build using their favorite tools. For example, AP Literature teacher Betsy Caldwell at Westwood Schools assigns a book to each of her AP students to review for the AP Exam and asks them to create "the multimedia artifact of their choice." One semester one student created a self-running PowerPoint to accompany his original song, another built a Flash video animation, and others used Movie Maker, Paint, Photo Story, and Pinnacle Studio. She had every student in the class create a different artifact, yet they were all multimedia and were all very original. Teachers can focus on content when students are allowed to choose their form of expression and have a variety of means in their repertoire.

TO INVENT

When students create a movie concept and pitch it to the class, they are required to invent. They should also be asked to invent in other ways. For example, in computer science they could invent a new way to access the Internet. In history, they could be asked, "What would Winston Churchill and Abraham Lincoln say if they had a conversation about the Vietnam War?"

Bold inventions will be required to improve our future. We need creative inventors like Daizi Zheng, who invented a way to power cell phones with a soda-pop battery,[50] or Pranav Mistri, who invented the wearable "sixth sense" computer. These are perfect projects to become part of one's learning legacy portfolio.

TO CONNECT

In George Siemen's connectivism theory of learning mentioned in Chapter 2, he says, "A learner can exponentially improve [his or her] own learning by plugging into an existing network."[51] In this case, it is very useful to use the Connection Planning Tool (Figure 3.3 on page 51) to plan ahead for diverse connections as part of the learning pathway of a class.

Connect across Time. Students should connect to their future selves by building a learning legacy. Is the work they are doing going to be archived and put in a place where they can retrieve it in the future?

See Pranav Mistri's Ted Talk on sixth sense http://tinyurl.com/ted-pranav

FLAT CLASSROOM™ FRAMEWORK

NAME OF PROJECT: A Whole New Mind—Arapahoe Live Blogging Project

WEBSITE URL: http://karlfisch.wikispaces.com

LOCATION: Ages 16–18, Colorado with Dan Pink and other experts from around the country

COMMUNICATION: Asynchronous—Live blog archive, recording of video; Synchronous—Live blog, live streaming, and interactions with educational experts

GENERATION: Current and older generation

INFORMATION: A New Mind; Online research; Interactions with subject matter experts

TIME: 2 months

LEARNING LEGACY: Recordings and archives of work

Principal Arthur Perry wrote in 1908, "Pride in the school and thought for its name and honor, is not to be gained in a day. It must become a matter of tradition and, once established, be handed down from one set of pupils to another."[52] Students want to leave their mark; let them.

Connect across Geography.   The student should have diversity in the places they connect. Are they connected with their class? School? District? Local Area? Region? Country? World? Space? Students participating in *Yes I Can Science* followed and asked questions of an astronaut on the Space Station![53]

Connect across Generations.   Are students doing meaningful work that allows them to connect and preserve learning from older generations in authentic learning experiences? Are they creating learning experiences for future generations (i.e., recording "time capsules" about today's experiences for others to learn from later)? Are they mentoring younger students? Do they have learning experiences with older students? Are they teaching older generations about things (e.g., technology) that they know?

Best-selling author Dan Pink connects with Karl Fisch's classroom for their "Pink Project" every year, and leading global collaborative researcher Don Tapscott links with the NetGen Ed™ project mentioned in this book every April. Music superstar Taylor Swift read a book as thousands of elementary-aged students tuned in to her webcast in late 2010!

Karl Fisch
@karlfisch
http://thefischbowl.blogspot.com

Connect to a Body of Knowledge.   Do students have the research skills and literacies that allow them to connect with teachers, other students, learning resources, subject matter experts, networks of learning, and learning communities? Are they allowed to connect, inquire, and learn? Is the channel of information open for students between them and these resources?

FLAT CLASSROOM™ FRAMEWORK

NAME OF PROJECT: Global Virtual Classroom—Web Design Contest

WEBSITE URL: http://www.virtualclassroom.org

LOCATION: Global

COMMUNICATION: Asynchronous—Web design work; Synchronous—collaboration and discussion with partners

GENERATION: peer co-creation; students on a team with other schools

INFORMATION: Knowledge on web design gleaned from a variety of sources

TIME: Several months

LEARNING LEGACY: Website and best practices recognized through an awards program

TO HAVE MEANING

Perhaps this best relates to the existential intelligence in Howard Gardner's theory. Ernie Easter's students in rural Maine participated with a Maine Online history museum to create living history artifacts. Students are tree banding and measuring trees for scientists at the Smithsonian Institute for the Shout Learning project[54] and participating in authentic research at the same time. Other students are participating in Taking IT Global's DeforestACTION project to protect rain forests.

Marsha Goren's students in Israel built a School of Kindness with two classes in the United States as part of the Global Virtual Classroom Project.[55] (Marsha is profiled in the case study at the end of this chapter.) This alliance of schools worked "to spread kindness in our schools, community, and the world—through acts of kindness." The students created a common website and interacted on NiceNet,[56] a free resource provided by technology professionals around the world.

When students see how content truly relates to the world, they are more willing to invest their time and energy into that content. How many students moan, "But I'll never use this" when tuning out on a teacher? Students have a choice. Projects with meaning help students want to be involved.

TO UNDERSTAND

Students want to learn! Teachers can interact with each student in a slightly different way based upon the student's needs (see Figure 7.12). It is vital that a rubric is provided for every project to make it easy to track the work of each student as a teacher moves around the room to coach and monitor where each student is in the process.

Joanna Chung, Chinese studies teacher at the Canadian International School of Hong Kong, partnered with Chung-Hsin School in Taiwan to teach Chinese. Joanna's student says, "The Wikispaces and Skype sessions doesn't [sic] make us just memorize some lines and type some random stuff, it actually helps us understand what we are learning through a fun and innovative way that we all like . . . it has helped me

SOCIAL NETWORK
NICE NET INTERNET
CLASSROOM ASSISTANT
http://www.nicenet.org

21st CENTURY SKILLS

C21 STANDARDS AND
ASSESSMENT

FIGURE 7.12 Student Readiness Level

Not Quite Ready	Ready	More Than Ready
During projects, spend one-on-one time daily with student	Specific rubrics	Mentors for others
Sit beside	Self-track rubrics	Awards (Hall of Fame) Competitions with other classrooms
Check off rubric items with student	Over-the-shoulder and verbal reporting to teacher daily	Make them "cool" by teaching cool stuff

improve my Chinese writing and reading skills."[57] There are other creative ways to deliver content, as shown in Figures 7.13 and 7.14.

TO EXCEL

It is especially important to give students ways to make more than a perfect score. The Flat Classroom and NetGen Ed™ projects both have awards programs for the video competition judged by dozens of educators around the world. In addition, teachers often give "Teacher's Choice" awards for the highest scoring projects. Other teachers create a "Hall of Fame" to give examples of best practice to students and to collect the best in one place for a learning legacy for their future students. Flat Classroom projects also have "Students' Choice" awards when appropriate.

In addition to awards, many students are motivated by learning something they consider cool—such as green screen video techniques or getting to use a "real production studio" for their filming, whereas others like being able to shoot at special locations. Every student wants to work on something that interests him or her. There are so

See Flat Classroom award winners at http://tinyurl.com /fcp-awards

See NetGen Ed™ Awards http://tinyurl.com /netgened-awards

FIGURE 7.13 Content Delivery Ideas

Facts/Dates/Time Lines/Events/Definitions
- Classtools.net
- Flashcard exchange
- Group document creation on Google Docs, Backchannels, and Group Notebooks

Details/Significant Individuals
- Wiki group projects
- Link sharing (Diigo)
- Creation of a OneNote or Evernote notebook

Events
- Blog posts of opinion questions
- Role playing
- Video search and embedding
- Interviews of people who experienced it (video)

FIGURE 7.14 Equivalent Products Matrix

If You Used to Do This . . .	Try This . . .
Report	Blog post, cooperative wiki
Skit or play	Digital storytelling, Aviary
Diorama or poster	Digital photography, VoiceThread, Flickr with Hotspots, or Glogster
Advertisement	Animoto movie, digital commercial wiki page, graphic ad embedded in Slideshare or slidecast
Model	How-to videos, www.jingproject.com, www.ustream.com, How-to wikis with resources
Mind map	Gliffy, Classtools.net, Mindmeister
Book	Publish on Lulu or create an ebook

many rewards possible in the differentiated classroom, and the dedicated teacher will customize those rewards based on his or her knowledge of student interests.

It is a great practice to issue press releases in the school's newspaper, on a news blog, or in parent communications to recognize students who create outstanding videos, artwork, or other electronic media that can be shared. Students need a way to make more than a perfect score: They want to excel!

SUMMARY

Albert Einstein said, "I never teach my pupils, I only provide the conditions in which they can learn." Teaching is about providing conditions in which students can learn and that means in some ways we must redefine the definition of teaching that took us through the 1900s into the new look of teaching that is more reflective of research-based best practices and the opportunities afforded us by technology.

Schools should be designed with the intention to allow students choices in how they learn, present, and collaborate with others, as reviewed in Ewan McIntosh's Seven Spaces of Learning. This can include the evolution of the media center into a Learning Commons approach or other approaches that consider the spaces. Schools aren't just about physical places with online space design as an important consideration for teachers. Administrators can make their environment conducive to choice and should be aware of the challenges presented in choice-rich environments. For success in student learning, a student-centered personalized approach should be the focus.

Students should be given choices and the ability to question, build, invent, connect, have meaning, learn, and excel in ways that promote an environment where learning flourishes. It is possible to build on solid research-based best practices and to learn from classrooms and teachers already leading the way globally, to have a classroom utilizing these concepts and have student confidence and achievement rise.

ESSENTIAL QUESTIONS

- What are the reasons for giving students choices in their learning?
- What are the characteristics of teachers in the choice-rich environment?

- Reviewing Ewan McIntosh's Seven Spaces of Learning. What types of spaces are underrepresented in the schools with which you work?
- How does administration affect the choices teachers are able to give students in their classrooms?

◀ Join the online conversation and share your answers at http://tinyurl.com/flatclass-ch7

FLAT CLASSROOM™ 15 CHALLENGES

CHALLENGE 10: GIVE STUDENTS A CHOICE

DO: Write a project plan where students are given a choice in their outcome and topic for a project.

If you are in a school: Do the lesson/project plan(s) with your students. Take notes about what worked and what didn't.

If you are not in a school: Secure potential for a guest teaching spot for your project or share the lesson/project plan(s) with your learning community on a wiki and ask for feedback.

SHARE: After completing the process, share your project plan on your blog or in a community lesson planning resource such as Curriki.[58] If you post it on an online public resource, share the link on your blog with your reflection. **The tag for this challenge is fcc10_choice. Use this when you blog, or share with your group.**

◀ Share what you did with your challenge at http://tinyurl.com/flat15-10

THE FLAT CLASSROOM™ DIARIES

Diary Entry 13

BARBARA STEFANICS, TEACHER, AUSTRIA, VIA EMAIL

Tim had been diagnosed with a form of Asperger's syndrome, which hindered both oral and written communication. He would stutter terribly—often struggling for minutes before he could say the one sentence that he needed to say. In class, we all waited because we knew that that one sentence would have real value and substance. On any written work or test, additional time would make no difference. The longest response he could manage would be only a few words, up to a sentence or two regardless of an extra allocation of time.

One day in the staff room (thank goodness for staff rooms), I bumped into Tim's English teacher. We shared our observations on Tim's problem, and she gave me the first clue that there was a chance for Tim to communicate normally under certain circumstances. She told me that strangely enough, Tim's stuttering did not occur when he was involved in drama. That was quite a surprise.

As part of the Horizon Project there were two breakthroughs that gave me a hint of how to actually get a more reliable assessment for Tim in his external examinations and overcome the communication problems. Both used technology.

All of the students in the Horizon Project were required to produce a video. Tim produced this video at home on his own in his room. It demonstrated that Tim using the technologies to create the video could communicate without hesitation or stuttering. This was the evidence that I needed to show that Tim could communicate just like any other student if he could use video or similar technology tools. Furthermore, Tim was awarded runner-up in the Horizon Project for his video.

The second indication I got was in the student meeting on Elluminate with Julie [Lindsay]. All of the students were expected to explain their outcomes of their research and the

Horizon Project. I simply could not believe it! Right before my very eyes, Tim was completely articulate. Unfortunately, it was such a surprise that I did not record Tim's response in Elluminate. We only had the real-time observation by me and the technician who was assisting me on this breakthrough for this student.

It was through the video and the observation from the Elluminate that it was possible to acquire special consideration for Tim to take his external examinations orally for two of his subjects and he achieved his international diploma. The Horizon Project and the use of technology in the project made a real difference for this student.

Diary Entry 14

JULIE'S JOURNAL ENTRY, SEPTEMBER 12, 2007

Today I had my grade 10 class for the third time this year. I really like this class. There is a good international mixture, mostly Arabic, but some Asian and European as well. They have a good sense of humor and are very quick and generally interested. I wanted to introduce the concept of a global project in a fun way so decided to play some of the student-created videos from both the Flat Classroom and Horizon Projects last year.

I started with Cannelle's zany overview for New Scholarship. She has the images moving around and people changing color and clips from 5 countries. The students are engrossed and exclaim at what they see. They ask questions about who was involved and what they did. I asked questions like, Have you ever created anything like this? Can you imagine collaborating with other students around the world? I then played Atif's video based on mobile technology in the year 2020. They seem quite fascinated by this and intrigued by the futuristic theme. I start to talk to them about how the Flat Classroom is an award-winning project and how it was based on Friedman's book. We discuss the flattening influences from the book and they take turns to add ideas and share stories.

I tell them we will be joining the project this year and they seem quite interested as to who will be involved. I think this was a good start. We also discussed logistics. How we can do this in two lessons per week and what we can do to fast-track into it.

The students tell me the cameras owned by the IT Department are too complicated and they have problems, especially with the firewire cable and compatibility with the PCs. They ask if they can use their own cameras. . . . Yes!, of course, use what you are comfortable with, bring your technology to school, let's work together on security for this, but don't use something that is cumbersome and detracts from the main focus of the project, which is to learn about other people, share what you know, together construct new knowledge and create a multimedia artifact in the shape of a digital story.

It is the stories that emerge from this project that will be remembered, not the ability of the students to manipulate complicated equipment or their knowledge of advanced features of software. Quick students who have ambition to put in more time can learn Premier, others can use Windows Movie maker. It makes no difference to me . . . as it is the story and the collaboration that is important.

CASE EXAMPLES OF GLOBAL COLLABORATION

Case Study 14

MARSHA GOREN,
teacher, founder of Global Dreamers—Israel

PDToolkit

for
*Flattening Classrooms,
Engaging Minds*
Read full Case Studies in
PDToolkit online.

In 1991 I wanted my students to become excited and interested in their learning and found that the Internet offered children the opportunity to collaborate with other students all around the world and become involved in real world, authentic learning opportunities that could be fun and truly meaningful. I am the creator of Global Dreamers website (http://www.globaldreamers

.org) and along with my students promote the vision of "world-wide peace." I am now a mentor for so many teaching professionals . . . .

The children have always been my inspiration and so I've tried to inspire them. It wasn't until the web took the world by surprise, though, that teaching became an exciting challenge, an unbelievable experience where collaborative learning comes alive in classrooms around the world, and my students have become learners and leaders; partners and participants through their Global Dreamers involvement.

Looking back I now realize the social innovation that Global Dreamers has brought. It was the different strategies we implemented which have helped our dream come true for the last nine years. Our work has helped to enrich and engage the lives of many of our global partners and friends around the world. This social innovative way of teaching and sharing tries to answer old problems that the world faced before the power of the Internet and technology touched our lives. It has also helped to change biased opinions by learning about others and has extended and strengthened the civil society and the future it may bring.

I was blessed to have a principal who believes in what we are doing; at first I am not sure she really even understood how far our work could go and how many educators and children would join us. She takes pride in our work and has many times announced that the value of work is amazing—more than any book lesson could ever give kids. The parents in my school realize technology and English can bring their kids to a higher level in the school system in Israel, so for the most part they are very supportive and immediately sign permission slips for their kids to participate in our work. I have never really had to deal with any problems, as they know and appreciate our work.

Case Study 15

CAROLINE CERVENY,
co-founder of Global Church Partnership Project

In this project, students from Australia (Our Lady of Mercy College, Burreneer, and All Saints Boys College [both] in New South Wales, Australia, and St. Petersburg Catholic High and Bishop Moore Catholic High School in Florida USA) linked together as they created videos profiling the life of priests in their areas. They created videos using the local software on their school machines and posted the final creation to YouTube; however, they needed to be able to share effectively. [According to Adrian Brown, Education Officer, Catholic Education Commission, New South Wales:]

Once judged ready for public viewing, [next] came the question of publishing and sharing. Google Earth was chosen as the appropriate vehicle. Google Earth is an astounding technology that allows the user to make virtual tours to almost any place on the planet. But in the case of this project it also served as a metaphor for the global nature of the work of the priests by mapping their stories against the globe itself. The digital stories could be effectively pinned at the places where their ministries actually occur and embedded in the environments where they are enacted—the hustle and bustle of seedy King's Cross in Sydney, the suburban parishes in Florida, the busy playing fields and buildings of Bishop Moore, St Pete's and Bosco in Engadine, NSW. Using street view, the simple lines of Mgr Gordon's Parish Church can be seen as well as the soaring towers of St Mary's Cathedral. Google Earth also allows the stories to be organized into a tour or pilgrimage, another appropriate metaphor for the Pilgrim Church.[59]

CHAPTER 8

Step 6
Creation

"Collaborative production is a more involved form of cooperation, as it increases the tension between individual and group goals. The litmus test for collaborative production is simple: no one person can take credit for what gets created, and the project could not come into being without the participation of many."

CLAY SHIRKY, *Here Comes Everybody*[1]

ADD FRIEND

CLAY SHIRKY
@cshirky
http://www.shirky.com

CHAPTER 8 WEB RESOURCES
http://www.flatclassroombook.com/creation.html

SHARE IT

Twitter hashtag for this book: #flatclass

Creating a Difference—A Story of Engagement

Two different countries, two different situations—but two different countries joined together by initiative, engagement, and the desire to create a difference. Atif, a Bangladesh student at International School Dhaka, and Beatrice, a Korean student from Korea International School, have never met offline or online. However, they share a common desire to use technology to make a difference in the world through sharing their ideas and creations with others globally.

When encouraged by his teacher, Julie, to enter a competition run by the BBC "Click Online" television show, Atif had little hesitation. Even when he had to make a late-night drive and sit outside the school gate to use the wireless network to upload the

See Beatrice and Will's team IMPACT Video (Inspirational Museum Promoting Arts by Children through Technology) http://tinyurl.com/fcc-impact

short video by the deadline, he was not deterred. When he was chosen as a representative example of the voice of youth and what they thought about social networking, specifically the social network ELGG in his case, he willingly shared his ideas about connecting for learning with the world.[2] His simple yet sincere video gave others around the world a glimpse into life in Bangladesh as well as pragmatic habits and attitudes of a student using cutting edge technology.

Three years later, as a participant in the 2009 Flat Classroom™ Workshop in Hong Kong, Beatrice overcame her shyness and worked in a team to envisage what the future might look like if we could harness technology for improving the world. She not only co-created an original idea, supported by a multimedia presentation, but upon returning to Korea, she blogged her experience along with an original image about using connection, communication, and collaboration to "flatten the world" (see Figure 8.1).[3] This image has subsequently been used, with permission, for Flat Classroom workshop promotion as the conference logo.

Beatrice also encouraged Will, a student from the United States, to enter an international film festival in Korea. Will was one of her partners at the Flat Classroom workshop but his life was changed when he received a runner-up award and an iPod for placing in the competition. Beatrice's collaborative spirit reached from Korea to Hong Kong to India to tiny Camilla, Georgia through the Internet and powerful face-to-face interactions.

FIGURE 8.1 Flatten the World (Designed by Beatrice from Korea)

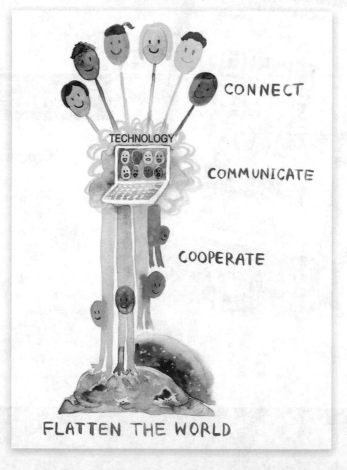

Both Beatrice and Atif were active rather than passive in their learning and sharing and they used imagination, creativity, and skill to develop artifacts that have made a difference to the people who watched, read, and viewed them. These are global citizens of the future who know how to communicate effectively and know how to share their creations so that others can also learn from their ideas and construct new meaning. They are creating their future one video, blog post, drawing, and connection at a time.

OVERVIEW OF CREATION

This chapter will discuss **Bloom's Taxonomy** and 21st Century Learning Objectives and how project methodologies and outcomes can be aligned to promote higher-order thinking and cover essential 21st century literacies. Examples from Flat Classroom projects as well as other experiences will share strategies for meaningful **co-creation** of artifacts.

In the Self section, we discuss creation as an aspect of higher-order thinking skills (HOTS), review recent research into the use of social media to create content, and look at 21st-century learning in a digital world from a teacher's perspective. Teachers will learn how to create their online identity and use social media to share and collaborate. This section emphasizes the importance of personal PLN development and creation tools as part of teacher learning, and finding ideas for beginning and advanced content publishing. Teachers must take a "learning by doing" approach as professionals and in the classroom.

In the School section, we discuss co-creation and its importance as part of collaborative production. There are opportunities to co-create within a school, between schools, and globally. Professional development should incorporate co-creation too. It helps teachers develop technology skills but also supports teachers understand instructional design methods that promote multimedia creation and co-creation through firsthand experience.

In the Student section, we start with individual innovation and creation and then move to co-creation. Curriculum objectives are aligned to example projects along with guidance for how to do it yourself.

 SELF   **Creating Your Online Identity**

WHY CREATE?

Experts such as Thomas Friedman[4] and Ian Jukes[5] discuss the changes in the workplace in the 21st century. New skills are needed to prepare students for the demands of the workplace, and the emphasis on memorization and rote learning is no longer valid. Modern working situations require a global perspective and an ability to work in teams, analyze problems, and provide solutions across time zones and cultures.

Students of today will need to become more entrepreneurial and align with contract-based working situations where changing careers and globalization are the norm.[6] A new skill set is evolving that includes global digital citizenship; information

ISTE STANDARDS

NETS.S 1
Creativity and Innovation

21st CENTURY SKILLS

C21 LEARNING AND INNOVATION SKILLS:
Creativity and Innovation

ADD FRIEND

IAN JUKES
@ijukes
http://www.ianjukes.com

fluency; the ability to connect, communicate, and collaborate; and the ability to solve problems. In addition, skills such as **ideational fluency** (the ability to produce ideas to fulfill certain requirements), originality, and flexibility are traits to be encouraged and developed in creative individuals. Creation isn't always a fun thing, but it is part of the job description of the modern worker.

Of special importance are creativity and creation and the role this plays in developing 21st century learning modes. The 21st Century Fluency Project[7] discusses *solution fluency* as the "ability to think creatively to solve problems in real time by clearly defining the problem, designing an appropriate solution, applying the solution, and then evaluating the process and outcome." It refers to *creativity fluency* as the "process by which artistic proficiency adds meaning through design, art and storytelling. It regards form in addition to function, and the principles of innovative design combined with a quality functioning product."[8] Creativity and creation are an attitude, an acceptance, and a realization that all participants have strengths and can find success.

New multimedia tools and the rise of social media have made it possible for anyone (with access) to create original and wonderful artifacts. The September 2010 Forrester report on Global Social Technographics[9] shows how consumers are engaging with social technologies. In the United States, for example, 23 percent of users are categorized as "creators" and do such things as publish a blog, upload self-created audio and/or video, publish a website, or post articles and stories online. This report indicates a decline internationally in the number of content creators since 2009. (The only country shown in the survey to be increasing their rate of creation is Japan, moving from 34 to 36 percent.) The implication is that fewer creators mean fewer ideas circulating, but there is an increase in "joiners" and awareness of the potential of social media.[10]

The Pew Internet Report on Teen Content Creators and Consumers in 2005 found 57 percent of all teenagers to be content creators.[11] The Pew Internet Report on Teens and Social Media in 2007 shows that 64 percent of online teens ages 12 to 17 said "yes" to at least one of possible five content-creation activities.[13] The impact of how we create, and what we create while making meaning out of information is discussed by Stephen Wilmarth, who identifies five socioeconomic trends that are influencing learning and teaching.[14] These include social production, social networks, a semantic web, a move into media grids and virtual learning, and non-linear learning. His discussion concludes with the notion that 21st century learning lends itself to a "bazaar approach" rather than a "cathedral approach," a chaotic rather than carefully crafted system that allows freedom for creation through informed best-practice adaptation of social technologies.

BLOOM'S TAXONOMY AND 21ST CENTURY LEARNING

The minimal cost of social media production and rise of social networks has encouraged many Internet users to become content creators. The semantic web (also called *Web 3.0*) is developing and allows creations to be more clearly labeled, shared, and discovered. More schools are removing the "walled garden" approach to learning.[15] All of this means that students and teachers are better equipped to use new technologies to their advantage and embrace creation as a desired higher-order thinking skill.

Bloom's revised taxonomy,[16] and more recently the work of Andrew Churches with **Bloom's Digital Taxonomy,**[17] puts "creating" as the top higher-order thinking skill (HOTS), with "remembering" as the lowest (LOTS). This taxonomy provides a summary of the learning process, from remembering to understanding, applying, analyzing, evaluating, and creating. The digital taxonomy continuum focuses on using the technology tools to facilitate learning and uses key terms/verbs for creating, such as *programming, filming, animating, blogging, video blogging, mixing, remixing, wiki-ing, publishing, video casting, podcasting,* and so on. As a 21st century skill, "creating," as supported by the emergence of the online digital world, poses the question, "Can the student create a new product or point of view?"[18] This is the challenge for all educators—how can we allow true creation, innovation, and freedom in the classroom, across the world? We want learners to identify and solve problems together by creating a new perspective, product, or artifact to share. What a challenge!

EXPLORE CREATION MODALITIES IN A DIGITAL WORLD

Gone are the days when you and your class are the only ones to see the effort put into lesson design, preparation, objectives, and resources. You are no longer an individual teacher creating with your students alone. Given the relatively new ease of online collaboration, co-teaching is possible in many ways, including globally. With online portfolios and networked material sharing *your* creations and involvements raise awareness and knowledge with others. Exploring creation modalities, however, starts with the essential question "What are you are trying to create and who do you want to share it with?" Table 8.1 shows a variety of digital creation modalities for educators to consider.

BECOME A PUBLISHER OF CONTENT

What are you willing to share? What are you not willing to share? Do you know who you are online? How do other people see you? How does this relate to your career as an educator? **Personal branding** is the process whereby people and their careers become regarded as brands.[19]

Bloom's Digital Taxonomy
http://tinyurl.com/blooms-digtax

TABLE 8.1 Digital Creation Modalities for Educators

Creation Modality	Individual Mode	Collaborative Mode / Co-Creation
Text-based document creation	Word processing software	Saving doc in a shared network location (e.g., SkyDrive or Dropbox creating Google doc)
Multimedia-based • Audio • Video	Audacity iMovie Garage Band Photostory	Voicethread Animoto Google Presentation
Multimedia-based • Animation	Photoshop Flash	Toondoo Scratch

In the context of education, this concept is not new. Although not fully embraced by all, digital technologies have great potential to improve relationships between stakeholders in the education process. Despite being a sensitive subject to those who see no correlation between marketing and education, brand management is being recognized as an essential skill for educators[20] who are realizing the value in their online content creation and contributions and developing entrepreneurial brands that are personal and transferable between locations and employers.

An excellent example of personal branding in education is that of Jeff Utecht.[23] As an international educator, educational technology specialist, and consultant (and one of the first Flat Classroom Project judges in 2006), Jeff has methodically developed an online brand that involves sharing his work, often with resources to download, and interacting with others using Web 2.0. He claims, "Educators want to be known for their ideas and their beliefs rather than simply their roles of educator, mentor, colleague."[24] His brand includes his iconic "Thinking Stick," which is in a similar vein to co-author Vicki Davis, who is widely known through her personal brand as the "Cool Cat Teacher."

Fast, immediate contact with your school community using technology narrows the communication gap and allows stories of success (personal and school) to proliferate. Yet many school websites don't have full information about their teachers, programs, or daily events. In fact, very rarely do you see links to personal branding spaces of educators. It continues to be a novelty for leaders in schools to be blogging and sharing their ideas routinely online, despite the fact that successful role models abound such as Paul Fochtmam, Shabbi Luthra, or David Truss. Rather than an imperative, the thought of personal branding is seen as a threat to many, and far too "out there" to be doable.

In today's world, every school has competition with many parents opting to educate their children online. Schools that exist in a competitive market are starting to see the value in using social media to "sell" their educational product, showcase educators and attract new teachers, and build strong alumni support for continued prosperity and valuable associations.

The new reality of education is described by Rob Jacobs, when he picks up on Seth Godin's 14 trends of new marketing as outlined in his book, *Meatball Sundae,*[21] but under the lens of education.[22] With regard to the use of technology to foster better communication between school and home, Jacobs asks, "Do you view it as a burden or an opportunity to spread your educational vision and message?" If it isn't a burden, then we should be using every tool we can to spread that message: Twitter, Facebook, Tumblr, YouTube, apps. We must put our message wherever the eyeballs of our stakeholders look on a consistent basis.

LEARN BY DOING

In order to be learning collaboratively with other educators and with students in an online community, we encourage "learning by doing" as the model for success. Refer to previous chapter text about developing your personal learning network, digital citizenship awareness, and digital footprint management. You need to establish your own online identity. Rather than be afraid, or disdainful, of having an online

presence, embrace it as a way to share and communicate and learn how to manage it. What will people find when they search your name? Likely you have a personal brand whether you know it or not, and people may find something that won't be you and it may not be something you like. For example, googling "Julie Lindsay" shows the handbag company, a .com of the same name. As Julie has become a prolific contributor in education, the volume of her personal work makes her more easily found in search queries.

Educators are socially responsible when they show professional activity, dialog, and interaction online. Showing students and skeptical adults the value in professional online behavior helps them understand the role it can play in their lives." It is not essential to be everywhere, but it is necessary to be somewhere online. David Truss talks about "facing Facebook" and how, although being someone with a large digital footprint elsewhere, he prefers not to focus on Facebook but considers it another valuable way to connect with some individuals.

In his book, *Me 2.0,* Dan Schawbel talks about the four steps to create your personal brand: Discover, Create, Communicate, and Maintain.[25] This can be translated into education and a learning environment, and here are our suggested steps for developing a personal brand.

ACTIONS TO DEVELOP YOUR PERSONAL BRAND IN EDUCATION

Action 1: Establish Your Online Identity!   Who are you? What words communicate who you are? Choose ways that are best for your situation through exploration of Web 2.0 tools. Remember that there are safe, private ways of joining in online conversations. If you join a professional website, it is OK to celebrate your successes and credentials. Your online identity should include:

- A personal profile and resume material (LinkedIn, Plaxo, Zerply, personal website or portfolio using tools such as Word Press or a wiki).
- An online avatar and ID that is identifiable (image and name). Your "name" is one of the most important decisions you make. It is best to keep this consistent between websites so people can find you (unless you don't want to be found).
- Identifiable presence with **micro blogging** (Twitter), social bookmarking (Delicious, Diigo), educational/social networks (Nings and collaborative wikis), multimedia services (Flickr, SlideShare, YouTube etc.), and, most importantly, a blog (Word Press, Blogger, Edublogs, Tumblr).

If you have already followed the steps created in Action 1, you are already well on the way to establishing your identity. Make sure you use one user name or ID everywhere so people know who you are.

Action 2: Create, Create, and Create!   Build an online presence that works to your advantage and that allows you to connect to support what you do. Create a culture of creativity for yourself and your students, and others around you. Upload multimedia, blog, tweet, bookmark, and so on. Use the tools to create a presence that includes your classroom work, your professional work, and parts of your life (e.g., travels and hobbies). What photos capture you? What videos tell your story? Be mindful that using software privacy settings allows you to control what you share and who sees it. Not everyone wants everything out there, and that's quite OK as well.

DIGITAL CITIZENSHIP AREA OF UNDERSTANDING
Habits of Learning

 **ISTE STANDARDS**

NETS.T 4
Promote and Model Digital Citizenship and Responsibility

DIGITAL CITIZENSHIP AREA OF UNDERSTANDING
Literacy & Fluency

21st CENTURY SKILLS

C21 LIFE AND CAREER SKILLS:
Initiative and Self-Direction

SOCIAL NETWORK
Linked In (professional networking)
http://www.linkedin.com

Zerply (professional networking)
http://www.zerply.com

 **WEBSITES**

Custom personalized dashboard
http://www.about.me

Action 3: Share as Part of a Group! Do not work in isolation. Reach out to colleagues; flatten your classroom walls by putting your ideas, your curriculum development, and your resources and innovations out there. Find like-minded educators to work with and collaborate with and bounce ideas off. Share resources and promote others as well, an important reason to share.

Action 4: Define What You Think. Does your online identity reflect what you think in a professional capacity? Do your blog and various uploads and interactions with others reveal you as a learner? Does it reveal your educational philosophy and development as an educator? Maintain your spaces regularly to show you are an active, vital educator, and design your footprint and brand so that you find a level of self-promotion you are comfortable with.

 **SELF-ASSESSMENT SURVEY**

PDToolkit
for
Flattening Classrooms,
Engaging Minds

See the survey results in the online PDToolkit before moving on to the next section.

Before moving to the next part of this chapter, we invite you to take this self-assessment survey. We also suggest you discuss these questions with colleagues, including your wider learning network, to determine your current level of confidence and ability with creation strategies.

1. **Have I have already started to create an online presence or digital footprint that may lead to developing a personal brand?**

   a. Yes   b. No   c. Maybe. I have a Facebook account—does that count?

2. **Do I encourage my students to blog and use the "social" side of social bookmarking in order to make connections?**

   a. Yes   b. No   c. Maybe

3. **Am I comfortable creating multimedia artifacts, such as audio and video files, or slideshows, and sharing these online?**

   a. Yes   b. No   c. Maybe

4. **Do I look for opportunities to co-create with other educators?**

   a. Yes   b. No   c. Sometimes

5. **Do I encourage the use of social media, in a variety of forms, to support learning in the classroom and to focus on creation?**

   a. Yes   b. No   c. Sometimes, but not successfully

6. **When I read an article, do I feel comfortable responding and sharing my thoughts in the comment?**

   a. Yes   b. No   c. Sometimes

7. **Do I use the same name in the many spaces where I operate?**

   a. Yes   b. No   c. Usually

8. **Do I have my bio posted on a main page that I link from all of my professional sites?**

   a. Yes   b. No

9. **Do I clearly determine the purpose of each of my online spaces (personal or professional) and work to keep them separate?**

   a. Yes   b. No   c. Usually

 SCHOOL Co-Creation Environments

Creating something meaningful with someone else can be very powerful. Called "collaborative production" by Shirky,[26] it is also referred to as the "melding of minds," "drawing on individual talents," or "the sum of the parts being larger than the individual parts themselves," and so on. Co-creation leads to a trust relationship that can lead to more complex and innovative creations between schools and globally.

  tweetable

Co-creation leads to a trust relationship that can lead to more complex and innovative creations between schools and globally. #flatclass

BUILDING TRUST FOR CO-CREATION

Without trust, you cannot have co-creation. If you don't trust someone to do their part, you're reluctant to trust them with any part of something that is important to your success and future. For the sum of individual efforts to happen, we must be willing to add our efforts to others. We need trust that:

 **ISTE STANDARDS**

NETS.T 4.
Promote and Model Digital Citizenship and Responsibility

NETS.S 5
Digital Citizenship

- The other person(s) will in fact do what you agree on
- As you build, each party will provide worthy and sensitive feedback on your contribution with the aim of overall improvement
- The final product acknowledges and reflects all contributions

 **21st CENTURY SKILLS**

C21 LIFE AND CAREER SKILLS:
Productivity and Accountability, Leadership and Responsibility

Building a global collaborative project requires a commitment from the teacher to the final product and outcomes. Teachers must also join in the creation of a learning community to support this growth. The habits of communication discussed in Chapter 2 will lead to trust. In a face-to-face world, these hurdles are jumped in different ways, and there is less room for misunderstandings. In a virtual, online world where every email and every discussion comment can potentially be misinterpreted, trust needs to be built through positive actions and compliance to a common goal.

Do what you say you are going to do, within the time you say you are going to do it. Be an active communicator and contributor and have the courage to co-create with other educators and students without the need for sole ownership of everything.

CO-CREATION IN YOUR PLN

When Julie went to teach in Qatar, she was invited to present to the Qatar Academy Board on future e-learning and technology needs throughout the school. It was her chance to share what was happening in other parts of the world and then propose new horizons. By reaching out via Twitter messages and emails to colleagues in other

View the video at http:// tinyurl.com/elearn-4life

A Week in the Life Blog
http://elementaryflatclassroom
.wordpress.com

See *50 Interesting Ways to Use Your Interactive White Board* in the Classroom Presentation http://tinyurl .com/50ways-iwb

NETS.T 5
Engage in Professional Growth and Leadership

NETS.T 1.d
Facilitate and Inspire Student Learning and Creativity

international schools, she received pictures and ideas to help co-create the final product. The resulting "E-Learning for Life"[27] video was an opportunity for everyone to witness a summary of ideas and proposals for improvement.

Co-creation via a blog is an excellent way to unite a learning community and focus on a common theme or topic. Teachers in the Flat Classroom Project for Elementary School Students "A Week in the Life . . ."[28] 2010 pilot decided from the start they wanted a collaborative, co-created blog to share their journey and reflect on the project.[29]

At Julie's school in Beijing, BISS teachers co-created on a blog during the digital portfolio pilot in 2010, sharing classroom experiences and ideas as wiki portfolios were introduced across the curriculum.[30] Information Technology in a Global Society (ITGS) teachers also co-create and document the progress of Inside ITGS in a blog.[31]

Google Docs and Google Apps are other global collaborative power tools. UK educator Tom Barrett uses Google Presentations to develop and share resources for his use, as well as anyone who has the link. This example, *50 Interesting Ways to Use Your Interactive Whiteboard in the Classroom*,[32] is licensed under Creative Commons Attribution, Share Alike, and Non-Commercial 3.0 and has been co-created by a number of educators. Tom openly asks for contributions and willingly shares the co-created work.

CO-CREATION IN PROFESSIONAL DEVELOPMENT (PD)

Professional development that uses co-creation as an infrastructure to not only develop better skills using collaborative technologies but also to re-design education itself and instructional design that promotes multimedia creation and co-creation is imperative in today's climate of change.

In fact, the very first time Vicki and Julie connected was through an online professional development opportunity co-creation wiki project. As part of the K–12 Online Conference in 2006, Vicki presented on "Wiki Collaboration across the Curriculum"[33] and Julie signed up to co-create a wiki on "Citizen Journalism Code of Ethics"[34] with Reuven Werber[35] from Israel. Julie's subsequent blog post[36] shows how this was a turning point in her view of Web 2.0 tools and wikis in particular, and their ability to support easy collaboration through a user-friendly interface as well as show legitimate research, evaluation, and synthesis skills. Add to this the practice of co-creation (content on the page, ideas, and feedback in the discussion) and the humble wiki becomes the tool of choice for many curricular needs. More importantly, there is now a new resource online (the co-created wiki page) that can be shared, updated, and used as needed.

Talking about 21st century learning is one thing, but providing an opportunity for educators and education leaders to come together, either virtually and/or in the same room, and create something together that can be used in the future is an exciting and inspiring approach. This is discussed further in Chapter 11, Challenge-Based Professional Development, but here are some essential examples now to show how this works.

Develop an Informal Community of Practice.   Julie organized educators in Qatar from all levels of education, met regularly on a weekend morning for the purposes of discussing 21st century learning. Their aim was to transform their educational practice.[37] Much discussion and co-creation of ideas and responses took place. Resources were shared via a wiki and meeting backchannel that also included virtual participants. The group decided to co-create a video that more effectively shared their development and journey. This video, simplistic in style but effective in message has been viewed about 1,000 times in less than two years and is a legacy for others to learn about the struggles with technology integration and 21st century learning in 2009.[38]

Design a Workshop for Co-Creation Opportunities. Then there is the opportunity to design collaborative learning experiences that encourage new instructional models based on co-creation and collaboration, and supported by new technologies. The "Flat Classroom Workshop"[39] and the "Create the Future Workshop"[40] are two key examples of this.

The key factor is co-creation of a product that can be implemented after the professional development has finished. For example the "Across the Globe"[41] project developed out of the "Create the Future Workshop" in Japan, October 2010, and you can see on the workshop wiki the co-creation of ideas, and the collaborative influences that finally birthed a fledgling project.[42] The "Flatten Your PD" idea developed out of the Flat Classroom Workshop in St Louis, July 2010, and was in fact co-created by real and virtual team members who worked diligently and effectively to set out their plans on the wiki.[43]

STUDENTS Innovation and Creation

To encourage creativity and innovation, give students access to tools and experiences that let them co-create and collaborate. Help students develop their own personal brand or brands for causes or projects.

OPPORTUNITIES FOR CO-CREATION IN THE CLASSROOM

True or false? Educators are natural collaborators and creators. Yes, we all attend meetings where we discuss curriculum, and we all need to write our class programs and lesson plans, but how often do you get to co-create with someone else? From something as simple as a statement on digital citizenship, to a unit rubric, to a set of class rules, to a presentation for the board of your school, each of these can be enriched through co-creation and reaching out to your extended learning network. This is not all about developing a global project (although that is a part of it); rather, it is about a mindset that allows the outside in and puts you out there. Let's look at some examples.

In the example shown in Figure 8.2, Vicki's grade 9 students wrote their class rules in a Google Doc on the first day. The class spent two days editing and discussing how the class should interact and remain safe online. After completion and sign-off, the rules were printed and the students signed them, along with their parents, as an agreement to stand throughout the whole year.

Our Flat Classroom Project Help wiki[44] is a co-created set of resources that support all projects, including "how to" pages, tutorials, important information for

FIGURE 8.2 Grade 9 Class Rules
Students collaborated in class to create a full set of guidelines. This is an example of one part.

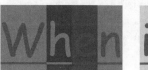

- Listen to your leader.
- Do not let another student do all the work. It is a group effort.
- Cooperate with your Co-workers.
- Give your Co-workers constructive criticism.
- Do not hover over classmates while they are working.
- Do not tell the leaders what to do, just give them suggestions.
- If two peoples have a problem, do not argue. Go to that person and work it out between yourselves, or go to your project manager or teacher.
- Leaders should not be bossy and should ask for input.
- Treat everyone with respect including yourself.
- Try not to get mad at people while you're working.
- Do not delete others people's work.
- Talk to your teammates about the ideas you have.

http://insideitgs.wikispaces.com

MADELEINE BROOKES
@mbrookes
http://www.technology
4thinking.com

moving forward in a project, students code of ethics, and more. Teachers and students from every project we run have the opportunity to use and contribute to the resources in "Wikipedia" style, collaboratively co-creating a better tool for learning each time.

The Inside ITGS collaboration between ITGS IB classrooms shows how curriculum can be co-created and developed jointly from anywhere in the world. Using a wiki-centric resource Inside ITGS co-founders, Julie and Madeleine, lead the co-creation of collaborative lessons and projects, essential resources, and shared artifacts. Students and teachers alike from different countries are editing, updating, discussing, and co-creating a live and dynamic resource that can be used for exam and project purposes.[45] As Madeleine shares with us on her blog,

> Our intention is to work together to develop and co-deliver the course, have our students communicate and collaborate with each other, encourage participation from ITGS schools around the world, as well as documenting our journey along the way. Our journey has begun! It is a journey that will explore the challenges of learning in the 21st century. Our vision is for our students will become "connected learners"; students who can seamlessly move between our physical classrooms and our evolving ITGS cyber-school and beyond.[46]

Another example of co-creation, this time using multimedia, is Julie and Vicki's K–12 Online Conference 2008 Keynote, "Time to Grow."[47] Created while Julie was in the Middle East and Vicki in the United States, the use of tools to upload and share videos, sound, slides, and narration stretched creative talents to the limit. When Vicki suggested they do a co-created green screen segment, it seemed almost impossible—but once again, nothing is impossible if carefully planned and communicated. So near the end of the 50-minute video, we appear in the same shot at the same time thanks to the genius of green screen technology.

CREATING A DIFFERENCE

Let's look at how we can encourage and support co-creation in a curricular sense with two different examples from the Inside ITGS collaboration and also the Flat Classroom Project. Both of these examples show the use of higher-order thinking skills while working with digital technologies.

To start the Inside ITGS class collaboration students were asked to introduce their virtual partner through creation of a one-minute multimedia artifact.[48] This involved making contact with the partner through the class network (Ning), communicating, and exchanging ideas and facts, and of course sound and video files as needed. The final artifact was to be uploaded to the Ning for review and final approval by the person the media was introducing. A variety of Web 2.0 tools could be used. Students were free to choose, as long as it could be accessible online to all and provide an opportunity for feedback and discussion. Some favorite examples include "Introducing Yae by Alejandro"[49] and "Introducing Ding by Queena."[50]

The Flat Classroom Project, as well as asking for co-created wiki research and sharing of content, takes co-creation of multimedia to the next level again where it requires that the final personal video from each student include an outsourced clip from another student not in the same class, or the same school.

The HOTS involved in this one are huge, requiring excellent communication skills and project management. Support and structure are provided by the use of the **design cycle** for project development, in conjunction with students being put into thematic selections such as story; social entrepreneurship; or innovation, invention, and prediction. Students need to design, plan, and create a 2- to 5-minute multimedia artifact where part of the presentation will be sent to them from somewhere else in the world. They need to communicate exactly what it is they want recorded, or else it will be a waste of time.

During this process, they also need to work through video format issues, uploading and downloading problems, issues to do with not having their out-sourced video request met, and a tight deadline for overall completion, not to mention dealing with other countries and situations where things can happen to interrupt workflow. A lot is learned about teamwork at a distance and reliable and responsible approach to planning and meeting workflow expectations.

Flat Classroom teachers have found it challenging also, as Ray Jones from Qatar stated,

> I am having my students film on cellphones, screencast, etc. . . . anything at their disposal. My mantra regarding the video production is to keep things simple and focus on a single message then (if time permits) branch out. . . . Video-making takes time to master . . . remember . . . it is the message that counts most, not flashy effects.[51]

View Time to Grow at http://tinyurl.com/time2grow

http://insideitgs.ning.com/profiles/blogs/introducing-partner-yae

http://v.youku.com/v_show/id_XMjAzMzg5OTIw.html

ISTE STANDARDS

NETS.S 2.a
Communication and Collaboration

NETS.S 4
Critical Thinking, Problem Solving, and Decision Making

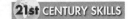

21st CENTURY SKILLS

C21 INFORMATION, MEDIA AND TECHNOLOGY SKILLS:
Information Literacy

A teacher from Montana, Jason Neiffer, expresses frustration:

> My students have all but given up but we are trying to fight our way back in. We are trying to be part of the video editing phase.[52]

Bruce in the Middle East states,

> Stick with it—we here in Saudi have had our own trying times wrapping our head around the project and figuring out how it works, but honestly, once they get going it is awesome . . . some words of advice—when your students develop their video idea, have them break it down into sections rather than an entire single shot."[53]

Working with multimedia in the classroom is challenging and exhausting; however, students delight at receiving an outsourced clip made especially for them, and their production is a joy to see. The anguish at losing work and having to start again, frustration with uploading or downloading, and glitches with movie-making software create an atmosphere of engagement and high activity within the class itself. When working with different computer formats (Apple, Wintel) and multimedia, find tools and methods that allow sharing and co-creating virtually.

As it states on the Project Help wiki page for outsourcing,

> The problems with outsourcing a video are the same as seen in the real world: lack of vendor dependability, time delays, time zone, communication barriers, and miscommunication. The knowledge learned in the experience of outsourcing is as important as the clip itself. Ask early. Follow up and talk to your teacher to get help if necessary. Make personal contact on the Ning. Those who wait often come up short. It is a fact of life.[54]

SUMMARY

Education needs to move past lower-order thinking into the highest level of thinking, which is *create*, according to Bloom's Taxonomy. This chapter began with Self—exploring one's self and how the individual teacher should create, including various modalities, becoming a self-publisher, and actions to develop your own personal brand. Then in the section titled School, co-creation environments were explored as teachers move to create the trust and opportunities required to enable co-creation to happen smoothly and fairly in the classroom and in professional development experiences.

Finally, co-creating *with students* was explored in Students, including many examples of co-creation and how it can inspire students and their teachers to make a difference and find meaning in their learning.

ESSENTIAL QUESTIONS

- What is a personal brand? What steps should you take to develop your own personal brand?

- How can co-creation be used in teacher professional development to help teachers build trust with the concept?

- How would one assess differently for co-creation than the traditional assessments done by teachers?

Join the online conversation and share your answers at http://tinyurl.com/flatclass-ch8 ▶

FLAT CLASSROOM™ 15 CHALLENGES

CHALLENGE 11: ALIGN YOUR PROJECT TO STANDARDS

DO: Using the project you created in Challenge 10, revise the project plan based on what you have learned. Align the project objectives with your course or another set of standards such as the ISTE NETS standards or the P21 Framework (cited throughout this book).

SHARE: Update your posting on Curriki[55] or your blog to include standards alignment and revisions. Reflect on your blog on the process of aligning with standards and what you have learned from this process. **The tag for this challenge is fcc11_align. Use this when you blog, or to share with your group.**

Share what you did with your challenge at http://tinyurl.com/flat15-11 ▶

FLAT CLASSROOM™ DIARIES

Diary Entry 15

JULIE'S DIARY, OCTOBER 1, 2007, QATAR. DISCUSSIONS ABOUT COMPLETING THE FLAT CLASSROOM PROJECT

This morning I had a session with my grade 10 class, with representatives from Germany, Malaysia, Aruba, Holl and, Qatar, Palestine, India and Qatar among 14 students, where we just talked about the project. We did not open computers or look at any multimedia. In fact I did something I rarely do these days, I distributed a handout with the Flat Classroom concepts and topics clearly described. While going through the essential requirements of the project I once again had the opportunity to marvel at how cutting edge this project is. This is not just on the edge for students, but also for teachers who are out there experimenting with new collaborative ways of developing curriculum and of communicating objectives. I told the students they would get out of this project what they put into it. They are excited and want to know when and how they can start communicating with their partners.

I have fast-tracked these students so much I forget that they are still so new to Web 2.0 . . . not even sure if I have shown them how to use the discussion tab on the wiki yet. They are confused by having to open the Ning, the wiki, and, of course, our class blogs on Eduspaces . . . ALL new tools for them. We talked about getting [along] with other people and the possibility that they may not "like" or have an affinity (or empathy, as Pink writes) with their team members but that they will still need to work through the project requirements. They told me this way of doing IT is completely different [from] anything they have done before. In previous years their classes have been application based with direct instruction in skill development. I laughed when they told me how each lesson was "open this," "do this," "save this," and so on.

Diary Entry 16

TIPS FOR TEACHING WIKIS: HOW I EXPLAIN IT TO STUDENTS[56]

VICKI DAVIS, Cool Cat Teacher blog, May 2010

Just sent this out to the Digiteen group and thought some of you working with wikis might like a few tips. (My students do call me the "wikinator." ;-))

Just a tip: To get started, I always break it down for the kids. I explain it like this.

Students, when we have a wiki, there are two phases: content creation and content editing and refinement.

1. Content Creation

If the page is blank, that is where we are now. You cannot pick up an invisible desk—likewise, if nothing is there, you cannot edit an invisible wiki— NOTHING IS THERE. So, our first job is to create content. I expect that today you should all add 150 to 200 words to this page and you will have a successful day.

Remember, that what you say should have citations by linking to the item on the Internet. Also, if you want to talk about *what* is on the page, do it on the discussion tab.

Remember that when you come to class you should first check the discussion tab and *respond*. People feel ignored if no one responds—even if you agree or say "hi"—they know you're there—the most motivated teams and best wikis have good "Web 2.0 leaders" who engage with their partners by responding. *Respond* to them.

In about three or four days we'll see that we're getting a lot on the page. At that point we all have to move to . . .

2. Content Editing and Refinement

Here is where you ask these questions as you edit . . .

Read the rest of this Flat Classroom Diary online. http://tinyurl.com /explain-wikis

---

CASE EXAMPLES OF GLOBAL COLLABORATION

PDToolkit
for
Flattening Classrooms, Engaging Minds
Read full Case Studies in PDToolkit online.

Case Study 16

Two global educators, HEATHER DAVIS (China) and LISA PARISI (USA) reflect on their work piloting the "A Week in the Life . . ." Project in 2010

ADD FRIEND

HEATHER DAVIS
@toadie1951
http://teachlesslearnmore.edublogs.org
LISA PARISI
@lparisi
http://lisaslingo.blogspot.com

LISA: "I work in a very high achieving school district. The priorities are high test scores that lead to top universities. So anything I bring into my classroom better fit into the curricular requirements. . . . Flat Classroom Project came to me. It was not created by me, nor was it something that was required. But I knew it was an important project to be part of."

HEATHER: "I teach at an international school in Beijing, China. . . . An international school does not provide education for local children but only for children who hold foreign passports. We use the National Curriculum of England as the foundation of our academic program and then build on that by incorporating many aspects of Asia and especially China to create a totally unique curriculum. . . . "

LISA: "By coming up with essential questions, I could guarantee that the project was rigorous and meaningful. No time for a cute "Say hello" project. Essential questions push the children into higher-level thinking. That's a plus for any classroom."

HEATHER: "It is imperative to me that I provide opportunities for my Grade 3/Year 4 students to establish relationships with other students using integrated technology in an authentic manner. . . . The main objectives that we are using in our classroom for the Flat Classroom Project involve predominately two subject areas—Geography and both oral and written Literacy. The majority of the children in my class are English as an Additional Language (EAL) speakers, so it was necessary to use the project as a vehicle to improve their communication skills."

LISA: "While they were learning about other children around the world, they were also learning communication skills. Edmodo gave them opportunities to learn to ask and answer questions, keep a discussion going, and contribute something more meaningful than "Yo." Then the wiki discussion gave them the chance to agree and disagree with others respectfully and politely. . . . Another important skill to be learned is how to work in a group collaboratively. This project gave the children opportunities to work, first in class with students they know, and then outside of class with students they don't."

HEATHER: "We began with Geography and Google Earth and learned where . . . the schools were located by taking a tour of the earth, stopping at each school. We quickly put together our bulletin board so that there was a visual reminder daily of our project. Language skills have developed as they

have done this task. Each student has had much to add about [his or her] life and culture that [he or she wants] to share with the other students."

LISA: "While this Flat Classroom Project was not created by me to be specifically fit into curriculum, by making a few adjustments and adding a few lessons into the day, it worked very nicely. I would be more than willing to participate again."

HEATHER: ". . . For me one of the greatest parts has been the relationships that have been developed with the other teachers in the project. . . . We all have the same goal, we all understand our students and this has created a support system I had not expected. . . . We share our successes and moments of not great success. . . it has provided a different aspect of Global Collaboration for me personally that I was not expecting."

Case Study 17

HONOR MOORMAN, teacher and dean of instruction, the International School of the Americas, San Antonio, Texas, USA, NetGen Ed™ Project 2010, Flat Classroom Project 2010

HONOR MOORMAN
@honormoorman
http://about.me/honormoorman

for
Flattening Classrooms,
Engaging Minds
Read full Case Studies in
PDToolkit online.

Participating in the Flat Classroom Project provides an amazing opportunity for students to do much more than just learn *about* the world. They're actually learning *from* and *with* peers and teachers from around the world. At the International School of the Americas, we emphasize collaboration and project-based learning. Students experience a multitude of small-group activities and interdisciplinary projects, so they typically enter my 21st Century Global Leadership class having already developed the requisite skills for effective face-to-face collaboration. But global collaboration via the web presents a whole new set of challenges and unique learning opportunities.

Before the project begins, students typically have lots of questions about what to expect. When I explain that they will each be working in a group comprised of students from several different states and countries, they often respond with a head tilt or a quizzical look that tells me they can't quite imagine how this will be possible. "Are we going to Skype with them all the time?" "Won't they be asleep while we're in school?"

As we begin working with the Flat Classroom Project wiki, students soon experience for themselves what it takes to

co-create original content and negotiate the collaborative writing process with teammates on the other side of the globe. Scott explained this beautifully in our virtual presentation for the 2010 Global Education Conference:

> The most pertinent examples of our collaboration are our wiki pages. We worked constantly to make sure we had the newest and most relevant information . . . shared [with] everyone . . . each group had to collaborate with the whole group . . . [and] our wiki was the collaborative culmination of our growth during the project.[57]

When I asked Sarah and Alix about the skills and habits of mind they felt students developed and practiced in the Flat Classroom Project, they mentioned openness.

SARAH: The whole basis of the project is on collective learning and trying to communicate with people across boundaries of different countries.

ALIX: I think it takes a really open-minded person to move beyond just what [she or he believes], and what people in [her or his] classroom, in [her or his] city believe, and listen to and accept someone from far away who experiences life completely differently. That's why expanding your networks to a global network is so important because being a child of the United States is absolutely different from what most children or adults in the rest of the world go through.

View a recording of 21st Century Literacy and Global Competence Flourish in the Flat Classroom Project, a virtual conference session by these students from the 2010 Global Education Conference
http://tinyurl.com/global-competence ▶

Step 7
Celebration

"The applause is a celebration not only of the actors but also of the audience. It constitutes a shared moment of delight."

JOHN CHARLES POLANYI

A Joint Celebration: Australia to Qatar

Perhaps the most moving moment of the Flat Classroom™ Conference held in Qatar in 2009 was when Anne Baird had her students from Australia presenting to the audience on Skype. As Julie introduced her, she said that Anne's students wanted to be at the conference in person but the Australian government in their region wouldn't allow the students to go to the Middle East.

The students gave blank stares of disbelief. Anne teared up and spoke:

> My students didn't know that [the government wouldn't let them come], but it is OK. My students, I didn't want to tell you that they wouldn't let you come because I thought it was wrong. I didn't want you to know because I didn't want you to be disappointed. But you know now, and you're here, and it is OK.

The other students and educators felt the dark pain but also the golden joy that the students could present via Skype. It was summer vacation in Australia and the students had come in from the gleaming sun to put together a stellar presentation and movie talking about the Digiteen™ Digital Citizenship project and the importance of teaching digital citizenship in schools. These kids came in to school in the summertime! To present! They worked

CHAPTER 9 WEB RESOURCES
www.flatclassroombook.com/celebration.html

SHARE IT

Twitter hashtag for this book:
#flatclass

ADD FRIEND **ANNE BAIRD**
@annieb3525
http://teachingwithtechnology.wikispaces.com

on presentation skills and technology skills in the summer because they wanted to. They *wanted* to connect, even though some adults deliberating in the dark feared what they did not know.

Anne's students were not in the Souk in 2009, but Anne was—building a bridge to the Middle East that her students will walk across tomorrow. We all celebrated their achievements.

OVERVIEW OF CELEBRATION

Somehow a project that just sort of fades out does not feel complete and leaves participants wondering what happened. Celebration represents a shared joy, a common achievement, and a mutual appreciation for a job completed together. It should be a meaningful part of the academic achievement; it certainly is a part of athletics in most schools. End strong and finish the race with a burst of speed and activity; but not just any activity will do or have a purpose. Figure 9.1, Celebration and Retrospection in Action, takes you through an overview of what we'll be sharing in this chapter.

In the section Self, learn why we celebrate at the conclusion of projects. At the heart of celebration is our adaptation of the Japanese kaizen approach for ongoing

FIGURE 9.1   Celebration and Retrospection in Action

Arrows represent how one type of celebration can feed into another when it is recorded and captured.

Self		School		Student	
Me	**My Students**	**Synchronous**	**Asynchronous**	**Synchronous**	**Asynchronous**
Why? • Kaizen • Retrospection • Closure • Sense of accomplishment • Learning • Feedback • Cement learning	**Public** • Hall of fame • Best of project	**Public** • Award events "The event is the award"	**Public** • Museums of excellence • Best-of-school press releases • Social media sharing • T-shirts/tokens/ memory minders	**Public** • Student award shows • Student summits • Showcases	**Public** • Student ratings of other student work "Students' choice" • Action project celebrations • Award archive
How do I do this personally? • Appropriate platform • Ongoing • Conclusion • Inquiry-based • Ask why, not who • Get real	**Private** • Student surveys • Teacher surveys	**Private/ semiprivate** • School leaders privately give students awards of recognition • Retrospective round tables	**Private/ semiprivate** • Certificates • Archive record encapsulating project • Archives of learning • Reflection spaces for teachers/ administrators • "Judging" and feedback to students	**Private/ semiprivate** • Popcorn conversations • Video recordings	**Private/ semiprivate** • Reflection spaces for students • Create next step for students • Personal project portfolios

improvement. Learn how you should reflect as a teacher and take away some simple methods to collect and process collaborative experiences for ongoing improvement. Recognize your students in positive, free ways that promote best practice.

Organizations are never stagnant: they are either improving or declining. Ongoing improvement is the topic of the next section, School, where we explore how to use culminating events and archives to consistently improve results. It is OK to make mistakes. It is not OK to ignore them and keep making the same errors. It is great to have successes. It is not OK to let them pass by without a flit of the eyes of those who matter in the learning process.

Every project should conclude with best-practice examples that embody excellence. In the Student section, we talk about how to recognize the best through awards and online galleries. Students' individual written reflections and verbal reflections become part of the celebratory learning process too. Learn how to prepare for online student presentations and keep them flowing and professional. Meaningful celebration and reflection is a catalyst to personal, professional, and organizational growth. Let's celebrate learning!

 SELF Personal Reflection and Celebration

Personal reflection and celebration is a vital habit of the successful 21st century person. Reflection and celebration becomes a consistent conclusion of student learning experiences and it is a powerful way to improve the results in your school and project. Even though *celebration* is the last of the seven steps to flatten the classroom, reflection is ongoing and should be present in all steps. The tagging, sharing and aggregation made possible by Web 2.0 gives us new ways to reflect in schools that most are yet to leverage. First let's understand why we do this and then how we celebrate and reflection personally. Then, lets see how we can recognize students publicly and privately as a teacher.

DIGITAL CITIZENSHIP AREA OF UNDERSTANDING
Habits of Learning

 **ISTE STANDARDS**

NETS.T 1.c
Facilitate and Inspire Student Learning and Creativity

WHY? PURPOSES FOR CELEBRATION AND REFLECTION

Ongoing Improvement (Kaizen). Socrates said, "the highest form of human excellence is to question oneself and others." This process of inquiry lies at the heart of **kaizen**, a Japanese term that means slow, steady improvement. We all get stuck in "ruts" and want to just keep things as they are. Ongoing improvement is a choice.

 tweetable
Even though celebration is the last of the seven steps to flatten the classroom, reflection is ongoing and should be present in all steps. #flatclass

Retrospection. It would be sad to retire and have it said, "she didn't teach 30 years, she taught 1 year 30 times." In order to progress, we have to intentionally plan for improvement. After major projects, some conduct a "postmortem." This term is repugnant in a learning environment because learning is organic and ongoing, and projects should be alive. Although student learning may conclude, the teacher and school should never stop learning and improving practices.

Closure. Knowing a project is done is important because in collaborative environments it is easy to have some participants just drop out. Once a teacher moves on to another module or unit of work, typically some students "evaporate" from the global project, and it is very noticeable. When everyone agrees on a date for a celebration event, it serves as a terminal point for closure on that project. The celebration is your finish line.

Students' feelings are often based on expectations shared by the teacher. This way, if some students are still finishing up reflections or other internal assessments based on the project past the celebration date, they won't take the absence of other students as a failure or a problem that teachers should be handling.

Sense of Accomplishment.   Because the teacher is the coach in this environment, he or she is often involved in the biggest struggles and problems. It is easy for the teacher to lose sight of the learning that has taken place. After every online **student summit**, teachers exclaim later in the teacher forum how much their students learned and how much joy it was to hear the students share. Teachers aren't mind readers. Having students present learning both verbally online and in a reflective manner, teachers realize what students are learning in a meaningful way. They hear the power and need to be reminded of it.

tweetable

Engaged teachers obtain and listen to student feedback at key points during a course, particularly after a collaborative . . . experience. #flatclass

Provide Feedback.   While listening to the students' perspectives, the teacher can ask herself or himself: Did the students have the outcomes I was planning for? Did the students have frustrations that I can prevent? Did the students have frustrations that were important for their learning process? Did some things happen unintentionally that were positive and need to be kept? Engaged teachers obtain and listen to student feedback at key points during a course, particularly after a collaborative project-based experience.

ISTE STANDARDS

NETS.T 2
Design and Develop Digital-Age Learning Experiences and Assessments

Cement Cooperative Learning Experiences (Jigsaw Effect).   The jigsaw effect is when the puzzle pieces *fit* together—when the students hear what the other students have done, they see it fit together and the "ah-ha" moment emerges. When students "divide and conquer" and deeply learn their aspect of the content, they become subject matter experts.

By presenting, other students take that learning and internalize it and put the pieces together in their own minds. Student summits are often one of the most transformative experiences for students—when they finally see the big picture. Often they say, "I wish I understood at the beginning," but the point is that they truly aren't ready to understand because the process leads them toward conclusions that they make on their own. Teachers try to give the big picture at the beginning but students can realize the context of the project when they see what other students have done and relate it to their own work. This is when students are truly writing the textbook for one another!

HOW DO I CELEBRATE AND REFLECT PERSONALLY?

ISTE STANDARDS

NETS.T 3
Model Digital-Age Work and Learning

Reflection begins with you. Teachers should write about their successes, struggles, and what they learned. It is great to do this on a learning space where students can see you be real and see your struggle for improvement. You're modeling a lifestyle of improvement. Teachers can also look at student reflections in order to shape theirs.

This way a student knows a teacher is listening through his or her personal writing and feedback. Flat Classroom teachers reflect about their struggles to teach on the same educational networks where students reflect on their struggles to learn. Let's look at characteristics of an effective personal reflection.

Appropriate Platform.   Know where to speak your mind. Use good judgment with where you are sharing and what you're sharing. Sometimes teachers get in trouble and even lose their jobs for sharing reflections in the wrong place. While schools should have private places for teachers to share thoughts and ask questions, most do not. It is better to write a reflection to yourself in Evernote or a private notebook than to write something on Facebook that a non-teacher or someone at your school would not understand.

Ongoing.   Effective reflection is ongoing. A daily journal of accomplishments and problems will be useful when you do your retrospection because it is easy to forget the struggles of beginning a project when you are six weeks later and at the end of a semester.

Inquiry Based.   Teachers are the original inquiry-based learners. We are problem solvers trying to reach the unreachable and unlock the complex psyche of a child. Make it a habit of asking questions and put your thoughts about answers. This is what makes a private online group helpful, because your inquiries can lead to responses from others.

Ask Why, Not Who.   It is human nature to want to blame someone for problems. Of course there are people involved! But the real question is why, not who. When you are reflecting on problems you should work to get at why. Why did that person get angry? Why did half the class not understand their assignment in week two? Why was it so hard to teach this concept in this way?

Publicly Praise.   The right time to name a "who" is when you want to praise someone. Praise should always be personal and specific. There's not enough encouragement in the world.

Privately Criticize.   When you criticize, even if you take the "who" out remember that others may not be as wise as you and will often want to know "who." Be wise when you criticize and where you do it.

Get Real.   All reflections aren't going to be perfect, pretty, or long. Sometimes a concise, "I taught xyz lesson today and am wiped out" is enough to give you a nudge to look back at that lesson when you do your retrospection.

MECHANISMS FOR REFLECTION, CELEBRATION, AND CRITIQUE

There are free, simple things you can do to recognize and collect feedback.

"Teacher's Choice" or "Hall of Fame" Feedback Mechanisms.   Awards programs aren't perfect. If a teacher notices or sees excellence, the creation of a "Hall of Fame" or

WEBSITES

http://www.evernote.com

DIGITAL CITIZENSHIP AREA OF UNDERSTANDING
Habits of Learning

21st CENTURY SKILLS
C21 LEADERSHIP AND RESPONSIBILITY

ISTE STANDARDS

NETS.T 2
Design and Develop Digital-Age Learning Experiences and Assessments

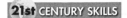
21st CENTURY SKILLS

21ST CENTURY LEARNING ENVIRONMENTS

"Teacher's Choice" awards are an excellent way to recognize best practice. "Best of Project" also works. This is as easy as a wiki page, blog post, or web page with links or copies of best practices.

Informal awards for student best practices give students a way to achieve more than a perfect score on the assessment. Recognize best practice but *never* give an award to just give an award—not everyone deserves it. The fastest way to make your awards impotent is to give one undeservedly. This also gives you a starting point the next time you start the same project.

NETS.T 5
Engage in Professional Growth
and Feedback

Verbal Feedback.   A major project by a student deserves more than a numeric grade. Their efforts deserve consideration, verbal feedback, and when it is excellent, an audience. Students want to know that a teacher looked at their project, especially if it took a long time to do. Numbers just aren't enough; they want to know they matter. Your response to a major project should show that you took the time to review and provide feedback. Even a "perfect" project should receive comment and suggestions for improvement. You give meaning through response in assessing student work.

Student Surveys.   Students need a private way to let teachers know about their learning on the project. It is true that students trying to make a perfect score do not want to upset the teacher by being disagreeable. Thus, students can complete an anonymous survey to provide feedback. It is also valuable for teachers who want to engage in authentic research and quantify the efficacy of a project to use this as an authentic research tool.

Teacher Surveys.   Teachers need to also be provided with an anonymous way to provide feedback to organizers. Although this can be tough "medicine to swallow" for project organizers, actively seeking feedback is an ingredient of a successful organization.

 # SELF-ASSESSMENT SURVEY

for
Flattening Classrooms,
Engaging Minds
See the survey results in the
online PDToolkit before moving
on to the next section.

Before moving to the next part of this chapter, we invite you to take this self-assessment survey. We also suggest you discuss these questions with colleagues, including your wider learning network, to determine your current level of confidence and ability with strategies that promote reflection and celebration.

1.   **When I complete a project or a semester/year, I typically (check all that apply):**

   a.   Take time to reflect and make notes in my personal, offline journal for the next time I do a project or unit of work.

   b.   Reflect with the class verbally to help summarize what was learned and not.

   c.   Give my class a lesson/day to share the learning of each individual student, sometimes recording this.

    d.   Encourage students to post their reflections on a blog or in a paper.

    e.   Give special recognition for those who achieve excellence in the project.

    f.   Move on to the next project with little fanfare, there is never time to celebrate or reflect.

    g.   Give students feedback in other ways such as a survey.

    h.   Don't have a way to retrieve student feedback.

2. **Do I recognize student personal excellence in my class?**

    a.   Yes   b. No   c. Maybe. I need to work on this.

3. **Do I personally reflect on project achievements?**

    a.   Yes   b. No   c. Maybe. I need to work on this.

 SCHOOL   **The Key Tactic That Improves Quality**

Schools and projects can celebrate and reflect in public and private ways to accomplish the objectives set forth in the last section. Teacher professional learning and collaboration is vital to school improvement. The Project Red 1:1 laptop research study (from Chapter 7) indicates that changing "management leadership by the principal" with monthly professional learning and collaboration between teachers as the second leading technology practice that improved learning the most. (It was just behind integrating technology into every intervention class.[1]) Change leadership is important and these practices built into the celebratory process will get you there.

EVENTS AND LIBRARIES OF LEARNING

Events are powerful tools when used well. They should also be recorded and become part of a public library celebrating learning.

Public Events.   You get what you celebrate. Do you wonder why everyone wants to be a star athlete or have a state winning team? Because they know they have accomplished something and because everyone loves praise for a job well done. Winning is addictive! However, motivation to learn is largely intrinsic because there are often very few extrinsic awards for learning besides a report card. If your parent doesn't care about grades, then a report card is even less motivating.

    This is one thing that Ron Clark, best selling author and principal of Ron Clark Academy, does so well. He is incredibly good at creating events that are the reward. From welcoming new students at his school with the entire school applauding to talking his way into getting his student's faces on the billboard in Time Square, he challenges educators to "[c]reate moments that will have a lasting impact on children's lives."[2] His school even has four "houses" (like those in Harry Potter) to celebrate and promote learning and include new students.

RON CLARK
@ronclarkacademy
http://www.ronclarkacademy
.com

Certainly moments of great athletic attainment are memorable but we have an imperative to create memorable moments of learning and inspiration in our schools. While some claim that the "pep rallies" in the United States designed to get students excited about doing well on standardized tests are an attempt of this, others (like the authors) think that it feels artificial because it isn't celebrating an accomplishment just an event.

The event should become the reward and can include mementos of learning, T-shirts, tokens, and other things that serve as "memory-minders" reminding the person of the achievement. Often coaches have vowed to shave their head or some other personal stunt as a result of a team's accomplishment. This is not to say that every principal should sharpen their razor and promise to lose their locks, but there are fun, free, creative things that can be done to celebrate learning. If graduation is your only academic ceremony, that just isn't enough.

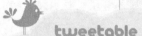

tweetable

We must create memorable moments of learning and inspiration. #flatclass

Libraries of Learning.   Websites are easy to make. Schools should create online "museums of excellence" and "best of school" artifacts. Memorization is easier to measure using standardized tests. How do you measure higher order thinking? Higher-order thinking at its best should be celebrated. What does it look like? Who did it? When a parent considers a school, they should be able to review projects and student work that the school considers to be the best. What are students creating?

The best events and activities that celebrate learning should be recorded and archived on a school's YouTube channel or website. A good school is much more than a test score.

Social Media Sharing.   Schools should use every opportunity and every venue to share their story. If something great has happened, tweet it, post it to your Facebook page, let people know. Social media is important because it gives your parents and students a chance to "like" what you're doing and tell the story through their networks. Use the "fans" of the school to tell your story. This motivates students who are part of these networks.

Principal's Choice.   School principals cannot be everywhere at once but can leverage their presence. This means that tools like blogs, email, Twitter, or Facebook fan pages are great ways to spread your vision and recognize best practice. A quick glance at thoughts and what you've shared as the school's accomplishment sends a powerful, public message about what you think is important. Excellent classroom learning practices should filter up to principals and administrators so everyone knows what excellence in learning looks like. Principals review test scores in detail, they should also look at projects.

Principals can also privately bring students and parents in for opportunities to recognize student accomplishment on individual projects. Political leaders are constantly bringing in people, presenting them with awards, and snapping a picture. This is because we remember those who remember what we've done. A principal's office shouldn't just be full of problems; it should be full of best practice and recognition of effort.

GROUP REFLECTIVE PRACTICES

Group Reflective Spaces.   Consider that reflection doesn't and often shouldn't be public especially if it is intended to identify problems. There is a big difference between explaining a problem and complaining. To pretend that problems don't exist is to lie. Yet, many schools suppress teachers from identifying areas that can be improved.

Schools should have educational networks with students and teachers and should also have smaller networks for professional development and sharing. Networks should have a clear purpose. Where is your school's network for reflection and improvement? Where is your community of best practice? We need such kaizen communities undergirded with positive, forward thinking problem explaining and solution driven conversation to help us move schools forward. Meetings dominated by the one or two outspoken staff members shouldn't be the only mechanism for providing feedback. Reflections can use words, pictures, videos but tags should be consistently used for all of them. Tags can give meaning with tag clouds as a great feedback mechanism for administrators. A tag cloud shows how often a term has been used as a tag by the size of the word. So, for example, if a lot of teachers are tagging their posts *copier,* someone can see that the copier is an issue at just a glance. Likewise, if there is a lot of conversation about math, that would emerge also.

Word Clouds.   Consider taking the blog posts and writings of students and pasting them into a tool such as Wordle to analyze meaning. It is a powerful summative tool, because not everyone tags properly.

Wordle
http://www.wordle.net

Retrospective Roundtables.   When a major project concludes, a roundtable of stakeholders is useful to discuss in retrospect the good and the areas that need improvement. Ideas for balancing conversation can be implemented to encourage listening to everyone in the room. For example, each participant could take three tokens upon entering the room (even principals) and when a person contributes to the conversation, the token goes into the middle. Everyone's tokens must be "spent" before the conversation opens for whoever wishes to speak. Quiet teachers are an important part of the conversation too and a wise administrator will include them.

Rubrics and "Judging." When rubrics are developed between project participants, a shared understanding of common goals supports a platform to have judging or an awards system. In collaborative projects, this provides teachers a measure of their students' performances versus that of other classrooms. Administrators can also know that teachers are achieving a level of excellence in their chosen medium when they see their students recognized in such a format.

ISTE STANDARDS

NETS.T 2
Design and Develop Digital-Age Learning Experiences and Assessments

C21 INTERDISCIPLINARY THEME:
Global Awareness

When external judges review project submissions, it can remove the personal bias that may be inherent in a classroom teacher's environment and provides opportunities for students who are dismissed by their peers and others in a face-to-face situation to be elevated in status because of their recognition by an external audience. This practice promotes personal excellence and improvement.

Learning Experiences through Judging.   In addition to the use of rubrics, open comments are important in providing feedback to students and teachers about best practice. For

See Malcolm's video at http://tinyurl.com/fcp-malcom

example, **meta-judge** Barbara Stefanics viewed the winning videos for every wiki page for the Flat Classroom Project 10-3 to determine overall winners. Her video winner was Malcolm from Canada. Barbara stated, "This video was very well done and very informational. I like the computerized voice for narration. It put me in a futuristic mood! Great graphics with the charts. Also, great analogy of comparing the old Internet to the new Internet . . . good source of outsourced video to explain Internet connectivity."[3]

In this example, students can see past the score into the nuances that allowed this video to win the project. This provides insight for the teachers and others educators who are following the project. Feedback of this nature can be provided by anyone. When something is identified as a best practice, state why. Also make sure everyone realizes that every project can be improved by pointing out any flaws.

ISTE STANDARDS

NETS.S 2.b
Communication and Collaboration

21st CENTURY SKILLS

C21 LEARNING AND INNOVATION SKILLS:
Communication and Collaboration

ADD FRIEND

TIM TYSON
@timtyson
http://drtimtyson.com

http://tinyurl.com/mabrymiddle

http://tinyurl.com/fcp-awards

![STUDENT] **Best Practices to Finish Up**

Celebration events such as awards shows and student summits give closure. The handshake is the starting line and the summit and awards shows are the finish line. Things can happen afterwards, but students and teachers alike know not to expect extensive collaboration.

AWARDS AND RECOGNITION OF BEST PRACTICE

Student Awards "Shows." Mabry Middle School under the leadership of Dr. Tim Tyson, had an annual event for their year-long student video project that was like an "Academy Awards" for students. Flat Classroom projects conclude every projects with an awards show recognizing the best videos and explaining why the top candidates were selected. For Flat Classroom projects, we work hard to let teachers know ahead of time if they have a student being recognized and who that student is so that they (and sometimes parents) can make time to be at the event. We've had students get up in the middle of the night or get special permission to exit one class to attend online ceremonies in the library and hear their award announced. Local schools usually put this in their local newspapers.

As already discussed, the teacher, principal, or schools can provide Teacher's Choice awards via a wiki or a blog post, and especially in person. Teachers have the power to give awards as they see fit for aspects of film or products. For example, one video may have excellent sound but for some other reason lost marks. The teacher could give an award for "best soundtrack" and another for "best use of creative camera angles."

Award Archive. Best of project awards and award ceremonies are powerful but it can't stop there. We have an awards page for our projects that showcases best student work. Science fairs often leave display boards up for a few weeks after the conclusion of the event. Student work can now be showcased in online museums of learning in perpetuity.

STUDENT REFLECTIONS AND SHARING

Action Reports from Students. Sometimes the students plan the best conclusions. It may involve printing T-shirts, issuing a press release, or holding an event, so don't be limited by the ideas here. In the Digiteen project, students plan their action project, and their culminating event is often held at school at which time they record and share what they did with the other students on an action wiki. When students summarize their own work and what worked and didn't work, it often gives them better feedback on this work than if the teacher had provided the same feedback.

DIGITAL CITIZENSHIP AREA
OF UNDERSTANDING
Habits of Learning

Student Rating Systems and Peer Review. The NetGen Ed™ project has Students' Choice awards where students nominate and vote on the best videos. Using Facebook-like ratings, where students are able to give stars to the videos of each other, are powerful ways to let students tell one another what they think. Peer review can be by rating or by leaving comments.

Individual Reflection and Celebration. Individual reflections, celebrations, and critiques are important, as students will be evaluating projects for most of their lives. Using hyperlinks to share work is also an important part of this so that students know how to write in ways that summarize their online work and document their performance as a future skill for success in the workplace or academia.

"Popcorn" or "Coffee Shop" Class Chats. Chris Morgan from Glenbrook Academy of International Studies in Iowa hosted a "popcorn conversation" where the students popped popcorn and sat down to discuss their learning. Vicki has taken students off campus to a local coffee shop to talk about learning in a casual environment. Informal celebrations involving food and conversation often provide esprit de corps as well as interesting learning by reflection after a project is concluded.

ACTION PROJECT CELEBRATIONS

The culmination of the Digiteen™ project is an action project back in the school community. This can take the form of an assembly presentation, a chance to talk to younger students about digital citizenship, a campaign to raise awareness about safety and security online, or in fact a number of other activities where students "take action" regarding digital citizenship. The aim is that the activity and ensuing celebration is student-directed and is a synthesis of their learning during the actual project.

USE YOUR IMAGINATION

Your celebration is limited only by your imagination. Be creative. Have fun. When students see that learning can be fun, they want more!

Best Digiteen Action Wikis
http://tinyurl.com/best-digiteen

Group Presentations. Having students present in a student summit with an audience is one of the most powerful experiences students can have. Not only do students learn the nuances of web conferencing and presenting, but they also learn netiquette for an effective backchannel. Many students do not realize that online teachers can see their private chats to one another, for example. They need to understand how to use these rooms in successful ways in their future. These can also be recorded and parents or administrators can be invited to attend "from their office" as a powerful way to demonstrate learning. (Consider it an online "assembly.")

SHOWCASE: FLAT CLASSROOM STUDENT SUMMIT

All classrooms participating in the Flat Classroom Project and the NetGen Ed™ Project are invited to run their own student summit[4] or join another summit as part of the end of project celebration. Flat Classroom project summits are currently held in real time in the virtual classroom, Blackboard Collaborate. They simulate a live presentation as all students prepare a graphic based on their topics, present their learning and field questions, and receive comments from the audience. The audience is often international, both teachers and students. The summit develops exciting synergy when students realize there are others in the virtual room apart from their immediate class.

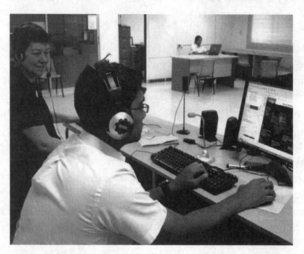

Julie Lindsay and Sabbab in Dhaka, Bangladesh, presenting in the first student summit.

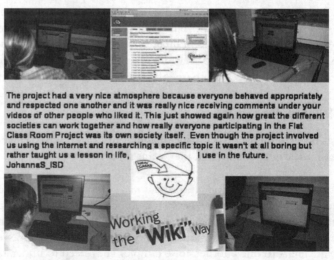

A typical student summit slide with photos and summary pictures that the student will discuss in their brief presentation.

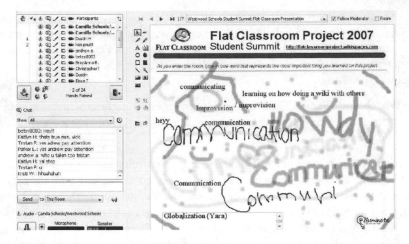

Students greeting each other in the 2007 summit.

Organizing a cross-class summit is a challenge, especially across time zones, but it's not impossible, and it's definitely worth it for the exposure and professional experience the students gain. Lacking international participants should not deter the class teacher. One strategy to flatten the learning in this type of celebration is to invite key people from the same school such as the head of the school, or other subject teachers, to come in from their office or own classroom using their computer. The students are always delighted, excited to interact in this relatively new learning mode and to see teachers taking an interest. Further flattening includes inviting parents, expert advisors, and judges to support students and provide constructive feedback on their presentation and ability to share learning.

View Student Summit Recordings
http://tinyurl.com/fcp-summits

PREPARING FOR A STUDENT SUMMIT: TEACHER AND STUDENT CHECKLIST

To ensure success when running a live online summit, the following suggestions will help managing teachers. Nothing beats preparation and rehearsal before going global, especially allowing students in to **sandbox** the virtual room first and work out any curiosities they may have. This means allowing time before the summit for students to play around (as in playing in the sandbox) and learn about the digital communication methods.

Pre-Summit Preparation. Preparation is the key to a successful online presentation. You'll find it takes several days of prep to be ready for your first presentation and at least one practice session.

DIGITAL CITIZENSHIP AREA OF UNDERSTANDING
Literacy and Fluency

Image. Students prepare a collage showing snapshots of their project and what it has meant to them (e.g., topic name, screenshots of their group, people involved, video images, key words, etc.). The collage can be prepared on a PPT slide and saved as a JPG file. It should also include the student's name—the same name the student has been known as during the project. Do not include full names. Upload this to a central location like a Ning network.

NETS.T.2
Design and Develop Digital-
Age Learning Experiences and
Assessments

C21 LEARNING ENVIRONMENTS

Script.   Students prepare a script so they can talk for 2 to 3 minutes about their topic, referring to the collage as needed (e.g., brief description of their topic, the group they were in, and the challenges, highlights, and learning outcomes, as well as advice for future participants). Without a script, students often get tongue-tied: Talking to a computer can be tough.

Create Whiteboard Slides.   The teacher, who must have moderator privileges in the room, preloads an opening slide for the summit, including school name, date, project, and running order.

Add Student Slides.   A teacher or student helper also preload student JPG images or slides to the white board. These images can be loaded to the educational network (Ning) first so that student managers can download easily and use them for the summit. Another option is to create a slide with the name of each student and let students go to their own slide and upload their image. This gives them experience with an interactive room and saves time. Do this several days before your first student summit, or at least the day before.

Save the Whiteboard.   The whiteboard group of JPG images is saved and downloaded onto your local computer for use the next time you log in. This is important because you can come back into the room later and easily load the file ready for the main summit. It also provides a valuable backup file that can also be sent to other moderators. Loading the whiteboard typically does not take long once it has been created as a separate file.

Rehearsal.   The class rehearses in the virtual room on a day before the summit to get used to using the tool and to gain confidence when presenting. This allows for some fun (but immature) sandbox activities like bombarding the whiteboard with graffiti and images. Remember to ask all students to login with this name protocol: first-name_schoolacronym particularly if you have many students. Also demonstrate the levels of control that you have in the room. (And mention that even if they "private chat" one another, the moderator in such rooms can typically see *everything*. This prevents future embarrassment in an online classroom. You cannot pass notes or talk behind an online teacher's back). Get all immature behavior out of their system and talk about how one acts in an online professional environment. Without rehearsal, a teacher is setting himself up for embarrassment.

Invite Stakeholders.   This is a great opportunity to invite administrators, superintendents, and parents to join you because they don't have to be physically present. You may have to involve your technology department to teach others how to dial in to the webinar, but that is a good thing! You can also tweet out the link to your network, but this is best done just before starting.

During the Student Summit.   Most student summits take this approach.

Start the recorder.   The recording controls provide record, pause and stop facility. You should always record—even if you're not going to publish—just in case you need it. Assess student presentations; it is helpful to rewatch because if you are moderator you can be focused on running the summit instead of assessing.

Introduction. One student is allocated the task of briefly introducing the school and location. (A prepared script helps with nerves!)

The moderator The teacher takes on the role of moderator, and may consider promoting one or two students to share this role. Otherwise, it is strongly suggested that another teacher be present to help moderate. Speaking from experience, it is very difficult to be master of ceremonies, moderate a class of students, and troubleshoot technical issues by yourself. The moderator can smooth transitions, and should also pose questions from the backchannel chat out loud so they will be on the audio recording.

Backchannel chat. Encourage good netiquette in the backchannel. If someone has a question, they should use the "at" (@) sign to ask the speaker a question. Typically each student should answer a question from the backchannel.

Technical facilitator. Find someone to help you troubleshoot technical problems ahead of time.

Student presentation. Each student takes a turn to "show 'n' tell," speak about her or his slide, and then answer any questions from the global audience that might be present. It is helpful to let students know who the next two to three presenters are so they can be on deck and ready.

Post-Student Summit. Summits are not over after the synchronous event. As we learned in Chapter 4, we must blend communications to include global partners. This means that you record the summit and share the learning asynchronously.

Recording processed and posted. The session is recorded and available for archiving and future retrieval.

Images loaded on student profiles. Students upload JPG images to the Flat Classroom Project Ning and tag them with the project code and school tag (e.g., FCP10-3, BISS) and appropriate copyright. This ensures that students retain the rights to their images. (Make sure you look at the terms of the service of your network, however, as some network operators reserve the right to use such images for purposes of sharing such as we have in this book.)

See Vicki's students present their Digiteen Action projects at the Global Education Conference 2011 http://tinyurl.com /gec2011-whs-digiteen

SUMMARY

tweetable

Innovation is fueled by reflection and the motivation of a project that ends well. #flatclass

Innovation is fueled by reflection and the motivation of a project that ends well. This chapter has shared many ways that individuals, teachers, and students can celebrate and critique a project for future success. Using both public and private mechanisms, it is important to have a mindset of kaizen, or "ongoing improvement," but also to cement learning through group reflection.

A variety of ways to recognize best practices are important to help teachers and students recognize "what the best looks like" as they pursue excellence in their work. Projects cannot just fade away; rather, they should have a clear endpoint so that teachers and students can move on with confidence, knowing that they successfully completed their task and are ready to move on to a new learning endeavor. Review Figure 9.1, "Celebration and Retrospection in Action," to plan ahead for how you will celebrate and improve.

ESSENTIAL QUESTIONS

- How should schools and classrooms implement strategies to promote kaizen?
- What role should teacher reflections play in providing feedback to their class? To other teachers? To project organizers? To administrators?
- What would be the impact on students if a project ended by just ceasing work without any of the suggestions in this chapter?
- How could involving students in designing their own closing event be beneficial?

◀ Join the online conversation and share your answers at http://tinyurl.com/flatclass-ch9

FLAT CLASSROOM™ 15 CHALLENGES

CHALLENGE 12: CELEBRATION AND SUMMATION

Do: Participate in a summit for your learning as part of your course or in one of our learning summits as shown in the schedule at www.flatclassroombook.com/ch9. The summit should be recorded, and you should have a graphic to present in the online classroom as you reflect on what you've learned.

Optional. If you do not have a course or group to present with, recruit three or four people in your learning community to attend your brief online presentation in a classroom. Share with them a summary of what you have learned and a celebration of your accomplishment!

SHARE: Blog about the process of presenting in an online classroom and summarize your presentation. Embed your graphic and a link to the recording of the presentation (if available.) Suggest at least one idea for a flat classroom-style project that relates to your content area. The tag for this challenge is fcc12_summit. Use this when you blog, or to share with your group

◀ Share what you did with your challenge at http://tinyurl.com/flat15-12 ▶

THE FLAT CLASSROOM™ DIARIES

Diary Entry 17

MARCIA ALESSI, NETGENED 2009 REFLECTION

 **ADD FRIEND**

MARCIA ALESSI
@mabengry

I've finally landed back in Los Angeles, although I'm not sure my feet have touched ground just yet! What a week it has been. Can you picture me sitting on the floor of a busy New York City Starbucks trying to get a connection so that I can download the Hippo OpenSim Viewer on that fateful rainy Monday morning of April, typing with one hand, holding my cell with the other as Leslie walked me through the Mac download process from Los Angeles where she was having her own technical difficulties which I gather happened all around the globe, and trying to set up her own laptop with six excited SPA NetGenners hovering 'round in the school library.

Eventually, only after an hour and fifteen minutes of downloading, was I able to get connected to the virtual ceremony and managed to catch the final thrilling moments. I'm not sure what the Starbuckers thought was happening as I talked to my students through a torrent of tears on the dirty and crowded floor. Probably a common sight in NYC :)

When I first read about this project two years ago, I never dreamed that despite our own technology challenges that we could enlist nine eighth-grade science students on a completely voluntary basis and compete so effectively to make education history. But that is what these students did. Because this project was done nearly 100 percent on student time and out of the classroom, some of our participants didn't submit videos. But as the learning curve flattens, just like the world, the next time more of them will feel comfortable doing so. What time was spent in the classroom was spent with students helping students, students enlisting advice from friends from the Middle East, Alaska, and Australia . . . just a keystroke away, and with Leslie and I mere supportive bystanders, cheerleaders, and occasional nudges . . .

To [student names omitted], who had no idea what their crazy teacher was asking them to "volunteer" for, but who jumped into this project within minutes, using Macs and PCs and all different sorts of movie-making formats, congratulations to each of you. These first steps of your digital footprint are now forever embedded in digital history. And to the parents who committed and permitted their children to take a risk and do something for nothing but the rewards of a new experience, thank you for trusting me with your children's learning. And last, to my principal, Sister Stella, whose vision is surpassed only by her unwavering support and enthusiasm for all that is good and best for the children of St. Paul's, a heartfelt thank you for believing in me.

A sampling of student comments:

I was confused at first and I didn't want to do it, but then I thought it was so cool that we could talk to kids from all over, and I would actually like to do something like this again.

I learned that we are in control of our future!

I learned how to work with people from around the world using technology.

I think this project was fun, and I am sad because it is over.

I thought it was neat to talk to other people throughout the world.

Diary Entry 18

"TELLING THE WORLD: FLAT CLASSROOM STUDENT SUMMIT IN PRACTICE," JULIE'S BLOG, DECEMBER 14, 2009[5]

This blog post posed three questions. Anne Mirtschin answered these as a comment to the post. Here is a summary of her answers:

Questions for Discussion Asked in Julie's Blog Post

1. How are you "flattening" your school and/or classroom by providing synchronous meetings between students globally? Is this considered important? Desired? Necessary? By you? Your colleagues? Your administration?

2. If experiences such as Flat Classroom Summits promote global citizenship and enhanced cultural understanding, how can we embed this practice into what we do everyday as educators? What has to change in education to make this possible?

3. Is it really possible to have an asynchronous online learning community when we see how powerful this virtual real-time handshake can be to all participants? What are the essential challenges of blending both asynchronous and synchronous modes across the world?

Read the rest of this Flat Classroom Diary online with the response from Anne to the other two questions at http://tinyurl.com/fcp-summit

Anne's Response via Comment to the Blog Post

Having just been involved in the latest FCP, I would like to endorse the fantastic learning outcomes that such involvement brings. To answer the questions:

1. I see "flattening my classroom" as essential. I teach in a small, rural, prep to year 12 school in country South Eastern Australia, where students are isolated geographically and culturally. The world is constantly flattening and skills for global interaction and communication are essential. The most obvious flattening occurs when my year 9–11 students join in one of the Flat Classroom projects. This enables students to interact, collaborate and work in virtual teams via wikis, Nings and actually meet in the virtual classroom via Elluminate. Synchronous meetings are a little difficult for us as we fall into the Asian time zones and language differences can provide a barrier to effective communications. However, we have successfully used Skype to videoconference with schools in Singapore, Malaysia, Philippines, Thailand, and China, etc., where English is taught as a first or second language. Another virtual classroom software—discoverE—has been used. If classes in the USA are willing to return to school in the evenings then connections can be made synchronously with Skype, discoverE, Elluminate or Coveritlive. My colleagues see it as important and are gradually making connections of their own. I have found it is important that they have ownership of the connections and communications. The administration also sees it as important and the International Division of our Department of Education also feel it is necessary. Although most would see it as essential, fear of the unknown, perceived lack of skills and understanding, time factors, etc., prevent many of them pursuing it further. . . .

Diary Entry 19

VIRTUALLY AWARDED . . . AND MORE! THE FULL VERSION CAN BE READ ON JULIE'S BLOG, APRIL 21, 2009.[6]

(This blog post talks about the NetGenEd Project 2009 Awards Ceremony held in a virtual world, where teachers and students joined together to celebrate and embrace emerging technologies . . . well, that was the plan, anyway. . . .)

Well, an hour before the official opening . . . and 30 minutes or so afterwards, we were continuing to get students into the grid, stabilize and start the awards. So much time had been put into this ceremony, through press releases, online meetings, judges and meta-judges determining the multimedia winners. Led by our very own virtual pioneer, Vicki Davis, who spent hours preparing the slideshow and making sure everyone who wanted to had access to the awards in the virtual world, we took the plunge . . . over the cutting edge . . . into something we all knew very little about . . . but something we now have a lot more confidence with. When I say "we" I mean the teachers involved in the project, as well as the students who had the opportunity to participate, including students from USA, Australia, and Qatar. As colleague and Flat Classroom teacher here at Qatar Academy, Sam Liberto, said he never thought he would be in a classroom asking students to edit their avatar and transport to a virtual island.

The language itself is alienating, but not anymore!

But, back to the panic. Well, as a lead presenter in the awards show, I was to pick up my newly created dress, get it on and arrive at the F.L.A.T.S looking glam and ready to go. Well, it took a few tries and some real help from Chris (dress provider and tech guru) to transport me to the box that contained the clothes. Ok, click on box, save clothes to inventory, now *wear* clothes . . . hmmm. Sounds easy, but then the grid wobbled, crashed. I tried again, wobble, crash. Message from organizers not to go in as too many participants were on the island flying and editing their appearance making it unstable. Panic. . . . but what if it starts and I don't have my dress on?? Managed to get in, put the skirt on, lovely green flowing skirt . . . but the top would not go on, not sure why.

As it turned out we managed to get through the awards and stream the audio into the Sim, but many participants did not manage to get in, including Vicki! . . . . The joys of technology! So, what did we learn? Well, I think we learned that . . .

Read the rest of this Flat Classroom Diary online. http://tinyurl.com /virtual-award-show

CASE EXAMPLES OF GLOBAL COLLABORATION

Case Study 18

Student Summit Transcript, Flat Classroom Project
2008—Westwood Schools

Following are some student reflections from a sample student summit. Note how students celebrated accomplishments, reflected upon learning, and shared critique about improvements that could be made.

Gracie: Hi, I'm Gracie. I'm in the group for Workflow Software, group 3B. I learned a lot about workflow software. It deals with businesses and schools and I made a video about how a student named Gracie has to complete a project in a week, but she has partners from around the world . . .

Joseph: My subject was workflow software and I had the fun factor. I made a video called "This and That" with Joseph, which is an interview of several people, asking them about workflow software and how it relates to them and their jobs. . . . You can have a person working in America and then he gets off of the project at 8:00. When he clocks out, the person from India clocks in in the morning and picks up where that guy left off . . .

Sarah: Hello everyone. My video is about the changing shape of information, which was uploading. I used Microsoft Surface and a semantic assistant. . . . Right now this isn't possible but we hope that soon it will be. I used green screen mainly for the picture backgrounds . . .

Taylor: Hello, I'm Taylor. I did a project called "Web 2.0 and the Tools for Sharing Information." My video was the iCoach, which was a personal trainer who can train from anywhere in the whole world . . .

Hillary: Hi, I'm Hillary. I made my video about the Shutterbug Sidekick that I used out on this project that we had earlier this year. It's a camera that can connect to the Internet and it can talk to people from around the world instead of everyone having to come to one place . . .

Case Study 19

"The Flat Classroom Project: A Celebration of Learning,"[7]
written by Pat D'Arcy, Head of Technology, ISDüsseldorf, Germany

When Julie Lindsay and Vicki Davis invited me to participate in the Flat Classroom Project a couple of years ago, I must admit I was a bit skeptical. Not about the concept. I was fully sold on the idea of "flattening" classroom walls, and introducing my students to the idea of linking hands and computers around the world. What troubled me was the doubt if I would be able to get it all together. The enormity of the concept is clearly evident from the project just finished, 2011-1, which had over 700 students from all around the world participating.

Of course participating in a FCP is frenetic, time pressured, quality demanding, total focus required; a marvelous microcosm of the real world outside the protective walls of the classroom. Through use of intelligent systems like Elluminate (Blackboard Collaborate), students from my classroom, in fact in my classroom, don their headsets with microphones, switch on the webcam, and see on their screens a list of participants in this real-time classroom experience with students

ADD FRIEND

PAT D'ARCY
@darcypat

from as far away as Beijing, Florida, Spain, Bulgaria, all joining them in the classroom on the screen, in Düsseldorf Germany. Then the challenge comes! Communicate, research one of the Web 2.0 tools involved, work in a team to produce a wiki page on the topic, work alone yet never alone to produce a multimedia presentation of some significant aspect of the flattener and how it might impinge on society. Invite a fellow participant to provide a film clip for you on your topic, and make a clip for someone else, then send it halfway round the world in the bat of an eyelid!

This Flat classroom project is a real celebration of all that is best about learning . . .

Read the full blog post at
http://tinyurl.com
/fcp-darcypat

Designing and Managing a Global Collaborative Project

CHAPTER 10 WEB RESOURCES
http://www.flatclassroombook.com
/project-design.html

SHARE IT

Twitter hashtag for this book:
#flatclass

"The more you have a culture that naturally glocalizes—that is, the more your own culture easily absorbs foreign ideas and best practices and melds those with its own traditions—the greater advantage you will have in a flat world."

THOMAS FRIEDMAN
The World Is Flat[1]

From Doha to Debate: "We Are Eracism!"

Four visionary students from four different countries came together at the Flat Classroom™ Conference in Doha, 2009; they brainstormed an idea that could ultimately change the world. "What if there was no racism?" they pondered, "What if we give teenagers all over the world an opportunity to express their opinions and ideas about issues in the current world?" From a simple altruistic ideal was born *Eracism*, meaning "erasing racism." The student team won an international vote and became the top project idea from the conference.[2]

Eracism is now a global debate project that students anywhere can join. Fashioned by digital storytelling pioneer Bernajean Porter, virtual world guru Peggy Sheehy, and debating in education expert Marcia Alessi, along with Julie and Vicki, the techniques for

See the original Eracism video at http://flatclassroomconference .ning.com/video/eracism-1

Read debate protocols and view Voicethreads at http://eracism .flatclassroomproject.org

C21 LIFE AND CAREER SKILLS:
Leadership and Responsibility

NETS.T 2
Design and Develop Digital-Age Learning Experiences and Assessments

asynchronous debate were created using Voicethread. The pilot topic, "Differences Make Us Stronger," attracted classrooms from different global regions and gave diverse communities a chance to debate in a **simulated synchronous** environment.

The two final teams then debated "live" in a virtual world using OpenSim, where they had to learn not only to debate, but also to operate avatars to add expression. Organizers, Reaction Grid, and Chester County, Pennsylvania, co-operated to allow a live audience to participate and vote live using a "voting chair" while also streaming the activities into Blackboard Collaborate for those to join who did not have access to the virtual world environment. Not only did Eracism promote understanding but it also challenged participants to innovate in creative ways and break down barriers in technology to simulate a synchronous environment in an inclusive way.

OVERVIEW OF DESIGNING AND MANAGING A GLOBAL COLLABORATIVE PROJECT

Teaching is an art, a profession, and a dedication to other people. Part of the craft is envisioning, designing, planning, and implementing experiences that provide new capabilities for the classroom and learning community. As simple as learning a new mathematical concept or as challenging as co-creating a video with someone on the opposite side of the world, designing a meaningful collaborative experience takes skill and knowledge of learning styles, team dynamics and the building symbiotic relationships. One must transcend the time differences, foster higher-order thinking, provide opportunities for cultural understanding, *and* make a product that impacts others in a positive way.

This chapter puts what you've learned so far into practice. Starting with the Flat Classroom™ Framework that you've seen featured throughout the book, we take the connection-planning tool from Chapter 3 and help you plan in a way that promotes diverse learning experiences for your students.

This chapter explores Flat Classroom pedagogy, including project design essentials, the seven steps of design principles, and project management strategies. Although the case study here is the Flat Classroom Project, this chapter sets up a methodology for success so that all readers can create global collaborations that work. It will be helpful to review Figure 10.8, the Classroom Project Design Chart on page 261, to review the content in this chapter.

FLAT CLASSROOM PEDAGOGY: GLOBAL COLLABORATIVE PROJECT DESIGN

Successful global collaborative projects start with planning and designing meaningful and understandable interaction. In order to encourage and invite others to collaborate on the structure, goals, time line, and particularly expectations, should be set out beforehand. According to Coughlin, the key to instructional design for global collaboration is a full understanding of interaction within collaborative learning and task complexity, as well as encouraging students to learn to solve more complex problems and think critically.[3]

The essence of collaboration can be seen even before a project commences as teachers across the world often come together to design appropriate outcomes for their classrooms. Well-designed projects are flexible enough to allow for innovation, but collaborative planning is best to accommodate the needs of all classrooms that are involved.

Using the concepts we've learned thus far and the framework we've used throughout this book, we can determine some basic elements of a project.

THE FLAT CLASSROOM™ FRAMEWORK: DECISIONS TO GET YOU STARTED

The Flat Classroom™ framework is built solidly on the connection-planning tool from Chapter 3. If you want to understand more about location, communication, generation, information, and time than the descriptions here, please refer to that chapter.

Project Name.   What's in a name? Everything. A good name is memorable, interesting, descriptive, and encourages participation. You can take lessons from marketers when designing your name: repetitive sounds, rhyming, double meanings, and succinctness. All of the things that go into the naming of a product or company go into name of a good project. Sometimes the name is there before the project but most often, it takes a while. We were two weeks into planning the Flat Classroom project before we found the perfect name! Take time to brainstorm. Keep a massive list. Involve students. You'll be glad you did.

Website URL.   Decide on the primary websites for your project. Go ahead and set them up. If a school will never be able to access your main collaborative site, you're wasting everyone's time. Do this as soon as you have the name of your project because it should be easy to remember. If it is long, you can shorten it to something brief using a **URL shortener**—something like tinyurl as used in this book. Buying a domain name has benefits because the site will be less likely to be blocked.

Determine the privacy and membership settings of the website and communicate it. How do people join? Who approves membership? Will it be a walled garden (Chapter 8) or publicly viewable?

Location.   Using the connection-planning tool, what is the targeted location for where the participants should be? Is it global? Is it within a certain region? Is it a certain geographic location?

Communication.   Specify clearly what type of asynchronous and synchronous communications methods you will use and how you will blend the two according to what you learned in Chapter 4.

Generation.   What are the specific ages of project participants? We do not use grade levels because they vary so much from country to country. Define any other age groups or targets that will work with the primary participants in some way.

It is a challenge to align classrooms from different countries and education systems globally. For example, a fourth-grade class in one country may be a different

age group in another country. Therefore, it is recommended to define participation in terms of age first, and then grade level or school section second. This distinction is necessary to give classrooms globally a chance to consider participating. You may also consider descriptive boundaries and recommendations, such as the project may be suitable for upper primary level, remembering of course that this may mean grades 4, 5, 6, or 7, depending on the system or country. Be careful of terms such as *freshman year*, as this has no relevance outside of the U.S. system. As another example, be aware that the term *high school* globally can mean anything from grade 6 to grade 13. Most U.S. educators have no idea what Grade 13 or KS1 is!

Information.   Look at the learning pathway. What information sources will be provided as students build their learning pathway for the project? This includes learning resources such as books or people, networks, subject matter experts, and communities.

Time.   What is the timeframe for this project? How long will it last? When is the handshake period? When is the culminating celebration? In terms of workflow, keep it synchronized. Synchronize the start and ending time of required outcomes as much as possible, understanding that schools have unique vacation schedules and events. Teachers must be careful not to let their unique needs interfere with the required outcomes on a project because other classrooms need collaboration.

If classrooms all edit the wiki at different times, it feels less collaborative and is, in reality, not collaborative. As long as disconnects and vacation times are communicated, this tends not to be an issue. Often, Flat Classroom Project teachers enter their class times in a Google calendar so that it can be seen easily who will be in class and working on a given day. Synchronizing participation between classrooms remains one of the top struggles in our global collaborative work to date.

Learning Legacy.   How will students leave a learning legacy from what they have done? Will it be a memory for themselves or a learning opportunity left behind for others? How will it be archived and stored? Be open to the idea that many local projects have an entrepreneurial bent. When students understand global issues and take local action, it can cost or make money. Great learning experiences can arise when students create and sell products with a purpose.

CURRICULUM PLANNING

Working "backwards by design," the approach encouraged by Wiggins and McTighe,[4] involves backward planning and "teaching for understanding" through identifying goals and learning outcomes and choosing activities or learning experiences to support this. For example, one outcome of the project may be a video or multimedia piece that demonstrates understanding of the topic researched. Activities and benchmarks identified during the project will have materials and skill development channeled to support this.

Communication of prerequisite skills, combined with the opportunity to sandbox tools as a class or an individual before jumping into collaboration is essential. Clarity in project outcomes, especially for each team or group, helps to propel the project forward with clear understandings.

Curriculum Integration and Alignment. Teachers should customize class outcomes to their school. Our Flat Classroom projects have attracted technology, speech, social science, composition, and movie-making courses: all in the same project. This is because teachers review the individual project and customize their class's participation to meet those outcomes.

A speech course may emphasize digital storytelling and online synchronous speech skills. A technology course may emphasize the understanding of global technology trends. A composition course may emphasize blogging and collaborative composition aspects of the project. As long as core, common outcomes are agreed on, a holistic approach provides a lot of flexibility.

Consider the main subject and curriculum areas to be invited to join this project. If it has a particular curriculum focus, this needs to be stated up front. If it is **interdisciplinary** or **transdisciplinary,** then provide examples of how it might fit into another school's curriculum.

For example, a project where water quality is being investigated and measurements shared could be appropriate for a science or humanities or even mathematics class. The fit depends on the needs of the teacher and the curriculum flexibility within the school. The project design needs to clearly state the topics to be covered, as this will help teachers determine if it is a fit for their class and how they may need to tweak their curriculum plans to be able to participate.

Guiding Question. A good guiding question directs the search for understanding and helps provide focus and coherence in a succinct phrase or sentence. The question should be overarching and provide scope for research within the confines of the intended outcomes. It must also drive the project to its natural conclusion—for example, what are the consequences of technology (information and communication tools) on how, when, and why we connect, collaborate, and create?

Project Aims. State clear aims for wanting global collaboration based on the curriculum integration objectives and guiding question.

Focus Questions. Create a list of essential questions crucial to the content and aims of the project. These questions should ensure teacher buy-in across different education systems, such as, "How can emerging technologies and enhanced connectivity improve learning and create extended communities?"

Standards Alignment. List any standards that are being referred to, such as ISTE NETS, C21, the standards used in this book, or U.S. Common Core standards.

Prerequisites and Skill Level. Any prior knowledge or skill prerequisites needed to start this project should be clearly stated, including digital literacy, familiarity with Web 2.0 tools, and digital citizenship requirements. It is wise to consider project modification if a more inclusive approach is desirable—for example, to accommodate classrooms that have limited access to certain online tools.

Required Outcomes. Global projects germinate when teachers agree on required outcomes of the project: things every classroom will do. Keep it simple. There should be

no more than two or three expected required outcomes. Include the learning experiences expected for each participant, such as creating a personal learning environment (perhaps a blog for reflection before, during, and after the project).

Optional Outcomes.   In addition to required outcomes, optional activities and outcomes can provide a richer and more differentiated learning opportunity for mixed groups of students. Decide at the start how the optional activities feed into assessment (if any) and how these can be made accessible for all.

Team Structure.   Teams should be structured based on what you want to accomplish. By nature, a grid like this helps each student's research project become slightly different and authentic in nature. Follow these four steps to help in designing a team grid.

Topic Alignment.   Teams should be aligned with the topics you want to cover. It helps to divide your theme into major topics and to cross-check that with the themes that you want to investigate for each topic.

Step 1: What are the main *topics* of the project? How many are there?
Step 2: What are the *subthemes*? How many are there? (Team numbers may also be put in here, e.g., team 1, team 2.)
Step 3: Create a simple table with *topics* as rows and *subthemes* as columns. This forms the basis of the grid.

For example, in the Flat Classroom project, we took the 11 flatteners and wanted to ensure that teams were small enough to be intimate, so we took Dan Pink's six senses of the conceptual age to create a matrix looking like that in Figure 10.1. This would provide for 66 groups maximum (11 topics × 6 subtopics = 66).

So, for example, students in team 2B would research the World Wide Web as their major topic and would create a video showing a new way that the World Wide Web could be used. We take this one step further by using the subgroups to determine the part of the wiki that students will edit. So, according to Figure 10.2 (page 242), a B student would write about "current news."

Step 4: Determine the overall *size* of the project collaboration and the agreed *team size*. These two factors are very important in determining the final team grid design. If you want smaller numbers in each team, then potentially more cells are needed across the grid.

ISTE STANDARDS

NETS.T 2
Design and Develop Digital-
Age Learning Experiences and
Assessments

NETS.S 2
Communication and Collaboration

Team Sizes.   Once the matrix is created, then teachers should determine the size of student teams. For example, if one wants to have 4 students per team, then 264 students is the maximum on this project. There are several considerations in sizing, however. If students are able to work on the research project only once a week, for example, more students are needed on a team in order to facilitate effective collaboration—otherwise, not enough edits are happening. If students are editing more, the teams would be smaller to prevent wiki wars from happening.

Figure 10.1 has all six subtopics (or columns) so we call it a "level 6" project. However, sometimes if a smaller group of students is going to be on a project, or if a school that had a large group of students drops out early in the project, it is necessary to make adjustments. To be ready for any contingency, we've designed our projects

FIGURE 10.1 Flat Classroom Project Matrix

	Categories of Video					
	The Story (Big Picture Topic Overview)	Innovation, Invention (Design)	Social Entrepreneurship (Meaning)	First-Person Narrative (Empathy)	Group Stories (Symphony)	How We Live (Play)
Connecting the World Online	1A	1B	1C	1D	1E	1F
World Wide Web	2A	2B	2C	2D	2E	2F
Work Flow Software	3A	3B	3C	3D	3E	3F
Uploading	4A	4B	4C	4D	4E	4F
Web 2.0	5A	5B	5C	5D	5E	5F
Globalization and Outsourcing	6A	6B	6C	6D	6E	6F
Google	7A	7B	7C	7D	7E	7F
PLE's Social Networking	8A	8B	8C	8D	8E	8F
Mobile and Ubiquitous Computing	9A	9B	9C	9D	9E	9F
Virtual Communications	10A	10B	10C	10D	10E	10F
Wireless Connectivity	11A	11B	11C	11D	11E	11F

The World Is Flat (row group label)

all the way from a Level 3 (3 subtopics × 11 main topics = 33 teams) up to a Level 6 project.

Creating a Team Grid in Practice.   Creating a team grid is just a matter of labeling meaningful rows and columns. Let's look at an example.

- *Digiteen™ 11-1 Team Grid:*[5] In Figure 10.3, we see the topics (across the row) = areas of awareness, and the subthemes (left-hand column) = core competency areas. The full grid provides for 55 cells (11 × 5) if needed. The core competency areas could be combined or even pruned to cater for a smaller project number.
- *"A Week in the Life . . ." 11-1 Team Grid:*[6] This grid provides six main topics cross-gridded with team numbers. This model is very easily expanded to include more teams using the same set of topics.

Be Attentive and Flexible.   You want to make sure that team sizes are not so large that some students no longer feel they are expected to participate (the bystander effect

FIGURE 10.2   Flat Classroom Project Design Chart

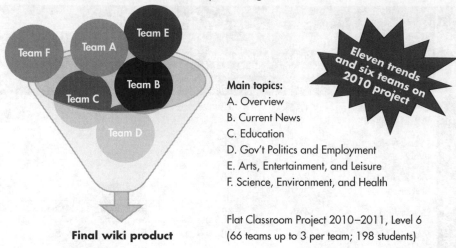

Main topics:

A. Overview

B. Current News

C. Education

D. Gov't Politics and Employment

E. Arts, Entertainment, and Leisure

F. Science, Environment, and Health

Eleven trends and six teams on 2010 project

Final wiki product

Flat Classroom Project 2010–2011, Level 6
(66 teams up to 3 per team; 198 students)

mentioned in Chapter 5), nor do you want teams that are too small. Small teams collapse if one or two other schools do not do their part or a student is out sick. We've found that five or six students is an ideal size for a team with no students from the same class in a subgroup.

We are very hesitant about letting students in the same classroom work together. They often ignore their other partners and resist collaborating asynchronously. If students in the same classroom edit the same wiki or project, they tend to want to sit together and one will not contribute effectively. Students who are not used to contributing will *beg* to get to work with someone in their own classroom. Each student should be accountable for work under his or her user ID and should make no excuses. Students have plenty of opportunities to collaborate locally, global collaboration in education is about learning how to collaborate globally. Take away the easy option and help students break out of the status quo by not allowing local partners for at least one global project a year.

21st CENTURY SKILLS

C21 LIFE AND CAREER SKILLS:
Productivity and Accountability

FIGURE 10.3   Digiteen™ 11-1 Team Grid

TEAM GRID/Project Matrix: Digiteen 2011-1
Teachers: Please add numbers as you add your students.

Row = Areas of Awareness Column = Core Competency Areas	1. Technical Awareness and Access	2. Individual Awareness	3. Social Awareness	4. Cultural Awareness	5. Global Awareness
A1: Safety	1. BrandonS_WJeff 2. FreddieA-MHS-2 3. nickf-rihs 4. PaulH-MHS-67 5. Kreslyn C - WHS 6. SooMinK-SFMS 7. MargaretB-CSRN 8. Ashley9-bard-Brkl-Mod	1. MyrandaB_WJeff 2. JonathanM STM 3. AndrewA-MHS-10 4. Daniella-rihs 5. Latosha_MSHS 6. Mehernaz- ASB 7. MatthewB - CSRN 8. Mitchell7-bard-Brkl-Mod	1. AlejandraC_WJeff 2. TaylorB-MHS-2 3. Jarw-rihs 4. KathrynP-MHS-67 5. I.T. - WHS 6. NelsonC-SFMS 7. JulianB-CSRN 8. Archibald-bard-Brkl-Mod	1. KevinC_WJeff 2. RobertB-MHS-10 3. joeyh-rihs 4. StephaniH-MHS-67 5. WildarW-JCSD 6. Malavika- ASB 7. JoseC-CSRN 8. Annabel7-bard-Brkl-Mod	1. GloriaG_WJeff 2. KrystalB-MHS-2 3. hannahg-rihs 4. ShariE-MHS-10 5. Eliza- ASB 6. MarieD-SFMS 7. JoeC-CSRN 8. Camryn8-bard-Brkl-Mod
A2: Privacy	1. JohnG_WJeff 2. EmilyM STM 3. AllisonB-MHS-10 4. kentanr-rihs 5. Amish- ASB 6. ColinC-CSRN 7. Laurel12-bard-Brkl-Mod	1. TashannB_WJeff 2. NickC-MHS-2 3. tyb-rihs 4. TylerR-MHS-67 5. Courtney - WHS 6. Camille- ASB 7. JosephF - CSRN 8. Nathaniel6-bard-Brkl-Mod	1. JonH_WJeff 2. BobbyC-MHS-2 3. Jordans-rihs 4. Hayas-whs 5. ElenaB-JCSD 6. Theo- ASB 7. MarcoE-SFMS 8. Jonathan-bard-Brkl-Mod	1. StephanieL_WJeff 2. KlaraB-MHS-2 3. thomasd-rihs 4. StephanieS-MHS-67 5. Tania- ASB 6. JohnW-SFMS 7. AbbyG - CSRN 8. Ayanna-bard-Brkl-Mod	1. EvieL_WJeff 2. RandyB-MHS-2 3. dariol-rihs 4. KyleS-MHS-67 5. Antonio- ASB 6. JocelynI-SFMS 7. Mikaylal - CSRN 8. Jayla10-bard-Brkl-Mod
A3: Copyright & Fair Use & Legal Compliance	1. MytinaL_WJeff 2. AllenJ-MHS-2 3. abbyb-rihs 4. BaylieS-MHS-67 5. Nadav- ASB 6. VincentK - CSRN 7. Mackenzie-bard-Brkl-Mod	1. JiahniL_WJeff 2. BobbyC-MHS-10 3. nicoleb-rihs 4. KristenS-MHS-67 5. Mimi- ASB 6. RyanL - CSRN 7. Virginia1-bard-Brkl-Mod	1. LanichaL_WJeff 2. KerrieC-MHS-10 3. taylora-rihs 4. KayleeS-MHS-67 5. Esha- ASB 6. ConnorMc - CSRN 7. Carlinda-bard-Brkl-Mod	1. MikaiahH_WJeff 2. NeftaliD STM 3. EricC-MHS-10 4. austing-rihs 5. LT W - WHS 6. Josh- ASB 7. ConnorM - CSRN 8. Kaleil7-bard-Brkl-Mod	1. KiarkN_WJeff 2. AmmalN-MHS-2 3. nathanw-rihs 4. Alex B - WHS 5. Alice V_MSHS 6. LilyO - CSRN 7. Fatima8-bard-Brkl-Mod

If a school drops out or problems happen, it is fine to combine teams and make adjustments during the handshake period.

Required and Optional Inputs. Establish what each student is expected to contribute during the project, and when. Also map out the benchmarks for this contribution and align them with the project time line. The challenge of "global" collaboration is determining from the start when each classroom is available and able to complete the work in between holidays, sports, and other interruptions.

Flexibility is needed, but an essential plan showing what is expected and when it is going to be delivered is a must. Does the project design include optional work for students? Consider including a design feature whereby students can opt to take on leadership responsibility or be more active in networking or providing resources for others. These options can apply to further course credit or recognition of enhanced engagement and motivation.

21st CENTURY SKILLS

C21 LIFE AND CAREER SKILLS:
Leadership and Responsibility

Assessment. Assessment is a difficult area for global collaboration, as most classrooms will have their own internal requirements. However, it is beneficial to all when common assessments are created for required outcomes so that students, either individually or in teams, can work toward the same goal. A rubric is an ideal tool to create and share globally.

ISTE STANDARDS

NETS.T 2
Design and Develop Digital-Age Learning Experiences and Assessments

With carefully constructed criteria and descriptors, participants in the project not only have a better understanding of what is required but also teachers can work this format into their own assessment. A common tool like a rubric is also necessary if the outcome is to be reviewed or "judged" externally. It must be clear that the product meets the criteria.

21st CENTURY SKILLS

C21 STANDARDS AND ASSESSMENT

Rubrics help determine best practices. If flawed artifacts rise to the top, then a rubric is flawed and needs to be adjusted. For example, we started seeing some videos with copyrighted content receive awards and realized that our rubric needed to be adjusted to require students to respect copyright. Now, a video with copyright concerns is disqualified from being able to receive a top award: copyright is that important.

Evaluation. When the project is over, it is important to evaluate its success, on different levels and from all stakeholders. Students can be encouraged to write final reflective blog posts, as can teachers. Peer review and continued interaction is encouraged as part of this reflection. Carefully constructed post-project surveys will provide valuable feedback and help in the redesign of the next implementation. All of the design steps discussed previously are points for evaluation and review.

ISTE STANDARDS

NETS.T 3
Model Digital-Age Work and Learning

CHECKLIST OF FLATTENERS: USING THE SEVEN STEPS TO REFINE OUR THINKING

We've now moved through the Flat Classroom framework and curriculum planning, but we have to consider the seven steps in more detail. We've shared creative ideas for integrating excellence in global collaboration. So, now that you've planned, let's refresh our minds with some things we need to do that we may have forgotten. This

checklist follows the Seven Steps to Flatten Your Classroom model and provides for effective 21st century project design that is inclusive of all learners and all learning situations.

Don't be overwhelmed; you can't do everything. However, sometimes a small adjustment prompted by such inquiry can make a big difference in your project's design.

SUPER-CHARGE YOUR PLAN WITH THE SEVEN STEPS

Step 1: Connection

- Do you have realistic expectations for yourself? For others? Can you maintain a healthy balance between your personal and professional lives?
- Using your connection-planning tool, relate this project to the other projects you are planning this year. Are there any experience gaps for students?
- Are the tools accessible to everyone? Have you defined the tools? Can you find alternatives?
- Set up your CMP (classroom monitoring portal) or, if your project is private, determine how the project will be teachersourced for prompt attention and how.
- Have you considered involvement of researchers? Is there any opportunity for citizen science?
- Have you considered the environmental impact of your project? What is the **carbon footprint** of your activities?
- If this is a technology-related course, have you given yourself some flexibility to allow your curriculum to be agile and responsive so that you can introduce some current technology trends and tools?

Step 2: Communication

- Protocols include the frequency and mode of connection. For example, will teachers connect every week to discuss project progress? Or maybe every day is necessary?
- What are the communication conduits that you will establish for teacher communications? Student communications?
- Will students be free to connect via Skype with team members themselves, or is this an expectation for a class activity? Will connections be teacher-initiated or student-led, or a combination of the two?
- What tasks will be teachersourced, and what are the expectations? How will teachers communicate when problems arise? How are holiday breaks communicated? How will teachers communicate to another teacher if a student is being flamed or bullied online during the project? What happens if one classroom joins the project and then does not communicate at all?
- How will you set teacher meetings? How will you record and share them? Are there any "sweet spots" when you're all typically online at the same time? Where will meeting recordings be saved?
- How will teams be established? When will the team grid go live?
- When is the handshake period, and how often will each classroom interact? How will students introduce themselves to team members?

C21 INTERDISCIPLINARY THEME:
Environmental Literacy

NETS.T 2
Design and Develop Digital-Age Learning Experiences and Assessments

Step 3: Citizenship

- What is your agreement on digital citizenship framework for analyzing activities on the project? (You need a common language to prevent semantic issues.)
- Do students know who can view their work and what the expectations for behavior are?

Safety, Privacy, Copyright, and Legal

- Do teachers know how to document (screenshot) and report issues? Does everyone have the administrative level on the websites in order to handle issues that may arise? Have you planned lead time for teachers to join spaces and be promoted before their students join a site? Who will approve student requests to join sites? What other people will be allowed to join the spaces? Are parental permissions and notifications handled?
- What are the basic privacy agreements about using full names and other information? Are there any schools with more strict requirements than the project has in place?
- What are the copyright guidelines of the terms of service for the websites that you are using? Are these guidelines communicated in a public way to participants?
- Are there any legal issues that teachers or students need to be aware of? (For example, when collaborating with China, students are told not to mention Tibet, as that will get the site banned in China, since Tibet would not be part of the project's aims.)
- Do you want to create a formal responsible-use guidelines document that meets the needs of the project? Depending on the size and scope of the project, this may include guidelines for being reliable, responsible, and ethical online learners for all participants; agreed standards for online networking; and agreed practice for copyright, intellectual property, fair use, and Creative Commons.
- Do you have a privacy policy?

Etiquette and Respect

- Are there any cultural issues that need to be discussed up front? Do students know what a cultural disconnect is and how to communicate when they feel offended?
- Are there any guidelines for profile pictures?

Habits of Learning

- Do students understand the habits they should have in order to learn as part of this project?
- How can they start and end class in ways that facilitate the ongoing success of the project and momentum?
- What type of PLN will be used for students?
- How can students keep a healthy balance in their learning and lives as they use technology? Are there any health issues relating to this topic of study or the particular technologies that will be used?

Literacy and Fluency

- Are students capable of performing the research tasks required, and do they know how to utilize technological websites? Are there things that can be done ahead of time to help students be more successful?

Step 4: Contribution and Collaboration

- How will you measure student contribution during the project?
- Are there opportunities for symbiotic learning relationships with other types of learners?
- Have you reviewed beginning-of-class and ending-of-class routines to encourage students to reach high levels of excellence on the project?
- Have you considered the bandwidth ability of other classrooms? Look at your design—are you a "bandwidth snob"? Have you set the bar for participation so high that the less affluent or less well connected cannot participate in your project?
- What are your expectations for student work outside of the classroom?

Step 5: Choices

- What types of choices will students be given? How will you let them bring their interests into the project?
- What choices in physical spaces will be offered? What electronic spaces are supported? How will choices be used to increase engagement?
- What is the current framework of participating classrooms? Does this framework show if classrooms are prepared for the project?
- What will be the students' home base?
- Will you use tags and, if so, how?
- Will you allow varied outcomes?
- Do you have different leadership options to help build proficiency in areas that are of interest to the students?

Step 6: Creation

- Do you have clear guidelines for format and submission of the final product(s)? Construct templates if needed.
- How will you move students to higher-order thinking with this project?
- How will students co-create? Can individual performance still be measured?
- What are your plans to provide support? Help files? How will you maintain communication between all participants as sounding boards and reviewers during this crucial stage?
- Will you have a "competition" or opportunity to share the work beyond the immediate participants?

Step 7: Celebration

- How will you and your students reflect? Will you have public and private ways for students and teachers to provide feedback? What will you do with the feedback? How will you be retrospective?

- What will be your culminating celebration? How will students and teachers present and reflect? Will you have student summits? Can you invite others to join in the celebration? How will you share your work?
- What will you do to determine best practices and share the results?

EXPAND YOUR AUDIENCE

Audience increases engagement.

Expert Advisors. Expert advisors (see Chapter 6) are invited into the FCP during the research and wiki development stage. Educators and experts from around the world help classroom teachers review wiki content and provide ideas and resources for students. They also leave comments and answer questions, thereby interacting with students, via the discussion tab. This can be a very enlightening part of the project, when a student realizes that learning does not merely involve people in his or her immediate vicinity and that conversations can take place on a completely new level independent of the classroom teacher or peers. Expert Advisor examples, Figures 10.4 and 10.5, show interaction between experts and students via the wiki discussion area.

FIGURE 10.4 Flat Classroom Project Expert Advisor Example 1

```
Google Takes Over the World    ▩ page   ▩ discussion   ▩ history   ▩ notify me
▩ Back to Discussion Forum   ▩ Monitor Topic   ▩ Lock Topic   ▩ Delete Topic
```

Expert Advisor Dennis Richards

dennisar May 28, 2010 12:27 am

Hi,

Just wanted you to know that I offered to help out FCP 10-2 as an expert advisor and Julie Lindsay asked me to check out your wiki page. I know you are close to completion, but I'll pass on what I notice for you to consider.

If you have any specific questions, leave them here.

For more about me, you can check out my profile on the bottom of my FCP Ning page here http://tinyurl.com/33e591y.

Dennis Richards

re: Expert Advisor Dennis Richards

dennisar May 31, 2010 5:44 am

I have recorded my comments regarding your work on the wiki page. Go here (http://vocaroo.com/?media=vB3QPhipGzf01bvlM) to listen to what I noticed about your page.

Source: Richards, D. (2010, May 27). Expert Advisor Dennis Richards. *Flat Classroom Project 10-2.* Retrieved June 8, 2011, from http://flatclassroom10-2.flatclassroomproject.org/message/view/Google+Takes+Over+the+World/24709983

FIGURE 10.5 Flat Classroom Project Expert Advisor 2

```
Google Takes Over the World   ▪ page   ▪ discussion   ▪ history   ▪ notify me
▪ Back to Discussion Forum   ▪ Monitor Topic   ▪ Lock Topic   ▪ Delete Topic
..........................................................................................................
Introduction for advisor Jamie McNamara

jamiemac3919  Nov 6, 2009 9:50 am

Hi, my name is Jamie McNamara and I will be one of the two advisors for the google
topic. I am a student at the University of Northern Iowa, which is located in Cedar
Falls, Iowa. I am a senior, majoring in elementary education, and minoring in
educational technology. I am looking forward to exploring all of your great ideas!!
Shu-hsiang and I will be reading over your materials and giving you feedback throughout
the project. If you have any questions contact one of us and we will try to help you
out as much as we can!!

..........................................................................................................

re: Introduction for advisor Jamie McNamara

sydnee15  Nov 6, 2009 11:15 pm

Hi Jamie, I was wondering if you could look at the C section about Politics, Government,
and Employment and give me some feedback. I would really appreciate it.

Thanks.

Sydnee
```

Source: McNamara, J. (2009, November 5). Introduction for advisor Jamie McNamara. *Flat Classroom 09-3.* Retrieved June 2, 2011, from http://flatclassroom09-3.flatclassroomproject.org/message/view/Google+Takes+Over+the+World/16490279

Sounding Boards. Sounding board classrooms are often younger students and their teacher who take one or two class days to view and provide feedback on the videos and/or wikis, typically on the wiki discussion tab, although this may be done in a variety of ways. Typically, younger students are not allowed full access to the Ning network because of their age, so the anonymous discussion commenting feature on the wiki is perfect for providing feedback in this case.

The sounding board process is a very easy, fun, and eye-opening way for younger students (upper elementary, middle, and lower high school) to participate in a global project. Basically, sounding boards act as peer reviewers for the students participating in the project. Small groups of students in the sounding board classrooms will review one Flat Classroom student group's work and offer very simple peer feedback. (See the Sounding Board Case Study in Chapter 6).

21st CENTURY SKILLS

C21 STANDARDS AND ASSESSMENT

Judges. Judges are recruited to use the project rubrics to determine a set of winners as well as an overall winner and to provide feedback to the teachers on the best practices. This is a very open sign-up process where a call is issued via the various networks and the official project blog and judges sign up for their area of interest. Care is taken to distribute videos evenly among judges, with most judges typically viewing 10 videos and every student video being viewed two or three times by different judges. A recent record of 279 videos submitted for one project saw some judges watching many videos over the space of a week.[7] Judges fill out the full assessment rubric online, via a Surveyshare form, for their top four choices.

Next, topic judges aggregate the choices, add their information, and the top four videos in each topic are finally determined by the review of the two initial judges and the topic judge. After the topic judging occurs, one meta-judge views all winning videos from each wiki to determine the top three and any honorable mentions of the project. The final winners are therefore vetted through a set of four judges to make it to the top.

This is a useful project for professors to use with their preservice teachers who are learning about digital storytelling or for teachers who want to volunteer their time and learn how video assessment works.

See award winners: http://tinyurl.com/fcp-awards

Rubric Design. The rubrics for the FCP were initially done by Julie Lindsay and Vicki Davis, but have been tweaked and worked over by many teachers, advisors, and assessment experts since then. The final products as shown in the PD toolkit reflect a group effort that has resulted in stronger rubrics.

21st CENTURY SKILLS

C21 STANDARDS AND ASSESSMENT

Each year, the rubrics go through a revision process as well as a discussion process from all teachers on the prior year's projects, as teachers edit the wiki and discuss any issues they found with the quality of the rubric. The goal of the rubrics is to encourage higher-order thinking skills and thus undergo revision as necessary. For more extensive information, please see the case study by Mark van 't Hooft, one of our leading advisors on rubric design, at the end of this chapter.

We recommend you review Chapter 1 again for a brief overview of other Flat Classroom projects and design features.

TRIED AND TRUE TIPS FOR TOP-NOTCH PROJECT MANAGEMENT

PROJECT MANAGEMENT DECISIONS

How Will You Meet with Teachers? It is important to build in effective management strategies to ensure all classrooms are supported and kept on the same track during a global project. Communication with classroom teachers is crucial here, as is regular and informative communication from project managers, as well as opportunities for teachers to feedback questions.

One strategy that works for *all* the projects under the Flat Classroom umbrella is regular (usually weekly) real-time meetings between the project manager/facilitator and the classroom teachers. A tool such as Blackboard Collaborate effectively supports this and meetings allow all stakeholders to come to an agreed understanding of the current status of the project and where it is going during the next workflow period of time. Whatever tool is used for these real-time linkups, the meeting must be recorded and shared with those who cannot attend.

What Tools Will You Use? Whether you are using a wiki, Edmodo, Voicethread, Google Docs, Ning, or other tool, it is essential that the learning framework be developed and set up prior to the project starting. Also, all participating teachers need a chance to orient themselves to the working environment before they bring in students. Flat Classroom projects rely largely on wiki templates to kick-start the landscape so that an entire project can be set up very quickly.

What Challenges Will You Face?   These include time zones, different school systems, keeping everyone connected and on schedule, and developing trust. Further issues hindering operations during global collaborations have been identified as[8]:

- Insufficient training and preparation of participating students
- Inexperienced classroom coordinators
- Lack of resources
- Use of colloquialisms and native language
- Effect of events (e.g., terrorist attacks on September 11, 2001)
- Parental influence (i.e., biases naturally inherent in the home)

NETS.T 2
Design and Develop Digital-Age Learning Experiences and Assessments

How Do You Plan for Success?   Overcome hindrances by avoiding complex instructions and design, using a class monitoring portal to monitor activity in the project, implementing tool skill set training, and having someone available to help sort out issues when they occur. The following strategies improved operations[9]:

- Preparing students to work in multicultural environments online
- Ensuring for student respect and awareness
- Having students who were well versed in social networking
- Monitoring Web 2.0 technologies to follow what the students were saying
- Using Web 2.0 to help students connect and understand each other
  - Educators giving students guidance, rules, and clear expectations
    - Student understanding of the global collaboration/Web 2.0 process
    - Having experienced classroom coordinators
    - Having a place for teachers only to connect to talk about the students as needed
    - Having a networking tool where conversations and a learning community can be established, and having clear entry points to scaffold success

You and your friends
are your own media.
#flatclass

SOCIAL MEDIA FINESSE

Marketing a project is an important skill; it attracts participants and contributors and it raises the profile of the project. Schools enjoy the publicity, and the wider school community becomes well informed of curriculum initiatives.

You and your online friends are your own media and can spread the word about your project. Teacher-run projects are some of the best because they are *owned* by several teachers who are committed to make it work. Project announcements typically include (1) project formation information, (2) project openings, (3) press releases (here who is participating), and (4) project awards and events. Project organizers should agree as to the syndication of each type of announcement. Depending on your goals, it can also be beneficial to be a reputable source of information about your topic, as that will give you influence that you can use to help others as well as your projects.

Project Website. Often, people look to see if a project is "legitimate" by looking for the official project website (see Figure 10.6). It is tempting to let this be where the students are working, but this may not be the best idea. For example, if it is a student wiki, people will mistakenly try to "join" the wiki to participate when, in reality, they can just read the content. Ideally, the project website should be editable by all organizers of the project. Students are also learning and educators may think student mistakes are due to a lack of integrity in the project and not realize that the learning process is ongoing.

Topics that should be included are a homepage with information about the project, an "about page" that tells about the project and organizers, information and links to your other projects, a list of sponsors (if any), an official blog for announcements, resources to share with others, a time line, testimonials, and links to past projects and work. We use Weebly, a service that lets all of the administrators of the project edit the website. Some decide to build and host their website on a content management system such as Wordpress. There are lots of options.

The "Official" Blog. It is best to have one blog dedicated to only project announcements and nothing else. This lets the bystanders who want to hear vital news follow your project without having to get everything else. It allows others to focus on what you're announcing and decide if they want to join in. This should be syndicated in multiple ways.

The official Flat Classroom Projects website at http://flatclassroomproject.net provides a blog where we add regular press releases (this also feeds into a Twitter posting). This is helpful, particularly for news media that may want to follow projects but do not wish to receive every small thing mentioned on other blogs. Everyone who administers the site can approve comments and post to the blog.

If it is available, you should add social media buttons to your blog that allow readers to easily send your information through Twitter, Facebook, Tumblr, Google+, or email.

WEBSITES

Weebly
http://www.weebly.com

Wordpress Free Blog Hosting
http://www.wordpress.com

Download Site for Wordpress software that you can install on your server
http://www.wordpress.org

FIGURE 10.6 Flat Classroom Website Sample Made with Weebly

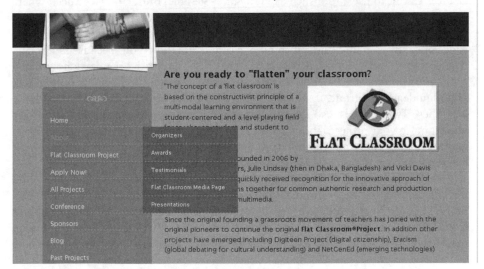

DIGITAL CITIZENSHIP AREA OF UNDERSTANDING

Etiquette and Respect

NETS.T 4
Promote and Model Digital Citizenship and Responsibility

The "Official" Email.   If you have several people running a project or if you need to post an email address on the web, you should create an email for the project. Share the email address and agree on who will check the account and respond at different times. Don't delete anything from the account. You might choose to have the organizer who is responding put her or his name into the response or **cc:** his or her personal account if this person is going to take over an issue.

This is also important because **email harvesters** troll the Internet with the goal of taking emails posted on web pages in order to sell them to **spammers.** If your project takes off you can end up with a lot of **spam** in your personal or work in-box.

When you email to a large group of people, make sure you send the message to yourself (the **To:** field) and blind carbon copy the recipients (**bcc:** field). This is good **netiquette** because:

- People don't like their emails given out without their permission.
- Many people don't understand the difference between **Reply** and **Reply All.** If everyone's email is in the To: or cc: field, and an uneducated person clicks Reply All, then everyone is stuck in the loop until it stops.
- If your message gets forwarded then the person who receives the forward will receive everyone's email that is in the To: or cc: field. If that email ends up in the in-box of an unethical person, they will harvest and sell your email. (This is also why people get mad at those who forward emails without removing the previous emails.) You will look unprofessional and people will not want to work with you because you have broken their trust.
- People will get angry and possibly report you as a spammer to their email company. Because email companies share lists of known spammers, your messages could start being delivered to the spam boxes of people who used to be able to receive messages from you.

Hootsuite
http://www.hootsuite.com

Seesmic
http://seesmic.com

Tweetdeck
http://www.tweetdeck.com

See the NetGen keynote: http://tinyurl.com/net-gen-keynote

Twitter.   Each Flat Classroom project has a Twitter account to make announcements, shout out recognition, and ask for volunteers. When projects have multiple organizers, it is easiest to use a tool such as Hootsuite, Seesmic, Buffer, or Tweetdeck where posts (called **tweets**) can be scheduled by participants so that you do not inundate people following your Twitter account. This is called **overtweeting** and when one person sends out too many posts, it can make others **unfollow** you. Because announcements often come in spurts, it is best to agree with the other organizers how many posts are appropriate and how far apart announcements will be scheduled. Talk about guidelines up front.

These Twitter tools also let you subscribe to and monitor the hashtags that are important to your project, both as sources of information for you and your students and for finding potential collaborators. Sending good information through the right hashtags will get attention for your project very quickly. Just don't be a **troll!**

The immediacy of Twitter allows almost instant recognition globally. Messages include requests for leaders, updates on project applications, news on live events, and more. The start of the student-generated keynote for the NetGen Ed™ Project 2010[10] shows classrooms around the world who recorded "Flat," "Class," "Room" through their teacher receiving an invitation via Twitter and other less orthodox means.

You can also make a **Twitter list** of the teachers that are collaborating together. This makes it easy for participants to start connecting with the other teachers with one click instead of having to follow everyone individually. Make sure that you add your personal Twitter account to the list.

Facebook. If you have a Facebook presence, projects should have a **Facebook fan page.** You don't want your project to be set up with a personal profile page. If a personal page is served as the project clearinghouse, then the **friending** process has opened a privacy doorway among teachers, educators, followers, fans, businesspeople, and the personal profile of each.[11] This is considered **overfriending** but fan pages resolve this issue. You can still write about the project on your personal account.

Fan pages can allow content sharing and posting as well as announcements, and are most appropriate for teachers and projects to connect project participants together. This is a great way to secure participation, but it is blocked in many schools. Once an announcement goes live on your fan page, it is fine for organizers who *like* the announcements posted on there to put them into their personal networks.

Press Releases. The effective press release is a template. Project organizers can insert their quotations and leave a paragraph or two for the local school to contribute. It is best to create this in a collaboratively edited document like a Google Doc that is most easily copied to a web page. (Wikis aren't.) This allows all schools to make sure their hyperlinks, information, and spellings are correct. Use blanks in the document for the insertion of the local school and information. A "formal" press release without these blanks should go on the project website.

Schools have used the press release to great advantage by faxing it to local newspapers, television, and radio stations. Teachers should involve administrators—the principal, the superintendent, the department chair—because the best press releases include quotations from a variety of people at the school. This should be done early enough in the project to allow media to come on campus and film or interview students if desired, but late enough so that students have a grasp of concepts. For a sample, see the press release for the 2010 project of "A Week in the Life . . ."

Encourage Cross-Posting. Organizers should realize that major project announcements should be shared in as many places as possible and should agree beforehand if it is OK to copy announcements verbatim from the official project website or if the announcements should be paraphrased. If it is OK to copy, more teachers will be willing to share. Great places to cross-post include the following.

Teacher Blogs. Organizers should share major project announcements on their own blogs, Facebook pages, and Twitter accounts. After all, this should be something they are excited about! Each teacher who blogs has his or her own "readership," and you should leverage the network.

School Websites. Press releases from projects are ideal for school websites and should be customized for each school by the local teacher and administrators and posted to the school website as well as sent to local media.

DIGITAL CITIZENSHIP AREA OF UNDERSTANDING
Safety, Privacy, Copyright, and Legal

NETS.T 4
Promote and Model Digital
Citizenship and Responsibility

http://tinyurl.com/awl-release

Automate Everything. Automate as much as possible. For example, for all of the Flat Classroom projects, we use Twittterfeed to automatically send updates to Twitter and Facebook every time we post. Project organizers should identify what items should be syndicated and sent everywhere and find the tools to send those out. You should be able to post on your blog and forget it. Just note that some services (e.g., Facebook) put announcements from services like Twitterfeed down on the priority list. So, for Facebook in particular, you may decide to type it directly on your fan page.

This allows organizers to post once and have the item sent to a variety of places. Additionally, services such as Feedblitz or Feedburner are excellent ways to syndicate content. This allows organizers to turn their official blogs into an email newsletter automatically.

LUCY GRAY
@elemenous
http://elemenous.typepad.com

Network. A variety of educational networks (some of which are our own, of course) provide the platform for connecting and communicating with experts and educators globally. Our Flat Classrooms Ning at http://flatclassrooms.ning.com is our essential community of practice for educators, and through this we broadcast messages and updates as well as add to blog posts. Other communities, such as the Global Education Collaborative,[12] led by Lucy Gray, provide an immediate community for sharing project needs.

If you post on your network, make sure that it is not blatant self-interest. If you only talk about yourself and never help others, people may view you as a troll and ignore, block, or worst of all, report you as a spammer. Trolls can kill collaboration because they are not interested in collaborating, but only in getting attention. It is OK to mention other projects and exchange ideas.

WORKED EXAMPLES

ISTE STANDARDS

NETS.T 2
Design and Develop Digital-Age Learning Experiences and Assessments

EXISTING COLLABORATIVE PROJECTS

Start Strong. The best way to explore and learn about global project design is to get involved with other global projects, preferably with your class, but also as an advisor, judge, researcher, organizer, or other role. This will provide experience and better understanding of essential design elements and workflow. We suggest as an entry point that you get started with other global projects before attempting to create your own (see Table 10.1).

tweetable

Designing educational collaborations takes knowledge of learning styles, team dynamics, and symbiotic relationships.
#flatclass

Resources to Find Global Collaborative Projects. There are many available opportunities to connect and collaborate, and connected teacherpreneurs (see Chapter 3) are always on the lookout for relevant projects that align with their curriculum. Table 10.2 provides a starting point of associations and networks where existing projects can be found and/or other educators who are willing to help design or pilot a project of independent design.

TABLE 10.1 Global Project Chart

Organization/Project and Description	Flat Classroom Framework
iEARN: The International Education and Resource Network This network supports projects designed by educators and students. Projects vary across age and curriculum areas and often have low technology requirements. They usually focus on sharing global experiences and cultural understanding. iEARN Learning Circles provide a structured and collaborative design that effectively joins six to eight classrooms for a period of time with the expectation of producing a website or document together.	Name of Project: iEARN Learning Circles Website URL: http://media.iearn.org/projects/learningcircles Location: Anywhere, 6–8 classrooms Communication: Asynchronous—Via forums and email; Synchronous—Teacher meetings and optional class linkups Generation: Similar age, K–12 connections Information: Learning network between classrooms Time: 6–8 weeks Learning Legacy: Website or document archived and left on iEarn Website
GSN: The Global SchoolNet This network has a set of projects, including the International School's Cyberfair and Doors to Diplomacy, which provide engaging topics and design structures that focus on classroom/group website creation. While encouraging community involvement and collaboration to create the project outcome by an individual classroom, the requirement does not mandate collaboration between classrooms. Peer and international expert review determine winners of these projects and prizes are awarded. GSN also has a project registry for finding partners.	Name of Project: International Schools Cyberfair Website URL: http://www.globalschoolnet.org/gsncf (http://www.globalschoolnet.org/gsnprojects) Location: Anywhere Communication: Asynchronous—Follow project guidelines on the website, connect with other classrooms as needed, not mandatory; Synchronous—Not as a rule Generation: Same school, similar age, 6–12 Information: Challenge project for a school class (e.g., environmental awareness) Time: Many months Learning Legacy: A website is created showcasing implementation of the chosen project
E-Pals Learning Space A remodeled version of what started as an email collaborative facility for classrooms to find each other globally. Encourages creativity, collaboration, and connectivity. Classrooms have their own groups, which include safe Web 2.0 communication tools, including email, blogs, wikis, forums, and media galleries.	Name of Project: E-Pals Website URL: http://epals.com and http://learningspace.epals.com Location: Anywhere Communication: Asynchronous—Via email, other tools as instigated by schools, virtual collaborative platform created by ePals; Synchronous—Chat forums, real-time sessions depending on school Generation: K–12, across schools Information: More informal way to find partners to correspond with to learn from Time: No time frame, open-ended Learning Legacy: Discussions, blogs, emails
E-Twinning E-Twinning is a European-based networking organization that allows only schools in the European Union to join. A recent research report found that after five years, eTwinning had nearly 4,000 projects run by 78,000 schools across 32 countries. Most used high levels of technology for production (e.g., digital video, websites, blogs).[13]	Name of Project: eTwinning Website URL: http://www.etwinning.net/en/pub/index.htm Location: Only schools in Europe Communication: Asynchronous—Wikis, blogs; Synchronous—Virtual real-time sessions if organized by teachers Generation: K–12, schools in Europe Information: Some formal programs, largely teacher-directed, provides a platform for connecting and collaborating Time: Various Learning Legacy: Many and varied artifacts

(continued)

TABLE 10.1 *(Continued)*

Organization/Project and Description	Flat Classroom Framework
My Hero This project promotes stories, writing, and multimedia about heroes in students' lives. Although stories are aggregated and shared on the network, typically this project is not collaborative. Students reflect on what a hero is and who a hero is in their own life.	Name of Project: My Hero Website URL: http://www.myhero.com Location: Anywhere Communication: Asynchronous—Students post information to be shared in the competition, forums; Synchronous—Award events, activities in the local classroom Generation: Peers, connection to other generations typically in the students' inner circle, depending on the heroes selected Information: Knowledge about how to create a webpage, upload art, comment, or create a video Time: Determined by local classroom Learning Legacy: Artifacts by individual students
Around the World with 80 Schools Founded in January 2009, this website requires that you be directly involved with students. The challenge is to connect with 80 different classrooms via Skype. Once completed you will be inducted into the hall of fame! Created by Silvia Tolisano.	Name of Project: Around the World with 80 Schools Website URL: http://aroundtheworldwith80schools.net Location: Worldwide Communication: Asynchronous—teachers post blog updates and artifacts; Synchronous—Skype Generation: Peers Information: Peers Time: Ongoing Learning Legacy: Memories that are posted and learning

TABLE 10.2   Networks That Share Global Project Opportunities

Description	URL
Connect All Schools: Resources for Collaborative Project Work	http://www.connectallschools.org/node/132295
Flat Classrooms Educator network for sharing and developing project ideas	http://flatclassrooms.ning.com
Global Education Collaborative	http://globaleducation.ning.com
Taking IT Global (see Case Study at the end of this chapter)	http://www.tigweb.org/tiged
Global Collaborative Project ideas inspired by the Learning 2.0 educational network.	http://globalcollaborations.wikispaces.com
Flat Classroom Project Databank, a place for Flat Classroom Certified Teachers and others to post their projects and attract classrooms from all over the world to participate.	http://projects.flatclassroomproject.org

FIGURE 10.7 Flat Classroom Project Design Chart

PROJECT PLANNING TOOL: PROJECT DESIGN ESSENTIALS

Flat Classroom Framework	
Design Essentials	**Description**
Project Name:	Interesting, descriptive name that encourages participation
Website URL:	• Easy link to website to share. • If it is long, use a shortener that is unblocked. • Allows others to make sure they have access before they sign up.
Location:	Location: What geographic or environmental locations are desired for this project!
Communication:	Asynchronous Synchronous
Generation:	What ages is this project targeted toward? Are there any other groups?
Information:	What shared information sources will be on the learning pathway of students?
Time:	What is the timeframe for this project? Handshake? Celebration?
Learning Legacy:	How will students leave a learning legacy from what they have done? Who is the audience?

Checklist of Flatteners

❑ Do you have realistic expectations? (Chapter 1)

❑ Have you considered involvement of researchers? Is there any opportunity for citizen science? (Chapter 2)

❑ Use your **Connection** Planning Tool and see how this project fits in with the big picture of your classroom activities this year. Are there gaps in your plan? Do you have some flexibility and agility in technology-related content to integrate new technologies? What level of global collaboration will you reach? Is teacherpreneurship expected? (Chapter 3)

❑ What **Communication** conduits will be used? What are plans for teachersourcing? When is your handshake, and what will happen? What student routines for beginning and ending class will support your plans? (Chapter 4)

❑ Have you determined your framework for analyzing digital **citizenship** decisions? Do your teachers understand how to document and share issues? (Chapter 5)

❑ How will you measure student **contribution** during the project? Are there opportunities to collaborate with others in symbiotic nontraditional learning relationships? (advisors, judges, authors)? (Chapter 6)

❑ What **choices** in physical environment and electronic spaces are supported? How will choices be used to increase engagement? What is your classroom framework of tools? What will be home base? Will you use tags and if so what are your standards? (Chapter 7)

❑ How will you move students to higher-order thinking in Bloom's Taxonomy with this project? How will students **co-create**? (Chapter 8)

❑ How will you and students reflect? **Celebrate**? As a group? Individually? How will you share your work? (Chapter 9)

Curriculum Planning, Standards Alignment, Inputs, and Outcomes	
Design Essentials	**Description**
Curriculum Integration and Alignment:	• Main subject • Curriculum areas • Interdisciplinary or transdisciplinary
Guiding Question:	What is the guiding question driving this project?
Project Aims:	State clear aims for wanting global collaboration based upon the curriculum idea and guiding question.
Focus Questions:	Create a list of essential questions crucial to the content and aims of the project to help with teacher buy in across different educational systems.
Standards Alignment:	List any standards that are being addressed in this project (i.e., ISTE NETS-S). You may want to include international standards here and use a separate planning document for your local standards.
Prerequisites and Skill Level:	Clearly state any knowledge or skill prerequisites needed to start the project including digital literacy, familiarity with Web 2.0 tools, and digital citizenship requirements.
Required Outcomes:	State what each student is expected to have created as a product by the end of the project and what learning experiences are supported (no more than 1–2).
Optional Outcomes:	Other optional outcomes for participants. (These can come from schools themselves.)
Team Structure:	How are teams going to be designed and structured to promote integration, collaboration, and co-operative learning?
Required Inputs:	State what each participant is expected to contribute to the project such as wiki collaborative content.
Optional Inputs:	Other optional inputs such as team leadership and management.
Assessment:	Create common assessments for required outcomes.
Evaluation:	Determine common evaluation techniques.

TABLE 10.3 Seven Steps Design Principles and Teaching Strategies for Flat Classroom Project

Connection	Teachers connect via the Flat Classroom Google Group as well as joining the Ning network and project wiki. Weekly online meetings in Elluminate are held, with times varied across time zones to cater to a global clientele. A Skype group is often used like a backchannel to connect teachers in real time as there is usually someone online somewhere who can respond. Teachers are expected to attend or listen to the recording of the online weekly meeting. The Google group is for "teacher only" discussion and feedback, and may include specific discussions about student issues. The Skype facility is for just-in-time connection and reaching out when support is needed immediately. Students connect via setting up a Ning profile and by joining the project wiki. Students are expected to connect with and friend their team members on the Ning network and to join the School group started by their teacher.
Communication	Students are encouraged to connect with other students via Skype, IM, or other means as and when needed. Guidelines for reliable, culturally sensitive, gender-appropriate, language-sensitive, context-aware communication are established through individual teachers and responsible-use agreements. Teachers and students are both encouraged to blog and leave each other messages to do with project expectations and development, especially messages of encouragement and collegiality.
Citizenship	Discussion is encouraged between teachers and students as to the best way to connect and communicate during the project. Each wiki has a lead editor who takes responsibility for ensuring that one type of English is represented across the page. Teachers refer issues to do with inappropriate digital citizenship to the project cohort of educators and action is taken immediately. (This is described in more detail in Chapter 5.)
Contribution and Collaboration	Wiki page development is the main area for contribution and students are expected to contribute collaboratively, not just add a paragraph of their work as an individual contribution. The discussion tab on the wiki is where students let the other team members know they have added or edited the page. Other discussions related to the project and topic take place in this area, too. The wiki history tab is where teachers can find documentation of student editing. Expert advisors and project teachers monitor and contribute in the wiki discussion area providing formative feedback, resources, and encouragement. Sounding board classrooms contribute reviews of almost complete wikis, leaving links and messages via the discussion tab. The multimedia artifact requires an outsourced clip, necessitating communication between students as to artifact design and needs for the clip.
Choice	Students choose to extend communication with their team members via other online tools to support project development and collaboration. The extended community can be invited to help support knowledge acquisition or technical skill development. There is complete choice as to how the multimedia artifact is created. All computer platforms and multimedia development software, both online and offline, can be used.
Creation	The personal multimedia artifact created by each student must include a short outsourced clip created by another student. The final video is to be no more than 5 minutes in length and include other requirements as per the video artifact rubric. It is to be uploaded to the Ning network and then listed on the master video wiki ready for judging. The collaborative wiki page is completed and tidied. Final videos are embedded into a separate wiki for each topic with template information for identification.
Celebration	Optional student summits are celebrations held in Blackboard Collaborate where each class, led by their teacher, presents. Each student creates an image collage and talks within the virtual classroom about her or his learning during the project to an international audience. The awards ceremony is the culmination of the video/multimedia artifact judging.

FLAT CLASSROOM PROJECT UNDER THE MICROSCOPE

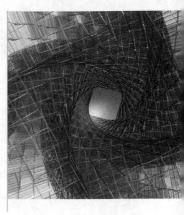

Let's now look at the Flat Classroom Project (FCP) as an example of global collaborative project design.

Checklist of Flatteners: Using the Seven Steps to Refine Our Thinking. See Table 10.3 (page 258) to examine the Flat Classroom Project from the perspective of the Seven Steps to Flatten Your Classroom and see where this now provides the scaffolding crucial for project success.

The Flat Classroom Project. Refer to Table 10.4 for project design essentials using the Flat Classroom Framework of the Flat Classroom Project. Figure 10.7 (page 257) provides the design essentials and Figure 10.8 (page 262) demonstrates the value of student video artifacts.

TABLE 10.4 Project Design Essentials for Flat Classroom Project

Design Essentials	Description
Project Name	Flat Classroom Project (Vicki and Julie brainstormed online when finalizing this name)
Website URL	http://www.flatclassroomproject.net—Main website http://www.flatclassroomproject.org—Wikis (each project has its own wiki, listed on the left) http://flatclassroomproject.ning.com—Educational network http://groups.diigo.com/group/flatclassroomproject—Diigo group *(optional)*
Location	Global
Communication	Asynchronous—Wiki, Ning, Diigo Bookmarking Group
Generation	Students ages 14–18 are the best choice; Grades 9–12/13, preferably grade 10 or above depending on maturity level and ultimately depending on skill level of the students. However, there is high expectation to be able to do effective research and to synthesize this research into collaborative content in "Wikipedia" style. Older generation—Expert advisors, judges Younger generation—Peer review and sounding board process
Information	*The World Is Flat* by Thomas Friedman *The World Is Flat 3.0* lecture by Thomas Friedman at MIT[14] *A Whole New Mind* by Dan Pink Teachers, peers, online authentic research Student PLNs using RSS *(optional)*
Time	The project runs for 10–12 weeks, with teacher handshake time before this. Here is a workflow example based on one of the three project cycles, FCP-01: January–April: 1. Application deadline: December 1 (previous calendar year) 2. Online teacher information meeting before January 15 3. Classroom and student handshake January 15–31 4. Wiki editing and collaboration: February 5. Nonparticipating classrooms removed from project: February 15 6. Classroom and student handshake January 15–31 7. Wiki editing and collaboration: February 8. Nonparticipating classrooms removed from project: February 15 9. Video pitches and creation: March 10. Celebration—Student Summits and video judging: April 1–15 Awards ceremony: After April 15 as determined by the project organizer

(continued)

TABLE 10.4 *(Continued)*

Design Essentials	Description
Learning Legacy	Videos, blog posts are shared in spaces. Award winners are posted on official website and released through the press release.
Curriculum Integration and Alignment	FCP is interdisciplinary, but with strong links to social studies/humanities and subjects that study global issues, and ICT impacts and developments such as Information Technology in a Global Society (ITGS, an International Baccalaureate Diploma subject). Also, due to the high level of technology involved and the fact that the final output includes a piece of multimedia, there are strong links to information technology, computer studies, and media design courses. Topics are taken from Friedman's work and include Connecting the World Online, World Wide Web, Workflow Software, The Changing Shape of Information, Web 2.0 Tools for Sharing Information, Globalization and Outsourcing, Google Takes Over the World, Personal Learning Environments and Social Networking, Mobile and Ubiquitous, Virtual Communication, and Wireless Connectivity. The multimedia artifact/digital story is also created according to a theme (based on Pink's work): Story; Innovation, Invention, and Prediction; Social Entrepreneurship; First-Person Narrative; Group Stories; How We Live (Play).
Guiding Question	"What are the consequences of technology (information and communication tools) on how, when, and why we connect, collaborate, and create?" The project is designed to develop cultural understanding, skills with Web 2.0 and application software, experience in global collaboration and online learning, and awareness of what it means to live and work in a flat world, all while researching and discussing the ideas developed in Friedman's book, *The World Is Flat*. Students also have the chance to interact with expert advisers and other classroom teachers and sounding board classrooms in a true flattened learning mode.
Project Aims	The essential aim is to immerse participants in a Web 2.0 environment, thereby developing transferable skills in emerging technologies.
Focus Questions	These provide essential discussion points and perspective on the project for all involved. For the FCP they include: • How can emerging technologies and enhanced connectivity improve learning and create extended communities? • How can we use "flattened" learning modes and emerging technologies to connect with other classrooms globally? • When we connect globally what can we do together that could make a difference to world as we know it? • How can we use multimedia to effectively convey a message? • What sort of products can be co-created via collaboration? • How can we best share our learning to a wider audience?
Standards Alignment	FCP covers all NETS.S and NETS.T C21 Standards
Prerequisites and Skill Level	The use of Web 2.0 technologies, wikis, blogs, and social bookmarking beforehand is an advantage. The learning curve is steep and participants (teachers and students) will be expected to network and collaborate online fluently. Research is a key component; therefore, some experience with academic research and copyright is necessary. The final product requires knowledge of application software to create a final piece of multimedia. Students and teachers will need an email account to sign up for the services used in this project.

TABLE 10.4 (*Continued*)

Design Essentials	Description
Required Outcomes	The FCP has four *mandatory* components for students: 1. **A written, audio, or video introduction** posted as a blog on the educational network. 2. **A written collaborative report using a wiki.** Students will edit the wiki and discuss the topic on the discussion tab of the page in teams 3. **A personal multimedia response (digital story/video)** (topic as assigned on the project matrix) 4. **A postproject reflection.** Students will post their reflection on the process to the educational network (Ning) The project design chart, Figure 10.2, shows how the team grid helps divide students further into topic areas on the wiki. For example, those in Team A will be responsible for co-creating the Overview section of the topic, and those in Team E will research and contribute collaborative work on Arts, Entertainment, and Leisure for the topic. The required project video artifact, Figure 10.8, is a combination of original multimedia material as well as an outsourced clip.
Optional Outcomes	Because it is such a multifaceted project and at times overwhelming for new classrooms, the FCP has some items that are optional. This practice takes the pressure off the beginning teacher to feel they must do everything, but at the same time provides opportunities for alternative class activities and modes of response leading to deeper learning. In this case the student summit presentations held in Blackboard Collaborate hosted by the teacher in their class, forum discussions and responses to keynotes, social bookmarking, and research using Diigo are optional.
Team Structure	The Friedman flatteners (11 identified for this project) are cross-gridded with themes taken from Pink's *A Whole New Mind*.[15] Students will be placed in mixed-classroom teams, preferably with no one from their class in the same team. Students will be assigned one each of the themes based on Pink's book (per the project matrix or team grid). Teams are typically no more than four or five students per grid, however there may be 20 or more students working on each of the flattener wiki topics. The project is scalable; if fewer classrooms enroll, then the project matrix uses fewer of the themes to create the mash-up. If more students sign up, more than one team grid can be used. The full FCP matrix, as in Figure 10.8, clearly shows the cross-grid between the flatteners and the concepts from Pink's book.
Required Inputs	Students are expected to "handshake" via the educational network and develop connections with their team members. Once on the wiki they collaboratively research and write a report, including embedded multimedia as appropriate. Engaged communication and evidence of collaboration is expected throughout, and will be shown by discussion on the Ning network and wiki. Each student is expected to help provide an outsourced video clip for another student who is preferably not in his or her class.
Optional Inputs	Each wiki topic page requests a student to volunteer to be the lead editor and therefore determine the type of English for that page (American, British, or other). Other optional inputs involving peer review and leadership tasks are at the discretion of the class teacher and the willingness of the students.
Assessment	Rubric-based assessment with two rubrics shared for all project classrooms (see the PDToolkit and the appendix for examples of rubrics).
Evaluation	Teacher survey, student reflective blog posts

FIGURE 10.8   Flat Classroom Project Video Artifact

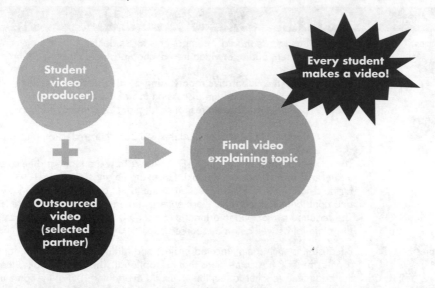

SUMMARY

This chapter is about turning knowledge into action. It may seem overwhelming, but the project planning tool is designed to help you begin your journey. If in doubt, start very simply. Keep your first project short, simple, and small, or connect it with an existing project. Also, keep your promises. Keeping promises is the kernel that blossoms into the development of your character, and it may determine whether others will work with you in the future.

Make this real, make it authentic, and remember that the first time a global project is implemented, the learning curve will be steep for all participants—especially you. Be prepared to accommodate differences with a flexible approach until the project finds its own level, usually by the second or third implementation.

ESSENTIAL QUESTIONS

- Consider a global collaborative project that interests you and relate it to the project design essentials. Are there any questions you have for organizers?

- How can we design learning experiences that embrace global education as well as enforce rigor and relevance? Are these the same?

- What role do social media play in the success of online projects in today's educational environment?

- Why are some projects more "successful" than others? How can we support the needs of participants bringing different countries, systems, and expectations?

- What are the characteristics of an engaged teacher and classroom in a global collaborative project?

◀ Join the online conversation and share your answers at http://tinyurl.com/flatclass-ch10

THE FLAT CLASSROOM™ 15 CHALLENGES

CHALLENGE 13: GLOBAL PROJECT DESIGN

 **21st CENTURY SKILLS**

C21 PROFESSIONAL
DEVELOPMENT

 **ISTE STANDARDS**

NETS.T 5
Engage in Professional Growth
and Leadership

DO: Through your personal learning network, suggest or join a group of people to pursue a plan for a global collaborative classroom project in a content area that interests you. Using the strategies learned in this book and the material from the chapter, design your project.

SHARE: Blog and post your project in the Flat Classromo databank (http://projects.flatclass roomproject.org), recruiting others to participate in the project. If you intend to use this idea now in the classroom, share with your colleagues and use your internal calendar to plan. **The tag for this challenge is fcc13_design. Use this when you blog, or to share with your group.**

Share what you did with your challenge at http://tinyurl.com/flat15-13 ▷

BONUS CHALLENGE 13: ENGAGE WITH SOCIAL MEDIA

Do: Using your learning network, connect and share your project from Challenge 13 with others (use the databank http://projects.flatclassroomproject.org), and, if desired, recruit participants for peer classrooms, expert advisors, mentors, and judges.

Share: Keep a journal or use a twitter hashtag to tweet out the results of your social media engagement efforts to help your project. **The tag for this challenge is fcc13b_social. Use this when you blog or to share with your group.**

Share what you did with your challenge at http://tinyurl.com/flat15-13b ▷

THE FLAT CLASSROOM™ DIARIES

Diary Entry 20

FLAT CLASSROOM PROJECT TEACHERS SHARE IDEAS ABOUT PROJECT DESIGN AND MANAGEMENT

Collated ideas from various Flat Classroom teachers.

KEVIN CROUCH and ERICA BARCLAY from the American School of Bombay:

 **ADD FRIEND**

KEVIN CROUCH
@kevincrouch
http://www.kevincrouch.net

ERICA BARCLAY
@ericakiersten
http://elementaryflatclassroom.wordpress.com/category/erica-barclay

Global collaborative projects require extra attention in a few areas to ensure a successful collaboration. . . . There are also critical organizational elements in setting up and participating in this project. In order to facilitate collaborative planning between teachers in different time zones, cultures, and schools, projects need to have clear guidelines, time lines and expectations.

When entering into a flattened learning environment, the learning outcomes should also be made clear. Depending on the desired outcomes, the project will be approached differently. One of the most exciting aspects of a flattened classroom is being exposed to applications and technology tools you may not have used or been aware of. There is no limit to variety of skills and literacies that can be integrated into these projects, and if you can master the organizational piece, you can make a pedagogical shift that will flatten the walls of your classroom for good.[16]

Read the rest of this Flat Classroom Diary from Kevin Crouch and Erica Barclay online. http://tinyurl.com/flat-keys. ▶

AARON MAURER (ELP Facilitator, Bettendorf School District, USA),
a Flat Classroom Certified teacher, writes about communication strategies.

This project [one Aaron created with a class in Japan] started off small by the basic electronic pen pal mechanics of sending a class letter to Japan and the teacher responding to the writing snail mail back and forth. Then we really started to become interested in the cultural differences between the two countries (once again nothing new here). We started to send pictures and realized the differences between America (society of "individuals") and Japan (society of "community"). We started to question school uniforms, food, words, family, etc. This led to making some movies back and forth. The movies then showcased the schools, what they buildings looked like, the scenery around town, the after school clubs.[17]

This was all awesome and very informative, but there was still not that instant communication and the frustration of a language barrier by my students using English words the Japan students were not familiar with and my students speaking zero Japanese. We brainstormed a possible solution.

AARON MAURER
@coffeechugbooks
http://www.coffeeforthebrain.blogspot.com

We are now experimenting with Twitter. The short quick phrases are ideal for language development. The communication is instant. We can still send pictures, ask questions etc. It has been a perfect tool. The one obstacle is that Twitter is blocked at school so I have to upload the tweets to Google Doc, then share in class, type up answers, go home and submit via Twitter. This has really helped bring down the communication barrier. As we tweet back and forth we can still work on the larger projects of videos, writing letters, etc."[18]

Read the rest of this Flat Classroom Diary from Aaron Maurer online. http://tinyurl.com/global-gossip

---

SUSIE THROOP, Marietta Center for Advanced Academics,
writes about the "A Week in the Life . . ." Elementary Flat Classroom project:

The first thing I did to introduce the project was to show the Edmodo site on my SMART Board to the class.

The teacher from Korea was the last to post. I clicked on the link in his post, which took us to his wiki. "Hey, that looks like our wiki," was the first response. Indeed it did. We watched the videos of his students as my kids sat on the edge of their seats. Next we brainstormed ideas for our virtual handshakes. The kids began posting and reading other students' posts.

The next thing that happened was the highlight of the day. Morgan said, "Where is Martha's Vineyard? Someone just commented on my post from Martha's Vineyard!!!"

SUSIE THROOP
@bsthroop
http://sthroop.wordpress.com

That made two things happen. First of all the students got onto Google Maps to locate [Martha's] Vineyard and second they all started chatting with kids their age 2,000 miles away. The students realized they could change their avatars—I had planned on introducing this, but they beat me to it. This all happened 2 days before our spring break. When I logged on to

Read the full diary entry from Susie Throop at http://tinyurl.com/my-first-day.

FLAT CLASSROOM™ FRAMEWORK

NAME OF PROJECT: Project Global Gossip

WEBSITE URL: http://coffeechug.wikispaces.com/Global+Gossip

TWITTER NAME: @Coffeechugclass

LOCATION: USA—Bettendorf, Iowa, Japan

COMMUNICATION: Asynchronous—Twitter (students pose questions), Woices (for introductions); Synchronous—each classroom

GENERATION: Peers (ages 10–14)

INFORMATION: Gathered from peers comparing various country (school systems, accents, societal norms)

TIME: Year-long collaboration or a one-time sharing (anyone can tweet answers to their Twitter account)

LEARNING LEGACY: Videos, Blackboard Collaborate recording, Twitter archive

Edmodo this morning, I noticed pages and pages of posts from my students—how cool is that?!

As the students left my class the first day they were all saying things like, "This is the coolest project ever!"

By recess time, other teachers were asking me what we were up to. They all want to participate in the project next year.[19]

CASE EXAMPLES OF GLOBAL COLLABORATION

for
***Flattening Classrooms,
Engaging Minds***

Read full Case Studies
in PDToolkit online.

Case Study 20

Rubric Design and Collaborative Learning,
MARK VAN 'T HOOFT,
Kent State University, Research Center for Educational Technology

 ADD FRIEND

MARK VAN 'T HOOFT
@dutchboyinohio
http://ubiquitousthoughts.wordpress.com

 **21st CENTURY SKILLS**

**C21 STANDARDS AND
ASSESSMENT**

Rubrics are alternative forms of assessment that list criteria (with associated levels of mastery or performance) against which a learning artifact is scored. As rubrics are usually distributed to learners before the start of a learning activity, they can be used as working guides or checklists. Rubrics are especially useful for project-based and collaborative learning activities such as the ones in the Flat Classroom Project, because they provide a common set of expectations for all members of a project group and describe exactly what a final product (such as a student-produced video) should look like at the various

performance levels. In addition, rubrics are flexible in that they can be easily revised over time, even if the learning activity does not change.

Key features of rubric design to support collaborative learning include:

• Determining the concepts to be taught and the criteria you will use to measure student learning.
• Creating a grid that includes these criteria and 3 or 4 levels of performance.

- Making sure that the criteria to be measured include both process (the collaboration) and end product. Decide how much weight to attach to each (i.e., are process and product equal in importance, or is one more important than the other)?
- Writing clear statements for each of the performance levels for each criterion. Statements that are unclear will confuse students and create issues when scoring projects against the rubric.
- Testing the rubric before issuing it to learners.

The ways in which students learn are constantly changing, and assessment of learning should reflect that. In the Flat Classroom Project, students are required to create a video about the impact of technology on our world. They do so while using Web 2.0 technologies to communicate and collaborate with group members who may be at different schools in different countries. It would be difficult to assess student learning in this scenario using conventional methods such as a paper and pencil test, but the use of a rubric offers a solution here. The current rubric evaluates the design and technical quality of the video,

the construction and synthesis of ideas related to the topic studied, and the level of collaboration within each group. As such, the rubric provides opportunities for authentic assessment and detailed feedback that transcends a simple numerical score. In addition, it gives students from different schools, countries, and cultures a common goal to work towards, and a set of criteria they can hold each other to.

What can educators designing their own projects learn from the Flat Classroom Project when it comes to assessment and rubrics? First, it is essential to test the rubric with a sample project. As our experiences in the Flat Classroom Project show, a rubric is never perfect, and chances are it will be revised one or more times.

For example, if it is difficult to be consistent when scoring multiple projects against a criterion, chances are the statements describing each level of performance need to be rewritten. Second, it is extremely important that students have seen the rubric and understand its purpose and contents *before* they start working on their group projects. This is especially important in projects like the Flat Classroom, because student expectations may differ from country to country and school to school.

Case Study 21

The TakingITGlobal Vision

C21 INTERDISCIPLINARY THEME:
Civic Literacy
Environmental Literacy

C21 LEARNING AND INNOVATION SKILLS:
Communication and Collaboration

Social networking is a way of life for youth today, with collecting friends on Facebook becoming a hobby like collecting stamps was in the past. Before the days of Facebook, Twitter, and even MySpace, TakingITGlobal (TIG) was founded to leverage the power of social media for making connections on a global scale, and set out to maximize this potential by using it as a tool to help youth understand and act on the world's greatest challenges.

TakingITGlobal[20] is an online social network unlike any other: a social network for social good. The site targets young people looking for ways to affect change on local and global scales, with a vision of youth everywhere being actively engaged and connected in shaping a more inclusive, peaceful, and sustainable world. Working toward this vision is an

MICHAEL FURDYK
@mfurdyk
http://profiles.tigweb.org/mfurdyk
KATHERINE WALRAVEN
@katwalraven
http://profiles.tigweb.org/kagawa

SOCIAL NETWORK
Taking IT Global
http://www.tigweb.org

army of staff members, interns, online volunteers, and hundreds of thousands of members. These members contribute to the site through its discussion boards on global issues, organize around causes that are important to them with the help of Action Guides, express themselves by contributing art and writing to TIG's Global Gallery and online publications, and the list goes on.

Supporting Global Education

The main TIG site in itself has much to offer teachers and students: There is an educational games section, an informative page for each country of the world, and dozens of global issues pages that are rich in content and resources. In addition to this, TIGed directly supports educators to bring global education into their classrooms. TIGed is a network of over 4,400 teachers and classes in 120 countries around the world.

These teachers collaborate with one another to open the walls of their classrooms and expose their students to people, cultures, and issues around the world. Major offerings of TIGed include a suite of teacher resources in global education, accredited professional development courses, and an award-winning virtual classroom platform that allows teachers to connect their classes with others around the world in the spirit of intercultural exchange and sharing.

Collaboration in Action

TIGed's space for collaboration is truly unique. Educators can seek out other teachers all over the world for the purpose of embarking on collaborative projects. Are you a Spanish language teacher in Arizona who wants to teach your students about the variety of cultures in the Spanish-speaking world?

Connect your class to others in Ecuador, Spain, Mexico, and Argentina—and see what happens! You could co-develop a whole unit online for all collaborating classes with the assignments posted in your TIGed collaboration space. Students can post their writing, share artwork, blog, and have video chat sessions with their fellow classmates around the world! TIGed's online classrooms are private and secure while providing students with access to unparalleled opportunities to work with global peers. Youth already have it in them to be the global citizens the world needs. Let's work together to provide them with the tools they need to make a difference, and they'll show us what taking education global can really do!

http://tiged.com

Challenge-Based Professional Development

> "The web of learning is part of a personal as well as a professional lifestyle. . . . What is clear is that this web of learning extends to all age groups, all walks of life, and learners in all corners of the world and beyond."
>
> CURTIS BONK
> *The World Is Open*[1]

 **ADD FRIEND**   **CURTIS BONK**
@travelinedman
http://travelinedman.blogspot.com

This is the story of how one random assignment can change the course of a teaching career.

The random assignment was my 12 weeks of student teaching in a classroom taught by Estie Cuellar. Estie had "met" Julie Lindsay and Vicki Davis virtually through a workshop she had attended over the summer and had signed up for a Flat Classroom™ project. She began asking me if I blogged, if I used Web 2.0 technologies. I had no earthly idea what she was talking about, but hey, I was a *student* teacher and willing to learn.

Nings, wikis, Diigo, Elluminate—so many new technologies— a whole new world opened up to me. I went from being a skeptic, to a believer, to an avid supporter. I made friends in Qatar, Germany, and Australia!

I explained what the term *cool beans* meant to a very confused group of international teachers. I also explained to a group in Japan that when my students said they like to "hang out and chill" with their friends, they are neither actually hanging, nor decreasing in temperature. We learned you don't include a picture of yourself exposing your back with a large tattoo covering it to male students in Saudi Arabia. We also learned that if you post a picture of Beyoncé in place of your Ning profile photo, some people will actually *think* you are Beyoncé, and you will attract a lot of male students clamoring to be your "friend" (true stories, all).

That first project I participated in was with nine students. Three years later, with my own classroom, I am now a Flat Classroom "veteran" preparing my students for the workplace using these technologies, and currently have a class of 27 students frantically preparing videos. But it has gone so far beyond the Flat Classroom Project, as I have now incorporated wikis, blogs, and Web 2.0 technology into every class I teach. I have a "support group" of FCP teachers that can always help me out when I am in a bind. I have a new group of educator "followers" on Twitter! Flat Classroom changed the way I teach.

KIMBERLY CLAYTON[2]

See Curt Bonk's high-energy overview of the evolution of Web 2.0 and the major educational innovations of the period at http://tinyurl.com/bonk-keynote

KIMBERLY CLAYTON
@kaclayton

NETS.T 5
Engage in Professional Growth and Leadership

21st CENTURY SKILLS

C21 PROFESSIONAL DEVELOPMENT

OVERVIEW OF CHALLENGE-BASED PROFESSIONAL DEVELOPMENT

Blended learning, e-learning, educational networks, just-in-time (JIT) professional development (PD), and online conferences are fairly recent additions to professional development for educators. In many instances, some of these modes of professional development have been overhyped at introduction and suffered from a backlash of those who "jumped in" only to find poor implementation of the technology and ineffective learning experiences. Additionally, new modes of professional development are emerging, including online volunteerism by preservice or student teachers as part of core courses and challenge-based conferencing.

This chapter explores emerging professional development modalities and examines current practice through specific case studies. It also looks at the design of a challenge-based experience for face-to-face and virtual participants and shares strategies for PD organizers to flatten and deepen the learning experience at future professional development sessions.

WHY EMBEDDING PD TRANSFORMS TEACHING PRACTICE

Much of the professional development of the past has been a "binge approach." Teachers are sent to professional development courses for 6 to 20 hours over a one- to three-day period. Overloaded, these teachers go back to their classrooms largely unchanged and without time to implement a significant portion of what they have learned. Or a school puts aside two PD days with guest presenters and a theme, but without the context of the participants' classroom and curriculum needs analyzed. This can be a wasted opportunity to grow further.

By using the pull technologies mentioned in *Step 1: Connection* (Chapter 3), many teachers are improving their practice by learning in small, incremental learning experiences and then immediately implementing what they've learned. They are now embedding their learning into their weekly experience.

Teaching strategies such as project-based learning mentioned in this book also apply to teachers. By embedding professional development as part of an extended project, teachers are implementing as they learn. This is why some schools, such as the middle school in Wells, Maine, are hiring "collaborative content coaches" like Cheryl Oakes so that teachers can be helped as they design and implement projects. Kim Cofino, for example, is the Technology and Learning Coach at Yokohama International School in Japan. What is needed is not necessarily a binge, 10-hour workshop, but rather, 15- to 30-minute tutoring sessions once a week, or ongoing connected learning with like-minded educators.

Embedding professional development means to integrate our learning into our doing. This happens either through learning in small bits of time during the working week or by attending face-to-face events where projects are used. Embedding professional development in our activities is key to transformational learning and gets us past traditional single-modality methods of delivery that require so much more effort. Context is the key to success here. Learning new skills within context, and being able to implement and apply those skills immediately is the goal.

Embedded PD means to integrate our learning into doing. #flatclass

OBSTACLES WE MUST OVERCOME NOW

Within a school setting, PD experiences should be designed that align with strategic goals, budgets, and curriculum needs. Obstacles to embedding PD in a teacher's weekly practice include a lack of vision and planning as well as confusion over curriculum priorities. School administrators and PD managers need to realize that the older models of teaching teachers are not working.

Rather than measuring professional development in units and putting restrictions on access, an enlightened approach is to mandate everyone have PD time across the working week. Teacher accountability and carefully constructed evaluation procedures can work together to support ongoing PD for all. Licensing agencies and organizations need to review some of the case studies below to determine how teachers can earn professional development credit for what are proving to be very effective, transformational learning experiences for all educators. There is a high demand for courses that practice what they teach. No more boring professional development leaders droning on about project based learning while educators take notes! If it works, do it! If it is the right way to teach, we should be using it to learn ourselves!

EMERGING PROFESSIONAL DEVELOPMENT MODALITIES

Tightening PD budgets are limiting support for 21st century skill development for all teachers. With a raised awareness that extra travel affects our carbon footprint and progress made in e-learning, schools should question the necessity of always needing the face-to-face mode to learn. The flexibility of learning at convenient times increases the attractiveness of online professional development for many teachers. Online communities, communities of practice, and blended learning opportunities provide scaffolds for online learning and therefore for teacher PD.

tweetable

Schools should question the necessity of being in the face-to-face mode to learn. Online communities provide scaffolds for PD. #flatclass

E-LEARNING

Course Delivery.   Often called "virtual learning" or "online learning" e-learning is rapidly becoming a part of the delivery of learning by major K–12 and post-secondary institutions. While including online content management systems such as Blackboard or Moodle, which have discussion boards and other features, these classes often also meet in online classrooms for study and learning.

Students in pure e-learning environments often seek multiple modalities of content and engaged professors. These environments have their problems, though. Vicki had several students attending a virtual high school for AP history and several had to drop the course because the teachers taught in a "regular" school during the day and only answered questions at night. The lack of support when they had questions made it unsuitable. The best e-learning environments are there 24/7 with engaged teachers and professors available when students need them.

Online Conferences.   Online conferences such as the K–12 Online Conference[3] or the Global Education Conference[4] are emerging as exciting ways for teachers around the world to share best practices in online meetings and a network. Some colleges are now offering credit for online conference participation. It was the first K–12 online conference in 2006 where Julie Lindsay and Vicki Davis first "met." The experience of meeting another like-minded educator via an organized online event can be life changing. Good online learning best practices are emerging as we write this book.

BLENDED LEARNING

Blended learning provides the "best of both worlds" according to many who prefer this method. Colleges use this procedure by having one meeting a week in an online classroom and face-to-face meetings for presentations and project work on an intermittent basis. Tests are often administered online as well. More recently, high school educators are using this method to engage students and provide alternative modes of communication. The Inside ITGS (Information Technology in a Global Society)[5] flattened classroom is a good example of this (see Appendix B for more details).

Many professional development organizations are using this blended learning method by kicking off an online course with a face-to-face meeting and often ending the course face-to-face as well. Examples of this include the CoETaIL course (Certificate of Educational Technology and Information Literacy)[6] and Powerful Learning Practice.[7] This saves travel expenses and allows participants to engage at a higher level. Additionally, the online work that is spread out through the length of the course allows educators to learn in a method that embeds their professional development.

ISTE STANDARDS

NETS.T 1.d
Facilitate and Inspire Student Learning and Creativity

NETS.T 3
Model Digital-Age Work and Learning

EDUCATIONAL NETWORKS

Online networks such as Classroom 2.0, Global Education Conference, EdTech Talk, and the Flat Classroom are emerging as places that provide webinars (often free) and online connections with other teachers. As of the writing of this book, attendance of free webinars and webcasts is a learning tool, but earning credit from active participation is just starting to emerge.

Teachers gravitate to these places to find answers and collaborators. Many projects are born from a tweet on Twitter! Educators get acquainted before going to conferences so when active participants in online networks attend a conference, they already have "friends." Conferences become more engaging and enjoyable as people who only meet face-to-face once a year connect throughout the year in online spaces.

SPEED ROUND PRESENTING AND PARTICIPATION

Speed Round Presenting.   The popular TED Talks have directly influenced conferences and professional development. In this format, participants are timed to give a speech (rarely over 20 minutes) according to the "rules" of the venue. Presentations are usually recorded and shared later. This method of presenting often replaces the single keynote, thereby allowing the participants to listen to four or five presenters in the span of time they would have heard one keynote. This takes advantage of a human's natural attention span (about 20 minutes) to provide variety and re-engagement with the lecture delivery method.

Speed Round Audience Participation.   Now the "smackdown" is becoming popular. At the Edubloggercon[8] event, held at the ISTE (International Society for Technology Educators) conference, a Web 2.0 Smackdown (first created by co-author Vicki Davis from the wrestling "smack downs" so popular in the southern United States) is held with participants lining up to present and a moderator timing participants to 2 or 3 minutes to share with the group a tool that they use. This often produces a lively, exciting exchange on ideas and is often accompanied by a backchannel.

In another derivative (aptly invented in China for the Flat Classroom Conference 2011), **Web 2 Kung Fu** is a system where audience members can learn from at least 10 other people in the audience. Audience participation turns onlookers into active learners. This could be done with any subject material. It always involves using the knowledge of the audience in power-packed sharing.

JUST IN TIME PROFESSIONAL DEVELOPMENT

Just-in-Time PD is about finding answers and learning resources when one needs and is ready for them. It can include such JIT sites as Atomic Learning, where one can search for a short video clip on how to perform a task in just about any type of software. Also, this system can be provided through live chats and through school system coaches and technology integrators who are available to coach teachers through project implementation.

The key feature is that this professional development, in whatever form it takes, should be available to the teacher "just in time." The power of micro blogging such as Twitter can be included here. Building an online responsive network is one way to reach out for help and learn every day.

ONLINE VOLUNTEERISM

Online projects like the Flat Classroom and NetGen Ed™ projects need volunteers to serve as expert advisors and judges. Professors of preservice and inservice teachers such as Dr. Eric Brunsell (see Chapter 1), Dr. Leigh Zeitz (see Chapter 6), or Eva Brown (Red River College in Winnipeg, Canada) have incorporated project-based volunteerism into the curriculum of their courses.

Dr. Brunsell had his students volunteer as expert advisors on the NetGen Ed™ project in 2009, where his students helped facilitate student teams on their wiki research, providing feedback and coaching them on content. Dr. Zeitz's students participate as expert advisors for the Flat Classroom projects and also as judges for the project. (A group of inservice students of Dr. Zeitz came to Beijing to help facilitate the 2011 Flat Classroom Conference.) Eva encouraged her students to participate as expert advisors, and as a class they delivered one of the very first Flat Learning Action Talks online. Each professor included "live" interactions with project organizers, Vicki and Julie, so that the preservice teachers could ask questions about teaching in online environments. This rich, embedded, project-based learning environment helped move past having class discussions about technology into the reality of teaching with technology. Preservice teachers can now learn by watching students learn and teachers interact in online spaces.

UN-CONFERENCES

Un-conferences are those where participants show up and often self-organize into sessions. Anyone posts what he or she wishes to present or facilitate and participants "vote with their feet." The sessions with the most votes are held and those without interest are removed from the program. Edubloggercon is an example of this technique and provides a rich way for educators using and interested in Web 2.0 tools to connect face-to-face before the conference begins. Often these educators present so heavily during the conference that they do not get to meet and share during the conference. Alternatively, it also gives those who are not presenting in the mainstream a chance to share and lead relevant sessions. The Learning 2.0 Conference,[9] held in Shanghai, China, also uses this approach to allow participants for at least two sessions each day to self-determine what they want to talk about and learn about from their colleagues.

SPECIAL INTEREST "AREAS" AT FACE-TO-FACE CONFERENCES

Larger, formal conferences create special-interest lounges. This encourages participants to gravitate toward areas where their hot topics are discussed (at ISTE, examples include virtual worlds, administrators, Bloggers Cafe) and often the interactive whiteboards at these areas erupt into spontaneous presentations that attract passersby as groups of people begin conversing about what they are doing.

CHALLENGE-BASED CONFERENCING

Perhaps one of the most exciting but very recent innovations is the advent of the challenge-based conference. The Flat Classroom conference has emerged as a prime

ISTE STANDARDS

NETS.T 5
Engage in Professional Growth and Leadership

WEBSITES

Learning 2.011
http://learning2.asia

WEBSITES

ISTE Conference
http://www.isteconference.org

example of this style of event where teachers and students attend the same conference and have mutually beneficial experiences with different learning outcomes.

In this format, participants each carry out a challenge that often spans the entire conference. As participants engage, short, intermittent presentations are given by facilitators to help participants understand the skills required for that particular phase of the project. This is embedded learning, and although the conference takes only two to three days, the process includes Just-in-Time instruction and facilitators coaching small groups of participants.

Project challenges create highly engaged experiences for those who want more than cerebral knowledge of the workings of the content matter. It has been observed in the Flat Classroom conference that some who prefer a 100 percent lecture format may not have "the energy" for participation. Most participants, however, find that they have learned content matter and more in a very deep, engaging way and established relationships with people in a powerful experiential, challenge-based learning experience.

THE HIDDEN CONFERENCE AT A CONFERENCE

Using live chats called a backchannel and hashtags, conference participants who are highly engaged with social media will often have their own version of a conference happening hidden from view by those who are not so connected. Savvy conferences will have organizers who stay connected to this backchannel or perhaps have one of their own for managing the conference.

At the Flat Classroom conference, there is a backchannel for discussion but often people will chat issues that conference organizers need to attend to in order to keep things running smoothly. Stories are emerging from non–social media savvy conference organizers of how even keynote speakers have been embarrassed by this hidden conference happening live on Twitter or in the formal or informal backchannel. Although you cannot control what happens in these spaces or shut them off, being there with real faces of your conference and contributing to the conversation will help you send the message that you are connected, savvy, and care about the experience for participants.

DESIGN OF POWERFUL TWENTY-FIRST CENTURY PROFESSIONAL DEVELOPMENT

Having conducted many project-based professional development experiences for educators, there are some key understandings needed in order to be able to design such experiences.

PREPARATION AND PLANNING

Sharing and Digital Citizenship Starts before Registration. Think about how you want participants to share. Ask them to give you their Twitter handle, Facebook ID, blog, or any information that they want to share. Ask their permission to share it with other participants. Consider using this information on nametags. Your goal is to help your participants move from being in your conference to being in each other's Twitter stream, Facebook groups, and personal learning networks as simply as possible. Help them connect easily.

Think about having participants set up a profile in your online network. They can give you their profile ID and you could generate a QR code on the name badge that would allow others to snap a picture and add his information to their address book on their phone, or follow him on Twitter. Make a Twitter list publicize the hashtag to let participants get acquainted before the conference. Make sure participants are aware of all official points of communication, including your conference's official blog, Twitter account, Facebook fan page, hashtag, the link for virtual participation (if any), and any groups where you'll be sharing (e.g., Flickr or Tumblr.) This may sound overwhelming to you, but if educators are expected to model digital age work and learning (ISTE NETS.T 3), then you need to make it part of their PD experience! You can talk all day about this technology stuff, but educators won't understand it until they see how it is used in real life.

Be on the alert for people coming to your conference who have done creative things and are natural leaders, and be willing to bring them into your circle of organizers. If teachers are supposed to "Facilitate and inspire student learning and creativity" (NETS.T 1) then you need to do it too!

Let participants know up front if they will be allowed to stream, film, or interview, and what will and will not be allowed. Imagine how angry someone would be to travel to an overseas conference with all of her or his video gear just to find out that no video recordings are allowed!

Be welcoming to beginners who may feel overwhelmed by terms like *QR code* or *Twitter handle*. One of the best examples of this is the ISTE Newbie project founded by Beth Still in 2008. What started as a project to bring a beginning teacher to the International Society of Technology Educators conference turned into a project that also welcomes first-timers to an excellent educational conference and brings them into the network.[10]

Set Realistic Expectations.   Know your audience and be realistic in what will be achieved in a short period of time. Try not to introduce too many new and potentially overwhelming ideas in a short space of time.

Prepare for Push-Back.   Though many students don't like it, many educators prefer lecture-based delivery. After all, many teachers *loved* school, and the traditional lecture-based method is how they learned. (Maybe that is why they are teachers.) So, one can expect that some of those teachers will feel uncomfortable in this new hands-on learning scene. Be prepared to work to meet the diverse learning needs of your audience just like a good teacher will do in her classroom.

Prepare to Get Their Attention and Reward Good Behavior.   In such environments, participants are going to do a lot of *talking*. This means that often when it is time for a facilitator to help participants move on to the next part of their project that they are not ready and may choose to keep on talking. It helps to get their attention by giving small rewards for good behavior by using stickers or a "commodity." At the Flat Classroom conference we use DigiDollars (see Figure 11.1). We use, three colors

DIGITAL CITIZENSHIP AREA OF UNDERSTANDING

Safety, Privacy, Copyright, and Legal

NETS.T 3
Model Digital-Age Work and Learning

NETS.T 5
Engage in Professional Growth and Leadership

NETS.T 1
Facilitate and Inspire Student Learning and Creativity

NETS.T 4
Promote and Model Digital Citizenship and Responsibility

DIGITAL CITIZENSHIP AREA OF UNDERSTANDING

Etiquette and Respect
Literacy and Fluency

ISTE Newbie Project
http://bethstill.edublogs.org
/newbie-project

FIGURE 11.1 DigiDollar

Source: Designed by Sarah Adams, Imagine That Solutions, Inc., Camilla, Georgia, United States.

of DigiDollars. One for presenters to give to students and educators. Another color for educators to give students and presenters for good behavior, and a final color for students to give to educators and presenters for good behavior.

We would bring everyone back to attention by giving out DigiDollars and recognizing those who did behaviors that we wanted to encourage others to do. Additionally, people would recognize presenters and one another for good behaviors. At the end of the conference, these DigiDollars were put in a box for drawings for prizes. (Note that any person writing his or her name on the color for their own category could not win a prize—this kept people from giving these to their friends or using their own dollars for themselves.)

Prepare for Apparent Chaos (It Isn't Really!). When introducing activities, participants are often very chatty. This is where getting attention via reward helps considerably and people will listen when you transition. When first introducing an activity and beginning the project you notice participants with varying attention spans, groups that are dominated by one or two people, or group concerns. This is where good facilitators are vital.

Every facilitator should be on hand at the project introduction phase (preferably one per for every two tables.) At this phase, you will get complaints, questions, and well-meaning people who inform you "this just isn't working; we need to do something else." All facilitators should be helping the newly formed teams work through their issues. If the project is well designed, stay the course; this is a natural part of the project introduction process. Afterwards, participants will realize that you have modeled for them what they will be doing in their own project based learning activities.

Prepare the Facilitators. Effective facilitators observe first. They should interject when they see some sort of group dysfunction (dominators, non-participants, upset participants, groups that are "stuck" or those that are off task). Facilitators should contribute (if needed) and move on. The best facilitators are no longer needed after the project has begun. As the conference progresses, they should be willing to back off from the groups to let them have their own ideas and autonomy. Often, by the end of Flat Classroom workshops, effective groups do not want intervention of any kind. "We've got it," they'll say; and they do!

Plan for Virtual Participation. Virtual participants should be able to sign up before the conference. Have people at the conference assigned to stream video, facilitate backchannel discussions, and speak up to advocate for a good experience in the backchannel. (This applies to the backchannel: For example, if someone says they are not hearing very well, you could speak up and politely tell the presenter.)

If virtual participants are going to participate on teams, plan ahead for their participation using tools like Skype and web conferencing. Include those who want to be included. In-person participants are energized by working with those in other places. It also teaches them to be considerate of those who cannot be there in person and teaches another valuable skill.

Plan for the Special Needs of Social Media. Working with bloggers is a bit of a paradox. On the one hand, they want to be a regular "rank and file" attendee. On the other hand, if you want them to "cover" the conference, they need access to the Internet and a quiet place to record if they are a podcaster or videographer.

There is another paradox: at technology conferences almost everyone is a social media broadcaster of some kind. If you required a certain number of Twitter followers or hits, you're missing the point that today's "nobody" is tomorrow's "somebody." The best advice is to get someone who understands the social media audience you have and to give people an easy way to contact you with special requests. Special interest "lounges" with special requirements also work well. For example, ISTE has a lounge for those who do virtual worlds with equipped workstations wired with high-speed access. Microsoft provides a quiet place to for bloggers to work at their Innovative Educator Forums and treats them as mainstream media. Done well, this is beneficial to a conference in the long run.

PROVIDE MECHANISMS FOR REFLECTION

The Flat Classroom conference uses an educational network (Ning) for reflection, videos, and photos from students. We schedule time in the conference for people to reflect in these spaces and also recognize those who reflect and share well. Often, late into the night, participants would stay up in these places sharing what they learned. We've had great reflections from parents, administrators, and others who aren't at the conference but are watching the events. This builds excitement.

Additionally, debriefing through surveys and facilitated feedback sessions are vital to learning how to improve the project in the future and also reinforce the learning that has happened. Recording these and reviewing them later (when organizers aren't so tired) are very useful tools for capturing improvements that need to happen and also for providing documentation to sponsors and supporters of the benefits of the challenge based learning experience.

Encourage Role Reversal. We've had students and educators join into one group with students as the leaders. Teams of two educators and one student were grouped to research a Web 2 tool and post their findings to a wiki. The teams wrote and designed a three-minute "elevator speech" (that you could give on a ride up in an elevator) that one person would deliver to every group in the room. Students were appointed lead facilitators of their groups to make sure everyone was on task.

NETS.T 2
Design and Develop Digital-Age Learning Experiences and Assessments

C21 LEARNING ENVIRONMENTS

http://www.microsoft.com/education/pil

SOCIAL NETWORK
http://flatclassroomconference.ning.com

C21 LIFE AND CAREER SKILLS:
Leadership and Responsibility

DIGITAL CITIZENSHIP AREA
OF UNDERSTANDING

Safety, Privacy, Copyright, and Legal
Etiquette and Respect

ISTE STANDARDS

NETS.T 4
Promote and Model Digital
Citizenship and Responsibility

ISTE STANDARDS

NETS.S 4
Critical Thinking, Problem Solving,
and Decision Making

21st CENTURY SKILLS

C21 LEARNING AND
INNOVATION SKILLS:
Critical Thinking and Problem
Solving

Educators said they enjoyed watching the students lead and became convinced that they often stifled student leadership by doing work "for" their students. This role reversal resulted in learning about technology and also student behavior in an up-close and personal way.

Specify Privacy and Sharing Policies.   If you have minor students present, consider their wishes (and their parents) in terms of photography and include policies for identifying people in photographs. Think through and model best practices when sharing. Also ask participants to select a copyright for their work and encourage the respect of copyright in all of your spaces. Make sure participants ask for appropriate permissions from others for quoting and using their work. Sharing is great but respect must underlie everything.

Be Creatively Inclusive.   Allow participants to use Google Translate or to translate for one another if they are having trouble communicating. At the Flat Classroom Conference 2009 in Qatar, one student was non-fluent in English. The group used Google Translate to overcome language barriers and allowed him to present in Arabic and have a student translate for him.

Project-based PD allows participants to use tools freely and to innovate to overcome barriers. Problem solving is part of global collaboration. Engaging others from the face-to-face relationships of participants can be very powerful, as seen in the Flat Classroom diary reflection from Anne Mirtschin shown at the end of this chapter. Everyone involved in a conference activity deserves respect, and it builds morale.

TIME TACTICS TO STAY ON TRACK

Start and End on Time.   Agendas should be posted on a wiki or website and edited as the conference moves along; however, organizers should resist the temptation to just let people work indefinitely.

Adjust the schedule but stick to the general outline of the plan or you will not finish. Additionally, participants need to know they can trust your schedule. When they cannot, they may start skipping or get overtired. Take care of your participants by giving them the time frame they signed up for. Let them end your conference inspired, healthy, and ready to go back to work.

DIGITAL CITIZENSHIP AREA
OF UNDERSTANDING

Etiquette and Respect

Be Flexible but Clear on Breaks.   With project-based learning experiences, participants can often come and go as needed for breaks, however, facilitators should point out the times for breaks to encourage participants to eat and take care of their personal needs. This helps prevent fatigue and keeps participants working well throughout the day. Don't assume they know it is time—project based learning can be very immersive and cause participants to enter a flow state. Some will refuse to take breaks, but most will stop to eat as the mental activity can often make people unusually hungry.

There Is Never Enough Time.   Parkinson's Law is that "Work expands so as to fill the time available for its completion."[11] There is never enough time! This is challenging because many participants will beg for more time. Give yourself some flexibility and be willing to shorten the presentations of presenters if required. It is a skill to learn when to give more time and when to hold firm on a deadline.

If one sees that teams will not be done, adjust requirements or help teams refocus on what is important. Often teams that are having trouble getting completion are trying to do too much. This is where facilitators are useful.

GOOD PD LEAVES A LEARNING LEGACY

Provide Mechanisms for Post-Project Connection. If you want participants to connect afterwards, Facebook fan pages and Twitter hashtags are a great way to help people find one another and track future projects. Also, encourage post-conference interactions via the educational networking environment used during the event. Good events have participants leave inspired; great events happen when participants have perspired. When the participants work, connect, and leave as changed practitioners in their field a good event has served its purpose.

Share and Archive Everything. Archive videos from the conference, the wikis, and everything else that is created. This allows for the conference to serve as a legacy to be interacted with and used by people in the future in ways we cannot as yet imagine. If you have a backchannel chat, it should be archived for others. Capture the links and learning that happened and preserve them. Make your event into an archive that can be experienced again as a learning experience or historical archive.

CASE STUDIES FOR EMBEDDING PROFESSIONAL DEVELOPMENT

CASE STUDY: THE FLAT CLASSROOM CONFERENCE

Epitomizing challenge-based PD, the Flat Classroom Conference includes students, educators, and education leaders across the world. The aim of the conference is to bring together geographically dispersed participants to share ideas while learning about and using Web 2.0 communication and collaboration tools in a flattened world. In addition, participants work on a project theme that can be taken back into their home school.

Each year's theme will inspire action and foster continued connections after the actual event. This improves global understanding and cement friendships for ongoing collaborations. It is also predicted that this will provide an opportunity for students and teachers together to 'create the future' through exploration of a global or social issue and developing an action plan to work globally to overcome this.

Structure. Two strands of the conference, Leadership Workshop and Student Summit, work separately but then come together for plenary and pitch sessions. The Leadership Workshop allows educators to explore methods and strategies that provide a fuller understanding of what it means to flatten the classroom while learning to lead an international global project. Instructional design for authentic collaboration and assessment, use of emerging technologies, and interaction with the Student Summit are key characteristics. The Student Summit provides an opportunity for skill

ISTE STANDARDS

NETS.S 2
Communication and Collaboration

ISTE STANDARDS

NETS.T 5
Engage in Professional Growth and Leadership

NETS.S 2
Communication and Collaboration

C21 INTERDISCIPLINARY THEME:
Global Awareness, Civic Literacy,
Health Literacy, Environmental
Literacy

development with Web 2.0 tools, 21st century research skills, educational networking and PLN development, advanced multimedia fluency, and above all leadership within a thematic action-based project that has measurable outcomes and actions for change within a flat world scenario.

The structure is designed so that each strand can work independently but then merge and come together for key activities, thereby learning from and with each other rather than in isolation.

In 2009 at the first conference in Qatar, students were asked to envision and create a project to improve a global social issue with global collaboration. Educators learned about twenty first century skills and teaching strategies as well as how to design global collaborations. The 2011 conference in China[12] saw a refinement of these essential activities with more emphasis on educators "doing." Educators and students served as audience, teacher, and coach to each other in a powerful learning experience managed by facilitators rather than traditional "presenters."

STUDENT SUMMIT 2011 THEME: "OUR GLOBAL FUTURE LIVING TOGETHER"

The Student Summit Action Project[13] involved working on a theme of environmental impact, based on influences such as Friedman's "Hot, Flat and Crowded." This included the challenges of big city living, urbanization, environmental changes, green and clean energy systems. The action phases that follow the design cycle of Investigate and Research, Design and Plan, and Create and Evaluate are shown in Figure 11.2. Initially students work through a cultural awareness session based on Hofstede's culture model. They then move into teams of four to five and brainstorm based on the theme and prepare project ideas to "pitch" to the Leadership strand. After the first pitch feedback, further refinement of team ideas leads to a presentation dealing with the pre-visualization of the production plan. This is known as Animatic, which is watched by educators and others around the world and voted on to determine the projects most likely to succeed. Student summit actions are detailed in Figure 11.3 (page 282), where Oral moves to Action and then to Video.

The final phase (Phase 4) has three strands: A, B, and C. Strand A, Movie-Making Production, is based on "Our Global Future Living Together" (for the top voted teams). Strand B is Closing Ceremony Planning and Directing. Strand C is Web 2.0 Elevator Speech collaborative work with Leadership Workshop.

LEADERSHIP WORKSHOP 2011: DESIGNING CURRICULUM TO EMBED GLOBAL COLLABORATION

The Leadership Workshop[14] (Figure 11.4 on page 283) not only analyzed the principles of effective global collaboration but also coached participants through the process of collaboratively designing a ready-to-go functioning project. This process included Web 2.0 Bootcamp opportunities and then focused on working in mixed school teams on Flat Classroom Project design pedagogy. This was also aligned with the better-known ADDIE model for curriculum design. (See the Case Study by Dr. Leigh Zeitz at the end of this chapter.)

FIGURE 11.2 Student Summit Work Flow from Flat Classroom Conference

WEBSITES

See the wiki that accompanied this flow. http://vflatclassroom .flatclassroomproject.org

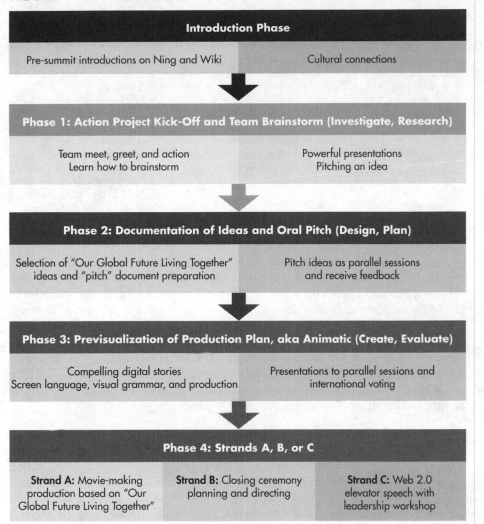

Introduction Phase

| Pre-summit introductions on Ning and Wiki | Cultural connections |

Phase 1: Action Project Kick-Off and Team Brainstorm (Investigate, Research)

| Team meet, greet, and action Learn how to brainstorm | Powerful presentations Pitching an idea |

Phase 2: Documentation of Ideas and Oral Pitch (Design, Plan)

| Selection of "Our Global Future Living Together" ideas and "pitch" document preparation | Pitch ideas as parallel sessions and receive feedback |

Phase 3: Previsualization of Production Plan, aka Animatic (Create, Evaluate)

| Compelling digital stories Screen language, visual grammar, and production | Presentations to parallel sessions and international voting |

Phase 4: Strands A, B, or C

| **Strand A:** Movie-making production based on "Our Global Future Living Together" | **Strand B:** Closing ceremony planning and directing | **Strand C:** Web 2.0 elevator speech with leadership workshop |

Merging Strands for Symbiotic Learning Experiences. Educators and students came together for the "project pitch" phase where students pitched ideas for global collaborative projects via rotation to tables of teachers. Teachers provided rubric-based feedback evaluating the student's pitches. Between tables, students were given three minutes to adjust and reorganize in response to the feedback of the teachers using a pitch rubric. After the pitch, students moved back to their strand for debriefing. Educators moved into a private room for a facilitated discussion about what they had learned from the projects proposed, the "round robin" method of feedback, and what they learned about students in a challenge-based environment. They also discussed the accuracy of the rubrics used.

ISTE STANDARDS

NETS.T 2
Design and Develop Digital-Age Learning Experiences and Assessments

FIGURE 11.3   Student Summit Actions

Oral All Teams	Animatic All Teams	Video 6 Teams
• 2 min. pitch • Repeats 10 times • Few or simple visuals only • Small group rotation • Feedback from Leadership Strand	• 4 min. pitch • Single presentation • Includes images, audio, and oral • Every team member must speak • Leadership Strand and Virtual Vote: "Project Most Likely to Succeed" (6 teams)	• 5 min. presentation, includes 3 min. video + 2 min. oral • Single presentation to full FCC attendees • Video uploaded to VT and embedded on wiki • Every team member should speak • International Vote: "Project Most Likely to Succeed" (1 team)

The following day student teams used the same rubric to provide feedback to the educators when they "pitched" their ideas for new global curriculum. The students used the same rubrics as talking points for providing feedback for the educators. What resulted was a powerful, authentic discussion where educators saw the value of project-based learning because they had seen the engagement in the eyes of students. Educators also "felt" the pressure and impact of the rubric design and could decide how they would do it in their classroom. Best of all, these projects were designed for students and teachers were able to get feedback from real students about the appeal and interest to them. So many times we've been at a conference and wish students could have a say. At great educational conferences you don't talk about students; you talk *with* them about the learning process.

tweetable

A conference with students and teachers needs plenary sessions where all ages can continue to learn together and build community. #flatclass

F.L.A.T.s.   It is important to build community during a conference, and an event that has both students and teachers needs plenary sessions where all ages can continue to learn together. Our **Flat Learning Action Talks (F.L.A.T.s)**[15] are such sessions where student teams and educators have 10 to 12 minutes to present an idea that will inspire and encourage action. Usually live, but it can be virtual (as in the students from Australia who Skyped into the Qatar event), the aim is to share a microcosm of learning across cultures and ages.

Involving Virtual Participants.   Another vital feature of the Flat Classroom conference and Flat Classroom workshops is how we involve the global community virtually. This is approached in two main ways: Level 1 is participation via application to be a full virtual team member (student or leader); Level 2 is participation via Flat Classroom online spaces, including streamed video, a backchannel, and access to media before, during, and after the event. In 2011, the conference was supported by Taking IT Global who set up a virtual Flat Classroom portal[16] for collecting and sharing media. Full details about virtual participation, as related on the wiki,[17] show the procedure for setting up a learning community to facilitate involvement in an event, using both synchronous (a preconference real-time meeting) and asynchronous methods (use of an online form to collect responses in a Cultural Scavenger Hunt, and a wiki to scaffold most team collaborations).

FIGURE 11.4 Comparison between the Leadership Workshop and Student Summit at the Flat Classroom Conference 2011

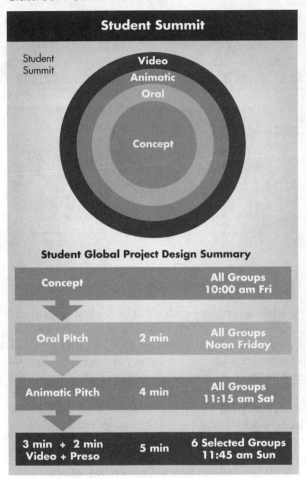

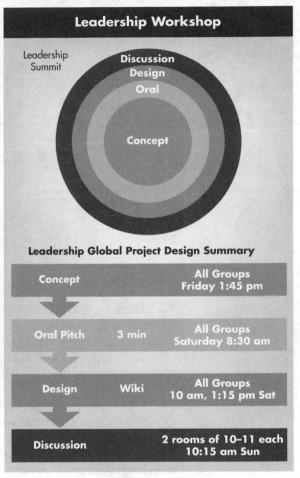

The key to successful virtual participation is to (1) have the Internet connection working consistently to avoid frustration to those wanting to connect in real time, (2) have people streaming video for synchronous viewers and supporting this with a backchannel for immediate feedback, and (3) provide an asynchronous collaborative environment with clear details about team composition. A student tech team based at the host school is crucial to this success as the team takes the main load for streaming the conference and monitoring the virtual spaces.

During the 2011 conference, as well as previous Flat Classroom workshops, virtual participants have very successfully worked with their "real-time" team members. For example, at the Flat Classroom workshop in India in 2010,[18] students attending in person used Skype to communicate with students from Germany and Japan and included them as full participants for project work. Although the virtual piece is another layer of organization and therefore time-consuming to set up, and has less

The top teacher project in Beijing 2011, "Tackling Transport Together" http://tinyurl.com/tackling-transport

Team Name: T-Cubed
Members: David (India), Stan (China), Iim (Indonesia), Salim (Oman)
Brainstorming Process: Click Here
Etherpad: _Click Here_

\
=

Project Name: Tackling Transport Together

Summary:
Students will be exploring the problems and solutions associated with transport. Students will first collect data about their particular transport issues and will virtually present that data to the other schools involved in the project. Each school with will then be assigned anotherschool's transport problems to offer solutions that help to solve the problem which results in an increase in environmentally friendly and efficient manner. The school will pitch their ideas to the original school and then collaborate to provide solutions to both schools.

Goals/Aims
1. Understand how transportation affects our daily life (own school).
2. Understand the effects of transportation on the environment (own school).
3. Identify factors affecting transportation time, cost and environmental impact
4. Identify possible solutions for the target school situation
5. Learn How transportation varies among different countries.
6. Identify possible solutions for another school situation
7. Use of appropriate technology and presentation techniques.

Topics for Investigation
1. Transportation issues in each school and city
2. Analysis of data/Data presentation techniques
3. Solutions to traffic problems

Photo by Stanley Covington

obvious or tangible results, it is a vital part of Flat Classroom philosophy and practice. It is also an inclusive PD model for community learning.

Outcomes. A Flat Classroom conference is a systematic model for challenge-based learning across cultures, genders, and ages. It relies on mixed teams (real and virtual) working together toward a common goal. It is process-based, challenge-based, action-based, and demanding, almost intimidating for some who like to escape for quiet reflection. With this conference there is no escape. If you do escape, your team is let down.

The true power of the challenge-based conference format, according to co-facilitator Kim Cofino, is in the networking and the collaboration and opportunity to be immersed in a technology-rich environment.[19] Outcomes therefore include a greater understanding of how learning takes place and how powerful independent action-based development can be. It also allows educators *and* students to realize they can equally change the current classroom paradigm, especially if working together.

Specific outcomes from the Flat Classroom conference include:

- *For the Students:* An opportunity to work in mixed teams to envision, pitch, refine, and present an action project for a global project that could be implemented in a classroom. Also, the final closing ceremony is entirely student-run and student-led and involves anything from musical and dramatic acts to final student videos based on the students' project ideas.
- *For Educators:* An opportunity to work in mixed teams to design new curriculum based on Flat Classroom methods and to gain feedback from students as well as conference facilitators. Also a chance to create strong networked ties with others to help make the envisioned project come alive in the near future.

Who Can Use This Model? This flattened model of challenge-based conferencing brings students into the conference along with educators. This model is being done in education, but it could be done in any format where the "receivers" and "deliverers" of a service learn, create, and share. The program shown in Table 11.1 is the Flat Classroom Conference 2011 Program and shows the Leadership Workshop and Student Summit successfully running apart and together at various times.

CASE STUDY: THE 23 THINGS[20]

Invented by librarian Helene Blowers, Public Services Technology Director for the Public Library of Charlotte & Mecklenburg County in North Carolina, USA. To date, over 250 organizations have conducted this program for their staff emulating the project that was licensed under Creative Commons. In this project, participants explore 23 things and reflect on them on their own blogs. Taking from 6 to sometimes 12 weeks, people going through this program embed their learning by exploring one Web 2.0 technology deeply and reflecting. This process seems to produce highly engaged, knowledgeable educators and participants who complete the project and report that it is more beneficial than the classes they have taken.

http://tinyurl.com/23things -original

CASE STUDY: MI CHAMPIONS PROGRAM

The premise of the MI Champions program (a PD program for Michigan teachers) is that teachers of core subjects who are novices at technology education apply to the program and are paired with a "coach." They have extra training in the summer and then are coached and encouraged and mentored. The program "kicks off" at MACUL, the Michigan statewide technology conference and takes one year. Participants (approximately 300 per "class") graduate during the next year's conference. This phenomenal program is an excellent example of embedding professional development and also providing highly engaging use of their technology conference by incorporating a "project" (the MI Champions program.)

MI Champions Program http:// tinyurl.com/mi-champion

CASE STUDY: UNIVERSITY OF NORTHERN IOWA

Leigh Zeitz took his students to St. Petersburg, Russia, to teach Instructional Design. These preservice teachers created their course, and, according to Dr. Zeitz, after the first day of teaching, stayed up late into the night redesigning the course the next day. This project-based learning also incorporated global awareness aspects, as the students had to learn course material (instructional design) well enough in order to teach it in a project-based format.

CASE STUDY: NORTH CAROLINA TWENTY-FIRST CENTURY CLASSROOMS

This project is an excellent example of project-based learning. Teachers apply for this grant to improve their classrooms with technology such as an interactive whiteboard and laptops. If they receive the grant, teachers are required to teach and mentor others about how they use the technology. Because the teachers are actively involved in requesting and designing how technology will be used, the project forces teachers to survey leading technologies. Additionally, teaching others has teachers collecting artifacts and self-assessing for improvement. This powerful project-based, grant-centered

TABLE 11.1 Flat Classroom Conference 2011 Program

Day and Time	Leadership Workshop	Student Summit
Thursday Feb 24 5pm-8:30pm		Opening of Student Summit
		Welcome dinner for students and accompanying teachers
		2-hour workshop
Friday Feb 25 8:30-12:00	Opening Ceremony Speed sharing session Bootcamps	Opening Ceremony Working on Oral Pitch
12:00-13:00	Oral Pitch session with students	Oral pitch session with Leaders
13:00-14:00	Lunch	Lunch
14:00-16:30	Leadership Cohorts	Pre-visualization of Production Plan
16:30-17:30	Flat Learning Action Talks	Flat Learning Action Talks
17:30-21:30	Conference Dinner	Conference Dinner
Saturday Feb 26 8:30-9:15	Leadership Oral Pitch session with students	Leadership Oral Pitch session with students
9:15-11:15	Leadership cohort sessions	Pre-visualization of Production Plan
11:15-12:15	Pre-visualization of Production Plan Presentations by students	Pre-visualization of Production Plan Presentations
12:15-13:00	Lunch	Lunch
13:00-16:00	Leadership cohort sessions	Team Projects: Strands A, B & C
16:00-17:00	Flat Learning Action Talks	Flat Learning Action Talks
Sunday Feb 27 8:30-11:15	Leadership Workshop sessions, some with students	Team Projects: Strands A, B & C
11:15-11:45	Refreshments and moving to Closing Ceremony	Refreshments and preparing for Closing Ceremony
11:45-12:45	Closing Ceremony	Closing Ceremony
12:45-13:00	Final Goodbyes	Final Goodbyes

approach is an excellent example of a grant that perhaps should also be a professional development unit of credit because of the study, work, and oversight required.

http://fcpteacher.flatclassroom project.org

CASE STUDY: FLAT CLASSROOM CERTIFIED TEACHER

The Flat Classroom Certified Teacher[21] course is totally online and brings educators from various parts of the world together for the common goal of learning more about how to become a Flat Classroom teacher. Over a 10- to 12-week period, participants meet online to cover 9 modules and work through the Flat Classroom Fifteen challenges. In addition, participants research global project design and management and pitch ideas for their own project. What is emerging now are competent and experienced global educators who know how to design and implement sustainable collaborative projects into their classroom.

SUMMARY

Challenge-based learning is becoming widely used as a delivery method in classrooms, but face-to-face professional development experiences are largely lecture-based. Imagine the hypocrisy of a 20-hour project-based learning seminar during which the presenter lectures for 20 hours! If a pedagogy works, use it!

This requires reframing the paradigm of teaching and conferencing to understand that conferences and professional development will look different during the process. It often appears chaotic, but powerful learning can also take place in this environment.

Nowadays, students are often included in conferences as a "novelty" of sorts. They are in the hallways and present-ing at poster sessions. There is great value in running student challenge-based learning experiences where educators can interact with and learn through experience about the teaching strategies they should be using in their classrooms and schools. Let teachers see students excited about learning. Let them witness it and want it to happen in their classrooms. This method alleviates fear.

In this chapter we share a different model of conferencing, but one that should be explored and used for those conferences that target rich, immersive experiences. It is time to stop talking about students and instead learn from them by talking *with* them.

ESSENTIAL QUESTIONS

- What are the evolving modalities of professional development?
- What are the main obstacles to embedded professional development? How can these be overcome?
- What are the advantages of combining students and educators in the same learning event?
- How has this chapter influenced the way you think about professional development in your learning community?

Join the online conversation and share your answers at http://tinyurl.com/flatclass-ch11 ▶

THE FLAT CLASSROOM® 15 CHALLENGES

CHALLENGE 14: CHALLENGE-BASED PROFESSIONAL DEVELOPMENT

DO: With a group of people in your learning community, consider how project-based professional development with educators and students can be used to teach both educators and students with mutually beneficial outcomes. Draw up at least a one-day schedule of what this would look like at your school or conference venue of your choice.

SHARE: Share the ideas of your group by hyperlinking to your draft and solicit feedback. The tag for this challenge is fcc14_pd. Use this when you blog, or to share with your group

◀ Share what you did with your challenge at http://tinyurl.com/flat15-14

BONUS CHALLENGE 14: CHALLENGE-BASED PD IN ACTION

DO: Plan and carry out your project-based professional development idea while encouraging feedback from participants.

SHARE: Share your plan, your learning and the outcomes on your blog and in our online idea bank. The tag for this challenge is fcc14b_action. Use this when you blog, or to share with your group.

◀ Share what you did with your challenge at http://tinyurl.com/flat15-14action.

THE FLAT CLASSROOM™ DIARIES

Diary Entry 21

FLAT CLASSROOM CONFERENCE TEACHER REFLECTIONS

From HEATHER DAVIS
Yew Chung IS, Beijing China
"Reflections on the Flat Classroom Experience" after Qatar 2009:

I, like many other westerners, was very nervous about going to the Middle East. As part of the generation that watched the American Hostage Crisis for 444 days during the Carter Administration, plus the growing wars and terrorism, I have been indoctrinated with a fear of men and women who wear robes and head coverings. Even in Canada, my heart would beat faster and I would be uncomfortable whenever I would see someone of Middle Eastern descent on the street.

How four days can change a person's viewpoint and comfort zone! I leave with an understanding that no stereotypes actually exist but are created by the media and by fear. I leave with an understanding that people all over the world are the same though the clothes and cultures may be different.

A love of family, country, and friends exists in all nations. A desire for a better world, a desire to solve our global problems together, a desire for information and education, and a desire to share openly and willingly exist. I leave with an appreciation of the elegance of the traditional dress. I leave with memories of laughter as we all shared common experiences.

I leave with the memories of the beautiful friendly eyes of the Qatari woman who were veiled, of their help and their willingness to help . . . .[22]

Read the rest of this Flat Classroom Diary online. http://tinyurl.com/qatar-memories.

From ANNE MIRTSCHIN
Hawkesdale P12 College, Australia
"All Eyes upon the Flat Classroom Conference" after Qatar 2009:

One of the really interesting outcomes of this experience was the involvement of parents. This was something unplanned and unforeseen, but ended up playing a key role in our connectedness. As we were on school holidays, the majority of planning and communication had to be made online. The girls had set up membership to the flat conference Ning and wiki prior to departure. Before they left, the girls became "the experts," helping their parents to register for the Ning, to join our school group and how to write messages, comments, and blog posts. This meant that parents experienced the conference with us. Photos and videos were uploaded daily, with blog posts written when possible. Parents commented regularly on all our pages and activities. They were able to watch the sessions that were webcast, and one parent stayed up until 1:00 a.m. to watch her daughter make her presentation. They even joined in on the Chatzy (http://www.chatzy.com) backchannel and could see the commentary going on behind the scenes. We received photos of the Australia Day breakfast, held in Hawkesdale as part of the Australia Day celebrations, an hour after it finished, as one set of parents had uploaded them to the Ning. They became part of our learning network.[23]

Read the rest of this Flat Classroom Diary online. http://tinyurl.com/qatar-memories2

DAVID W. DEEDS, IT manager and teacher
at Changchun American International School
Flat Classroom Conference: "Working Hard, Having Fun," after Beijing 2011:

Despite "warnings," I guess I went [to the Flat Classroom conference in Beijing] expecting the usual laidback academic event, but I was in for a substantial . . . and refreshing . . . surprise. I found myself almost having to jog from one activity location to the next . . . only on the job is my schedule busier! At one point during the symposium, I passed a newly met colleague in the hallway and asked him if he was working hard. He replied: "Working hard, having fun!" This phrase would make a fitting tagline for the conference.

Approximately 250 teachers and students from 45 schools in 14 different countries participated in the Flat Classroom Conference (FCC), which was completely unlike any other education symposium I've ever attended before.

DAVID W DEEDS
@dwdeeds
http://www.indeeds.com

Read the rest of this Flat Classroom Diary online. http://tinyurl.com/beijing-memories

What makes the FCC different . . . perhaps, I dare say, unique? As I've already mentioned, you don't get to simply warm a chair . . . everyone participates in the process. And I do mean EVERYONE . . . there's no place to hide . . . believe me, I tried . . . they kept finding me. At some point, each teacher and student found him/herself talking in front of an audience . . . it was as if Toastmasters did hazing. "Get ready to speak . . . wait for it . . . SPEAK!"[24]

Diary Entry 22

FLAT CLASSROOM CONFERENCE STUDENT REFLECTIONS

STEVE R.
"My Experience and Reflection" after coming to Qatar 2009:

First of all, I have made friends from all over this beautiful world that we live on. From Australia to Oman to Ethiopia to this beautiful country of Qatar. And one thing I have to say is that no one and I mean no one should ever judge someone on their stereotypes. Why is it that I get along with the people from this conference? Why is it that I can make people laugh over here? It is because we are all humans. Yes I know that there are cultural differences but that doesn't mean that we are completely different. We share so many characteristics. I am extremely happy that I have made friends from all around the world and I hope to see them again sometime in the future.

Second of all, I have learned many qualities that I can use in the future since I plan on going into the business world.

I have learned how to present something more effectively. I have learned many different aspects of having a successful campaign and that is something I can hold to value for the rest of my life.[25]

Read the rest of this Flat Classroom Diary online. http://tinyurl.com/steve-qatar ▶

TAMMAM G.
"My Experiences, Tell Me Yours" after the Qatar Conference 2009:

Right, I'm so hyper right now, my brain is rushing with all the new experiences that occurred today, which is why I might be erratic in telling you all about [them]. . . . All right, I met Edgar today, and right off from the beginning, we kept talking and talking and talking, and we were still talking right about when Mrs. Vicki told us to move on to our third person!!! And we were cut off!!!

We turned to Xayneb and Emiley, and THEY were still talking. I mean, I never travel a lot, I don't exactly have the luxury of visiting the world every summer or something, but I've

seen my share, but to actually meet and INTERACT deeply with somebody from . . . Pakistan and Australia, is absolutely amazing, and cool . . . having a bunch of well taught and intelligent people come together, to bash stereotypes, and to sit around

Read the rest of this Flat Classroom Diary online. http://tinyurl.com/tammam-qatar

and come up with ideation ideas, relating I.T. and the Flat Classroom to environment, economy, etc. . . .[26]

CASE EXAMPLES OF GLOBAL COLLABORATION

PDToolkit
for
Flattening Classrooms, Engaging Minds
Read full Case Studies in PDToolkit online.

Case Study 22

"Create the Future,"[27] Project-Based Workshop
KIM COFINO and JULIE LINDSAY

The "Create the Future" Workshop has evolved through the collaborative work of Julie Lindsay and Kim Cofino. Both of these educators realized the need for a more effective hands-on approach to professional development that immersed participants into a challenging scenario and instigated activities and expectations that encouraged collaboration and teamwork within a project-based learning environment.

Over three years this workshop was developed through experience in running school-based professional development sessions, while introducing new technologies and new ways of thinking about learning using technology. From the wiki, the theme of the workshop states:

Participants will work in teams on ideas and objectives including Web 2.0 skill building, global collaboration and project management, designed to flatten the learning experience. Breakout sessions will include building a personal learning network and digital portfolio development, digital citizenship best practice, and enhancing your web 2.0 toolbox. This workshop is designed to open doors to new modes of teaching and learning and focus on the learner (teacher and student) as a communicator, collaborator, and creator.[28]

As a result of the Create the Future workshop, participants:

- Understand the power of Web 2.0 tools and learn how to choose the right tool for the task.
- Appreciate the potential of globally collaborative projects for students and teachers—increasing internationalism, intercultural understanding, and global awareness.
- Build a network of interested and enthusiastic colleagues, both face-to-face as well as virtual participants.
- Experience a hands-on workshop model where student-centered, project-based learning is fully integrated with a technology-rich environment. The strategies, structures, and techniques in this model are easily applied to the classroom setting.

In addition to the current, relevant, and forward-thinking content of the workshop, the format is truly innovative; with teachers collaborating to design a globally collaborative unit intended to be implemented in the classroom immediately. The collaborations that begin between teachers at Create the Future result in exciting and engaging global projects that connect students around the world using the most relevant and effective technology tools.

The Create the Future workshop format helps give teachers a framework for implementing technology-rich global collaborations in the classroom, as well as bridging the gap between teacher skills, knowledge and understanding of new tools, and best-practice pedagogy. The learning from the workshop does not finish at the end of the face-to-face sessions, as projects designed at Create the Future are shared on the collaborative wiki with space for discussion, feedback, and reflection. Teachers are encouraged to continue connections beyond the scope of the initial workshop and to continue connecting their students.

Combining effective use of technology tools, project-based learning, backward design, hands-on experiences, and tangible outcomes makes the Create the Future workshop format highly relevant and readily applicable to the classroom practitioner.

Read about this workshop at http://createthefuture .wikispaces.com

---

Case Study 23

Leadership Strand Uses the Flat Classroom Development Process
DR. LEIGH ZEITZ, University of Northern Iowa, USA

PDToolkit
for
Flattening Classrooms,
Engaging Minds
Read full Case Studies
in PDToolkit online.

The Flat Classroom Conference Leadership Workshop enabled educators to actually experience developing a Flat Classroom Global Collaborative Project. The cohort broke into teams of similar teaching interests. Each team identified a theme for its project and then established goals. Having determined its direction, each team developed its project activity, or methods of interaction. These methods of interaction defined the character of the project. They might include interpersonal exchanges, information collection and analysis, or problem solving.[29]

Having originated their general idea, it was time for these teachers to sell it to their greatest critics—students. The day before, students had presented their ideas to the teachers. Now the tables were turned and the students were the evaluators. Some of the educators were intimidated. They created a 3-minute sales pitch and presented it to six groups of students to refine their ideas from a student's perspective.

Ideas in hand, it was time to actually create a project description using the Flat Classroom Project Design template (Chapter 10). This template provides an interested educator with the basic information needed for participating in a Flat Classroom project. It defines the goals and standards as well as the intended students' age and skills. The project's expected inputs and outcomes are described as well as how it will be assessed and evaluated. It is a final blueprint for the experience.

It takes an active process to create such a product. We organized our development method using the ADDIE (see Figure 11.5) instructional design model.[30] ADDIE adds the verbs to the process: Analyze Design, Develop, Implement, and Evaluate.

Using a predesigned template available through the Flat Classroom Conference wiki, all the groups organized their projects:

FIGURE 11.5 ADDIE Chart

Analysis	Aims of the project
	Topics for investigation
	Student levels and/or age
	Prerequisites and skill levels
	Link to curriculum
Design	Method of interaction
	Mode of working
	Challenges
Development	Identify the activities
	Identify the technologies
	Create a time line
	Define the final product
Implementation	Logistics
	Will students participate?
Evaluation	How will success be measured?

WEBSITES

Examples of teacher-generated global project designs can be found on the **Flat Classroom Conference wiki** at
http://conference2011.flatclassroomproject.org

Further examples include the award winning:

Tackling Transport Together:
http://tinyurl.com/tackling-transport

LIPS (Local Issues People Share):
http://conference2011.flatclassroomproject.org/LIPS

- The groups analyzed their students' curricular needs to create a project that could fulfill these requirements.
- The design process provided the project's character. The educators used the student feedback to refine the structure for the project. They identified potential challenges as well as possible remedies.
- Given direction, it was time to actually develop the project. The teachers identified the necessary activities along with the technologies needed. They created a time line with periodic benchmarks for ongoing assessment. The final product of this project was described.
- Implementing the project was not possible, but the groups identified the collaborative connections with

other classrooms that would have to be made and other necessary steps for the actual implementation.

- The success of the project (and the students) must be evaluated. The educators created rubrics for assessing the results. Plans for using these results to evaluate the project as well as provide feedback for the students were explained.

The educators were fun to watch as they created their projects. Just like their students, they began by muddling around in ideas and possibilities. Personal professional needs were balanced with the group's interest. Some groups collaborated from the beginning, whereas other groups had problems finding a project that satisfied all of their needs.

Ultimately, each group designed and developed a single project that was represented on the group's wiki page. These projects were evaluated by Dr. Zeitz and his team of University of Northern Iowa graduate students. A final three projects were selected and presented in a general assembly of the conference.

In the end, all of the educators were winners. They experienced a design and development process that they could use to create these projects at their own schools. They laid the foundation for their future experiences in global education.

Rock the World

"Nobody can go back and start a new beginning, but anyone can start today and make a new ending."

MARIE ROBINSON, Teacher,
From Birth to One[1]

Let's tell the story of a student whose life completely changed course through global collaboration and videography in 2011. Hear his full story in the words of his teacher at the end of this chapter in the case study.

Domingo is a very shy and quiet student in inner-city Texas and is considered at risk because he is a non-native speaker from a low-income family. His life changed when he won a major award for his online video for Flat Classroom™.

After the project, Domingo applied for a prestigious work/study program in the local area. The introverted student was simply brimming with a deep, newfound knowledge of how the world works. The interviewers said they were impressed with his "passion and knowledge of the importance of 'flattening' our world through communication" and he was accepted into the program.

Domingo walked across the stage and received his high school diploma in June 2011 just as this book was preparing to go to press. In the end, he had to complete some lacking coursework the night before graduation via computer so he could graduate. But his technological communication skills were sharp and such an obstacle would no longer limit him. Although he didn't have the Internet at home, the digital divide no longer lived in his mind because his school had bridged the gap. His school had made room in their curriculum knowing that sometimes world knowledge can be as important in a child's life as content knowledge that the child will forget when walking on a stage. The one, practical, business course that put aside the memorization and tests for 6 weeks to fully immerse him in learning changed his life.

CHAPTER 12 WEB RESOURCES
http://www.flatclassroombook.com/
rock-the-world.html

SHARE IT

Twitter hashtag for this book:
#flatclass

You see, now Domingo is the pride of his family. He started at Montana State University in September 2011 on a full scholarship. He is the first one in his family to go to college.

Breaking the cycle of poverty requires intervention. We cannot continue to pound the passion and connection out of learning and expect students like Domingo to want to advance their education. When we demolish the digital divide and genuinely teach students the concrete things that are prerequisites for success in today's interconnected world, we change the course of history one child and one family at a time.

Isn't it about time that we realize that in order to interrupt the downhill momentum of the life of most at-risk children that we must help them look up and see their world in a new light? We need to turn their eyes toward a teacher who will help them see the big pictures of life so that they can draw their own future on the halls of time. Domingo did not have the money to travel and yet he saw the world through the sights and sounds of a solid global collaborative experience while seated in a desk chair in inner-city Texas.

He saw the world, and perhaps, most important of all, the world saw him. Here's to you, Domingo, and the millions of students just like you waiting for a relevant education to open their eyes to the potential between their own ears.

OVERVIEW OF ROCK THE WORLD

It is time to rock the world with a massive improvement in our educational systems. We've been experiencing the birth pains for some time now. A new day of learning is being born. Some have already experienced this rebirth in their learning techniques.

This is more than just something nice to do; rather, it is an imperative. First we will examine the facts. Trends show that to be employable and successful you will have to achieve a postsecondary education. Competition to attract learners is increasing. The trends that shook the music industry in the 2000s are hitting education like a sledgehammer. Understand how to use the trends in this book to make your school competitive and to sell this new pedagogy to stakeholders who want proof. Second, learn what is next for you as a person. Change starts with you, and now that you've made it all the way through this book don't let it stop here. We'll give you a few quick, short steps to catapult your learning forward. You see, the next chapter of this book is *you*. You will write it. Open up the back cover and write your name at the top of the page. Write Chapter 1. Now, start your story. Who knows, you may quote the words you pen in the back cover of this book at the beginning of the book you write about your journey.

Finally, make sure you read our section entitled "If You Only Read One Thing, Read This!" You'll be glad you did.

SUCCESS IN THE TWENTY-FIRST CENTURY: THE PEOPLE AND SCHOOLS THAT WILL SURVIVE AND THRIVE

PEOPLE WHO DON'T GO TO COLLEGE HAVE A BLEAK FUTURE

By 2018, about two-thirds of all employment in the United States will require some college education or better (see Figure 12.1).[2] With the excessive drop-out rate in the

United States, this same report predicts that the U.S. "post-secondary education and training system will fall short by 3 million or more post-secondary degrees."[3]

How will this shortfall be met? With the global average of "expected years of schooling" at only 11 years in 2008, the world is falling short of the education level required to sustain growth.[4] As seen at the website in the margin, recent data from the Organisation for Economic Co-Operation and Development (OECD) shows that in countries such as Turkey, Portugal, and Mexico over half of their students drop out before graduating from high school. These countries are severely limiting their country's ability to attract these growth-sustaining jobs. Education is the raw material needed to produce prosperity and development in our world.

With students disengaging from learning,[5] how can we make students learn? The answer is that we cannot. We cannot make a child learn any more than we can make them eat broccoli if they don't want to!

If we can captivate their interest in some way during the school day, we give them a reason to come to school beyond the obligatory requirements of local law. An energetic, curious child is as unstoppable as a river downstream of a rapidly melting glacier. This entire book is about harnessing a child's innate curiosity. We believe that the principles shared here can unlock a generation of disenfranchised students who are in education systems that have obscured meaning behind the definitions they are memorizing. There is no time to debate the whys—let's learn how to engage and reach them!

http://tinyurl.com/oecd-grad-stat

DIGITAL CITIZENSHIP AREA OF UNDERSTANDING

Habits of Learning:

tweetable

Education is the raw material needed to produce prosperity and growth in our world. #flatclass

FIGURE 12.1 Education Level Requirements of Employment in the United States, 1973–2018

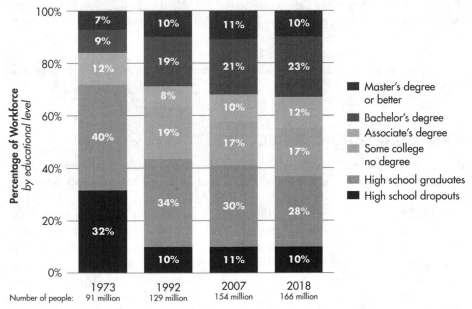

Source: Carnevale, A. P., Smith, N., & Strohl, J. (2010, June). *Help wanted: Projections of jobs and education requirements through 2018.* Retrieved from http://www9.georgetown.edu/grad/gppi/hpi/cew/pdfs/FullReport.pdf

CREATING A COMPETITIVE ADVANTAGE FOR YOUR SCHOOL

A rapid change is coming to education. The school you are competing against is no longer the one around the corner; today, it can be anywhere in the world. Students are staying home in droves to be "homeschooled," when in fact they are "cyber-schooled" by using the vast resources of teachers and websites to learn and become well educated.

Teachers are the competitive advantage of a successful school. They always have been and will continue to be. An excellent teacherpreneur has parents fighting to get in his or her classroom and administrators know it. If you have enough of these teacherpreneurs in one place, you have parents lining up to get in your school.

BUILDING YOUR LEARNING PATHWAY: WHAT'S NEXT?

Can a student be well educated if she or he never has contact with other students outside their classroom, school, or district? Can a teacher be well rounded if he or she never has contact with other teachers outside their classroom, school, or district?

21st CENTURY SKILLS

C21 INTERDISCIPLINARY THEME:
Global Awareness

Many of you will teach online and will have students from around the globe in your classroom. Others will bring the world into the classroom in rich, meaningful ways that enhance learning. All of you will want to work for competitive organizations—the other educational organizations that are not competitive will have layoffs at some point and you'll want to be the best in order to stay employed.

Either way, lifelong learning is essential for you to be your best. You will leave the pages of this book behind and move to your next learning endeavor. But if we can leave you with a learning pathway for global collaboration, you are set to collaborate for the rest of your teaching career.

Can one book change your life? Perhaps.

Can introducing you to a powerful network of information and friends change your life? Absolutely!

So, my teacher, my friend: meet your future by meeting each other.

MAKE CONNECTIONS THAT COUNT

ISTE STANDARDS

NETS.T 5
Engage in Professional Growth and Leadership

21st CENTURY SKILLS

**C21 PROFESSIONAL
DEVELOPMENT**

If you learned one thing, we hope it is that you need to connect. Build your learning network and connect to it as part of your weekly learning habits. Apply what you learn.

Don't feel any pressure to learn like anyone else. Some use Twitter and some hate it. Some use an RSS reader and others break out in a rash when they hear the term. The point is: Are *you* learning? Do you have ongoing connections with others to help you embed your professional development into your weekly routine? If students are the greatest textbook ever written for students, then teachers are the greatest book ever written for teachers! Write the book. Read the book. Be the book. Reading about best practices and sharing them are part of being a professional educator in the twenty-first century.

IMPROVE YOUR LIFE WITH CONVERSATION

Have you joined networks of learning? It is time to make "time for new ways of working with colleagues."[6] Join formal networks scattered through this book and the informal networks surrounding hashtags like #edchat or #flatclass on Twitter or on Facebook fan pages.

DIGITAL CITIZENSHIP AREA
OF UNDERSTANDING
Literacy and Fluency:

When networking, remember that it is a two-way street. Those who share receive so much in return. When you comment, communicate, question, and engage, you become involved. When you become involved, your ability to collaborate multiplies exponentially. When your "friends" on networks truly become friends in your life, you get much more out of face-to-face conferences and events. It is a new way of networking but can make your life and profession more engaging and inspired.

If sharing multiplies your life, then when you share nothing, you are multiplying by zero. Many who get nothing out of Twitter put nothing meaningful into Twitter. It isn't about who follows you; it is about who you help. Helpful people are credible people. Few people are that interesting but we are always interested in people who are interested in helping us be better people.

tweetable

If sharing multiplies your life, then when you share nothing, you are multiplying by zero. #flatclass

HABITS TO SUPER-CHARGE YOUR PROFESSIONAL CAREER THAT YOU MUST START NOW

Change Your Habits, Change Your Life.   Look in the mirror. You are a product of every decision you have made so far. This is where you are. You are here, right now. Where you are tomorrow will be a product of your decisions you make starting this moment. Where you are in a month is a product of your decisions you make between now and that time. You can change.

In this book we've talked about a lot of habits of being a successful global collaborator and certainly there are some that nudge at you that need to become part of your routine. Vicki has a problem keeping up with email—Julie doesn't! So, Vicki has on her "habit list" every day "in-box zero," which nudges her to go to her email and make sure she's read and answered everything!

DIGITAL CITIZENSHIP AREA
OF UNDERSTANDING
Habits of Learning

This is not about Hercules clearing out the Aegean stables. (They were a mess, so he diverted a river and cleaned it out in a day!) You cannot add global collaboration into your classroom overnight, however you can decide to build your learning pathway and to make it a habit to read your PLN for three 10-minute sessions a week!

Go back and reread the quote at the beginning of this chapter. This was on the board at the weight loss meeting where Vicki finally had met her goal of losing 30 pounds! She wept because she had made a new ending for herself instead of just accepting the status quo!

This applies to you! You cannot start a new beginning but you can start today and make a new ending! This applies to our world! We can begin today to make a new ending to the things that we see are wrong. So, you think that your students don't understand people from other countries? *Start changing their minds today!* You think that you have unsupportive parents? *Start working on way to build parent*

support today! You think you're not reaching the students for learning effectively? *Make changes today. TODAY. TODAY!*

Many times when a student is not going to do an assignment, she or he will look in your eyes and say, "OK, I'll try to get this done by tomorrow." This usually means: "No, I'm not going to do it." As Yoda says in *The Empire Strikes Back*, "Do, or do not—there is no try." Make up your mind.

Your future is usually not written in the bold one-time move, although that has certainly happened. Your future is written in the habits that you do every day through the consistent determination to move forward and improve something, whether it is your health, your wealth, or your classroom. If you can find someone who has done it successfully and emulate him or her consistently, you are going to be incredible.

DIGITAL CITIZENSHIP AREA OF UNDERSTANDING

Habits of Learning

Make Learning a Habit. Lifelong learners stay relevant and competitive. Now that you've constructed your learning pathway, which should include a personal learning network, take time to read it two or three times a week. Decide now: When am I going to look at my PLN?

Join a group of teachers in your field to serve as part of a formal learning community (some call these **Critical Friends Group**, or mentors). Although traditionally this is within a school, it could be online. Joining a group of teachers to share and learn from is an important practice for ongoing improvement in your practice. Decide now: What steps will I take to form or join a learning community? Who is someone I can ask to join me? How can we meet every month?

Volunteer to lead a book club and teach others what you've learned here. Extend your learning and experience by sharing and facilitating.

ISTE STANDARDS

NETS.T 3
Model Digital-Age Work and Learning

NETS.T 5
Engage in Professional Growth and Leadership

21st CENTURY SKILLS

C21 PROFESSIONAL DEVELOPMENT

Share Because You Care. Share with your colleagues and with others in your profession as part of what you do. If you have a great lesson plan, put it in your state's online repository (if they have one), post it in a learning network, or put it in Curriki (an online curriculum wiki). Invite feedback and let people take it and "mash it up" and add enhancements for their own classroom.

It should become part of the professional practice of the modern educator to actively share best practices with other educators as part of what he or she does. This can take many forms but also it should be part of your habits. Share with parents what you are doing. Make it easy for people to communicate with you. Share because you care.

Be an Original "You," Not a Poor Copy of Someone Else. In the United States one of the greatest singers who ever lived is a man named Elvis Presley. With a black pompadour and glitzy jewels on his costumes, he is copied by many people imitating him and wishing they could be Elvis. How many amazing musicians have wasted the career they could have had by trying to be Elvis instead of just being "me"? Instead of being a priceless original Joe, Tom, or José, they spent their lives being a cheap knock-off of Elvis! Why?

In your journey into global collaboration you will have your own story. You have a choice right here and right now. Don't be a knock-off of someone you admire, be an original "you." You are somebody and the most important teacher in the world to your students. Are you going to put this book down and wait another five years and wish you'd done something? Are you going to have to wait until somebody else does it first? Are you going to miss this major trend because you are scared or you just don't think it is important?

Or are you going to join the growing numbers of us who know this is the way to go? Are you going to tell your own story, win your own awards, and look down at a conference one day while you are presenting about your project to see one of us authors in the audience learning from you and applauding your work?

We do not know where we are headed but we do know this: With you as part of the change, we will all be better than if you are not part of the change. Join us. Take this self-assessment survey to begin to write your own book and determine where you go next with your learning.

SELF-ASSESSMENT SURVEY

PDToolkit

for
Flattening Classrooms, Engaging Minds
Fill out this survey online or see the survey results online at PDToolkit.

We invite you to take this self-assessment survey. It is available online so you can give us the feedback! Please help us improve! We also suggest you discuss these questions with colleagues, including your wider learning network, to determine your current level of confidence and ability with putting it all together so you can Rock Your World!

1. **What features of this book have you used? (Check all that apply)**

   a. I read this whole book!

   b. Self-Assessments: ___ None ___ Some of them ___ All of them

   c. Flat Classroom Fifteen: ___ None ___ Some of them ___ All of them

   d. Flat Classroom Ning Network (http://flatclassrooms.ning.com)

   e. Tweeted questions to @flatclassroom

   f. Tweeted using the book's hashtag #flatclass

   g. Gone to webpages for the chapter and read information

   h. Interacted with the book's authors in some way

   i. Used QR codes to view a webpage for this book on my handheld device

   j. Blogged or shared something from this book with someone else.

2. **Which planning tools have you begun to use?**

   a. Connection planning tool (Step 1: Connection and Step 2: Communication)

   b. The five phases of flattening your classroom (Step 1: Communication)

   c. The "Planning Pie" to reach the different intelligences (Step 5: Choice)

   d. The project planning tool

   e. I looked up UDL (Universal Design for Learning) and used that format

   f. Something else I invented or learned from this text

3. **What are some ways you have built a learning pathway as it relates to best practices in teaching? What are some of the items in your pathway? (See Step 1: Connection)**

(continued)

Self-Assessment Survey *(continued)*

4. **How often do you look at information in your learning pathway each week?**

   a. Never

   b. 15 minutes a week

   c. 20 to 45 minutes a week

   d. More than 45 minutes a week

5. **Will you send an email to the authors giving feedback on this book with something you liked and one suggestion for improvement right now to fcbook@flatclassroom.org? Or will you send feedback on twitter to @flatclassroom or via the hashtag #flatclass?**

   a. I sent an email.

   b. I sent a tweet.

   c. I don't give feedback on books.

6. **List the next three things you want to learn more about as a result of this book.**

IF YOU ONLY READ ONE THING, READ THIS

So, we had to have a title that would get you to read the last page, the last thing. This is perhaps the most important.

YOUR "BIG THREE" R&D

ISTE STANDARDS

NETS.T 5
Engage in Professional Growth and Leadership

21st CENTURY SKILLS

C21 PROFESSIONAL DEVELOPMENT

If you've read the whole chapter, you've just taken the survey and looked at the results, and by now you should clearly know what is next for you in learning. Now unleash the power of the Big Three.

This practice will transform your teaching and career. Choose three things you want to learn more about in global collaboration. Choose three. That's it. Three. We eat by taking small bites. We learn the same way.

Following the Georgia Educational Technology Conference in 2005, Vicki made a list of the next three things she wanted to learn: #1 Wikis, #2 Blogs, #3 Social Bookmarking. Within a week, her award-winning class wiki was created. Within two weeks she created the Cool Cat Teacher blog. Her story began the moment she distilled her action down to a small, manageable list of next items to learn. You can't do it all, but you can do something. For many years in a row after attending the ISTE (formerly NECC) conference in the USA, Julie listed the most important three things she wanted to learn more about and introduce to her classrooms and teachers in other parts of the world. She continues to do this each year, three things, not five, not ten. Start with three only. This big book is here because each author started with small steps of progress.

What are your next three steps about which you want to learn?

My Big Three
These are the next three things I am going to learn more about.
1. _____
2. _____
3. _____

Write them down. Share them in one of your networks, but do them and move ahead.

TAKE THE FIRST STEP

Your journey into global collaboration begins with one step. What will it be? Put a star by the item on your big three list that will be the first thing you do. Put it on your calendar or list now.

TELL YOUR STORY

When you have a success or triumph or even a problem, we would love for you to share with us as we continue to write, blog, and share the story of global collaboration. Please email us at story@flatclassroom.org, or blog it at flatclassrooms.ning.com. Good luck! If you finished the Flat Classroom™ Fifteen, make sure you go to our network and let us know by creating a final post linking to all of your work. Congratulations!

SUMMARY

Act. Do. Be you. Choose three. Your lifelong journey starts now. Rock the world.

ESSENTIAL QUESTIONS

- Describe the items in your learning pathway concerning global collaboration in the classroom. Which item has helped you in the most positive way?
- What are your Big Three? Which one will you start on first and when?
- How could you create a formal learning community for ongoing improvement?

Join the online conversation and share your answers at http://tinyurl.com/flatclass-ch12. ▶

FLAT CLASSROOM™ 15 CHALLENGES

CHALLENGE 15: TELL YOUR STORY

DO: Take the survey at http://www.flatclassroombook.com/final-book-survey .html. Share your best story of learning and global collaboration with other teachers through a blog post or other means.

SHARE: If you are on Twitter, please tweet the book authors @julielindsay and @coolcatteacher with a link to your story #flatclass and fc-complete—an example tweet is shown in the tweetable:

tweetable

Hey @julielindsay @coolcatteacher fc-complete Here's my story of global collaboration http://tinyurl.com /my-fcp-story #flatclass

The tag for this challenge is fc-complete. Use this when you blog, or to share with your group

◀ Share what you did with your challenge at http://tinyurl.com/flat15-15

THE FLAT CLASSROOM™ DIARIES

Diary Entry 23

VICKI DAVIS,
Flat Classroom Diary Entry, September 4, 2007

I just logged into the Google Doc that Julie and I are using to write our diaries of our journal into our second year of collaboration AND JULIE'S IN HERE TOO! So often, we are so close that it is like we're touching hands—and yet, we are now 7 hours' time difference. We've got to get used to this new time zone, I'm so used to checking in with her at 5:00 a.m. and at 8:00 p.m.! This will be a whole new routine.

Last year, it was just two classes, but now we're looking at more. The students are definitely NOT ready for a full-scale, large team like we have in the Horizon Project and yet we want to integrate students into this group project. We want to get some sort of duplicable content, and yet I scratch my head and ask, "Is anything truly duplicable anymore?" How can all teachers move into a world full of collaborative group work? Although I have a textbook and test banks and such, there is still a very fluid component to my curriculum reflective of the dynamics in the world today. How can teachers who are used to (or told to) get everything out of a prepackage do such projects—or can they? How can unempowered teachers do such a project? I don't think they can.

I look at my list of what Julie and I need to get done in order to bring this project together and feel like we are too late. There isn't enough time—and yet, there is never enough time. We've had to pull back the time frame in order to include the southern hemisphere, which gets out of school in mid-November and so we again are adjusting to a new time. The whole time zone and hemisphere issue is something that we learn in elementary school but isn't truly understood until it is experienced. That is why I think the experiential knowledge of such projects could perhaps be more important than the content.

I struggle with a total lack of understanding from many about what it takes to pull something like this together and it is so easy to let the urgency of teaching, the managing of 100 computers, and the handling of the student information system get in the way of this truly important project. Whether anyone appreciates the importance of this project (and I think many do, although most don't really know what we're doing—yet), with all of my being, I know how vital it is to teach global collaborative skills so that my students can be part of the "Symphony" described in Dan Pink's masterful book, *A Whole New Mind.*

With that being said, I think it is a Whole New Classroom that we enter now. Perhaps Julie and I (and Barbara and John and whoever out there joins in this year) will build this new classroom together as we work to smash down walls and preconceived notions in the minds of the future of the world. This is where we need to go both at the high school level and college level . . . and the workplace is already there.

Although thousands of pundits will arise to dispute the realism of being able to do such projects and the need for them . . . I predict those pundits are the ones who profit from keeping the world divided or are scared of a place where the kids make up their own minds and reject stereotypes that have been handed down for generations. It is so important to put a face and heartbeat on the world as it becomes personalized, for detachment has truly caused some of the greatest tragedies that have happened on this beautiful globe.

Will something happen to derail this whole project? Will the obstacles keep us from tearing down walls to make this happen? Will changes in job responsibilities or teaching load derail us? All I can say is that I'm going to give everything to this with the knowledge of this: Although Julie and I and the others are busier than ever . . . we've trod down this path when it was much harder and this time last year, I didn't even know Julie.

So, the possibilities are limitless. I became a teacher so I could change the world of even one student . . . and if one is changed that is enough . . . however if what I do in this classroom can change the world of thousands or even hundreds of thousands of other students . . . I shall work to open the walls of my classroom . . . for truly, it is not about me but about exposing my students to the incredible "out there" of which they know so little. And when "out there" comes "in here" . . . unbelievable change can truly happen.

Diary Entry 24

JULIE LINDSAY, October 6, 2007

I was sharing some Flat Classroom experiences with colleagues last night over dinner. We were talking about curriculum reform and School 2.0 requirements. It dawned on me that we need to be creating these opportunities for students to interact with others and communicate and collaborate in order to learn more about what life is like in all parts of the world. We need to be promoting innovation and creativity and moving into higher-order thinking rather than robotic-style teaching. My Grade 10 Flat Classroomers this semester were meant to do a unit of work focusing on Adobe Premiere and video making. I 'transformed' this unit into the Flat Classroom Project so that we could participate. This means we will not be learning Premiere in any depth, unless students choose to take on that task. This means I will not be following the original unit plan; I am doing this with permission. But hey, what would you rather be doing, learning Premiere or helping to dispel the myth that all Middle Easterners are terrorists via a proactive network of youth who are the future of this world?

CASE EXAMPLES OF GLOBAL COLLABORATION

Case Study 24

Some "Big Three" Items from Teachers
VICKI DAVIS. July 2009 after a Flat Classroom Workshop in St. Louis

for
Flattening Classrooms, Engaging Minds

Read full Case Studies in PDToolkit online.

Reply by Martha Bogart on July 9, 2008,[7] at 9:13 p.m.

My items for intentional R&D:

1. Second Life—don't know ANYTHING about this, and want to learn it
2. Back Channel Chats—want to incorporate them in the staff development that I do
3. Ning—have started one and want to continue with it and make it more robust

Reply by Jim Leesch on July 11, 2008, at 4:33 a.m.

Ok. . . My Big Three:

1. Create a couple of different Nings for the upcoming year—one for faculty use and one for my advisory group.
2. Research Elluminate and try it out for possible use in faculty meetings.

3. Learn how to use and upload Jing screencasts effectively. This may have uses for trying some "reverse" schooling.

Reply by Sharleen Berg on July 12, 2008, at 11:20 a.m.

My Big 3 list for R&D:

1. Ning vs. Wiki? Deciding which would be best in starting a Smartboard resource for our staff
2. Connecting . . . spend time finding resources for teachers new to Web 2.0
3. Continue work on 23 Things on a Stick project - Web 2.0

Share your "Big Three" here:
http://tinyurl.com/fcp-big3

Case Study 25

 "Domingo's Story," KIM CLAYTON, Westside High School, Houston, TX, USA

PDToolkit
for
**Flattening Classrooms,
Engaging Minds**
Read full Case Studies
in PDToolkit online.

I also wanted to share a follow-up on one of my students—Domingo, who was the Grand Prize winner for his multimedia piece—so that you will truly understand what an impact this project can have in students' lives.

Domingo is an extremely shy and quiet student considered at risk because he is not a native English speaker and is from a low-income family. With my encouragement and with confidence bolstered from his success in the FCP, he applied for the GeneSys Works program, which is a work/study program that places at-risk students in an professional work environment.[8] Domingo was accepted into the program for the next year and truly impressed the interviewers with his passion and knowledge of the importance of "flattening" our world through communication. This is a student whose life will be changed because of the knowledge and skills he took away from this project.

Thank you to the entire Flat Classroom community for the ability to participate in this project and all for the hard work that Julie and Vicki do!

[Kim emailed an update to this story just as we were going to press. We wanted to share this with readers. What a great way to end this book!]

Must update you on Domingo—I had the pleasure of watching him walk across the stage to receive his high school diploma last week. It almost DIDN'T happen. He failed a semester of pre-calculus in the fall and needed to make it up. He finished the coursework via computer *the night before* graduation. He will attend Montana State University on a full scholarship to study agriculture. He is the first in his family to attend college. Domingo, and the many other Domingos out there who are just looking for a teacher to push them, are the reason I became a teacher. So much more rewarding than the world of banking I left behind.

Flat Classroom™ Project Rubric Assessment

There are *two different* rubrics featured as part of the Flat Classroom™ Project.[1] The first one, "Video Artifact," covers Criteria A and B and is to be used by all classrooms for assessing the multimedia artifact. It will also be used by the judges for the digital story/video awards.

The second rubric, "Engagement, Reflection, and Evaluation," (Criteria C and D) is optional for teachers to use at the conclusion of the project.

The first and second rubrics have been designed to complement each other, hence the progression from Criteria A to D.

Rubric 1: Video Artifact

Student work will be assessed against two criteria related to the objectives of the Flat Classroom Project. This is an individual mark assessed by the judges for a "best multimedia artifact." Individual teachers can also use this rubric for class assessment as they need it.

OBJECTIVES

- To *create* a video that communicates with a general audience and is based on the theme of The Story; Innovation, Invention, and Prediction; Social Entrepreneurship; First Person Narrative; and Group Stories (Symphony) or How We Live (Play)

- To actively *share* original content about the topics being *researched and analyzed.*

Description	Marks
Design and Technical Quality	30
Synthesis and Construction of Ideas	36
TOTAL	**66**

TASK DESCRIPTION

Students will work individually to create one video in each of six categories for each topic. There are six types of videos:

- *Group A Video:* The Story (Group A). These videos explain the topic. They may be distinct or a multipart series, but they must explain the topic at hand, including the latest research and findings from the wiki.

- *Group B Video:* Innovation, Invention, and Prediction (Group B). These videos should include an innovation, invention, or prediction based on the trend that is shown. Some questions that *may* be covered: Where will this trend take us? How do you envision the future? Do you think this trend will be replaced with another? What inventions are needed because of this trend?

- *Group C Video:* Social Entrepreneurship (Group C). A social entrepreneur is defined as "someone who recognizes a social problem and uses entrepreneurial principles to organize, create, and manage a venture to make social change."[2] In these videos you will select the social cause of your choice and, using the information learned about your trend, create a video about how the trend you analyzed can be used to spark change in that area. If you find current organizations involved that you wish to share as part of your video, please discuss this with your teacher before writing it into your script.

- *Group D Video:* First-Person Narrative (Empathy) (Group D). In this video, you will tell a story of a person involved in the trend.

- *Group E Video:* Group Stories (Symphony) (Group E). In this video, you will tell a story of a group or groups of people as they are impacted by this trend.

- *Group F Video:* How We Live (Play). In this video, you will show how "play is becoming an important part of work, business and personal well-being, its importance manifesting itself in three ways: games, humor and joyfulness."[3]

DESCRIPTORS

Criterion A: Design and Technical Quality

Criteria	5–6	3–4	1–2	0	Max Points Awarded
Use of multimedia tools to express ideas	Effective	Sufficient	Limited	The work does not meet the standard described in other levels.	6
Sound quality and balance between music/video and voice-over (if any)	Clear; no or little distortion of sound; easy to understand, adequate pace. Appropriate balance is achieved between music/sound and voice at all times.	Mostly clear; may have some distortion of sound or pace may be too fast or too slow therefore interfering with understanding of narration. Music/sound or voice may be used rather than both and generally a good balance is achieved.	Difficult or impossible to hear or understand; use of audio may be limited and ineffective.	The work does not meet the standard described in other levels.	6
Special effects and transitions	Special effects and transitions are used creatively and specifically to enhance the final message.	Special effects and transitions enhance the final message to a limited extent.	Special effects and transitions do not enhance or interfere with the final message.	The work does not meet the standard described in other levels.	6
Clip editing process	All or most video clips and images have been effectively edited to improve the impact of the artifact.	Some video clips and images have been edited which has improved the impact of the artifact to a limited degree.	Video clips and images have been poorly edited and do not enhance the impact of the artifact.	The work does not meet the standard described in other levels.	6
Length of video	Between 1 and 5 minutes long; maintains interest and is an appropriate length for the message conveyed.	(no marks in this section)	(no marks in this section)	Under 1 minute or over 5 minutes.	6

Criterion B: Synthesis and Construction of Ideas

Criteria	5–6	3–4	1–2	0	Max Points Awarded
Fit with submission theme ("story," "innovation, invention, and prediction," "social entrepreneurship," "first person narrative," "group stories" or "play")	Excellent fit	Adequate fit	Limited fit. Video may fit better with a different theme than what it was submitted under.	The work does not meet the standard described in other levels.	6
Construction of content	Systematic synthesis of information is clearly based on topic research.	Some synthesis of information based on research on the topic.	Synthesis of information is superficial and not clearly related to research on the topic.	The work does not meet the standard described in other levels.	6
Organization and presentation of content	Content is presented in a way that is creative or tells a story that makes a point or teaches a lesson; well-crafted introduction and an effectively structured progression of topics or story.	Content is presented in a way that tries to be creative or tell a story; reasonably well structured progression of topics or story including an introduction.	Presentation is poor and interferes with understanding of content and is poorly organized; there may be an introduction and some attempt to structure topics.	The work does not meet the standard described in other levels.	6
Editing of content	Content is by and large free of spelling/grammatical errors and technical glitches.	Content may contain minor spelling/grammatical errors and/or an occasional minor technical glitch.	Content contains many spelling/grammatical errors and/or a number of technical glitches.	The work does not meet the standard described in other levels.	6
Evidence of collaboration	Yes. There is evidence of collaboration beyond merely sharing a piece of video; outsourced video is included, source is credited and the use of it may or may not be seamless.	(no marks in this section)	Yes. Outsourced video is included, source is NOT obviously credited and the use of it may or may not be seamless.	The work does not meet the standard described in other levels.	6

Student work will be assessed against three criteria related to the objectives of the Flat Classroom Project.

This is an individual assessment done by teachers to be used for "collaboration and engagement" awards and for class assessment as needed. As with the rubrics above, this rubric can be adapted to meet the assessment demands of different academic systems (e.g., increasing the number of points to make a combined total of 100 in conjunction with Criterion A and B).

OBJECTIVES

- To *collaborate* and *interact* with classrooms around the world on the theme of *"the flat world"*

as technology develops and has more impact on our everyday lives.

- To involve students in higher-order learning and using higher-order thinking skills that include organization, *peer review,* and *reflection* activities as well *as synthesis* of ideas, *analysis,* and evaluation of trends, *creation* of webpages, and multimedia products.

Criteria	Description	Marks
C	Online Interaction and Engagement with the Project	3
D	Reflection and Evaluation	4
	TOTAL	**7**

DESCRIPTORS

Criterion C: Online Interaction and Engagement with the Project

Level	Descriptor (for maximum marks)
0	The work does not meet the standard described in level 1–2.
1–2	Communication with team members and teachers was infrequent. There is little evidence of being a considerate partner and of providing feedback, or contributing ideas to the project. The wiki page editing and multimedia artifacts were partially completed by the deadline. Some organizational skills were demonstrated.
3	Communication with team members and teachers was frequent. There is evidence of being a considerate partner, providing feedback, and effectively communicating ideas to the project. The wiki page editing and multimedia artifacts were completed by the deadline. High-level organization skills were demonstrated.

Criterion D: Reflection and Evaluation

The reflection could be in written or oral form and could:

- Discuss the main social and ethical issues related to the topic and weigh up the main ideas.

- Propose ways to improve the student's performance and evaluate the strengths and weaknesses of the project.

Level	Descriptor (for maximum marks)
0	The work does not meet the standard described in level 1–2 or the essay exceeds 800 words.
1–2	Some attempt has been made to discuss and evaluate the main social and ethical issues related to the topic. There is evidence of some analysis of the project from a personal viewpoint. The reflection includes proposals for personal improvement and a few suggestions for enhancing work for this type of project. There is some attempt to cite references and use tagging and hyperlinks.
3–4	Discussion and evaluation of the main social and ethical issues related to the topic is comprehensive. A high level of analysis of the project from a personal viewpoint is evident. The reflection includes proposals for personal improvement and well-considered suggestions for enhancing work for this type of project. All references are cited, and tagging and hyperlinks are used appropriately.

Global Collaboration and the International Baccalaureate

This appendix provides a brief overview of how Flat Classroom™ projects and pedagogy can be embedded into the International Baccalaureate (IB) programmes. It is aimed at current, practicing teachers in the Primary Years Programme (PYP), the Middle Years Programme (MYP), and the Diploma Programme (DP), as well as teachers who are interested in finding out more about integrating projects into their curriculum.

Introduction to the International Baccalaureate

The International Baccalaureate runs three frameworks: Primary Years Programme, Middle Years Programme, and Diploma Programme.[1] The IB philosophy is based on education being holistic, multicultural, and transdisciplinary with an emphasis on international education, inquiry learning, and global citizenship. It fosters communication and collaboration within and beyond the classroom walls with a community approach that encourages all learners to look globally as well as act locally. It draws on "a recognizable common educational framework, a consistent structure of aims and values and an overarching concept of how to develop international-mindedness."[2]

How the International Baccalaureate Relates to Flat Classroom Projects

The IB Learner Profile provides a tool for whole school reflection and analysis and asks teachers to reflect on their classroom practice and assessment methods, as well as daily life, management, and leadership in order to support inquiry-based learning within a holistic framework.[3] Read more about the Learner Profile and how Flat Classroom projects support this concept. After completing the very first Flat Classroom Project in 2006, Julie writes in her blog about the Learner Profile, and how the project supported learning about new IT

tools that would allow students to use multimedia to express their ideas.[4] It was a whole new learning paradigm that needed independent, responsible, and brave students and teachers to see it to completion.

Further development of the collection of Flat Classroom Projects clearly follow the aim of all IB programmes, which is to "develop internationally minded people who, recognizing their common humanity and shared guardianship of the planet, help to create a better and more peaceful world."[5]

How Can International Baccalaureate Schools Get Involved?

Flat Classroom projects are suitable for IB programmes at age-appropriate levels. The holistic nature of the pedagogy and the supportive learning environment builds a global community of practice whereby students and teachers gain cultural awareness. It also enhances technical and IT skills related to global collaboration using Web 2.0 tools for connection, communication, collaboration, and creation.

There are a number of accessible entry levels to Flat Classroom projects and some examples are shared in this appendix. To begin the journey, educators are encouraged to join our network, flatclassrooms.ning.com, and interact with others globally. It is through this network that we announce opportunities to join projects or to support projects by being an expert advisor, a judge for final products, a sounding board, or a provider of feedback on issues and challenges individuals and teams are facing with projects in session.

We also run the Flat Classroom certified teacher course a few times each year and invite educators to consider joining this to learn firsthand how to run a Flat Classroom before, during, or after implementing a project into their curriculum. Contact Flat Classroom organizers at fcp@flatclassroom.org with further questions. Further information about all projects can be found at flatclassroomproject.net.

EXAMPLE 1: FLAT CLASSROOM PROJECT—MYP TECHNOLOGY

Classrooms around the world have adopted this project for Humanities/Social Studies, Politics, Global Studies, History, and other curriculum areas. MYP Technology and DP Information Technology in a Global Society (ITGS) easily adopt this unit, as on the surface it is about technologies, has a final product, and also requires access to computers to work through the collaboration and creation of multimedia.

Transdisciplinary Potential A greater depth of knowledge and understanding could be achieved if a Humanities/Technology/Global Studies/English cross-curriculum approach was adopted, especially with the Dan Pink concepts as the influence for video creation.[6]

Excerpt from Year 5 / Grade 10 MYP Technology, 10- to 12-Week Unit

Project Name: Emerging Technologies and Global Collaboration—Flat Classroom Project

Area of Interaction: Human Ingenuity

Significant Concept: Students will understand that learning can be collaborative and include others beyond the immediate classroom.

Guiding Question: How can we use information technologies to connect and collaborate and co-create products?

Essential Focus Questions

- How can emerging technologies and enhanced connectivity improve learning and create extended communities?
- How can we use "flattened" learning modes and emerging technologies to connect with other classrooms globally?
- When we connect globally, what can we do together that could make a difference to the world as we know it?
- How can we use multimedia to effectively convey a message?
- What sort of products can be co-created via collaboration?
- How can we best share our learning to a wider audience?

Project Overview Students will use emerging technologies to connect, collaborate, and create a product that communicates their ideas for the current and future use of IT and collaborative learning. Not only will students study the concepts found in Friedman's *The World Is Flat,* but they also will model those concepts through participation in a global, collaborative project (Flat Classroom Project). The end product will be a multimedia artifact communicating their ideas according to the team/topic given. In addition, students will co-author a wiki page on their topic, collaborate with other students globally, and present in a virtual classroom, sharing about their learning.

Reflection on the Flat Classroom Project Shared by Pat D'Arcy, Head of Technology, MYP Technology teacher, ISdüsseldorf, Germany

> The Flat Classroom Project is not a normal day-to-day experience, yet in the deeper sense of classroom experiences it is of course a perfect example of the real thing! Individual responsibilities, responsibility to a small group world wide, work with someone you may never see; developing trust and respect. All the ingredients of the IB Learner Profile are included in a tremendous 12-week experience."[7]

EXAMPLE 2: DIGITEEN™ PROJECT—MYP TECHNOLOGY

Transdisciplinary Potential This project is relevant for all five MYP levels and could be adapted for upper PYP years. The focus is on global citizenship when using digital tools and is applicable across all curriculum areas. There is also potential to combine this with a community and service project as a grade level or a topic-based team.

Excerpt from Year 4 / Grade 9 MYP Technology, 10- to 12-Week Unit

Project Name: Digiteen™ Project

Area of Interaction: Community and Service

Significant Concept: Students will understand that learning online requires responsible and reliable behaviors.

Guiding Question: How can I become a responsible and reliable citizen when using technology?

The full MYP Technology Unit Plan, "Emerging Technologies and Global Collaboration: Flat Classroom Project," can be found online with additional resources, including "Learning Experiences" and "Teaching Strategies." http://tinyurl.com/MYPflatclassroomproject

Essential Focus Questions

- What are the issues with being online?
- How can I make others in my community aware of the importance of being a conscientious digital citizen and behaving appropriately when using technology and online resources?
- What action can I take to promote *digital citizenship in the community*?

Project Overview The Digiteen Project is a global collaboration between classrooms around the world. This unit asks students to explore the concept and practice of digital citizenship and challenges them to share their findings with other members of the project community. The students will collaborate with other classrooms around the world to explore and discuss digital citizenship themes and to add their research and ideas to a collaborative wiki. They will then formulate ideas for an action-based project in the local community that shares their research and new learning and raises awareness of digital citizenship issues.

WEBSITES

The full MYP Technology Unit Plan with resources can be found online.
http://tinyurl.com/MYPDigiteen

EXAMPLE 3: NETGENED™ PROJECT— INFORMATION TECHNOLOGY IN A GLOBAL SOCIETY (ITGS)

As described on the NetGenEd™ 2011 Project Wiki:[8]

In this project, students will study and "mash up" the results of the 2011 Horizon Report from the New Media Consortium and Educause[9] and Tapscott's book *Grown Up Digital: How the Net Generation Is Changing Your World*.[10] Students will study the current research and create wiki-reports with their student partners around the world analyzing current trends and projecting future happenings based on this collaborative analysis. The students, who assume roles such as project manager, assistant project manager, and editors of the various wikis, manage this project.

After compiling their wiki reports based on current research, and encouraged by "expert advisors" (subject matter experts in the industry), students will then create a video where students envision the future of global social action based on their research in current global technological trends.

Resources

NetGenEd™ Project website: http://www.netgened
.org

Reflections on Global Collaboration Andrew Churches, ITGS teacher and examiner, reflects on his class involvement in the NetGenEd Project:

For the last 3–4 years in February and March my students IB1 ITGS (first year International Baccalaureate, Information Technology in a Global Society) students have participated in a global educational project called NetGen Ed. The ITGS syllabus call on the students to examine and reflect on the impact that information technology in its many forms has on different aspects of society.

The aspects include health, education, science, and alike. The syllabus requires the students to consider many ethical issues based around information technology. They examine and investigate digital citizenship, equality of access, security, reliability and much more. The contents of the syllabus changes with the evolution of the technologies that we see emerging and disappearing on the web. In short ITGS is a dynamic and evolving course, with huge relevance to our young digital citizens.

The NetGen Ed™ project is a perfect match. Investigating 6 current trends defined from the Horizon Report and linking these to the characteristics of the 21st century learner (as defined by the research of Canadian Don Tapscott), with an in-depth focus on education, the project sees students from round the world collaborating and co-operating for not only their own goals but also for the groups goals. Digital citizenship and netiquette are not theoretical, but essential to the interactions the students have. Understanding of collaborative tools is not based around a simple classroom extension, rather is the lifeblood of this dynamic project. The students must work together to be able to complete their personal tasks and outcomes.

The NetGenEd™ project is the foundation of my course; it establishes the norms I expect in my classroom of collaboration and co-operation, respect and resourcefulness, adaptability and imagination. What a way to start a year.

EXAMPLE 4: INSIDE ITGS

Inside ITGS is a collaborative project that aims to document exploration and delivery of the IB Diploma course, Information Technology in a Global Society (ITGS). Inside ITGS co-founders Julie Lindsay (BISS) and Madeleine Brookes (Western Academy, Beijing) have been involved with ITGS for a number of years and have often shared resources and ideas. Using Flat Classroom pedagogy, the idea is to take class collaboration to the next level by providing a learning community where students in both schools can collaborate, share ideas, and learn together. Other schools have also been invited to participate in projects along the way. Guidelines have been established,[11] including registration protocols, an approach to being a global digital citizen, and teacher expectations.

Tools to structure the collaboration include:

- A teacher blog, insideitgs.net, to record endeavors and become a living resource that is accessible for all ITGS teachers and students from around the world. It is also a resource that other ITGS teachers can dip into, contribute to, and thereby become part of this grass-roots, international learning community.
- An educational network, insideitgs.ning.com, to support the online learning community.
- A collaborative wiki for information delivery, student-authored content, and collaboration projects: insideitgs.wikispaces.com.

Inside ITGS is structured so that classes can work together for extended periods of time, beyond the typical global project design. Different assignments and activities provide scope for students to learn with and from their global partners.

Reflection on Global Collaboration through Inside ITGS: Inside ITGS One Year Later Madeleine Brookes, ITGS teacher and examiner, ADE, HS Technology Integrator

We started Inside ITGS knowing that online communication is easy. We knew that our students can easily communicate even here in China where many tools such as Facebook and YouTube are generally not available; our students use tools such as Skype, iChat, and MSN constantly to spontaneously conduct their social lives around the clock in both synchronously and asynchronously. One year later, we found that having our students develop their online communication skills to collaborate to extend their learning was a major challenge.

In a traditional, MYP enquiry-based classroom, students can easily form groups to work collaboratively; students tend to know each other's strengths and weaknesses and relationships can be quickly developed or deepened. Contrast this to an online environment where students are brought together online from two or more classes, albeit in the same city without the benefit of visual cues through body language as well as informal exchanges, and our first challenge arose: How do we quickly get the students acquainted and "related" online? Our "Introducing" assignment, plus a face-to-face meeting including a shared lunch, certainly helped get this started. Over the year, we have worked hard trying to build the relationships; we have had many online meetings using Elluminate although we are now looking to explore Second Life as we feel this will be a more inclusive and participatory tool.

A second factor is the shift from synchronous to asynchronous learning, which is essential when working with schools on different continents and time zones and, as we found, different timetables even within the same city. Students have to be much more flexible in their approach; be highly visible and available online inside and outside the school day and willing to dip in and out of their collaborative assignment over a period of a few days instead of just planning a single chunk of time to get their "individual" task done.

Overall, training the students how to use the tools technically required very little instruction compared with [training] our less-tech savvy adults; our "training" investment was in how to harness the power of the tools to be more productive and collaborative.

So Inside ITGS one year later: We start afresh with a new group of students in a few months; at this point I have no idea how many classes and from how many schools. I wonder if we will we have the same initial challenges or will we find that our newer students will be further down the line?

The ISTE NETS and Performance Indicators for Students (NETS•S)

1. Creativity and Innovation

Students demonstrate creative thinking, construct knowledge, and develop innovative products and processes using technology. Students:

- **a.** apply existing knowledge to generate new ideas, products, or processes
- **b.** create original works as a means of personal or group expression
- **c.** use models and simulations to explore complex systems and issues
- **d.** identify trends and forecast possibilities

2. Communication and Collaboration

Students use digital media and environments to communicate and work collaboratively, including at a distance, to support individual learning and contribute to the learning of others. Students:

- **a.** interact, collaborate, and publish with peers, experts, or others employing a variety of digital environments and media
- **b.** communicate information and ideas effectively to multiple audiences using a variety of media and formats
- **c.** develop cultural understanding and global awareness by engaging with learners of other cultures
- **d.** contribute to project teams to produce original works or solve problems

3. Research and Information Fluency

Students apply digital tools to gather, evaluate, and use information. Students:

- **a.** plan strategies to guide inquiry
- **b.** locate, organize, analyze, evaluate, synthesize, and ethically use information from a variety of sources and media
- **c.** evaluate and select information sources and digital tools based on the appropriateness to specific tasks
- **d.** process data and report results

4. Critical Thinking, Problem Solving, and Decision Making

Students use critical thinking skills to plan and conduct research, manage projects, solve problems, and make informed decisions using appropriate digital tools and resources. Students:

- **a.** identify and define authentic problems and significant questions for investigation
- **b.** plan and manage activities to develop a solution or complete a project
- **c.** collect and analyze data to identify solutions and/or make informed decisions
- **d.** use multiple processes and diverse perspectives to explore alternative solutions

5. Digital Citizenship

Students understand human, cultural, and societal issues related to technology and practice legal and ethical behavior. Students:

- **a.** advocate and practice safe, legal, and responsible use of information and technology
- **b.** exhibit a positive attitude toward using technology that supports collaboration, learning, and productivity
- **c.** demonstrate personal responsibility for lifelong learning
- **d.** exhibit leadership for digital citizenship

6. Technology Operations and Concepts

Students demonstrate a sound understanding of technology concepts, systems, and operations. Students:

- **a.** understand and use technology systems
- **b.** select and use applications effectively and productively
- **c.** troubleshoot systems and applications
- **d.** transfer current knowledge to learning of new technologies

The ISTE NETS and Performance Indicators for Teachers (NETS•T)

Effective teachers model and apply the National Educational Technology Standards for Students (NETS•S) as they design, implement, and assess learning experiences to engage students and improve learning; enrich professional practice; and provide positive models for students, colleagues, and the community. All teachers should meet the following standards and performance indicators. Teachers:

1. Facilitate and Inspire Student Learning and Creativity

Teachers use their knowledge of subject matter, teaching and learning, and technology to facilitate experiences that advance student learning, creativity, and innovation in both face-to-face and virtual environments. Teachers:

a. promote, support, and model creative and innovative thinking and inventiveness

b. engage students in exploring real-world issues and solving authentic problems using digital tools and resources

c. promote student reflection using collaborative tools to reveal and clarify students' conceptual understanding and thinking, planning, and creative processes

d. model collaborative knowledge construction by engaging in learning with students, colleagues, and others in face-to-face and virtual environments

2. Design and Develop Digital-Age Learning Experiences and Assessments

Teachers design, develop, and evaluate authentic learning experiences and assessments incorporating contemporary tools and resources to maximize content learning in context and to develop the knowledge, skills, and attitudes identified in the NETS•S. Teachers:

a. design or adapt relevant learning experiences that incorporate digital tools and resources to promote student learning and creativity

b. develop technology-enriched learning environments that enable all students to pursue their individual curiosities and become active participants in setting their own educational goals, managing their own learning, and assessing their own progress

c. customize and personalize learning activities to address students' diverse learning styles, working strategies, and abilities using digital tools and resources

d. provide students with multiple and varied formative and summative assessments aligned with content and technology standards and use resulting data to inform learning and teaching

3. Model Digital-Age Work and Learning

Teachers exhibit knowledge, skills, and work processes representative of an innovative professional in a global and digital society. Teachers:

a. demonstrate fluency in technology systems and the transfer of current knowledge to new technologies and situations

b. collaborate with students, peers, parents, and community members using digital tools and resources to support student success and innovation

c. communicate relevant information and ideas effectively to students, parents, and peers using a variety of digital-age media and formats

d. model and facilitate effective use of current and emerging digital tools to locate, analyze, evaluate, and use information resources to support research and learning

4. Promote and Model Digital Citizenship and Responsibility

Teachers understand local and global societal issues and responsibilities in an evolving digital culture and exhibit legal and ethical behavior in their professional practices. Teachers:

a. advocate, model, and teach safe, legal, and ethical use of digital information and technology, including respect for copyright, intellectual property, and the appropriate documentation of sources

b. address the diverse needs of all learners by using learner-centered strategies and providing equitable access to appropriate digital tools and resources

c. promote and model digital etiquette and responsible social interactions related to the use of technology and information

d. develop and model cultural understanding and global awareness by engaging with colleagues and students of other cultures using digital-age communication and collaboration tools

5. Engage in Professional Growth and Leadership

Teachers continuously improve their professional practice, model lifelong learning, and exhibit leadership in their school and professional community by promoting and demonstrating the effective use of digital tools and resources. Teachers:

a. participate in local and global learning communities to explore creative applications of technology to improve student learning

b. exhibit leadership by demonstrating a vision of technology infusion, participating in shared decision making and community building, and developing the leadership and technology skills of others

c. evaluate and reflect on current research and professional practice on a regular basis to make effective use of existing and emerging digital tools and resources in support of student learning

d. contribute to the effectiveness, vitality, and self-renewal of the teaching profession and of their school and community

PARTNERSHIP FOR
21ST CENTURY SKILLS

Framework for 21st Century Learning

The Partnership for 21st Century Skills has developed a vision for student success in the new global economy.

21st Century Student Outcomes and Support Systems

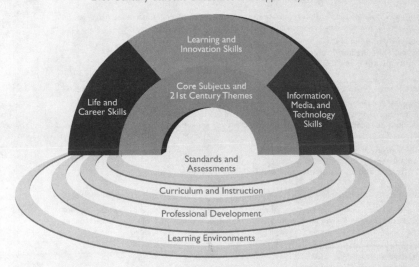

21ST CENTURY STUDENT OUTCOMES

To help practitioners integrate skills into the teaching of core academic subjects, the Partnership has developed a unified, collective vision for learning known as the Framework for 21st Century Learning. This Framework describes the skills, knowledge and expertise students must master to succeed in work and life; it is a blend of content knowledge, specific skills, expertise and literacies.

Every 21st century skills implementation requires the development of core academic subject knowledge and understanding among all students. Those who can think critically and communicate effectively must build on a base of core academic subject knowledge.

Within the context of core knowledge instruction, **students must also learn the essential skills for success in today's world, such as critical thinking, problem solving, communication and collaboration.**

When a school or district builds on this foundation, combining the entire Framework with the necessary support systems—standards, assessments, curriculum and instruction, professional development and learning environments—students are more engaged in the learning process and graduate better prepared to thrive in today's global economy.

Publication date: 12/09

177 N. Church Avenue, Suite 305   Tucson, AZ 85701   520-623-2466   www.21stcenturyskills.org

Core Subjects and 21st Century Themes

Mastery of **core subjects and 21st century themes** is essential to student success. Core subjects include English, reading or language arts, world languages, arts, mathematics, economics, science, geography, history, government and civics.

In addition, schools must promote an understanding of academic content at much higher levels by weaving **21st century interdisciplinary themes** into core subjects:

- **Global Awareness**
- **Financial, Economic, Business and Entrepreneurial Literacy**
- **Civic Literacy**
- **Health Literacy**
- **Environmental Literacy**

Learning and Innovation Skills

Learning and innovation skills are what separate students who are prepared for increasingly complex life and work environments in today's world and those who are not. They include:

- **Creativity and Innovation**
- **Critical Thinking and Problem Solving**
- **Communication and Collaboration**

Information, Media and Technology Skills

Today, we live in a technology and media-driven environment, marked by access to an abundance of information, rapid changes in technology tools and the ability to collaborate and make individual contributions on an unprecedented scale. Effective citizens and workers must be able to exhibit a range of functional and critical thinking skills, such as:

- **Information Literacy**
- **Media Literacy**
- **ICT (Information, Communications and Technology) Literacy**

Life and Career Skills

Today's life and work environments require far more than thinking skills and content knowledge. The ability to navigate the complex life and work environments in the globally competitive information age requires students to pay rigorous attention to developing adequate life and career skills, such as:

- **Flexibility and Adaptability**
- **Initiative and Self-Direction**
- **Social and Cross-Cultural Skills**
- **Productivity and Accountability**
- **Leadership and Responsibility**

21ST CENTURY SUPPORT SYSTEMS

Developing a comprehensive framework for 21st century learning requires more than identifying specific skills, content knowledge, expertise and literacies. An innovative support system must be created to help students master the multi-dimensional abilities that will be required of them. The Partnership has identified five critical support systems to ensure student mastery of 21st century skills:

- **21st Century Standards**
- **Assessments of 21st Century Skills**
- **21st Century Curriculum and Instruction**
- **21st Century Professional Development**
- **21st Century Learning Environments**

For more information, visit the Partnership's website at www.21stcenturyskills.org.

PARTNERSHIP FOR
21ST CENTURY SKILLS

Member Organizations

- Adobe Systems, Inc.
- American Association of School Librarians
- Apple
- ASCD
- Blackboard, Inc.
- Cable in the Classroom
- Crayola
- Cisco Systems, Inc.
- Corporation for Public Broadcasting
- Dell, Inc.
- EF Education
- Education Networks of America
- Educational Testing Service
- Gale, Cengage Learning
- Hewlett Packard
- Houghton Mifflin Harcourt
- Intel Corporation
- JA Worldwide®
- K12
- KnowledgeWorks Foundation
- LEGO Group
- Lenovo
- Learning Point Associates
- Leadership and Learning Center
- McGraw-Hill
- Measured Progress
- Microsoft Corporation
- National Education Association
- National Academy Foundation
- Nellie Mae Education Foundation
- netTrekker
- Oracle Education Foundation
- Pearson
- Project Management Institute Educational Foundation
- Quarasan!
- Scholastic Education
- Sesame Workshop
- Sun Microsystems, Inc.
- The Walt Disney Company
- Verizon

acceptable use agreement (AUA): An agreement between a network owner and the users of that network about the appropriate use of the network typically done to protect the network owner from legal action. (Also called an Acceptable Use Policy [AUP] or Fair Use Policy.)

accessibility: The ability for technology to be accessible by people with disabilities.

app: A program that one can download and install on a personal device via the Internet.

asynchronous communications: Communicating with others over a period of time. Whether in person or through technology, this mode of communications often has participants leave some sort of "message" to another.

augmented reality: Reality that is enhanced by an electronic source of information often using GPS. Using geotagging, specific places on the earth can be tagged (hardlinked) with information for others to retrieve while at that location.

authentic research: Original questions and answers posed by learners. Once relegated to the highest attainment of learning, authentic research is now seen as a valued part of learning at all levels, as it demonstrates through experience and scientific methods.

avatar: The visual second or third representation of a user ID in a virtual world or online.

backchannel: A live chat that often accompanies a live presentation or ongoing group activity. It serves as a way for information to flow in real time between participants.

beta test: A trial conducted in the final stages of product development, typically done by people not connected with its development.

bcc: The recipients of an email message entered in this field are "blind carbon copied" and will not be able to see each other and will not be listed on the email.

blog: Short for "web log," this is an online web-based journal.

Bloom's Digital Taxonomy: An update to Bloom's Taxonomy that encompasses emerging technology advances and their impact on classroom practice and the aim of encouraging higher-order thinking skills.

Bloom's Taxonomy: A classification of student learning objectives. The revised (2000) taxonomy is: Remember, Understand, Apply, Analyze, Evaluate, and Create.

brand monitoring portal (BMP): A portal that uses RSS to collate current information posted in public websites in an easy-to-read single webpage to facilitate monitoring of your "brand." Schools, organizations, and people can have a brand.

bystander effect: A phenomenon in which individuals do not react to an emergency situation when other people are present. This effect (also called *Genovese syndrome*) demonstrates that the more people that observe an event needing intervention, the less likely any one individual is to intervene. It is a problem in global collaboration because others can wrongly perceive that someone else has noticed a problem and expect "every-one else" to act. Community members should be taught that if they notice inappropriate behavior in a network it is their responsibility to act.

Can-SPAM Act: A 2003 U.S. law that requires businesses that use commercial email for marketing to give the recipients the right to have such businesses stop emailing them and that gives harsh penalties for violation. One may use listserv groups such as Google groups to share email because people can easily subscribe or unsubscribe.

carbon footprint: The measure of the impact our activities have on the environment.

cc: The recipients are "carbon copied" on an email message. Their email becomes part of the message itself and can be seen by those who the message is forwarded to.

CIPA: Children's Internet Protection Act (CIPA) requires schools and libraries receiving funding from the U.S. government for Internet access from the e-rate program to certify that they have an Internet safety policy with technology protection measures that restrict access to material harmful to minors. See http://tinyurl.com/cipa-info

citizen scientist: Typically a volunteer with no formal scientific training who joins in a research project or scientific work to perform research tasks such as observation, measurement, or computation.

classroom monitoring portal (CMP): The use of an RSS reader to monitor a public online classroom and bring all sources of information into an easy-to-read single webpage.

claymation: Using clay figures to create stop motion photographs that can be turned into movies.

co-creation: The joint creation of a final product while working with partners.

collaborative contribution: a contribution (of any form) made by a collaborative participant, which leads to the emergence of shared understandings and contributes explicitly or implicitly to the collaborative output.

community of practice (CoP): A group of people who share an interest in a subject or problem and collaborate over an extended period of time in a social learning experience.

communication conduit: The communication channels through which ideas and work flow between teachers and students on a project.

content management system (CMS): A collection of procedures and systems used to manage work flow in a collaborative environment.

COPPA Act: Children's Online Privacy Protection Act of 1998 (United States) prohibits the collection of market research information (or "profiling") of children under age 13 for any websites operated in the United States or serving children in the United States. For this reason, many websites require a potential user to certify that she or he is 13 years or older (usually with a check box). Although this is a U.S. law, many U.S. websites are used by those in other countries who must comply with the services they offer to those outside the United States.

Critical Friends Group: A concept developed by the National School Reform Faculty (NSRF). The original model is 6 to 12 teachers and administrators who commit to work and learn together for a two-year period with the aim of establishing student learning outcomes and increasing student achievement.

cross the midline: When a person moves an object across his or her field of vision and body from one side to the other, an action that is theorized to help connect the different sides of the brain.

crowdsourcing: The act of having tasks typically done by individuals to a community or group of people. Typically this is done through an open call to "all comers," but it can also be done through a community.

cyberbullying: Bullying behavior that occurs in technological modes of communication.

cyberstalker: A person who monitors the online behavior of another person, group of people, or organization, in order to stalk or harass the person. This can sometimes move into the realm of cyberbullying, but often it is harassment intended to cause fear or shame in the victim(s). A mild version of this is "creeping"—a slang term students use for someone who pays more attention than is normal to another person's page.

dead text: A term that denotes extended paragraphs of text without hyperlink or citation. Dead text should be a warning sign that an Internet source may be representing information to be true that is not verified by a valid source. If the text is dead, one must look at the author of the resource to determine his or her reliability.

deep web: Also called the "invisible web," this consists of the websites that are not indexed on public search engines. Many academic databases cannot be searched by public engines even if they are free.

design cycle: The use of a logical approach to creating a product, including Investigate, Design, Plan, Create, and Evaluate.

differentiated instruction: A pedagogical approach that provides students with multiple means of learning, constructing meaning, and producing evidence of learning.

Digidollar: A paper currency used at the Flat Classroom conference to motivate participation.

digital citizenship: Norms of online behavior. A person practicing effective digital citizenship understands the technology and can relate her or his behavior choices according to social, cultural, and global norms.

digital divide: The many divisions between those people who have access to technology and those who do not.

digital fluency: The ability to find and critically evaluate online information and to use this information effectively, efficiently, and ethically.

Digital Millennium Copyright Act (DMCA): A U.S. law that implemented two international treaties from the World Intellectual Property Organization (WIPO) to protect certain works from other member countries. Because of this law, many U.S.-based websites actively scan publicly uploaded content for copyright violations and will remove content even if the author claims rights under "fair use."

document camera: A specialty digital camera used for showing documents on a digital projector. This has become an electronic replacement for the "opaque projector."

dual encoding: A theory of cognition initiated by Allan Paivio that supports the dual-route theory of reading, both of which contend that when information is delivered through visual and auditory means, learning can be improved.

eBook reader: An electronic book reader that allows the user to download electronic books and manuals to read, to search, and to take notes in them.

educational network: An online network created for the purpose of social learning.

email harvester: An automated service that trolls through websites and forwarded emails to retrieve emails for the purpose of selling the email address to businesses or sending spam.

ethnocentrism: The belief in the superiority of one's own ethnic group.

Facebook fan page: A Facebook webpage to link the fan(s) of a celebrity, product, or cultural issue.

Facebook like: The process of "liking" something on the web, which sends it through your Facebook updates and is viewable by your friends.

file name extension: The characters after the last period in a file that determine the type of file and thus what software program can use the file. Although somewhat technical, understanding file extensions has become part of the modern language of the socially media savvy student and educator.

filtering: The process of filtering the Internet to minimize the risk of viruses and inappropriate content from reaching students and teachers. Many U.S. schools use CIPA as an excuse to indiscriminately block websites, but global collaboration typically requires flexible Internet filtering by IT staff.

Flat Learning Action talks (F.L.A.T.s): A short action-based presentation that uses both media and word to convey a message or share an idea.

folksonomy: A system that takes the entry of tags by users and makes meaning from the classifications. In folksonomy, users can tag any way they choose but some loose taxonomies are sometimes agreed upon by users to create meaning and share resources (e.g., the hashtag).

follow: To follow the updates of a person on a social media website. This is one-way communication in that you can follow a person and he or she may not follow you back.

freemium: A website or service that is free for basic features but can require payment to unlock advanced features or increased capacity. Typically, you will be asked before any charges are made to your account, which are usually put onto a credit card. Trialing a freemium service is typically a good way to see if you like a service before paying.

friending: The process of asking a person to friend you on a social website. This is a two-way relationship in which both people have to join into the relationship.

geotagging: The insertion of GPS coordinates into an electronic artifact.

global awareness: An awareness of the nuances of individual, social, cultural, and national differences between various parts of the world.

global collaboration: To work with someone in a location other than your own (typically in another country) to produce or create something.

global competence: The cross-cultural skills and understanding needed to communicate outside one's environment and to act on issues of global significance.

global positioning satellites (GPS) coordinates: Global positioning satellites triangulate off each other to determine the exact latitude and longitude of the position of a technology device that is GPS enabled.

"glocalization": The concept of thinking of an issue on a global basis but acting locally to improve that issue in one's local sphere of influence.

Google AdSense: A service that generates ads based on the words used on a webpage. This is one of many ad-supported services used to fund "free" sites in the hope that the money from "click-through" traffic will offset the cost of providing the service. Teachers must carefully monitor the "free" services using such advertising methods, because a teacher could be teaching how to write a term paper and Google AdSense could generate an ad selling term papers.

Great Firewall of China: The colloquial reference to the Golden Shield Project run by the Chinese government to censor and monitor Internet users within their borders.

handshake: The process of establishing strong connections between project participants.

hashtag: A word preceded by the number sign (#, called a *hash*) used to aggregate conversations on Twitter.

hidden curriculum: A term coined by Henry Jenkins in his MacArthur report *Confronting the Challenges of Participatory Culture* that refers to things learned by those with access to technology that are hidden from those without access.

higher-order thinking skills (HOTS): Higher-order thinking skills as defined by Bloom's Taxonomy.

home base: A place where students begin their online interactions within a course and that is the center of the online classroom.

ideational fluency: The ability to produce ideas to fulfill certain requirements

identity theft: Stealing personal information, typically with the intent to defraud.

intellectual property: A work that is the result of creativity to which one has rights. Typically one may apply for a patent, copyright, or trademark for this type of work.

interdisciplinary: Relating to more than one area of knowledge or subject/discipline.

International Baccalaureate (IB): Formerly the International Baccalaureate Organization (IBO), an international educational foundation headquartered in Geneva, Switzerland.

interpersonal skills: Skills required for relationships with other people.

intrapersonal skills: One's relationship with oneself.

intrinsic motivation: The incentive to take on an activity for the enjoyment of the activity itself rather than external benefits (or extrinsic motivation).

jigsaw: A cooperative learning strategy where each learner masters knowledge in a part of the learning puzzle and comes together with the other learners to share.

kaizen: A Japanese business philosophy of continuous improvement.

learning climate: The tone or atmosphere of the teaching setting.

Learning Commons: The creation of a common space for learning resources and learners with a strong consideration for aesthetics and diverse learning experiences.

learning environment: The spaces inhabited by students, such as learning centers, online spaces, and the materials, supplies, and resources available, including the administrative effect on that environment.

learning styles: Some researchers hypothesize that each person has preferred modalities (*see* VAK modalities) and that when multiple modalities are used in instructional design, learning is improved.

machinima: The use of 3D environments such as video games to create animated videos.

malware: Software intended to cause harm to a person's technology device. It can include spyware, Trojan horses, and viruses.

media diet: A constantly pruned set of publications that keeps people informed about what matters most to them professionally and personally.

meta-judge: An independent judge who reviews the work of other judges to determine overall winners.

micro blogging: A form of blogging that limits updates to just a few characters.

mp3: The standard file extension for a compressed music file.

Multiple Intelligence: Gardner's Theory of Multiple Intelligence was proposed by Howard Gardner in 1983; it hypothesizes that humans have many different forms of intelligence.

multisensory learning: Learning with more than one sense engaged.

netiquette: Internet etiquette.

new media: Communications methods that have arisen from the Internet and twenty-first century telecommunications technologies.

OAR (Open Archive Record): A data file ending in .oar as the file extension that includes everything in an Open Sim virtual world. Using this file type, one can catalog and save past virtual worlds and then use the server space for another purpose.

offshore outsource: To contract with a foreign entity to perform work in lieu of an inside source.

Open Sim: An open source virtual world program that is free for download and installation based on Second Life and undergirded by LSL (Linden Scripting Language).

outsource: (1) obtain (goods or a service) from an outside supplier, especially in place of an internal source; (2) contract (work) out.

overfriending: Indiscriminately adding friends to a social media site, which can result in negative consequences, including mixing groups of friends that are best treated separately. Overfriending is a problem for educators, particularly if they friend students and adults who can access each other depending on privacy settings.

overtweeting: Sending a large number of tweets that noticeably fill the Twitter stream of those who follow you. Some consider this rude and it typically results in being unfollowed.

Pareto's Principle: Named after Vilfredo Pareto, this "law of the vital few" states that approximately 80 percent of the effects come from 20 percent of the causes. It can be applied in the classroom. If 80 percent of learning happens from 20 percent of your activities as a teacher, what would happen if you did more of the most beneficial activities (the 20%)?

parody website: A website that appears authentic but is actually intended to be a humorous spoof.

peer-to-peer learning: Cooperative learning between peers. A terminology derived from peer-to-peer (p2p) networks that allow file sharing.

personal branding: Social media has resulted in the fact that individual people can be seen as a "brand" by other people online.

personal learning network (PLN): The creation of a network of resources or participation in an online network personalized to the specific needs of the individual learner.

pharming: A hyperlink that looks like it is taking you to one website but is really taking you to another. Sometimes just going to a malicious website is enough to install a virus on your computer. To watch for pharming, put your mouse over a hyperlink to see if the hyperlink that is spelled on a page is the actual link that you will go to.

phishing: An email claiming to be from a reputable source sent with the sole purpose of stealing personal information from the recipient.

Privacy Policy: A legal document that discloses how a party uses the data provided by customers or users.

problem-based learning: A pedagogical approach that is inquiry based and makes use of solving problems as the center of instructional design.

project-based learning: A pedagogical approach that is student centered and uses a project or open-ended assignment at the center of instructional design.

project manager: The person assuming responsibility for the management and output of a project as well as reporting on group dynamics and motivating team members to contribute.

project plan: A plan for the creation, management, and assessment of a project-based learning module in the classroom.

QR code: A quick response code that can be scanned by a mobile device to allow easy entry of data such as a website, phone number, or text.

render: This literally means "to cause to become." To render a file means to turn it from a file that can be opened in a software program (e.g., Audacity or iMovie) to a file that can be universally opened by others (e.g., an mp3 or a movie that can be seen on YouTube).

Reply: The function in email that allows responses to the person who sent the message.

Reply All: The function in email that replies to the person who sent the message and everyone else to whom the message was publicly sent (everyone listed in the To: and cc: fields of the original message).

research-based best practices: Classroom pedagogies that have been verified by research.

reverse mentor: The reversal of the typical mentoring relationship where a person who may be considered an authority figure learns from one with lesser formal authority.

rip: To remove a file from one source (like a CD or DVD) and move it to another location. While this can sometimes be done by electronic "pirates" it can also be done for legitimate classroom reasons and is an important skill for all movie makers and audio editors.

RSS: "Really Simple Syndication" or "Really Simple Subscription," this technology delivers information to a webpage or app that has subscribed to updates.

rubric: A scoring tool for subjective assessments with a set of criteria and standards linked to learning objectives.

sandbox: A time period where students are allowed to explore a tool while there is limited pressure to produce an outcome.

screenshot: A picture of the screen of a technological device.

search engine–enabled Socratic teaching: Teaching with questions where students are allowed to search for answers using search engines.

Second Life: Founded by Linden Labs, this virtual world has typically been the de facto standard for virtual world environments hosted in online servers.

serendipity: An aptitude for making desirable discoveries seemingly by accident.

simulated synchronous: An environment that is asynchronous but is designed to "feel" synchronous or live to participants. Innovations in this area help participants "feel" the energy of a live connection without the live connection actually happening.

social networking: The use of an online network to connect, share, and communicate with other people.

Socratic teaching: The method of teaching by asking questions; first used by Socrates.

sounding board: A person or group whose reactions to suggested ideas are used as a test of their validity or potential for success before they are made public.

spam: Unwanted email or electronic communications.

spammer: A person or organization that sends unwanted email.

spyware: Software installed on a computer, usually through a webpage, that spies on the actions and behavior of the user; often the first step leading to further harm or identity theft.

standard messaging service (SMS): The delivery of text-only messages to a mobile phone.

student summit: A real-time gathering of students to share learning, take action, and celebrate the work done together. This can be done online in a virtual classroom or virtual world.

synchronous communications: Communicating with another person in real time.

tablet device: A device that is typically a flat standalone unit that allows one to access the web and interact with other resources via wireless or sync technologies.

tag: A term used to label a piece of information or artifact. Typically created for retrieval, cataloging, archiving, and aggregating meaning, tagging has evolved into many types of tags. including the hashtag used on social media sites. An artifact may have many tags.

tag cloud: The process of taking tags and organizing them graphically so that tags used with more frequency are of a larger proportionate size than those used less frequently.

tagging standard: An agreed-on method of tagging or taxonomy, often based on a course of study.

taxonomy: A system of classification that uses standards allowing the sharing and standardization of information. As people agree on standard tags to use in social media, a taxonomy emerges.

teacherpreneur: A teacher who creates intellectually profitable learning experiences customized to student learning needs and accepts accountability for the outcome.

teachersourcing: A practice involving a group of teachers who come together to provide monitoring and maintenance functions in online learning environments to provide an ongoing, visible role of teachers in a learning community.

technopersonal communications: Personal relationships where technology is the channel of communication. Technology adds context and meaning to communications beyond that which the original sender may have intended and requires a level of proficiency in the technology to prevent misunderstandings and promote accurate dialog.

Terms of Service (TOS): The terms that users agree to in order to use a service. If a user disagrees or does not comply with the terms, the service can be discontinued without notice.

terraforming: The act of shaping land, typically in a virtual 3D world.

think-pair-share: A cooperative learning strategy developed by Frank Lyman beginning with a thought-provoking prompt, then pairing with a partner to discuss answers and observations, and afterward sharing findings with the larger group.

To: Who an email message is sent to. Every email requires one To: recipient, so when sending to a large group, send it to yourself and blind copy the others to protect their privacy.

transdisciplinary: The crossing of and joining together of many disciplines to create a holistic approach.

transparency: The practice of openly disclosing motivations, associations, and relationships in an ethical way that inspires trust in online spaces. This often implies you share publicly and don't hide in private spaces. It means everyone can see through you—you've disclosed everything.

Trojan horse: This type of program installs a "back door" that lets a person get onto your technology device. These often "pretend" to be something they are not (e.g., antivirus software, a free game, or screensaver) and get the user to click install.

troll: This Internet slang is a derogatory term for a person who posts inflammatory, wasteful, or off-topic messages in an online community.

tweet: A single 140-character (or less) message sent through Twitter.

Twitter list: A list of people on Twitter. By following the list, you can go to the lists page and see what the people on that list are doing without having to follow them.

un-conference: An un-conference is a facilitated, participant-driven conference centered on a theme or purpose.

unfollow: When someone unsubscribes and will no longer receive your updates.

Universal Design for Learning (UDL): An instructional method designed to present information and content in different ways, differentiate the ways that students can express what they know, and stimulate interest and motivation for learning.

URL shortener: An online service that shortens the website address into a more succinct or easy to remember web address. This works using a service called URL forwarding. You have to be careful because sometimes shortened URLs are actually pharming ploys.

userid: Also called a username, this is an identifying name of a person on a technology-enabled system.

VAK modalities: Visual, Auditory, and Kinesthetic modalities that help educators design learning to reach all types of learning styles.

video compression: To reduce the quality and quantity of data typically in order to upload and share video online.

virtual world: A 3D multidimensional environment created or hosted on a server that allows users to create avatars and interact in a customized environment.

virus: A program that makes a technological device not function properly.

walled garden: A closed set of information services for users. In education, this usually refers to not allowing outsiders to access or see any online activity of students in the school.

.wav: The standard file extension for a music file on a CD.

Web 2.0 Smackdown: Term originated by Vicki Davis. Participants have a short time frame to share an idea, a tool, or a class example using Web 2.0 technology.

Web 2 Kung Fu: Term originated by Vicki Davis in Beijing, China, for a speed sharing activity. It is a method to allow audience members to share quickly with each other their favorite tools and their uses in the classroom.

web quest: An inquiry-based activity where some or all of the information comes from web-based resources.

white list: A list of email addresses or websites that can always be accessed through a firewall.

wiki: Taken from the word meaning "quickly" in Hawaiian, wikis were invented by Ward Cunningham and are a fast way for multiple people to create a webpage document together while tracking changes and contributions of each member of the page.

wiki war: This occurs sometimes when more than one person is editing a wiki page and work is lost by the person who saves first; also called "edit wars.".

word cloud: The process of taking the words in a document and organizing them graphically so that words used with more frequency are of a large proportionate size than those used less frequently.

PREFACE

1. Flat Classroom Certified Teacher. (n.d.). *Flat Classroom Certified Teacher*. Retrieved June 3, 2011, from http://fcpteacher .flatclassroomproject.org

2. Davis, H. (2011, June 2). Connect yourself: Build a learning pathway: Teach less learn more. Retrieved June 2, 2011, from http://teachlesslearnmore.edublogs.org/2011/06/02 /connect-yourself-build-a-learning-pathway

CHAPTER 1

1. Flat Classroom Conference: A Vision of the Future. (2009, September 15). Retrieved May 1, 2011, from http://youtu.be /A6X3uFYBRDA

2. Ramos, Steve (2009, February 7). Being back in Houston Texas for about a week and a half. Retrieved May 30, 2011, from Flat Classroom Conference Ning, http:// flatclassroomconference.ning.com/profiles/blogs /being-back-in-houston-texas

3. Singleton, M. (2009, September 28). Miller's "The World Is Flat" reflective blog post. Retrieved May 30, 2011, from Flat Classroom Project Ning, http://flatclassroomproject.ning .com/profiles/blogs/millers-the-world-is-flat

4. Friedman, T. L. (2005, 2006). *The world is flat* (Vol. 2, p. 8). London: Penguin Group.

5. Tye, K. (2003). World view: Global education as a worldwide movement. Retrieved July 31, 2010, from http://www.questia .com/googleScholar.qst?docId=50020

6. Marks, O. (2009, July 10). Global collaboration competitive success: Old dogs, new tricks and the shift index. Retrieved July 31, 2010, from http://www.zdnet.com/blog/collaboration /global-collaboration-competitive-success-old-dogs- new-tricks-the-shift-index/728

7. Coughlin, E., & Kajder, S. (n.d.). The impact of collaborative, scaffolded learning in K–12 schools: A meta-analysis. Retrieved July 30, 2010, from http://www.cisco.com/web/ about/citizenship/socio-economic/docs/Metiri_Classroom_ Collaboration_Research.pdf

8. Ito, M. (2008, November 15). White paper: Living and learning with new media: Summary of findings from the digital youth project. Retrieved July 30, 2010, from http://digital youth.ischool.berkeley.edu/report

9. The transformation of education through collaboration. (n.d.). Retrieved July 31, 2010, from https://learning network.cisco.com/servlet/JiveServlet/download/6757-5 -8682/Transformational_Instruction.pdf

10. Hargadon, S. (2009, December 16). Educational networking: The important role Web 2.0 will play in education. Retrieved July 31, 2010, from http://www.scribd.com/doc/24161189 /Educational-Networking-The-Important-Role-Web-2-0- Will-Play-in-Education

11. Coughlin & Kajder, The impact of collaborative, scaffolded learning in K–12 schools.

12. Reed, J. (n.d.). Global collaboration and learning— EDTECH: Focus on K–12. *Welcome to EDTECH™*. Retrieved April 6, 2011, from http://www.edtechmag.com /k12/events/updates/global-collaboration-and-learning .html

13. Cofino, K. (2010, March 20). Creating a culture of collaboration through technology integration. Retrieved April 6, 2011, from http://kimcofino.com/blog/2010/03/20/creating- a-culture-of-collaboration-through-technology-integration

14. Partnership for 21st Century Skills. (2004). Collaboration skills. Retrieved June 21, 2010, from Partnership for 21st Century Skills: http://www.p21.org/index.php?option=com_content& task=view&id=263&Itemid=132

15. International Society for Technology in Education. (n.d.). Standards. Retrieved April 6, 2011, from http://www.iste.org

16. Lindsay, J. (2006, October 13). Re: *My students weigh in on Friedman's flat world* [Web log comment]. Retrieved May 31, 2010, from Cool Cat Teacher Blog: http://coolcatteacher .blogspot.com/2006/10/my-students-weigh-in-on-friedmans- flat.html

17. Gragert, E. (2009, August 15). Education update: Preparing Latino students for college success. Retrieved July 30, 2010, from http://www.ascd.org/publications/newsletters /education-update/aug09/vol51/num08/Guest-Editorial.aspx

18. Lindner, M. (n.d.). Edward T. Hall's cultural iceberg. Retrieved June 3, 2011, from http://www.constantforeigner .com/iceberg-model.html

19. Story contributed by David Truss, http://pairadimes .davidtruss.com, http://about.me/davidtruss

20. Hagel, J., Brown, J. S., & Davidson, L. (2010). *The power of pull* (p. 26) [Kindle edition]. New York: Basic Books.

21. Friedman, *The world is flat*.

22. International Cyberfair. (n.d.). Retrieved May 7, 2011, from http://www.globalschoolnet.org/gsncf

23. Lindsay, J. (2006, December 15). Flat Classroom Conversations: Part 3. Retrieved April 6, 2011, from http://123elearning .blogspot.com/2006/12/flat-classroom-conversations-part-3 .html

24. Pink, D. H. (2006). *A whole new mind: Why right-brainers will rule the future*. New York: Riverhead Books.

25. Service Learning. (n.d.). Retrieved June 3, 2011, from http:// www.iseek.org/education/service-learning.html

26. Horizon Report. (n.d.). Retrieved May 7, 2011, from http:// www.nmc.org/horizon

27. NMC. (n.d.). Retrieved April 6, 2011, from http://www.nmc .org

28. What Is EDUCAUSE? (n.d.). Retrieved April 6, 2011, from http://www.educause.edu

29. Eracism—Flat Classroom Conference. (n.d.). Retrieved April 6, 2011, from http://flatclassroomconference.ning.com /video/eracism-1

30. Information Technology in a Global Society (ITGS) for the International Baccalaureate Diploma.

31. Zilber, E. (2009). *Third culture kids: The children of educators in international schools*. Woodbridge: John Catt Educational.

32. Terry Freedman is an independent educational ICT consultant in the UK. He publishes the ICT in Education website at www.ictineducation.org and an e-zine, Computers in Classrooms, at www.ictineducation.org/newsletter. He is also an educational advisor for Flat Classroom.

33. Dr. John Turner is an international educator, originally Head of Technology at Presbyterian Ladies College, Melbourne, for many years. He is currently Head of Educational Technology at the Canadian International School, Hong Kong. He is also an educational advisor for Flat Classroom.

CHAPTER 2

1. Warlick, D. (2006, 24 June). Flat world, flat web, Flat Classrooms. Retrieved June 21, 2010, from http://www .slideshare.net/dwarlick/flat-world-flat-web-flat-classrooms . Slide 10.

2. Brian Mannix is also a Flat Classroom Certified teacher, having graduated from the 10-3 pilot class.

3. Leader of the year. (n.d.). Retrieved April 6, 2011, from http://www.techlearning.com/section/LeaderoftheYear

4. Gee, J. P. (n.d.) New digital media and learning as an emerging area and "worked examples" as one way forward, p. 41. Retrieved June 1, 2011, from http://www.scribd.com/doc/18943052/New-Digital-Media-and-Learning-as-an-Emerging-Area-and-Worked-Examples-as-One-Way-Forward

5. According to a personal interview with Vicki Davis, October 28, 2010.

6. For citizen scientists. (n.d.). Retrieved June 1, 2011, from http://science.nasa.gov/citizen-scientists

7. Constructivism. (n.d.). Retrieved June 4, 2011, from http://www.funderstanding.com/content/constructivism

8. Siemens, G. (2004, December 12). Connectivism: A learning theory for the digital age. Retrieved June 4, 2011, from http://www.elearnspace.org/Articles/connectivism.htm

9. Read Craig Union's complete research dissertation as well as excerpts: http://tinyurl.com/fcbookresearch1

10. Levinson, D. J. (1950). *The authoritarian ethnocentrism*. New York: Harper & Brothers.

11. Papert, S. (1993). *The children's machine: Rethinking school in the age of the computer.* New York: Basic Books; Papert, S. (1993). *Mindstorms* (2nd ed.). New York: Basic Books.

12. Friedman, T. L. (2007). *The world is flat: A brief history of the twenty-first century* (3rd ed.). New York: Picador.

13. References for this research summary can be found at the end of the "Short version" abstract: http://tinyurl.com/fcbookresearch1

14. See a current list at http://tinyurl.com/flatclassroomresearch

CHAPTER 3

1. Herold, D. M., & Fedor, D. B. (2008). The realities of change. In *Change the way you lead change: Leadership strategies that really work* (p. 13). Stanford, CA: Stanford Business Books.

2. Lewis, C. S. (n.d.). C.S. Lewis. Retrieved August 26, 2011 from http://www.famousquotes.com

3. Fahmy, S. (2010, January 13). Self-control is contagious, study finds. Retrieved January 15, 2010, from http://www.physorg.com/news182627098.html

4. Rizzolatti, G., et al. (1996). Premotor cortex and the recognition of motor actions. *Cognitive Behavior Research* (3), 131–141.

5. Blowers, H. (2006, August). 23 things. Retrieved June 1, 2010, from http://plcmcl2-things.blogspot.com

6. Louis, K. S., & Marks, H. M. (1998). Does professional community affect the classroom? Teachers' work and student experiences in restructuring schools. *American Journal of Education, 106,* 532–575.

7. Tracy, Brian. *Five tips for creating successful habits*. Retrieved June 2, 2011, from http://www.timeforlifenow.com/blog/business-development/five-tips-for-creating-successful-habits

8. Hagel, J., Brown, J. S., & Davison, L. (2010). *The power of pull* (p. 35) [Kindle edition]. New York: Basic Books.

9. Bergman, Michael K.. (2001, August). White paper: The deep web: Surfacing hidden value. *Journal of electronic publishing.* 7(1). Retrieved from http://hdl.handle.net/2027/spo.3336451.0007.104

10. Hagel, Brown, & Davison, 9.

11. For more information on RSS Readers, see RSS Tutorial http://rss-tutorial.com/rss-select-an-rss-reader.htm.

12. "How to Develop a Brand Monitoring Platform (for Free)" by Trevor Jonas of Social Media Today covers this topic effectively. Administrators reading this text should consider setting up a Brand Monitoring Platform as part of their challenge for this Section. (See http://www.socialmedia today.com/SMC/190607.) This topic is covered briefly in the chapter on designing a flat classroom project under the topic "Harnessing Social Media to Facilitate Grassroots Connections."

13. Hurst, M. (2007). *Bit literacy.* (p. 65) [Kindle edition]. New York: Good Experience Press.

14. Sadoski, M., & Paivio, A. (2004). A dual coding theoretical model of reading. In R. B. Ruddell & N. J. Unrau (Eds.), *Theoretical models and processes of reading* (5th ed., pp. 1329–1362). Newark, DE: International Reading Association.

15. Winograd, D. (2010, June 1). The iPad could be the best mobile accessibility device on the market. Retrieved June 20, 2010, from http://www.tuaw.com/2010/06/01/the-ipad-could-be-the-best-mobile-accessibility-device-on-the-ma

16. Hagel, Brown, & Davison, *The power of pull,* 22.

17. MI Champions Grant. (n.d.). Retrieved June 14, 2011, from http://www.macul.org/grantsawards/michampionsgrant

18. Gamerman, E. (2008, February). "What makes Finnish kids so smart." Retrieved from http://online.wsj.com/public/article/SB120425355065601997.html 3/11/2010

19. Confronting the challenges of participatory culture. (n.d.) McArthur Report, p. 3.

20. For more on technology ecology, see Confronting the challenges of participatory culture, McArthur Report, p. 8.

21. Email to Vicki Davis, used with permission.

22. Johnsen, W. H. Retrieved June 2, 2011, from http://quotationsbook.comquote/35768/#axzz1OBTP0pBN

23. Lindsay, J. (2008, May 12). Are you really there?? Retrieved June 11, 2011, from http://123elearning.blogspot.com/2008/05/are-you-really-there.html

24. Davis, V. (2010, April 22). Cool cat teacher blog: Class chats: Connecting elementary kids in powerful ways (Spread the word!). Retrieved August 26, 2011, from http://coolcatteacher.blogspot.com/2010/04/class-chats-connecting-elementary-kids.html

25. Hellyer, C. (n.d.). Horizon Project sounding board review. Retrieved June 5, 2011, from http://taradaleint.wikispaces.com/Sounding+Board+Peer+Review

26. Hellyer, C. (2007, March 26). Peer review for The Horizon Project. Retrieved June 11, 2011, from http://teachingsagittarian.com/2007/05/peer-review-for-the-horizon-project

27. Hellyer, C. (2009, August 10). Skype tips virtual room 231. Retrieved June 11, 2011, from http://inside.isb.ac.th/rm231/skype-tips

28. Hellyer, C. (n.d.). Horizon Project sounding board review. Retrieved June 5, 2011, from http://taradaleint.wikispaces.com/flatclassroom+project+soundingboard+review

29. Hellyer, C. (2010, March 6). Student projects—Flat Classroom 2010, Mumbai, India. Retrieved June 11, 2011, from http://teachingsagittarian.com/2010/03/student-projects-flat-classroom-2010-mumbai-india

CHAPTER 4

1. Jenkins, H. (2009). *Confronting the challenges of participatory media* (p. 41) [Kindle edition]. Cambridge, MA: MIT Press.

2. von Wahlde, N. (2010, October 26). Our first day in Prague. Retrieved April 10, 2011, from http://elementaryflatclassroom.wordpress.com/2010/10/26/our-first-day-in-prague. Nancy vonWahlde is a Flat Classroom certified teacher and wrote this while helping to pilot the first "A Week in the Life . . ." Elementary School Flat Classroom Project in 2010.

3. Tina Schmidt, third-grade teacher, St. Ignatius of Antioch School, Yardley, PA.

4. Choi, J. (2008, May 11). Day 57—Desperation. Retrieved July 31, 2010, from http://horizonproject2008.ning.com/profiles/blogs/1990909:BlogPost:22359?id=1990909%3ABlogPost%3A22359&page=2#comments. Note: This Ning is now defunct.

5. Communication theory and multicellular biology—*Integrative Biology* (RSC Publishing). (n.d.). Retrieved June 15, 2011, from http://pubs.rsc.org/en/Content/ArticleLanding/2011/IB/c0ib00117a

6. Cauchon, C. (1994, September 1). Whistler's mutter. Retrieved December 6, 2010, from http://psychologytoday.com/articles/199409

7. http://quotecosmos/subjects/1098/Self-talk. Retrieved December 6, 2010.

8. Retrieved December 6, 2010, from http://psychology.about.com/od/educationalpsychology/ss/multiple-intell_8.htm

9. Cauchon.

10. Carnegie, D. (1936, revised 1981). *How to win friends and influence people*. New York: Simon & Schuster.

11. Cherry, K. (n.d.). Interpersonal intelligence—Multiple intelligences. Retrieved June 15, 2011, from http://psychology.about.com/od/educationalpsychology/ss/multiple-intell_7.htm

12. Jenkins, *Confronting the challenges*, pp. 41–49.

13. Mehrabian, A., & Weiner, M. (1967). Decoding of inconsistent communications. *Journal of personality and social psychology*, 6(1), 109–114. doi:10.1037/h0024532. PMID 6032751

14. Seigenthaler, J. (2005, November 29). A false wikipedia story. *USA Today*.

15. Wikipedia to Require Contributors to Register. (2005, December 6). National Public Radio. Talk of the Nation story summary and radio broadcast.

16. http://www.ala.org/ala/aboutala/offices/olos/olosprograms/preconferences/docs/info_lit_standards.pdf. Retrieved December 6, 2010.

17. http://www.focalpointglobal.org; http://www.globaleducationconference.com/recordings.html; https://sas.elluminate.com/drtbl?sid=gec2010&suidD; http://www.focalpointglobal.org

18. Jayson, S. (2009, January 29). From business to fun: What different generations do online. Retrieved November 28, 2010, from http://www.usatoday.com/tech/webguide/internetlife/2009-01-28-online-generations_N.htm

19. 25% of teens use social networking daily and 11% use email daily. (2009, September). Pew Research Center's Internet & American Life Project surveys; Lenhart, A. (2010, November 30). Facebook messages—Some say it's an "email killer," others disagree; Pew internet data shows us where email stands today among youth. Retrieved from http://www.pewinternet.org/Commentary/2010/November/Pew-Internet-Data-Provides-Context-for-the-Facebook-Messages-Announcement.aspx

20. Nurmi, N. (2010). World-wide work stress: Multi-case study of the stress-coping process in distributed work, p. 51. Retrieved from http://lib.tkk.fi/Diss/2010/isbn9789526033563/isbn9789526033563.pdf

21. Davis, V., Oakes, C., Peters, S., Wagner, J., & Hammond, D. (2007, October 2003). Women of Web 2.0 show #44. Retrieved July 31, 2010, from http://edtechtalk.com/node/2337

22. Mannix, Brian. (2010, December 6). Personal Interview via email.

23. Taxonomy is the process of classification and is used by scientists, librarians, and people from just about every field. In this case, we are classifying students. It is an excellent juxtaposition to the concept of folksonomy or meaning that emerges as many people classify data according to their own thought process.

24. Eric von Hippel, MIT Professor, as quoted in Kaufman, W., (n.d.). Crowd sourcing turns business on its head, NPR, retrieved December 6, 2010.

25. Howe, J. (June 2006). The rise of crowdsourcing. *Wired*. Retrieved December 6, 2010, from http://www.wired.com/wired/archive/14.06/crowds.html

26. For more on outsourcing, read *The four hour workweek* by Timothy Ferris.

27. We use Clocklink (http://clocklink.com) to insert a clock and appropriate time zone on the home page of each wiki.

28. Lenhart, A., Sousan, A., Smith, A., & Macgill, A. (2008, April). Writing technology and teens (p. 6). Retrieved July 31, 2010, from http://www.pewinternet.org/Reports/2008/Writing-Technology-and-Teens.aspx

29. Ibid., p. 4.

30. Fresco, A. (2005, October 13). Texting teenagers are proving "more literate than ever before." Retrieved from http://www.timesonline.co.uk./tol/life_and_style/education/article584810.ece.

31. Ibid.

32. See the article "American and British English differences" on Wikipedia for more information at http://en.wikipedia.org/wiki/American_and_British_English_differences.

33. See a complete list of David Barton's Words that could be confusing and embarrassing in the U.K. and United States at http://www.systms.demon.co.uk/ukus.htm

34. In our first article that we wrote together, Julie and Vicki had a battle over *analyze* until they realized that both spellings were correct. Now, they determine the primary audience to determine the form of English used.

35. Whitaker, T. (2004). *What great teachers do differently* (pp. 115–116). Larchmont, NY: Eye on Education.

36. Darley, J. M., & Latané, B. (1968). Bystander intervention in emergencies: Diffusion of responsibility. *Journal of personality and social psychology, 8*, 377–383.

37. Kitty Genovese was a victim of a stabbing by a serial rapist and murderer during a half hour attack that was witnessed by as many as 38 witnesses who failed to intervene. The fact that everyone saw many people observing caused everyone involved not to intervene in the event.

38. Manning, R., Levine, M., & Collins, A. (2007). The Kitty Genovese murder and the social psychology of helping: The parable of the 38 witnesses. *American Psychologist, 62*, 555–562. (PDF, 149 kb)

39. Choi, Day 57—Desperation.

CHAPTER 5

1. Couros, A. (2007, December 3). Understanding digital citizenship. Retrieved July 30, 2010, from http://educationaltechnology.ca/couros/721

2. Rheingold, H. (2002). *Smart mobs: The next social revolution*. Cambridge, MA: Basic Books.

3. Tapscott, D. (2008). The net generation comes of age. In *Grown up digital: How the net generation is changing your world* (p. 9). New York: McGraw-Hill.

4. Internet Crime Complaint Center. (n.d.). Internet crime prevention tips. Retrieved August 3, 2010, from Internet Crime Complaint Center: http://www.ic3.gov/preventiontips.aspx

5. Available at http://www.cafepress.com/coolcatteacher. All rights reserved, Cool Cat Teacher, LLC. Used with permission from Cool Cat Teacher, LLC.

6. Creative Commons, (2011). Retrieved August 11, 2011, from http://creativecommons.org.

7. Creative Commons license choice. (2011). Retrieved August 11, 2011, from http://creativecommons.org/choose

8. Churches, A. (n.d.). Digital citizen AUA. *Edorigami*. Retrieved June 15, 2011, from http://edorigami.wikispaces.com/Digital+Citizen+AUA

9. *Cerveza* is Spanish for "beer." Retrieved June 15, 2011 from http://en.wikipedia.org/wiki/Cerveza.

10. Available from http://iste.org at http://www.iste.org/images/excerpts/DIGCIT-excerpt.pdf

11. Media and technology resources for educators. (n.d.). Retrieved June 15, 2011, from http://www.commonsensemedia.org/educators
12. EAST Initiative. (n.d.). Retrieved June 15, 2011, from http://www.eastinitiative.org/howeastworks/Research.aspx
13. Dionne, J. (n.d.). Retrieved June 15, 2011, from http://www.pikifriends.net
14. Virtual world digital citizenship for middle schoolers. (2008). Retrieved June 15, 2011, from http://digiteen2008.wikispaces.com/Virtual+World+Digital+Citizenship+for+Middle+Schoolers
15. St. Stephen High School (2010). Retrieved June 15, 2011, from http://digiteen10-2.flatclassroomproject.org/St.+Stephen+High+School
16. Super social safety team 2009-2010 computer fundamentals class, W. S. (2009). Retrieved June 15, 2011, from https://docs.google.com/View?id=ah4zsdj46b66_32c853ngg7
17. Ibid.
18. EAST > About & Contact. (n.d.). Retrieved September 3, 2011, from http://www.eastinitiative.org/AboutContact
19. EAST Initiative. (n.d.). Eureka springs robotics team wins PTC design award. Retrieved June 15, 2011, from http://www.eastproject.org/NewsUpdates/NewsStory.aspx?Id=903
20. EAST Initiative. (n.d.) Student PSA featured by Craig O'Neill. Retrieved June 15, 2011, from http://www.eastproject.org/NewsUpdates/NewsStory.aspx?Id=896
21. Mtn. Pine EAST students documenting effects of oil spill (2010), Retrieved June 15, 2011, from http://www.eastproject.org/NewsUpdates/NewsStory.aspx?Id=967
22. All referenced studies may be found at http://www.eastinitiative.org/howeastworks/Research.aspx

CHAPTER 6

1. Retrieved from http://www.quotesdaddy.com/quote/785040/ryunosuke-satoro/individually-we-are-one-drop-together-we-are-an-ocean
2. Cox, C., & Cuvelier, C. (2006, December 13). Virtual communication. Retrieved September 3, 2011, from http://flatclassroomproject2006.wikispaces.com/Virtual+Communication
3. Collaborative contribution. (n.d.). Retrieved October 22, 2011, from http://collaboration.wikia.com/wiki/Collaborative_contribution
4. Ibid.
5. Klossner, J. (2010, April 22). I lurk, therefore I am. Retrieved July 31, 2010, from http://fcw.com/blogs/john-klossner/2010/04/john-klossner-social-network-lurking.aspx
6. Current statistics can be found at http://www.messagelabs.co.U.K./intelligence.aspx
7. Shernoff, D. J., Csikszentmihalyi, M., Schneider, B., & Shernoff, E. S. (2003). Student engagement in high school classrooms from the perspective of flow theory. *School Psychology Quarterly, 18,* 158–176. Retrieved July 13, 2010, from http://www.cedu.niu.edu/~shernoff/pdf/shernoff.spq.pdf
8. Retrieved July 31, 2010, from http://digiteen.ning.com
9. Retrieved July 31, 2010, from http://digiteen.ning.com/forum/topics/will-technology-be-the-key-to
10. Retrieved July 31, 2010, from http://digiteen.ning.com/forum/topics/what-is-digital-literacy
11. Tapscott, D. (2008). *Wikinomics S.l* (p. 18). New York: Penguin.
12. Wenger, E. (2006). Communities of practice. Retrieved April 6, 2011, from http://www.ewenger.com/theory/http://www.ewenger.com/theory
13. Retrieved April 16, 2011, from http://collaboration.wikia.com/wiki/collaborative_media
14. For example, the Ning platform went to a user-pays model in August 2010; Wikispaces provides a free model but the umbrella private label service is far superior and conducive to managing projects.
15. Kaplan, S. (2002). Building communities—Strategies for collaborative learning. Retrieved April 6, 2011, from http://www.astd.org/LC/2002/0802_kaplan.htm
16. Devaney, L. (2010, March 16). Digital access, collaboration a must for students. Retrieved April 6, 2011, from http://www.eschoolnews.com/2010/03/16/digital-access-collaboration-a-must-for-students/?ast=55
17. Tapscott, *Wikinomics.*
18. Retrieved from http://qataracademy-it.wikispaces.com/Grade+10#Grade%2010%20Information%20Technology-The%207%20%27Cs%27%20for%20Surviving%20the%20Flat%20Classroom%20Project-Contribute
19. Index of Quick Guides. (2005). Retrieved April 7, 2011, from pre2005.flexiblelearning.net.au/guides
20. Warlick, David. (2010, October 20). Flat Classroom 10-3 keynote—Flat Classroom Project. Retrieved April 16, 2011, from http://flatclassroomproject.ning.com/video/david-warlick-flat-classroom
21. Freedman, T. (n.d.). 2008 keynote—Embedded flatness. Retrieved April 16, 2011, from http://flatclassroomproject2008.wikispaces.com/keynote
22. Bonk, Curt. (2009, October 8). Bonk's The world is open: FCP 2009-3 keynote—Flat Classroom Project. April 16, 2011, from http://flatclassroomproject.ning.com/video/curtbonkdr-curt-bonks-the
23. Keynote: No future left behind. (2009, March 4). Retrieved from http://www.youtube.com/watch?v=kra_z9vMnHo
24. The student perspective—Will it be done by you, or to you? (2010, May 3). Retrieved April 16, 2011, from http://flatclassroomproject.ning.com/video/flat-classroom-project-keynote
25. Retrieved April 16, 2011, from http://flatclassroom10-3a.flatclassroomproject.org/message/view/Wireless+Connectivity/29044011
26. Barbara Stefanics, meta-judge for Flat Classroom Project 09-3. http://flatclassroom09-3.flatclassroomproject.org/Awards
27. Torsten Otto, meta-judge for Flat Classroom Project 09-2. http://flatclassroom09-2.flatclassroomproject.org/Awards
28. Retrieved April 16, 2011, from http://netgened2010.flatclassroomproject.org/Teams
29. Retrieved April 16, 2011, from http://coolcatteacher.blogspot.com/2011/03/web-20-leadership-for-students.html
30. http://www.animoto.com
31. Retrieved April 16, 2011, from http://flatclassroom09-3.flatclassroomproject.org/Introductions
32. D-a-l-i-a-n - H-a-n-d-s-h-a-k-e . (2011, March 31). Retrieved April 16, 2011, from http://flatclassroomproject.ning.com/video/dalian-handshake
32. Retrieved from http://tinyurl.com/yaraprofile
33. Diigo is currently blocked in China, but the RSS feed from Diigo bookmarks can be accessed.
34. Retrieved April 16, 2011, from http://digiteen10-3b.flatclassroomproject.org/Tagging+Standards
35. Open Source Video Platform. (n.d.). *Kaltura.* Retrieved April 16, 2011, from http://corp.kaltura.com
36. A typical rubric set http://flatclassroom10-3a.flatclassroomproject.org/Rubrics
37. Created collaboratively by Phil Macoun, Aspengrove School, Canada, and other Digiteen 2008 teachers (a Flat Classroom Project). http://digiteen2008.wikispaces.com. Available online at http://tinyurl.com/digiteen08rubric
38. Retrieved June 13, 2011, from an email sent to Julie. Used with permission.
39. Retrieved June 13, 2011, from http://flatclassroomproject.ning.com/profiles/blogs/2010-whs-student-reflective

40. Macoun, P. (2008, October 25). Digi Teen stories. Retrieved June 13, 2011, from http://macoun.edublogs.org/2008/10/25/digi-teen-stories

41. Retrieved from http://flatclassroomproject.ning.com/profiles/blogs/928031:BlogPost:13290

CHAPTER 7

1. Hall, T., Strangman, N., & Meyer, A. (2009, November 2). Differentiated instruction and implications for UDL implementation. Retrieved December 31, 2010, from http://aim.cast.org/learning/historyarchive/backgroundpapers/differentiated_instruction_udl

2. Boaler, J. (1998). *Open and closed mathematics approaches: Student experiences and understandings journal for research in mathematics education, 29*(1), 41–62.

3. Edutopia staff. (2001, November 1). PBL research summary: Studies validate project-based learning. Retrieved December 31, 2010, from http://www.edutopia.org/project-based-learning-research

4. Sadoski, M., & Paivio, A. (2004). A dual coding theoretical model of reading. In R. B. Ruddell & N. J. Unrau (Eds.), *Theoretical models and processes of reading* (5th ed., pp. 1329–1362). Newark, DE: International Reading Association.

5. Pavio, A. (n.d.). Dual coding theory. Retrieved December 31, 2010, from http://tip.psychology.org/paivio.html

6. Bradford, John. (n.d.). Using multisensory teaching methods. Retrieved December 31, 2010, from http://www.dyslexia-parent.com/mag30.html

7. Gardner, H. (1983, 1993). *Frames of mind: The theory of multiple intelligences.* New York: Basic Books.

8. Retrieved from http://www.howardgardner.com/docs/Can%20Technology%20Exploit%20Our%20Many%20Ways%20of%20Knowing.pdf

9. Visser, B. et al. (2006, September–October). "g" and the measurement of multiple intelligences: A response to Gardner, *Intelligence, 34*(5),507–510.

10. Information on Eugene Griessman retrieved December 31, 2010, from http://www.presidentlincoln.com/Brochure-5pages-Ring.pdf

11. Ibid.

12. Ibid., p. 13.

13. Maiers, A., & Sandvold, A. (2010). *The passion-driven classroom: a framework for teaching & learning.* Larchmont, NY: Eye on Education.

14. Friedman, T. L. (2007). *The world is flat* (p. 314). New York: Farrar, Straus and Giroux.

15. Bloom's revised taxonomy of higher order thinking. (n.d.). Retrieved December 31, 2010 from http://www.kurwongbss.eq.edu.au/thinking/Bloom/blooms.htm

16. Autor, D. H., Levy, F., & Murnane, R. J. (2003, November). The skill content of recent technological change: An empirical exploration, *Quarterly Journal of Economics, 11*(4), 1279–1333. Charts available at http://www7.nationalacademies.org/cfe/Technological_Change_and_Job_Polarization_Presentation_PDF.pdf

17. Keller, Helen. (n.d.).1-love-quotes.com. Retrieved August 29, 2011, from http://www.1-love-quotes.cpm/quote/893231

18. Retrieved from http://www.nuance.com/dragon/index.htm

19. Brian, M. (2011). Stevie Wonder sings Steve Jobs' praises for iOS accessibility. Retrieved October 20, 2011, from http://thenextweb.com/apple/2011/09/15/stevie-wonder-sings-steve-jobs-praises-for-ios-accessbility

20. Whitaker, T. (2004). *What great teachers do differently: Fourteen things that matter most* (p. 55). Larchmont, NY: Eye on Education.

21. Israel, S. E. (2009). *Breakthroughs in literacy: teacher success stories and strategies, grades K–8* (p. 194). San Francisco: Jossey-Bass.

22. Breaux, A. L., & Whitaker, T. (2010). *50 ways to improve student behavior: simple solutions to complex challenges* (p. 83). Larchmont, NY: Eye On Education.

23. Retrieved August 29, 2011, from http://www.telegraph.co.uk/news/uknews/1380915/Computers-to-replace-teachers.html

24. Goebel, J. (2008). *Reimagining education* (p. 85). ONEFamily Outreach, LLC.

25. Laptops vs. lectures, Let's ban lectures! Retrieved August 29, 2011, from http://itmanagement.earthweb.com/columns/article.php/3870346/Laptops-vs-Lectures-Lets-Ban-Lectures.htm

26. Proof that the best of us can be taken: Microsoft Firefox professional. (2007, February 12). Retrieved January 1, 2011, from http://coolcatteacher.blogspot.com/2007/02/awful-offensive-advertising-for.html

27. Halpin and Croft, cited in Freiberg, H. J. (1999). *School climate: measuring, improving, and sustaining healthy learning environments* (p. 3). London: Falmer Press.

28. Ewan McIntosh (edu.blogs.com) runs a boutique media and learning consultancy working with schools and government worldwide. He hails from Edinburgh, Scotland. The copyright of this text remains © Ewan McIntosh 2010, but perpetual rights are granted for its inclusion in Flat Classroom™ book project of Vicki Davis and Julie Lindsay. The author asserts his moral right.

29. Loertscher, D. V. *Taxonomies of the school library media program.* Salt Lake City, UT: Hi Willow Research and Publishing.

30. Retrieved from http://www.schoollibraryjournal.com/article/CA6610496.html

31. Loertscher, D., Koechlin, C., & Zwaan, S. (2008). *The new learning commons: Where learners win!* (p. 10). Salt Lake City, UT: Hi Willow Research and Publishing.

32. Loertscher, D. V., & Diggs, V. (2009). From library to learning commons: A metamorphosis. [Case Study]. *Teacher Librarian, 36*(4), 32–38.

33. McIntosh, E. (2010, October 10, 2010). Clicks & bricks: When digital, learning and physical space meet. Retrieved October 20, 2011, from http://edu.blogs.com/edublogs/2010/10/-cefpi-clicks-bricks-when-digital-learning-and-space-met.html

34. Beijing (BIS) International School. Retrieved from http://www.biss.com.cn

35. VoiceThread was unblocked a few months later, but confidence had been lost with teachers. A slow reimmersion is in process.

36. It is best to have tags without spaces because spaces are not search friendly. That is why the tag "turnin" is used instead of "turn in." Another option is to use the underline or minus (e.g., "turn-in" or "turn_in").

37. Handheld Augmented Reality Project (HARP). Accessed June 15, 2011, from http://isites.harvard.edu/icb/icb.do?keyword=harp

38. Hartgill, M. (n.d.). Establishing dominance and crossing the midline. Retrieved October 10, 2010, from http://www.kidzworld.co.za/art_midlinecrossing.htm

39. Rosen, L. D. (2010). *Rewired: Understanding the iGeneration and the way they learn* (p. 108). New York: Palgrave Macmillan.

40. Harvard University. (2007). The river city project. Retrieved June 15, 2011, from http://muve.gse.harvard.edu/rivercityproject/index.html

41. Retrieved from http://ramapoislands.edublogs.org/2010/01/28/a-special-ed-class-takes-the-leap

42. Julie's classroom framework based specifically on 2009–2011 at Beijing BISS International School

43. Retrieved June 15, 2011, from http://www.studywiz.com

44. Retrieved June 15, 2011, from http://lindsay-technology.biss .wikispaces.net for grades 9 and 10; http://itgs.wikispaces .com for grade 11.

45. Ed Hallisey, Principal, Putnam Valley Middle School. (2010, March).Interview with Vicki Davis.

46. Devaney, L. (2010, June 23). Study reveals factors in ed-tech success. *eSchool News.* Retrieved January 2, 2010, from http://projectred.org/uploads/eSchoolNews_ProjectRed.pdf

47. Parkinson's law. (n.d.). *The Economist.* Retrieved June 15, 2011, from http://www.economist.com/node/14116121?story _id=14116121

48. Bonk, C. J. (2009). *The world is open: How web technology is revolutionizing education.* San Francisco: Jossey-Bass.

49. Wiggins, G. P., & McTighe, J. (1998). *Understanding by design* (p. 27). Alexandria, VA: Association for Supervision and Curriculum Development.

50. Eco-friendly phone for Nokia by Daizi Zheng. (n.d.). *DeZeen.* Retrieved June 15, 2011, from http://www.dezeen .com/2010/01/07/eco-friendly-phone-for-nokia-by-daizi-zheng

51. Retrieved June 15, 2011, from http://www.connectivism.ca /about.html

52. Perry, A. C. (1908*). The management of a city school.* New York: The Macmillan company. Page 304.

53. Retrieved from http://www.yesican-science.ca

54. Retrieved from http://www.shoutlearning.org

55. Retrieved from www.virtualclassroom.org

56. Retrieved from http://www.nicenet.org

57. "053578" Student of Joanna Huang, the Chinese Studies teacher at Canadian International School of Hong Kong and about their collaboration to learn Chinese with Chung-Hsin School in Taiwan.

58. K–12 Open Curricula Community. (n.d.). *Curriki.* Retrieved May 22, 2011, from http://www.curriki.org

59. More reading on this topic at http://issuu.com/cyberpilgrim /docs/ic_april_2010_no_1

CHAPTER 8

1. Shirky, C. (2008). *Here comes everybody: The power of organizing without organizations* (p. 50). New York: Penguin Press.

2. Atif's video for Click Online retrieved from http://tinyurl .com/atifvideo (http://video.google.com/videoplay?do cid=6974394175099109918#)

3. Park, B. (2009, September 23). From a Flat Classroom to a flat world. Retrieved June 8, 2011, from http://flatclassroom conference.ning.com/profiles/blogs/from-a-flat-classroom-to-a-1

4. Friedman, *The world is flat.*

5. Jukes, I., McCain, T. D., & Crockett, L. (2010). *Understanding the digital generation: Teaching and learning in the new digital landscape* (pp. 62–63). Kelowna, BC: 21st Century Fluency Project.

6. Ibid.

7. 21CFP—The fluencies. (n.d.). *21st Century Fluency Project.* Retrieved June 8, 2011, from http://www.committedsardine .com/fluencies.cfm

8. Jukes et al., *Understanding the digital generation,* p. 66.

9. Rousseau-Anderson, J. (2010, September 28). The latest global social media trends may surprise you. Retrieved May 28, 2011, from http://blogs.forrester.com/jackie_rousseau_ anderson/10-09-28-latest_global_social_media_trends_may_ surprise_you

10. Perez, S. (2010, September 29). Social networking users are creating less content. Retrieved June 8, 2011, from http:// www.readwriteweb.com/archives/social_networking_users_ are_creating_less_content.php

11. Lenhart, A. (2005, November 2). Teen content creators and consumers. Retrieved June 8, 2011, from http://pewinternet .org/Reports/2005/Teen-Content-Creators-and-Consumers.aspx

12. International study urges organizations to adapt to Web 2.0 "phenomenon." (2007, June 25). Retrieved June 8, 2011, from http://www.digitalcommunities.com/articles/International-Study-Urges-Organizations-to-Adapt.html?page=2

13. Lenhart, A. (2007, December 19). Teens and social media. Retrieved June 8, 2011, from http://www.pewinternet.org /Reports/2007/Teens-and-Social-Media.aspx

14. Wilmarth, S. (2010). Five socio-technology trends that change everything in learning and teaching. In H. H. Jacobs, *Curriculum 21: Essential education for a changing world.* Alexandria, VA: Association for Supervision and Curriculum Development.

15. Ibid.

16. Churches, A. (n.d.). Bloom's digital taxonomy. *Edorigami.* Retrieved June 8, 2011, from http://edorigami.wikispaces .com/Bloom%27s+Digital+Taxonomy

17. Ibid.

18. Jukes et al., *Understanding the digital generation,* p. 69.

19. Personal branding. (n.d.). *Wikipedia.* Retrieved June 8, 2011, from http://en.wikipedia.org/wiki/Personal_branding

20. Jacobs, R. (2008, July 22). Education innovation: 14 trends of the new educational reality (Part 1:Trends 1–7). Retrieved October 24, 2011, from http://educationinnovation.typepad .com/my_weblog/2008/07/14-trends-of-the-new-educational-reality-part-1-trends-1-7.html

21. Godin, Seth. (2007). *Meatball sundae: Is your marketing out of sync?* New York: Portfolio, 2007.

22. Jacobs, Education innovation.

23. Utecht, J. (n.d.). Consultant author. Retrieved June 8, 2011, from http://www.jeffutecht.com

24. Utecht, J. (2010, March 22). Personal branding—Know who YOU are. *U-Tech Tips.* Retrieved June 13, 2011, from http://www.utechtips.com/2010/03/22/personal-branding-knowing-who-you-are

25. Schwabel, D. (2011, April 7). Four steps to personal branding success. *Your Daily Digest on Productivity and Life Improvements—Stepcase Lifehack.* Retrieved June 13, 2011, from http://www.lifehack.org/articles/management/4-steps-to-personal-branding-success.html

26. Shirky, Here comes everybody, p. 50.

27. Lindsay, J. (2007, November 20). E-learning for life. Retrieved November 20, 2007, from http://youtu.be/Mua83YBW9QA

28. Retrieved June 8, 2011, from http://aweekinthelife.flatclassroom project.org

29. Retrieved June 8, 2011, from http://elementaryflatclassroom .wordpress.com

30. Retrieved June 8, 2011, from http://bissportfolios.edublogs.org

31. Retrieved June 8, 2011, from http://www.insideitgs.net

32. Retrieved June 8, 2011, from https://docs.google.com/present /edit?id=0AclS3lrlFkCIZGhuMnZjdjVfMTA2YzlmbThq& hl=en_GB

33. Wiki collaboration across the curriculum. (2006, October 23). *K12 Online Conference 2010* . Retrieved June 13, 2011, from http://k12onlineconference.org/?p=38

34. What is citizen journalism? (n.d.). K12 Wiki. Retrieved June 13, 2011, from http://k12wiki.wikispaces.com/Citizen+ Journalism+Code+of+Ethics

35. http://twitter.com/reuw

36. Lindsay, J. (2006, November 1). K12 wiki winners! *E-Learning Journeys.* Retrieved June 3, 2011, from http://123elearning .blogspot.com/2006/10/k12-wiki-winners.html

37. 21C Learners. (n.d.). Qatar Academy wikispaces. Retrieved June 8, 2011, from http://elearning.qataracademy.wikispaces .net/21C_Learners

38. Lindsay, J. (2009, February 21). 21C learners create the future? Retrieved June 8, 2011, from http://youtu.be/mVNBebzs0j4

39. Lindsay, J. (July, 2010). *Flat Classroom Workshop 2010.* Retrieved June 8, 2011, from http://flatclassroomworkshop 2010.flatclassroomproject.org

40. Lindsay, J., & Cofino, K. (2010, October 2). Create the future. Retrieved June 7, 2011, from http://createthefuture .wikispaces.com

41. Retrieved June 7, 2011, from http://acrosstheglobe.wikispaces .com

42. Retrieved June 7, 2011, from http://createthefuture.wikispaces .com/Team+Japan

43. Retrieved June 7, 2011, fromhttp://flatclassroomworkshop 2010.flatclassroomproject.org/Flatten+your+PD

44. http://helps.flatclassroomproject.org

45. http://insideitgs.wikispaces.com

46. Brookes, M. (2010, August 21). The ITGS cyber-class is here. *Technology for Thinking.* Retrieved June 14, 2011, from http://www.technology4thinking.com/2010/08/21/the-itgs-cyber-class-is-here

47. http://dotsub.com/view/6ebab07e-1cae-44cd-bc02-6c4201286291 and http://k12onlineconference.org/?p=293

48. Introducing! (n.d.). Inside ITGS. Retrieved June 14, 2011, from http://insideitgs.wikispaces.com/Introducing!

49. Introducing partner, Yae Fukushima. (2010, September 6). Inside ITGS—Information Technology in a Global Society. Retrieved June 14, 2011, from http://insideitgs.ning.com /profiles/blogs/introducing-partner-yae

50. Introducing Ding Chen, Queena. Retrieved December 3, 2011, from http://v.youku.com/v_show/id_XMjAzMzg5OTIw .html

51. Jones, Ray, teacher, Qatar Academy, Doha, Qatar. From Flat Classroom Google Group, November 15, 2008.

52. Neiffer, Jason, teacher, Capital High School, Montana, USA. Flat Classroom Google Group, November 10, 2010.

53. Doig, Bruce, teacher, Riyadh, Saudi Arabia. Flat Classroom Google Group, November 11, 2008.

54. http://helps.flatclassroomproject.org/OutSourced+Video +Help

55. K–12 Open Curricula Community. (n.d.). Curriki. Retrieved May 22, 2011, from http://www.curriki.org

56. Davis, V. (n.d.). Tips for teaching wikis: How I explain it to students. Cool Cat Teacher Blog. Retrieved June 14, 2011, from http://coolcatteacher.blogspot.com/2010/05/tips-for-teaching-wikis-how-i-explain.html

57. Brogan, S. (2010, November 18). 21st Century Literacy and Global Competence Flourish in the Flat Classroom Project [virtual conference session]. 2010 Global Education Conference. Retrieved from http://www.globaleducationconference .com/recordings.html

CHAPTER 9

1. Project Red. (2010). Project Red key findings. Retrieved October 21, 2011. Slide 6.

2. Clark, R. (2011). *The end of molasses classes: Getting our kids unstuck: 101 extraordinary solutions for parents and teachers.* New York: Simon & Schuster. Page 52.

3. Davis, V. (n.d.). Flat Classroom Project 10-3 Awards. Retrieved May 14, 2011, from http://www.slideshare.net /coolcatteacher/flat-classroom-project-103-awards

4. All about a Flat Classroom student summit. (n.d.) Flat Classroom Projects Help Wiki. Retrieved December 3, 2011, from http://helps.flatclassroomproject.org/Student+Summit

5. Lindsay, J. (2009, December 14). Telling the world: Flat classroom student summit in practice. E-Learning Journeys. Retrieved May 14, 2011, from http://123elearning.blogspot .com/2009/12/telling-world-flat-classroom-student.html

6. Lindsay, J. (2009, April 21). Virtually awarded. . . . and more! E-Learning Journeys. Retrieved May 14, 2011, from http://123elearning.blogspot.com/2009/04/virtually-awardedand-more.html

7. D'Arcy, P. (2011, June 6). The Flat Classroom Project, a celebration of learning—flat classrooms. Retrieved June 9, 2011, from http://flatclassrooms.ning.com/profiles/blogs /the-flat-classroom-project-a

CHAPTER 10

1. Friedman, T. L. (2005). *The world is flat: A brief history of the twenty-first century.* New York: Farrar, Straus, and Giroux, p. 325.

2. Eracism. (2009, January 27). Retrieved June 11, 2011, from http://flatclassroomconference.ning.com/video/eracism-1

3. Coughlin, E., & Kajder, S. (n.d.). The impact of collaborative, scaffolded learning in K–12 schools: A meta-analysis. Retrieved July 30, 2010, from http://www.cisco.com/web /about/citizenship/socio-economic/docs/Metiri_Classroom_ Collaboration_Research.pdf

4. Understanding by design. (n.d.). Wikipedia. Retrieved August 4, 2010, from http://en.wikipedia.org/wiki/Understanding _by_Design

5. Digiteen 11-1 team grid. (2011, January 1). Retrieved June 10, 2011, from https://docs.google.com/View?id= ah4zsdj46b66_152g9f

6. "A Week in the Life . . ." 11-1 team grid. (2011, January 1). Retrieved June 6, 2011, from https://docs.google .com/document/d/1T_UdKwKq-qdpmZGk5ONKALylf MUMMl-INDwY8JOqkoU/edit?hl=en_GB&authkey= CI3AqsIJ#

7. Master list of videos. (n.d.). Flat Classroom Project 11-1. Retrieved May 7, 2011, from http://flatclassroom11-1.flat classroomproject.org/Master+List+of+Videos

8. Union, C. (2011, June 3). Research summary on the Net Generation Education 2009 and 2010 and Horizon 2008 projects. Retrieved December 3, 2011, from https://docs.google .com/document/pub?id=1ZTLv4u2Ly5nhQaA2k

9. Ibid.

10. NetGen Ed 2010 keynote. (2010, April 7). NetGen Ed 2010. Retrieved June 16, 2011, from netgened2010 .flatclassroomproj

11. Davis, V. (2011, March 25). Facebook Friending 101 for schools. Cool Cat Teacher Blog. Retrieved June 16, 2011, from http://coolcatteacher.blogspot.com/2011/03/facebook-friending-101-for-schools.html

12. Gray, L. (n.d.). The Global Education Collaborative—The official social network of the Global Education Conference. Retrieved June 16, 2011, from http://globaleducation.ning.com

13. Galvin, C. (2009, December 5). eTwinning in the classroom: A showcase of good practice (2008–2009). *eTwinning: The Community for Schools in Europe.* Retrieved July 31, 2010, from http://resources.eun.org/etwinning/80 /PUBLICATION_eTwinning_in_

14. Friedman, T. (n.d.). MIT World speakers: Thomas L. Friedman. Retrieved June 16, 2011, from http://mitworld.mit.edu /speaker/view/402

15. Pink, D. H. (2006). *A whole new mind: Why right-brainers will rule the future.* New York: Riverhead.

16. Crouch, K., & Barclay, E. (2011, May 17). Keys to flattening your classroom. *Elementary Flatclassroom.* Retrieved June 11, 2011, from http://elementaryflatclassroom.wordpress .com/2011/05/17/keys-to-flattening-your-classroom

17. Maurer, A. (2011, May 17). A little project sharing. Flat Classrooms. Retrieved May 28, 2011, from http://flatclassrooms .ning.com/group/flatclassroomcertifiedteacher111/forum /topics/a-little-project-sharing-in

18. Ibid.

19. Throop, S. (2011, June 5). My first day. Elementary Flatclassroom. Retrieved June 11, 2011, from http://elementary flatclassroom.wordpress.com/2011/06/05/my-first-day

20. TakingITGlobal. (n.d.). Retrieved June 3, 2011, from http:// www.tigweb.org

CHAPTER 11

1. Bonk, C. J. (2009). *The world is open: How web technology is revolutionizing education.* San Francisco, CA: Jossey-Bass, p. 31.
2. Contributed by Kimberley Clayton, Texas, USA.
3. K12 Online Conference. (n.d.). Retrieved May 26, 2011, from http://k12onlineconference.org
4. 2010 Global Education Conference. (n.d.). Retrieved December 3, 2011, from http://globaledcon.weebly.com
5. About Inside ITGS. (n.d.). Retrieved June 11, 2011, from http://insideitgs.wikispaces.com/About+Inside+ITGS
6. About COETAIL. (n.d.). Retrieved May 28, 2011, from http://www.coetail.asia/about
7. Home. (n.d.). Powerful Learning Practice. Retrieved May 28, 2011, from http://plpnetwork.com
8. About. (n.d.). EduBloggerCon. Retrieved May 26, 2011, from http://www.edubloggercon.com
9. Learning 2.011. (n.d.). Learning 2.011. Retrieved December 3, 2011, from http://learning2.asia
10. History of the ISTE Newbie Project. (n.d.). Retrieved June 16, 2011, from https://sites.google.com/site/istenewbieproject
11. Parkinson, C. N. (Nov 19, 1955). Parkinson's Law. *Economist.*
12. Flat Classroom Conference Home Page. (n.d.). Retrieved June 16, 2011, from conference2011.flatclassroomproject.org
13. Student action project. (n.d.). Flat Classroom Conference 2011 Wiki. Retrieved June 20, 2011, from conference2011.flatclassroomproject.org/Student+Action+Project
14. Leadership overview. (n.d.). Flat Classroom Conference 2011 Wiki. Retrieved June 20, 2011, from http://conference2011.flatclassroomproject.org/Leadership+Overview
15. Flat learning action talks (FLATs). (n.d.). Flat Classroom Conference 2011 Wiki. Retrieved June 20, 2011, from http://conference2011.flatclassroomproject.org/F.L.A.T.s
16. Flat Classroom Conference 2011—Virtual Conference. (n.d.). Retrieved June 16, 2011, from http://flatclass.tigweb.org
17. Virtual participants. (n.d.). Flat Classroom Conference 2011 Wiki. Retrieved June 20, 2011, from http://conference2011.flatclassroomproject.org/Virtual+Participants
18. ASB Unplugged Flat Classroom wiki. (n.d.). Retrieved June 20, 2011, from asbunplugged2010.flatclassroomproject.org
19. Cofino, K. (2011, March 4). Not your grandma's conference. Always Learning. Retrieved May 1, 2011, from http://kimcofino.com/blog/2011/03/04/not-your-grandmas-conference
20. 23 Things. (n.d.). Learning 2.0. Retrieved June 15, 2011, from http://plcmcl2-things.blogspot.com
21. Information about the Flat Classroom Certified Teacher course is found at http://tinyurl.com/flatclassteachercert or from http://fcpteacher.flatclassroomproject.org
22. Davis, H. (2009, February 1). Reflections on the Flat Classroom experience. Flat Classroom Conference Ning. Retrieved August 5, 2010, from http://flatclassroomconference.ning.com/profiles/blogs/reflections-of-the-flat
23. Mirtschin, A. (2009, February 28). All eyes on the flat classroom conference. Flat Classroom Conference Ning. Retrieved August 5, 2010, from http://flatclassroomconference.ning.com/profiles/blogs/all-eyes-on-the-flatclassroom
24. Deeds, D. (2011, March 5). Flat Classroom conference: "Working hard, having fun." inDeeds! Retrieved May 28, 2011, from http://www.indeeds.com/?p=1
25. Steve R. (2009, January 26). My experience and reflection. Flat Classroom Conference. Retrieved May 28, 2011, from http://flatclassroomconference.ning.com/profiles/blogs/my-experience-and-reflection
26. Tammam, G. (2009, January 24). My experiences (tell me yours). Flat Classroom Conference Ning. Retrieved August 5, 2010, from http://flatclassroomconference.ning.com/profiles/blogs/my-experiences-tell-me-yours
27. Cofino, K., & Lindsay, J. (n.d.). Create the Future. Retrieved May 14, 2011, from http://createthefuture.wikispaces.com
28. Ibid.
29. Harris, J. (2001). Structuring Internet-enriched learning spaces. *Learning and Leading with Technology,* 28(4): 50.
30. Molenda, M. (2003). The A.D.D.I.E. model. *Education Technology: An Encyclopedia.* Santa Barbara, CA: ABC-CLIO.

CHAPTER 12

1. Robinson, M. (n.d.). Maria Robinson quotes. Retrieved June 15, 2011, from http://thinkexist.com/quotation/nobody_can_go_back_and_start_a_new_beginning-but/174633.html
2. Carnevale, A. P., Smith, N., & Strohl, J. (2010, June). Help wanted: Projections of jobs and education requirements through 2018. Georgetown University Center on Education and the Workforce. http://www9.georgetown.edu/grad/gppi/hpi/cew/pdfs/FullReport.pdf. Page 24.
3. Ibid., p. 119.
4. OECD. (2010). Education at a glance: 2010 OECD Indicators. Paris: Organisation for Economic Co-operation and Development. Chart A.1.1, p. 26.
5. Olson, K. (2009). *Wounded by school: Recapturing the joy in learning and standing up to old school culture.* New York: Teachers College Press.
6. Boss, S., & Krauss, J. (2007). *Reinventing project-based learning: Your field guide to real-world projects in the digital age.* Eugene, OR: International Society for Technology in Education, p. 7.
7. Davis, V. (2008, July 9). Your "big 3" R&D. Flat Classrooms Ning. Retrieved June 14, 2011, from http://flatclassrooms.ning.com/group/stlouisworkshopjuly2008/forum/topics/2090574:Topic:1698?commentId=2090574%3AComment%3A1994&groupId=2090574%3AGroup%3A
8. Interns for IT, engineering, drafting, accounting jobs. (n.d.). Genesys Works. Retrieved June 9, 2011, from http://www.genesysworks.org

APPENDIX A

1. Rubrics were redesigned in April 2010. We acknowledge the tireless dedication to excellence as shown by volunteers Steve Madsen and Mark van 't Hooft in assisting with this process.
2. Social entrepreneurship. (n.d.). Wikipedia. Retrieved June 16, 2011, from http://en.wikipedia.org/wiki/Social_entrepreneurship
3. Pink, D. H. (2006). *Portfolio: A whole new mind: Why right-brainers will rule the future.* New York: Riverhead Books, p. 188.

APPENDIX B

1. Three programs at a glance. (n.d.). The International Baccalaureate. Retrieved May 28, 2011, from http://www.ibo.org/programmes/index.cfm
2. Academic programs. (n.d.). The International Baccalaureate. Retrieved May 28, 2011, from http://www.ibo.org/general/what.cfm
3. IB Learner Profile. (n.d.). The International Baccalaureate. Retrieved May 28, 2011, from http://www.ibo.org/programmes/profile
4. Lindsay, J. (2007, May 21). The Flat Classroom Project, the learner profile, and school 2.0. E-Learning Journeys. Retrieved May 28, 2011, from http://123elearning.blogspot.com/2007/01/flat-classroom-project-learner-profile.html
5. Learner profile guide. (2008). The International Baccalaureate. Retrieved May 24, 2011, from http://www.ibo.org/programmes/profile/documents/Learnerprofileguide.pdf
6. http://flatclassroom11-2.flatclassroomproject.org/Topics
7. D'Arcy, P. (2011, June 6). The Flat Classroom Project, a celebration of learning. Retrieved June 13, 2011, from http://flatclassrooms.ning.com/profiles/blogs/the-flat-classroom-project-a
8. About this project. (2011, March 29, 2011). Flat Classroom Projects. Retrieved September 11, 2011, from http://netgened2011.flatclassroomproject.org/About+this+Project
9. Johnson, L., Smith, R., Willis, H., Levine, A., & Haywood, K. (2011). *The 2011 Horizon Report.*
10. Tapscott, D. (2009). *Grown up digital: How the net generation is changing your world.* New York: McGraw-Hill.
11. http://insideitgs.wikispaces.com/Guidelines+for+participation+as+an+Inside+ITGS+Class.